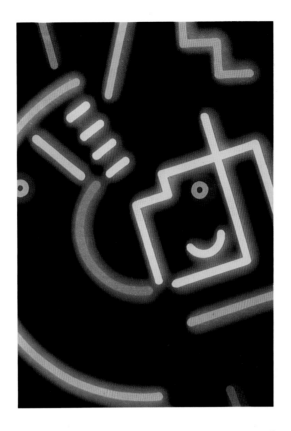

69th Art Directors Annual
and
4th International Exhibition

ADC Publications Inc.

Board of Directors
Dorothy Wachtenheim, President
Pearl Lau, Vice President
Jim Craig, Marketing & Promotion
Hugh O'Neill
Phil Thurman

ADC Executive Director
Diane Moore

Editors
Jeri Zulli
Jonathan Gregory

Hall of Fame Copy
Daniel M. Forté

Database Consultant
Marie Gangemi

Interior Design
Ryuichi Minakawa

Cover and Section Dividers Design
McRay Magleby
Lily McCullough
Linda Sullivan

Published in 1990 by
RotoVision SA
Route de Suisse 9
CH-1295 MIES/VD
Switzerland
for
The Art Directors Club Inc.
250 Park Avenue South
New York, NY 10003

While ADC Publications Inc. has made every effort to publish full and correct credits for each piece included in this volume, errors of omission or commission sometimes occur. For this ADC Publications Inc. and Rotovision SA are most regretful, but hereby disclaim any liability.

Since this book is printed in four-color process, a few of the images reproduced here may appear slightly different from their original reproduction.

ISSN: 0735-2026
ISBN: 2-8230-6041-1
Printed in Hong Kong

Media Conversion and
Digital Composition by:
I, CLAVDIA, Inc., New York, New York

Distributed to the trade in the
United States & Canada by
Watson-Guptill Publications
1515 Broadway
New York, NY 10036

International Distribution
RotoVision SA
Route de Suisse 9
CH-1295 MIES/VD
Switzerland

RYUICHI MINAKAWA

Ryuichi Minakawa, the *Annual's* interior designer, is art director of the Toppan Printing Company of America. He has also been involved in a similar manner with the 64th, 65th and 68th editions of the Art Directors Club *Annuals,* Volumes 7 through 11 of the *One Show* annuals, and *Illustrators 32,* the annual of The Society of Illustrators. At Toppan, Minakawa is responsible for the overall graphic production of *Graphis* magazine and the Graphis annuals.

Minakawa was born in Kumamoto, Japan. He is a graduate of the Art Center College of Design in Pasadena, California, and, prior to his current position with Toppan, worked for several major graphic design firms, specializing in corporate identity, logos, and package design.

Minakawa lives in New York City and is a member of the Art Directors Club.

SAUL BASS

Art Directors Club Hall of Famer and this year's designer of the 4th Annual International Call for Entries, Saul Bass has had a profound effect on visual communication. A designer and developer of numerous trademarks and corporate identity strategies, Bass's work for *Fortune 500* companies reads like a *Who's Who.* Alcoa, AT&T, Celanese Corp., Quaker Oats, United Airlines and Warner Communications are just a few of the clients who have benefited from his graphic design expertise.

In addition to his extensive and highly successful work as a designer, Bass, based in Los Angeles with his partner Herb Yager of Bass/Yager & Associates, has had an accomplished career as a filmmaker, motion picture graphic designer and title creator. Who can forget the shower sequence from "Psycho" or the final battle scene from "Spartacus"? Bass directed special feature sequences for these classic films as well as many others.

His penchant for creating opening title graphics—as he did for over forty of Hollywood's most memorable motion pictures—is a credit to Bass's unique visual style and innovative technique. For example, "The Man With the Golden Arm," "Seven Year Itch," "Vertigo," "North By Northwest," "Psycho" and "It's A Mad, Mad, Mad, Mad World" contain some of the more unforgettable opening credits in film history.

Who's Who in America lists over 12 honors and doctorates under Bass' name from various organizations around the world. His work appears in the permanent collections of museums from New York to the Far East. It's only fitting for Bass to contribute his design to the club's 4th Annual International Competition.

MCRAY MAGLEBY

A 1966 graduate of the University of Utah, McRay Magleby, this year's national Call for Entries designer, has won numerous national awards in graphic design. His work has often appeared in *Graphis, CA Annuals, Art Direction, Print* Case Books, Japan's *IDEA* Magazine, AIGA and the *Art Directors Annuals.*

He is currently art director of the Brigham Young University Graphics Department, a position he has held since 1969. Mr. Magleby supervises a staff of ten designers and produces publications, books and posters for the university.

Many of his posters, originally designed for BYU, are currently being sold in galleries and reproduced on greeting cards. Magleby is also a professor of art at the University of Utah, where he teaches graphic design and illustration. In 1985 he was selected to receive the Distinguished Teaching Award.

CONTENTS

HALL OF FAME MEMBERS

1972
M. F. Agha
Lester Beall
Alexey Brodovitch
Rene Clark
A. M. Cassandre
Robert Gage
William Golden
Paul Rand

1973
Charles Coiner
Paul Smith
Jack Tinker

1974
Will Burtin
Leo Lionni

1975
Gordon Aymar
Herbert Bayer
Cipe Pineles Burtin
Heyworth Campbell
Alexander Liberman
L. Moholy-Nagy

1976
E. McKnight Kauffer
Herbert Matter

1977
Saul Bass
Herb Lubalin
Bradbury Thompson

1978
Thomas M. Cleland
Lou Dorfsman
Allen Hurlburt
George Lois

1979
W. A. Dwiggins
George Giusti
Milton Glaser
Helmut Krone
Willem Sandberg
Ladislav Sutnar
Jan Tschichold

1980
Gene Federico
Otto Storch
Henry Wolf

1981
Lucian Bernhard
Ivan Chermayeff
Gyorgy Kepes
George Krikorian
William Taubin

1982
Richard Avedon
Amil Gargano
Jerome Snyder
Massimo Vignelli

1983
Aaron Burns
Seymour Chwast
Steve Frankfurt

1984
Charles Eames
Wallace Elton
Sam Scali
Louis Silverstein

1985
Art Kane
Len Sirowitz
Charles Tudor

1986
Walt Disney
Roy Grace
Alvin Lustig
Arthur Paul

1987
Willy Fleckhaus
Shigeo Fukuda
Steve Horn
Tony Palladino

1988
Ben Shahn
Bert Steinhauser
Mike Tesch

1989
Rudolph de Harak
Raymond Loewy

1990
Lee Clow
Reba Sochis
Frank Zachary

It is no simple task to identify figures in our profession as illustrious as those who have already been elected to the Hall of Fame; but the Selection Committee has identified three people whose qualifications well match those already chosen.

They represent different aspects of our profession:

Lee Clow—for his ground breaking work in advertising.

Reba Sochis—for her influence and inspiration to a whole generation of designers.

Frank Zachary—for his extraordinary career as an editorial art director and editor.

There is also a Special Award being presented to **Robert Weaver**—for his equally impressive accomplishments as a teacher and illustrator.

For an organization to survive, it must have a history to believe in and standards to aspire to. Clow, Sochis, Zachary and Weaver provided these standards and history for us, in accordance.

Through these awards, we celebrate and thank them for their contributions.

Milton Glaser
Hall of Fame Selection Committee Chairman

Lee Clow

This is the city, Los Angeles, California. It's a magical place known for burritos, celebrities, Disneyland, Dodgers, earthquakes, EST, freeways, palm trees, smog, tofu, valley girls and—advertising? There are ten million stories of people who work and play here. Lee Clow is one of them and this, is his story...

Born in Los Angeles in 1943, Lee Clow literally grew up at the beach. He credits his first grade teacher, Mrs. Rice, with recognizing his artistic potential. It all occurred very serendipitously with a little drawing of a boat Clow had made in class. It seems little Lee loved boats and realistically portrayed it right down to the curling eddies of smoke rising from its stack. Mrs. Rice immediately noticed his uncanny knack for detail and told Lee's mom of his impending future as an artist. As a result, Mrs. Clow encouraged her son to continue drawing and painting.

As Clow got older, he began to hone his artistic skills. He attended Santa Monica City College and received a two-year degree. His parents simply could not afford to send him to the more prestigious Art Center College of Design. Years later, as irony would have it, Clow was asked to teach there! It was also during this period that Clow's distinct California personality crystallized.

According to Clow, "I spent a lot of time at the beach surfing. If the temperature soared above 80 degrees and the waves were four feet high, I didn't bother going to class!" He was eventually drafted into the Army at the height of the Vietnam War. Clow's illustrative abilities got him assigned to the White Sands Missile Range in New Mexico. After his tour of duty was up, he went back to school, taking design courses at Long Beach State.

After the Army, he was hired as a paste-up artist at a local design studio. His first agency art directing position was with NW Ayer's west coast office. Frustrated by "only okay work getting produced," Clow remained there a couple of years.

Inspired by the creative revolution of the just-completed decade of the sixties, Lee Clow was deeply influenced by the DDB team approach to advertising. At the time, it certainly caused a frisson of excitement, sending much needed shock waves of creativity throughout the industry. Wanting to have his cake and eat it too, Lee Clow set out to search for the perfect west coast agency that aspired to DDB's principles. He simply refused to trade in his bathing trunks for a Brooks Brothers suit.

Clow stumbled upon a young California agency called simply Chiat/Day whose creative credo was, "Let's do good ads." Back in 1971, it was two years young, had a staff of 30 and billings just shy of $15 million. Lee Clow was determined to work there. He got his book together and launched a campaign of persistence. Phone calls, letter writing and kind pestering eventually led to a scheduled interview with Jay Chiat's associate, Hy Yablonka.

Clow, pumped for his big chance, waited patiently for Yablonka, who forgot about the meeting, instead opting for a long lunch. Resolved to seeing Yablonka at any cost, Clow staked out the building's lobby poised for his return. They met. Although Chiat/Day was not hiring, Yablonka did give him a great deal of time and constructive criticism.

In January of 1973, Lee Clow's tenacity finally paid off. He was hired by Chiat/Day as an art director. Clow recalls meeting Jay Chiat a day before he was to begin work. Chiat simply told him in his inimitable style, "Work hard and maybe you'll do some good ads."

Clow, under Jay Chiat's unorthodox working environment, was given great opportunities to grow. The agency was and still is, according to Clow, "a great forum of free association fostering creativity."

For someone whose formal training was in art and design, Lee Clow literally taught himself advertising. The on-the-job training provided by his boss, Jay Chiat, coupled with his well-thumbed prized possessions: a collection of New York Art Directors Club and Communication Arts *Annuals* from the 1960s, Lee Clow began his career in the world of advertising. So in tune with the swell of creativity spawned in the sixties, Clow even today goes back in time for help in creating new concepts when he needs inspiration.

In 1977, Lee Clow began his trip up the ladder at Chiat/Day. Notorious for shunning titles and the limelight, Clow was nonetheless promoted to associate creative director. In 1982, he became creative director of the Los Angeles office and two years later, he was named president, chief creative officer (and senior art director) of Chiat/Day/Mojo.

Clow attributes his success to Jay Chiat's anti-establishment concepts of horizontal management. "You must have a combination of talent and a good environment to work in, in order to excel," Clow says. Witness the open air atmosphere of Chiat/Day's offices. All are equal in size with no closed doors. Management is always accessible to both staff and clients. They really do consider themselves family.

The list of risk-taking entrepreneurial clients the agency has served over the years proved to be perfect foils for Clow's unique and quirky creativity. His work for Apple Computer, California Cooler, KCBS, KNBC, Nike, Nissan, Olympia Beer, Pacific Northwest Bell, Pioneer Electronics, Pizza Hut, Porsche and Yamaha helped create a counterculture and state of mind in advertising that quickly spread across the country like a forest fire. It was advertising California style; it simply could not be ignored or duplicated in the button-down corridors of Madison Avenue. Through his clients, Lee Clow taught us that "California Dreamin" was no longer just a song reminiscent of pop culture, but a very serious and viable force advertising could not resist recognizing.

All one has to do is flip through the new coffee table book, *Chiat/Day, The First Twenty Years* to see Clow and his agency's incredible metamorphosis unfold. His Apple Computer "1984" spot. A concept so fresh, yet disturbing, it's been heralded as a classic from both a cinematic and advertising standpoint. Clow's irreverent "lifestyle" spots for California Cooler seem very autobiographical. Who better can portray a bunch of well-tanned surfers partying, dude?

Clow's most upbeat slice of California life shines through in his "I Love LA" spot for Nike. Randy Newman in an old red Buick, cruising down the boulevards singing, "From the South Bay to the Valley, from the west side to the east side, everybody's very happy 'cause the sun shines all the time." It's intercut with a wonderful montage of celebrities and ordinary people shot against a beautiful and glitzy LA background.

Lee Clow openly admits, "I haven't yet done an ad I'm totally happy with. When I reach that stage of the game, I guess I'll retire and go into the aluminum siding business." For Clow, as long as the forces of passion and insecurity tug at his creative psyche, he'll continue to search for that "all elusive, perfect ad."

Interestingly enough, Lee Clow has two heroes he's quick to mention: Walt Disney and Hobie Alter. Hobie Alter, you ask? Who's he? Alter's name graces many a surfboard and catamaran—the Hobie Cat, for one. Clow idolizes Disney because of his natural artistic abilities and uncompromising determination to succeed regardless of life's roadblocks. Alter because he reached a point in his life that permitted him to attend board meetings in shorts and sandals!

In order to maintain harmony and stasis between his career and private life, Lee Clow still enjoys surfing, cruising to Catalina Island with his wife of 21 years and yes—attending meetings in his ever present shorts and sandals! He also finds great solace commiserating with his two dogs on the finer points of advertising, especially after interminable client meetings. "It's very therapeutic," Clow says.

Lee Clow's stark individualism makes him a prime candidate for the "guru" of the west coast school of laid-back advertising. When asked to comment on his induction into the New York Art Directors Club Hall of Fame, Clow paused for a moment and said, "It's quite an honor, yet—ironic, too. Since my goal was to do good ads *without* having to move to New York."

From $15 million in billings to $1 billion; from 30 employees to 1500, Lee Clow is still Lee Clow and Chiat/Day is now Chiat/Day/Mojo.

Should you happen to see a large, bearded man decked out in shorts and sandals engaged in an animated conversation with two dogs on a sandy beach in Venice, California, chances are it's Lee Clow. He's probably in the midst of explaining to them his philosophy of life. With apologies to Carl Lewis's Nike spot, "Never give up. There's no telling how far you can go…"

Chiat/Day wants to join a motorcycle gang.

It takes a tough bunch to handle a motorcycle account. But Chiat/Day has what it takes.
Speed. Balance. Savvy. Talent. Everything.
Except a client.
That's where Yamaha comes in. Between your innovative products, planning and marketing expertise, and our proven advertising and creative abilities, we can sell motorcycles, accessories and snowmobiles like nobody else's business.
And if we can't, you'll get your money back.
That's right. You read it correctly. If we can't increase your sales, we'll refund the difference on a percentage basis from any media commissions or fees we may have earned.
Chiat/Day isn't afraid to join a motorcycle gang. Especially Yamaha's.

Yamaha ad, 1973

SPARE TIRES.

How often do you fire up your car for a trip to the post office? Or go off camping and end up exploring in your eight-miles-per-gallon camper?
Often enough, we suspect, to be a prime customer for the Yamaha Chappy. An extra set of wheels that's fleet, fun and frugal.
The Chappy can handle most anything from city streets to country trails. And you can handle the Chappy—thanks to the wide, stable tires; rigid, low-center-of-gravity frame; and automatic transmission with dual-range final drive.
The Chappy sports a peppy two-stroke engine that's both tough and reliable. And our patented Autolube system automatically premixes gas and oil so you don't have to.
You'll find the suspension is responsive. The instrumentation is informative. And the long, wide seat is very, very comfortable.
The mileage? Phenomenal. Up to 118 mpg.
The price? Very spare.

THE CHAPPY FROM YAMAHA
In certain states, Chappy is not street legal.

Yamaha ad, 1973

KCBS-TV ad, 1976

Apple Computer, "1984" TV spot, 1983

Take Macintosh out for a test drive.

Since we introduced Macintosh,™ we've been telling you it's the first business computer anyone can learn to use overnight.
Now we're going to prove it.
By giving you a Macintosh to use. Overnight.
Right now, anyone who qualifies can walk into a participating authorized Apple dealer, and walk out with a Macintosh Personal Computer.
No purchase necessary.
It's our way of letting you test drive a Macintosh in the comfort of your own office, home, RV, hotel room, dorm room or whatever.
And really experience, first-hand, how much your finger already knows about computing.
Simply put, in less time than it takes to get frustrated on an ordinary computer, you'll be doing real work on Macintosh.
Because the hard part of test driving a Macintosh isn't figuring out how to use it.
The hard part is bringing it back.

Apple Computer ad, 1984

Apple Computer ad, 1984

Chiat/Day is working on your car.

Porsche ad, 1984

And Professor Porsche expects still more.

The windows in Professor Porsche's office in Zuffenhausen overlook a courtyard.

A courtyard lined with Porsches parked in a patchwork of colors and model designs.

Not shiny new cars, but the ones that have already met foul weather and potholes. Survived the winding kilometers between summer picnics and winter ski trips.

To Professor Porsche, these are very important Porsches.

Because when he stands at this window, hands crossed behind his back, rocking from toe to heel, and looks down at the cars in the courtyard, he imagines.

He is reminded of how much is yet to be accomplished.

It is the reason Professor Porsche drives his company much the same way one drives his cars.

With passion. Respect. Conviction.

The result, cars that set new expectations of what a car ought to be.

Cars like this one.

Porsche's latest project, the 959. Or, more affectionately known as the "Gruppe B" car.

A car powered by the same 6-cylinder, horizontally opposed, twin overhead cam engine used in Porsche's 956 race car. Producing 400 hp.

A car with such a sophisticated

drive train you can actually dial in the power to each of the four wheels.

A car with a self-adjusting suspension system that automatically lowers it as speed increases.

Top speed: no one really knows. Yet.

And as far as Professor Porsche is concerned, it really doesn't matter.

Because no matter how close to perfection the Gruppe B car comes, there will be another day when he stands at his window.

And imagines.

959 (Gruppe B) 6-cylinder, horizontally opposed, four overhead camshafts, four valves per cylinder, water/air-cooled rear engine with twin intercooled turbochargers. 2850cc's, 400+ hp. Estimated top speed: 188+ mph.

Porsche ad, 1984

Pizza Hut, "Doug & Bob" TV spot, 1985

California Cooler TV spot, 1985

Nissan "Z" intro TV spot, 1989

Nike ad, 1984

Reba Sochis

Paccione

Oscar Wilde once wrote, "It is through art and through art only, that we can realize our perfection." Reba Sochis is the personification of Wilde's statement.

Born in Philadelphia, Pennsylvania, Reba Sochis grew up expecting to follow in her sister's footsteps: go to the university and study to become a teacher. Certainly, the proper profession for a proper young lady and most acceptable to our country's social attitudes at that time. Always interested in art, Sochis, however, saw her future develop differently. Not wanting to be confined to a classroom, she convinced her parents to allow her to enroll in the Philadelphia Museum School of Art.

The year was 1929. The country was about to be thrown into the depths of a great depression. Fortunately, Alexey Brodovitch had just joined the school's faculty. He was to be a great influence in her approach to graphic design. His teaching methods were as unique as he was. Brodovitch did not dwell on technique, focusing instead on the philosophy of design. According to Sochis, "The more he tried to provoke his students, the harder we worked," a character trait many an assistant would also lovingly attribute to Reba Sochis.

By 1934, she moved with her husband to New York City. In the midst of the Depression, to supplement their income, Sochis freelanced as a designer, creating various book jackets for small publishing houses. She eventually landed her first job in editorial layout design at *Esquire* Magazine, where she recalls being given the opportunity to experiment and take risks. After *Esquire*, Sochis headed for *Charm* Magazine.

By the end of World War II, she was hired as an art director for a large design firm in New York called Beacon Studio. Sochis resumed her career in what was, with the exception of her only female counterpart Cipe Pineles Burtin, then art director at *Seventeen* Magazine, the unchartered world of women in design. Interestingly enough, the same tandem remain the lone female members in the ADC Hall of Fame.

She was the only woman responsible for a staff of over 20 men. Sochis looks back on her pioneering days at Beacon as being a "jewel of a job." She attributes this to the fact that she never looked upon herself as a threat to the men and their jobs. Sensing this, they quickly accepted Sochis for her talent. She immediately became one of the boys without ever having to sacrifice her femininity. As long as her high standards of work were not compromised, there were no wrinkles at Beacon Studio.

One of Beacon's biggest accounts was Talon Zippers. Quite pleased with Sochis's elegant work for their promotional pieces, the client encouraged her to open her own studio. Late in 1949, Reba Sochis ventured out on her own with Talon as her first and only account. Because of the plethora of promotional materials Talon required, Sochis was swamped with work. She needed to hire a talented assistant and fast! Her first full time employee was a 19-year-old Pratt junior named George Lois. Lasting over 40 years, the mutual love and admiration both still have for each other is steadfast.

Mention Lois to her and you hear only superlatives. Lois also reminisces about his first boss: "In just one day working for Reba, you could learn more than in four years at Pratt or Cooper Union. She was the toughest boss in the world, but she was also the sweetest woman you could hope to know."

As Sochis's reputation for quality design grew, so did her studio, necessitating the hiring of more assistants. She turned it into a wonderful greenhouse of talent, recruiting Pratt and Cooper students as full and part time assistants. Among those who benefited from Sochis's tutelage, eventually moving on to outstanding careers in their own right, were: Seymour Chwast, Bob Gill, Kit Hinrichs, Steve Horn, Andrew Langer, Gilbert Lesser, Rick Levine, Tony Palladino, Tony Russell and Bob Tucker.

Reba Sochis instilled in her young assistants a motivational work ethic seldom seen today. She was able to mold them because, "They were young and talented and had no negative work habits to begin with." Known for being a perfectionist, Reba Sochis nurtured a generation of designers that certainly owe her an immense debt of gratitude:

Seymour Chwast: "For the short time I worked for Reba Sochis her dedication to design and craft amazed me. She would endlessly fuss over the letter spacing of type for a letterhead....Reba accepted only perfection."

Bob Gill: "Reba designs like an angel and swears like a cab driver. What more can anyone want in a role model? I love her."

Steve Horn: "Reba Sochis is the best thing since chopped liver! She began by putting the fear of God in me. In the short time I worked there, she gave me a well-rounded education that's proved invaluable. I learned more from Reba Sochis in nine months than most people learn in a lifetime."

Andrew Langer: "Reba Sochis was not an easy person to work for. When she liked your work, you received quiet praise. When she didn't, she really let you have it! Reba's a very stubborn person. But then the best usually are."

Rick Levine: "Reba Sochis influenced me greatly as a graphic designer. Her work was new, exciting and fresh. She taught me how to layout a page with great elan."

Tony Palladino: "Reba was a peer of mine, a work friend. A determined woman devoted to the quality of communication—which was a difficult role for a woman. She made us 'tough' guys think differently about women in design. Reba would rivet you against the wall about clear, intelligent communicative messages—and hold you to it. You couldn't walk away from Reba with a half-assed truth. You had to love her for that."

Tony Russell: "Met Reba the day after arriving in New York from England in November, 1963. Working with her and knowing her design standards cushioned the culture shock and persuaded me to stay. I value her friendship still."

The work Reba Sochis turned out from her atelier was flawless and the envy of conceptual designers. Her list of satisfied clients was a tribute to her professionalism. Sochis's work for Talon, Borghese, Bulkley Dunton, Lincoln Center, New York Telephone, Pappagallo, Revlon, JP Stevens and Shell Oil are marvels of detail and fine design.

A case in point was a shopping bag she produced for the newly launched Pappagallo shoe stores. In order to achieve the visual look of an intricate mosaic pattern, Sochis and her assistant, Andrew Langer, literally cut thousands of small tile-like pieces from sheets of gold paper. Each had to be positioned onto a mechanical with a tweezer! It took them weeks to complete the project, but the end result was a striking work of art.

For a Lincoln Center corporate fund raising brochure, Sochis decided to use safety paper, more commonly referred to as checkbook paper. Indeed, a very subtle, yet effective method of getting people in the mood to donate money.

More often than not, her incredible work was also the result of time being on her side. The majority of her jobs did not require deadline-insertions; thus, if Sochis was not pleased with a particular design, it was completely scrapped and redone from scratch.

At one point, she was asked to teach at Pratt. Sochis never realized how much she disliked teaching until actually setting foot in a classroom. After one semester, Sochis left Pratt, preferring instead to instruct eager young assistants from the comforts of her own studio.

Today, Reba Sochis is active in design, advertising and promotion. She selectively works on a wide variety of challenging projects.

According to Sochis, enlisting students from design schools presents a problem. "The George Loises and the Bob Gills simply don't exist anymore. The high caliber of young talent is not as prevalent as it once was."

Reba Sochis readily admits to being a demanding taskmaster. But it's done out of a deep-rooted love and respect for her craft. In an era of computer-generated design amidst a get-it-done-yesterday world, it's comforting to know that there are people like Reba Sochis. As long as she still cares, that twinkle in her eyes will continue to light up the design world.

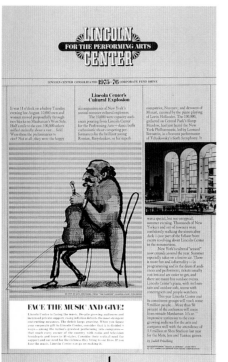

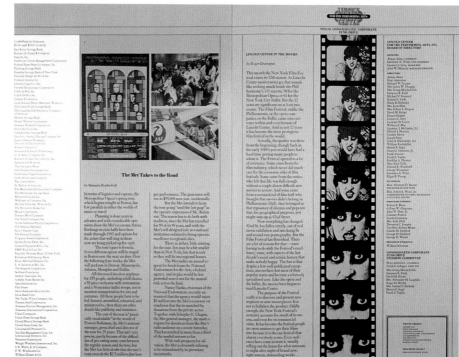

Lincoln Center brochure cover

Lincoln Center brochure, inside spread

Pappagallo Shoe Shops, placemat

Pfizer trade ad

Bulkley Dunton trade ad

Bulkley Dunton corporate brochure

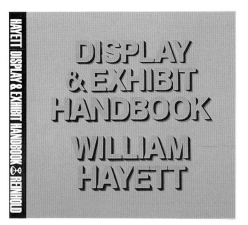

Hayett book jacket

Hayett book endpapers

Talon traveling exhibit

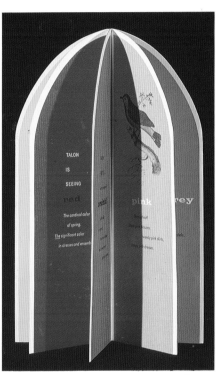

Talon spring color promotion

Delman Shoes newspaper ad

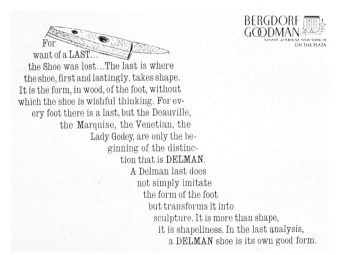

Delman Shoes newspaper ad

Frank Zachary

Jonathan Becker

Countless people are probably asking themselves the following question: "Who the heck is Frank Zachary?" If ever there was an unsung hero who totally epitomizes the specialized craft of magazine editing and art direction, or as he puts it, "graphic journalism," Frank Zachary is that hero. He is living proof of the old geometry theorem, "The whole is equal to the sum of its parts." Indeed.

Born in 1914, the son of Croatian immigrants, Frank Zachary grew up near Pittsburgh, Pennsylvania wanting to become a writer. His mind loved to wander beyond the confines of the local steel mills to poetry and tales of science fiction. At the age of 18, Zachary gathered together a portfolio of short stories he'd written and took them to Henry Scheetz, who owned a

weekly magazine called the *Pittsburgh Bulletin Index*. Scheetz was genuinely impressed with Zachary's indefatigable drive and enthusiasm, character traits still very much in evidence today. Zachary was hired on the spot! Not as a printer's apprentice, but as an all-purpose news hound. His growing list of responsibilities included: copy boy, beat reporter, layout artist and photographer. Zachary covered everything from society balls and golf tournaments to hard news stories.

While Frank Zachary was busy reporting the news for the *Bulletin Index,* the soon-to-be famous novelist John O'Hara became the magazine's editor. Nine months later, O'Hara left to pursue his career and Zachary replaced him as editor. To supplement both his experience and income, Frank Zachary also became the Pittsburgh correspondent for *Time, Life* and *Fortune* Magazines. This didn't sit too well with his boss at the *Bulletin Index.* They soon parted company.

In 1938, at the age of 24, Frank Zachary headed for New York City with $50 in his pocket. Through the aid of young Cyrus Sulzberger of the *New York Times* family, he was hired at Carl Byoir's public relations agency. Zachary found himself doing bland press releases for a variety of clients.

Feeling cramped and mired in a slump, he left the firm and went to work for Grover Whalen, the master publicist and showman. Client: The 1939 New York World's Fair. Zachary gained on-the-job experience unmatched anywhere—a far cry from those trite news releases he was accustomed to writing. As assistant director in charge of World's Fair magazine publicity, Frank Zachary fed countless feature stories and ideas to magazines on every "hook" imaginable. It was at the fair that he met and befriended a fellow PR writer responsible for radio publicity. His name was Bill Bernbach, the man who ten years later went on to open the legendary advertising agency Doyle Dane Bernbach.

After the World's Fair began to lose its luster and public attention shifted to crumbling world events outside the Fair's Utopian facade, Zachary moved on to organize a number of events for the United China Relief Fund. By 1942, the United States, already enmeshed in the global conflict, needed talented people to help bolster its patriotism. Frank Zachary was hired by the Office of War Information (OWI), where he helped create various propaganda publications to raise morale. He worked with a gifted group of people, from novelist Howard Fast and artist Ludwig Bemelmans to art directors Tobias Moss and Bradbury Thompson. Their combined efforts produced *USA* and *Victory* Magazines. It was Frank Zachary's job as editor and picture coordinator that was to distill his creativity into even greater accomplishments.

After the war, Zachary, already supporting a wife and two daughters, needed to earn more money—hopefully via editing a magazine. He became east coast editor for a monthly publication geared to tyro photography called *Minicam*. Zachary lobbied to change the target audience and format of the magazine. He won. *Minicam* became a wonderful vehicle for professional and artistic photography. He concentrated on stories detailing the stylistic and technical wizardry of Ansel Adams, Harry Callahan, Arnold Newman and others. It was then that Zachary purchased the name of "Modern Photography" for $200, soon replacing *Minicam* as the magazine's title.

While Zachary was preparing an article on *Harper's Bazaar's* master art director Alexey Brodovitch, he became totally amazed and immersed in Brod's style and the "art" in art direction. They became close friends and eventual colleagues.

In the late 1940s, Zachary decided to leave *Modern Photography* and wound up working at a Curtis Publishing Company test publication simply called Magazine "X". It was to be a tabloid similar to *Life*, heavy on features packed with photography. Its title became *People* and Zachary was to become senior editor. Curtis executives, fearing it would lose money to *Life* and compete against its own *Saturday Evening Post*, abruptly cancelled *People*. Instead, Curtis Publishing concentrated its efforts on a faltering travel magazine called *Holiday*, whose editor was Ted Patrick, Zachary's old OWI crony.

By 1948, Frank Zachary, disillusioned with the seemingly impossible task of putting together a successful magazine, took a job once again with Grover Whalen, this time to publicize the golden jubilee of New York's consolidation of five boroughs into one city. The 50th anniversary celebration was rivaled only by the 1939 World's Fair. Whalen, Zachary and crew pulled out all the stops on this project. Everything from the biggest parade in New York history to a monstrous fireworks display in midtown Manhattan helped make this celebration a tremendous success.

In 1949, Frank Zachary left Whalen for the last time. Zachary, along with friend and former *Modern Photography* colleague George Rosenthal, Jr., decided to collaborate on a glossy, *Graphis*-type magazine showcasing the best in graphic design, illustration and photography. Rosenthal got his father to put up $25,000, and the large 9 by 12 inch publication was christened *Portfolio*. No expense was spared to make it one of the most beautifully produced magazines of its day. From paper stock to specially tipped-in inserts, *Portfolio* was a visual feast not to be missed! Stories and artwork featured painters, photographers and graphic designers who specialized in contemporary visual communications. Zachary and Rosenthal lured Alexey Brodovitch to become the magazine's art director. They paid him a whopping $3000 an issue. Paul Rand also got into the act, designing an "absolutely exquisite" letterhead. *Portfolio* was indeed a labor of love.

Reality set in, however, when it came time to pay the bills. Zachary and Rosenthal decided to help defray costs by selling advertising space in the magazine. The ads turned out to be crude and detracted from the overall impact of the publication. So as not to destroy its cachet, advertising was dropped from its pages. This, and Rosenthal Sr.'s decision against further funding, led to the demise of *Portfolio*. From 1949-1951, three glorious issues were produced. Prized as collectors items today, *Portfolio* remains one of the greatest achievements in modern day magazine content and design.

Always seeming to be at the right place at the right time, Frank Zachary was offered the position of picture editor of *Holiday* Magazine. In 1951, *Holiday* was in trouble and needed a fresh injection of creativity. Realizing the challenge involved in turning *Holiday* around, Zachary accepted the job. To him, "The picture *is* the layout." If you have a great image it need not be overshadowed by the type. With that in mind, Zachary began experimenting with layouts of photographs and illustrations a la Brodovitch. Using almost cinematic principles of motion, scale and visual imagery, he transformed a stale and floundering format into a graceful one. Frank Zachary was *Holiday*'s tonic!

According to Zachary, "You're only as good as the people you surround yourself with." He's quick to mention that the success of *Holiday*, as well as the success of other endeavors, may not have been attained if the caliber of illustrators and photographers were not top-notch. Among those whom he is especially indebted to are: Slim Aarons, Henri Cartier-Bresson, Robert Capa, Jean-Michel Folon, George Giusti, Burt Glinn, Edward Gorey, Tom Hollyman, Arnold Newman, Robert Phillips Ronald Searle and John Lewis Stage.

For *Holiday*, Zachary developed what he termed environmental portraiture. Common by today's standards, it rocked editorial photography in the fifties. Case in point: an article on New York's master builder, Robert Moses. A studio shot simply could not capture the essence of the man. For dramatic effect, Zachary thought it would be apropos if Moses could be photographed against the backdrop of New York City. He commissioned Arnold Newman to shoot Moses standing tall on a girder, rigged precariously out over Welfare Island! Needless to say, it was environmental portraiture at its best.

After being passed over as editor of *Holiday* in 1964, Frank Zachary left the magazine for: the world of advertising? Yes! At Mary Wells' request, he was made president of Pritchard-Wood, a McCann-Erickson subsidiary with nine branch offices throughout the world.

Based in New York, Zachary, sensing his lack of ability to succeed in advertising, stayed only eight months at Pritchard. He then moved to McCann's experimental Center for Advanced Practice, an in-house think tank dedicated to new and innovative marketing techniques. There, he worked closely with Bill Backer and Henry Wolf.

Zachary, a fish out of water, decided to return to *Holiday* as art director in 1969. It was too much too late. *Holiday* had once again hit the skids after he left in 1964, and its popularity continued to decline. Attempts to revive it proved futile, and *Holiday* was sold, with Zachary's assistance, to a businessman named Marty Ackerman. Ackerman also bought *Status* Magazine, and for Zachary's help in acquiring *Holiday* rewarded him with the position of editor. Zachary performed his magic once again, making *Status* a spirited publication.

When his *Status* contract expired, he left to join *Travel & Leisure*. In 1972, after making his imprint there, Frank Zachary came full circle and was offered the plum job of editor-in-chief at *Town & Country* Magazine, a position he has held for 18 years.

Under Zachary, *Town & Country*'s focal points have shifted to a very successful combination of high society with emphasis on trends in fashion and graceful living. He also spiced it up with a dash of highbrow satire. When Zachary took over as editor-in-chief in 1972, *Town & Country* had a circulation of 120,000 and $3 million in gross revenues. Today, it boasts a circulation of over 440,000 and gross revenues in excess of $32 million.

At the age of 76, Frank Zachary is the oldest editor-in-chief of any US publication. He remains as vibrant as the magazine he presides over. Zachary's concepts and designs have forever changed the way magazines are produced, read and enjoyed. Blessed with the innate ability and drive to adapt design considerations to societal changes, imbued also with a unique brand of graphic sense, Frank Zachary is truly the gin-in-the-punch of modern day magazine design.

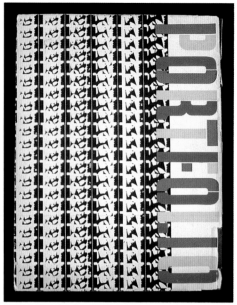

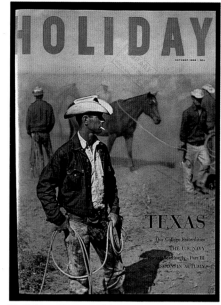

Portfolio, *1948-1950; cover: Herbert Matter*

Jazzways, *1950; cover: Paul Rand*

Holiday, *1951-1964; cover: John Lewis Stage*

Holiday, *1951-1964; photo: Henri Cartier-Bresson*

Holiday, *1951-1964; cover: George Giusti*

Holiday, *1951-1964; photo: Arnold Newman*

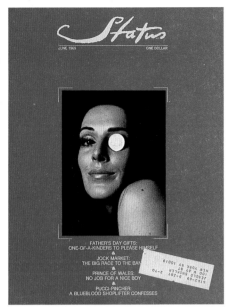

Status, *1969-1971;*
cover: Henry Wolf, Salvador Dali

Travel & Leisure, *1971-1972;*
cover: Ronald Searle

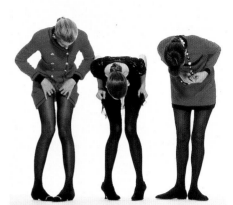

Town & Country, *1972-Present;*
photo: Jerry Salvati

Town & Country, *1972-Present;*
cover: Norman Parkinson

The Kings of Hollywood: Clark Gable, Van Heflin, Gary Cooper & James Stewart, Hollywood, 1958.

Town & Country, *1972-Present; photo: Slim Aarons*

Town & Country, *1972-Present; photo: Victor Skrebneski*

ADC Hall of Fame

Special Award

Robert Weaver

Saul Leiter

Talent runs in Robert Weaver's family. His brother Fritz is the extremely gifted television and Shakespearean actor. Robert is the wonderfully versatile illustrator whose striking images have graced the pages of the country's most respected magazines. His work came to the forefront of American illustration at a time when the country needed a graphic conscience. Robert Weaver, through his cleverly placed brush strokes or pen in ink, was our conscience—whether we knew it or not.

Born in Pittsburgh, Pennsylvania in 1924, Robert Weaver attended the Carnegie Institute of Technology in his hometown and the Art Students League in New York. After serving overseas in the military during World War II, Weaver did not immediately return to his native soil, opting instead to settle in Venice. He spent two years studying at the Academia Delle Belle Arti. Amidst the beauty of Renaissance antiquity and canals dotted with gondolas, Robert Weaver continued to master his drawing technique.

By the mid-fifties, Weaver arrived back in New York armed only with a modicum of confidence and a battered book filled with color mural sketches. He dropped them off at *Town & Country* Magazine. The publication's art director, Tony Mazzola, was intrigued by his work and hired him to illustrate several manuscripts scheduled to appear in subsequent issues of the magazine.

In what has become almost a folklorish tale of naivete, Weaver, knowing little of the technical jargon used to put a magazine together, misunderstood Mazzola when he was asked to "omit bleeding and stay out of the gutter." Weaver took this to mean no violence or harsh visuals! Finally

explaining the terminology to Weaver, Mazzola proceeded to use him on a number of occasions. For Robert Weaver, the thrill of seeing his work appear in print and admired by countless people became an "addiction" that lasted four decades.

His work was showcased in every major editorial publication. Readers of *Charm, Esquire, Fortune, Life, Look, Playboy, Seventeen, Sports Illustrated* and *TV Guide* were constantly treated to Weaver's social portraitures. From visually covering the Kennedy campaign in *Esquire* to the last days of Ebbets Field for *Sports Illustrated*, Robert Weaver's work, though commissioned for specific and timely publication, remains timeless.

Because of his vivid visual style, magazine art directors put very little in the way of restrictions on him. Weaver is particularly indebted to ADC Hall of Famers Leo Lionni and Henry Wolf for encouraging him to "break the rules."

Weaver's talent did not stop at illustrating for magazines. His increasing popularity spilled over into the world of promotion and graphics as a record jacket illustrator. Weaver's portrayals of jazz personalities, from traditional to bebop, are especially noteworthy. Whether it was a study of vibrophonist Milt Jackson hunched over his instrument or of alto legend Charlie Parker playing the blues, Robert Weaver captured the true essence of the music through his memorable visuals.

His work has won him a myriad of recognition in the form of articles, awards and gallery exhibits. Weaver was inducted into the Society of Illustrators Hall of Fame in 1985. He's been a visiting professor at Syracuse University and for over 30 years has taught illustration at New York's School of Visual Arts. Silas H. Rhodes,

chairman of the board of SVA, characterized Weaver's unmistakable style by saying, "In a triumph of principle, Robert Weaver's art *is* the fine art of illustration."

A typical class will no doubt hear Weaver talk about his craft and wax philosophical on a variety of topics, be it the preservation of our environment or the beauty of baseball. He encourages his students to split from the ordinary and take chances. Weaver regularly brings in people for his students to study and draw. They range from street people and ordinary people to dancers and Guardian Angels, all representing the fabric of our society depicted via the sketch pad.

As tribute to his dynamic body of work, the School of Visual Arts has had two very successful Weaver exhibitions: a retrospective in 1977 and a more recent show encompassing his extraordinary dimensional collages.

Realizing that times change and magazines can no longer provide a forum for his talents, Weaver has turned to the book format, which offers him a wider canvas with which to express himself. A variety of projects, his dimensional collages and teaching duties keep him busy.

A close friend of Weaver's, and one of the nation's best illustrators, Jim McMullan paid tribute to him this way:

Perhaps it is impossible to speak of Weaver's drawing as a quality distinct from the special kinds of connections he makes in his work; for that same synthesis of surface and subject occurs in the ideas that animate his paintings. They are ideas which remind you always of the immutability of the two dimensional surface while taking you simultaneously on a wild mental journey of associations. The way in which he manipulates your view of the surface in the painting and of the idea "surface" in the objects painted is very much the way a magician shows you the handkerchief; 'Here it is, this flimsy piece of cloth—I wave it about—It is all rather insubstantial—But, presto! A bouquet of flowers.' In Weaver's case, the handkerchief might be the paper he is drawing on, or the paper he draws. He insists on its paperness only to prestidigitate the effect of some other reality and finally to return you to the paper.

A very gentle, soft spoken man, Robert Weaver speaks and creates with great emotional eloquence. For his great contributions and achievements, changing the direction of illustration and publishing while sharing his vision with hundreds of grateful students, the Art Directors Club Hall of Fame takes great pride in presenting him with this recognition. Leave it to Weaver...

ADVERTISING

Zoo visitors, please remember: ugly animals like being looked at, too.

When you take a look at some of our not-exactly-what-you'd-call-cuddly animals here at the Zoo, always try to remember one thing.

Ugliness is in the eye of the beholder. Please keep this in mind when you first behold the warthog.

The bat is one of the most misunderstood mammals. Nature needs fruit bats to help pollinate plants.

The warthog may look a little odd to you. But, in nature, almost everything has its purpose.

Take those lumpy bumps on the sides of a warthog's head (it's not called a warthog for nothing, you know). They protect the warthog as it digs up the ground

SAIGA
Saiga tatarica

Don't think of it as a large nose. Think of it as a small air filter and heater.

looking for tasty roots.

And they also protect the males when they bang their heads together to compete for a female.

The warthog also has a stringy, scraggly tail that sticks up in the air when it runs. Some people think that it acts like a little flag to the other warthogs running behind in the tall grasses.

So you see?

Ugly to you, maybe.

Very useful to a warthog.

WARTHOG
Weight: up to 200lbs.
Length: 5' Height: 28" at shoulder
Tusks: Upper pair can curl upward to 12" or more in length.

After you've seen all you want to see of the warthog, walk over to Hoof and Horn Mesa and look for an animal called the Russian saiga (you can't miss it, just look for a big nose).

In Siberia where the saiga lives, it's bitter cold in the winter and very dusty in the summer. When the saiga breathes, the large nose works as a heater and air filter.

TWO-HEADED SKINK

If you're a skink's enemy, you're never really sure which end to attack first.

Over on the other side of the Zoo, stop by Reptile Mesa where we have the tortoises and alligators. And check out the two-headed skink. So named because its back end looks like its front end, and vice versa.

In the wild, this tends to confuse a skink's enemy, at least long enough for the skink to get both of its ends out of there.

Why don't you come and see some of these things for yourself?

When you find out why some animals are different-looking, maybe you'll start looking at them a little differently.

What big eyes a gecko has. All the better to see you with at night, my dear.

And then you'll feel the way we do. That there's really no such thing as an ugly animal.

Although the warthog comes very, very close.

Just when you thought you'd seen everything.
The San Diego Zoo

Pygmy hippos. Isn't that like saying jumbo shrimp?

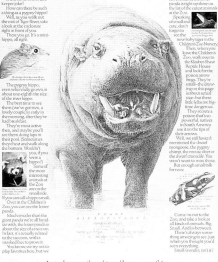

Is this some sort of zoo-keeper joke? How can there be such a thing as a pygmy hippo? Well, as you walk out the exit of Tiger River, take a look at the enclosure right in front of you. There you go. It's a mini-hippo, all right.

The pygmy hippo, even when fully grown, is about one-eighth the size of the river hippo.

The best time to see them (we've got two, a lovely couple) is early in the morning, after they've had breakfast.

They're most active then, and maybe you'll see them doing laps in their pool. (Sometimes they cheat and walk along the bottom.

you, if you were a hippo?) Some of the most interesting animals at the Zoo are on the small side. If you can call a hippo small.

Over in the Children's Zoo, you can see the lesser panda.

Much smaller than the giant panda we're all familiar with, the lesser panda is about the size of a raccoon. In fact, it's actually related to the raccoon, with a masked face to prove it.

You know, we try not to play favorites here, but we

have to admit the lesser panda is right up there on the list of the cutest animals at the Zoo.

Speaking of small and cute, don't forget to see the new baby tiger in the Children's Zoo Nursery.

Then, when you leave the Children's Zoo, walk over to the Klauber-Shaw Reptile House and look for the poison arrow frogs. They're small—the drawing on this page is about actual size—but these little fellas are big-time dangerous.

They secrete a poison that's so powerful, natives in South America use it on the tips of their arrows.

Well, we still haven't mentioned the dwarf mongoose, the pygmy chimp, the mouse deer or the dwarf crocodile. You won't want to miss those.

But enough small talk for now.

Come on out to the Zoo, and take a look at all kinds of animals. Big. Small. And in-between.

There's always something amazing to see. Just when you thought you'd seen everything.

Small wonder, isn't it?

Just when you thought you'd seen everything.
The San Diego Zoo

Visit our convenient new location in the jungles of Asia.

You won't need a passport, any of those painful shots or that insect repellent that smells like turpentine. Just come and visit new Sun Bear Forest at the Zoo.

We've re-created an Asian rain forest complete with more than 4,000 plants. A lush aviary. Cascading waterfalls and quiet pools of water.

And it's the new home for some of the most mysterious, elusive animals in the world.

The sun bears from Malaysia. And the lion-tailed macaques from India.

The sun bear is the smallest bear in the world. It gets its name from the mark on its chest that resembles a setting sun.

Maybe you'll see them climbing on the fallen logs in their new home.

There's even a big tree with a honey dispenser timed to release honey, as a special treat for the bears (and

a treat for you, to watch).

And speaking of trees, even the trees in Sun Bear Forest are mysterious.

There's one called the sacred fig tree. Also called the strangler fig of Asia. As it grows, it wraps its branches around other plants, strangling them.

If you walk around the corner, you'll see some of the rarest monkeys in the world.

No more than 2,000 lion-tailed macaques are thought to be alive in the wild.

We're very proud to be able to give ours a big, new home like this.

We've designed it to fit their playful nature, with trees and vines to swing on, tall grasses to hide in, and cool, rushing streams for wading.

As you can probably tell, we're pretty excited about Sun Bear Forest.

And the best part is, you don't have to go to Asia to see it.

It's right here, at the always-changing, always-amazing, just-when-you-thought-you'd-seen-everything Zoo.

Sun Bear Forest At The San Diego Zoo.
Just when you thought you'd seen everything.

ADVERTISING

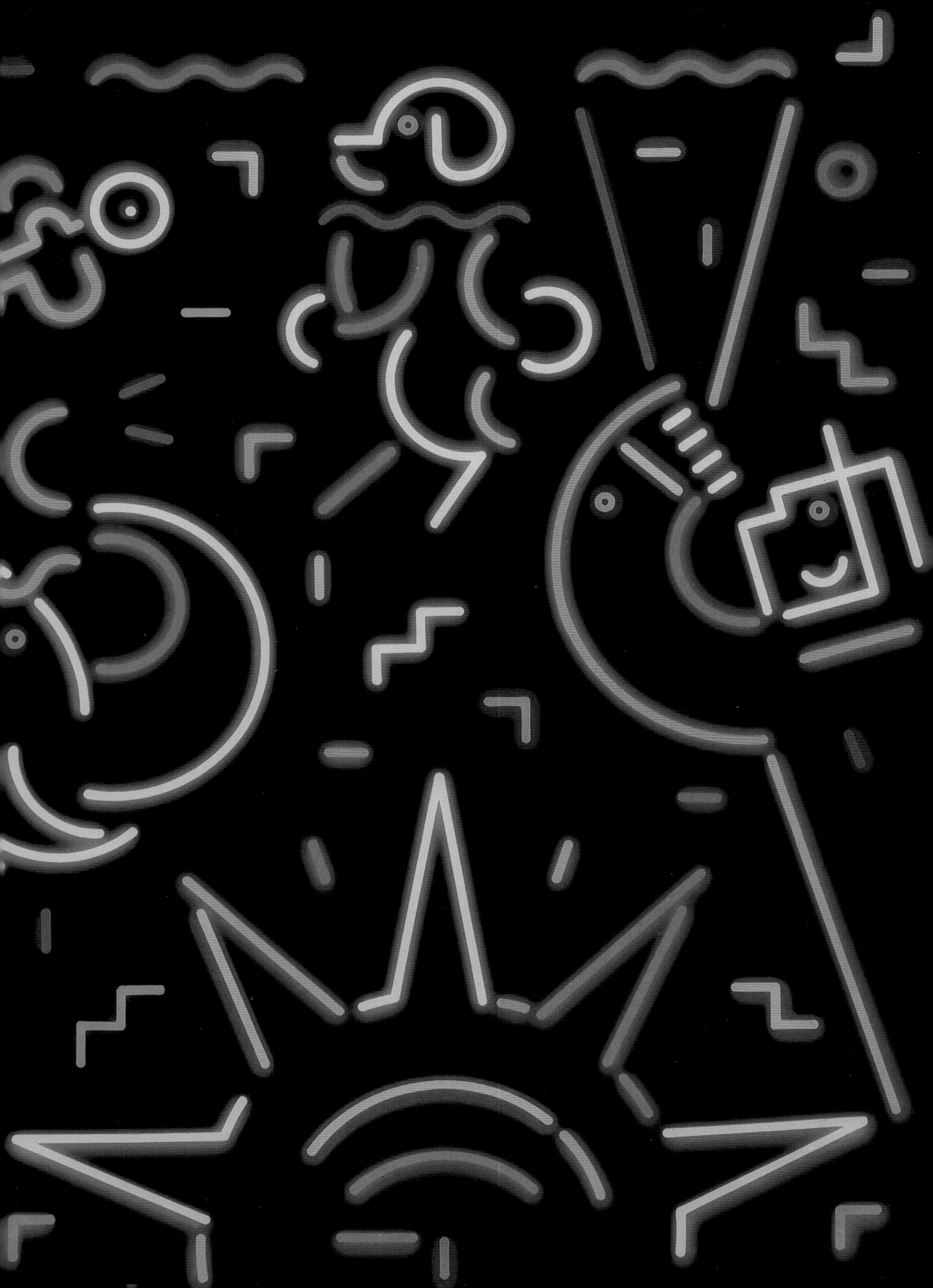

When people at work ask what you did over the weekend, you can always tell them you helped save the planet.

If you've always wanted to help endangered animals, but never knew what you could do to help, we have a very simple suggestion.

Get everyone into the car and come out to the Wild Animal Park.

Here, you can not only have a good time, you can spend your time doing some good.

That's because your attendance and support helps us help the animals.

We provide a haven where endangered animals can live their lives and raise their families, safe from a world that's closing in fast.

As you ride an electric monorail through two valleys, you'll see good things happening out here. You'll watch hundreds of animals living as they would in the wild. Animals sharing the land, babies that have just been born, herds that have room to run.

Later, take in the serenity of a waterfowl lagoon. Enjoy our animal shows. Pet a Persian gazelle. Or observe the antics of a gorilla troop.

And when the day's over, you won't just leave the Wild Animal Park. You'll leave it a little better off.

The San Diego Wild Animal Park. The rarest of animals. In the rarest of places.

To visit us, take I-15 to the Via Rancho Parkway exit and follow the signs. Or call 747-8702 for more information.

The San Diego Wild Animal Park

Most amusement parks offer a pleasant escape from life. We offer a pleasant return to it.

Come to the San Diego Wild Animal Park, and come back to life.

You'll see rhinos and zebras and wildebeests and animals you don't even know the names of (don't worry, we'll tell you) roaming the landscape.

As a silent, electric monorail carries you on a five-mile trip through two valleys, you'll see things rarely seen outside Africa or Asia.

Maybe you'll watch two giraffes "sparring" with their necks. A newborn gazelle, looking at its mother for the first time. A water buffalo, its head poking above the water, looking at you.

Or you can set out on your own, and walk down a hiking trail, through an Australian rain forest, over a suspension bridge, past African flowers.

Maybe you'll just stand there. Fascinated. For longer than you'd ever imagine, as you see a gorilla troop equally fascinated with a newborn family member.

You can pet a blackbuck antelope. Take home a tillandsia plant. Or watch animal shows with everything from eagles to bears, opossums to kangaroos.

If you want to get away from life for a little while, start by coming back to it.

At the San Diego Wild Animal Park. The rarest of animals. In the rarest of places.

To visit us, take I-15 to the Via Rancho Parkway exit. Or call (619) 480-0100 for more information.

The San Diego Wild Animal Park

If the Serengeti had a backyard, this is what it would be like.

Come to the Wild Animal Park, and you can go on a remarkable trip.

During our 50-minute monorail tour, you'll see the wildlife of Africa and Asia.

And you'll see more wild animals in those 50 minutes than many people see in a lifetime.

They're everywhere you look.

Herds of wildebeest, blackbucks and deer. All running free in our 1,800-acre preserve.

As you ride, and look, and listen, you'll begin to understand why we're here. To provide a sanctuary where endangered animals can live and breed in peace. So, even though the animal world keeps getting smaller and smaller, there will always be a place, a safe place, for them to live.

After you take the monorail tour, there's still plenty to do and see. A gorilla mother playing with her baby. You can take in the new Australian Show and African Marsh exhibit. Or just explore things on your own as you walk along the Kilimanjaro Trail.

Later, you can take home an exotic artifact from our gift shop. And you'll take home something else, too. An unforgettable picture of what life must be like in the wild. At the San Diego Wild Animal Park. The rarest of animals. In the rarest of places.

To visit us, take I-15 to the Via Rancho Parkway exit. Or call (619) 747-8702 for more information.

The San Diego Wild Animal Park

2 Gold

Art Director: John Vitro
Creative Director: Jim Winters
Photographer: Jim Brandenberg
Copywriter: John Robertson
Agency: Franklin & Associates
Client: San Diego Wild Animal Park

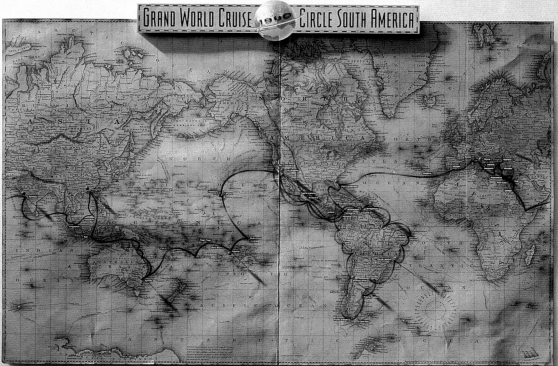

3 Gold
Art Director: David Page
Creative Director: Jeffrey Goodby
Rich Silverstein
Photographer: Harvey Lloyd
Aaron Jones
Duncan Sim
Copywriter: David O'Hare
Agency: Goodby, Berlin & Silverstein
Client: Royal Viking Line

Perception.

Reality.

For a new generation of Rolling Stone readers, a mouse is not a furry little animal that processes cheese. The mouse we're talking about processes information. And last year, the mouse population, especially among Rolling Stone readers, was on the rise. Rolling Stone readers purchased more than $657 million worth of personal computer equipment and software during 1988. That ain't cheese. If you want to catch your share of that action, bait your trap in the pages of Rolling Stone.

RollingStone

Perception.

Reality.

For a new generation of Rolling Stone readers, it isn't necessary to munch on magic mushrooms to appreciate contemporary American literature. Rolling Stone readers turn the pages of America's best sellers at the rate of 13 million books a year. If you're looking for a highly educated, discerning audience for your advertising message, you'll get great reviews in the pages of Rolling Stone.

RollingStone

Perception.

Reality.

Bummer, Bullwinkle. For a new generation of Rolling Stone readers, mousse is a hair care product, not the star of a Saturday morning cartoon. Last week, Rolling Stone readers used mousse and other hair care products more than 76 million times. If you've got health and beauty products to sell, rack up the sales with your ad in the pages of Rolling Stone.

RollingStone

4 Gold

Art Director: Houman Pirdavari
Creative Director: Pat Burnham
Photographer: Jim Arndt
Rick Dublin
Copywriter: Bill Miller
Agency: Fallon McElligott
Client: Rolling Stone

If the Serengeti had a backyard, this is what it would be like.

Come to the Wild Animal Park, and you can go on a remarkable trip.

During our 50-minute monorail tour, you'll see the wildlife of Africa and Asia.

And you'll see more wild animals in those 50 minutes than many people see in a lifetime.

They're everywhere you look.

Herds of wildebeest, blackbucks and deer. All running free in our 1,800-acre preserve.

As you ride, and look, and listen, you'll begin to understand why we're here. To provide a sanctuary where endangered animals can live and breed in peace. So, even though the animal world keeps getting smaller and smaller, there will always be a place, a safe place, for them to live.

After you take the monorail tour, there's still plenty to do and see. A gorilla mother playing with her baby. You can take in the new Australian Show and African Marsh exhibit. Or just explore things on your own as you walk along the Kilimanjaro Trail.

Later, you can take home an exotic artifact from our gift shop. And you'll take home something else, too.

An unforgettable picture of what life must be like in the wild. At the San Diego Wild Animal Park. The rarest of animals. In the rarest of places.

To visit us, take I-15 to the Via Rancho Parkway exit. Or call (619) 747-8702 for more information.

The San Diego Wild Animal Park

5 Silver

Art Director: John Vitro
Creative Director: Jim Winters
Photographer: Jim Brandenberg
Copywriter: John Robertson
Agency: Franklin & Associates
Client: San Diego Wild Animal Park

Last Year Wendee Weichel Beat A Competitor That Tried To Kill Her.

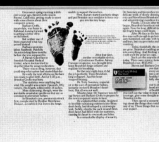

On May 25, 1988, Steven And Barbara Crofts Had A Baby They Weren't Expecting.

The Day Maryanne Blake Took A $75,000 Bike Ride.

This x-ray is not for those with weak stomachs. It shows how Maryanne's hand was broken and nearly severed from her arm.

The steel rods were in this x-ray are part of the external fixator which held Maryanne's wrist motionless so broken bones could heal.

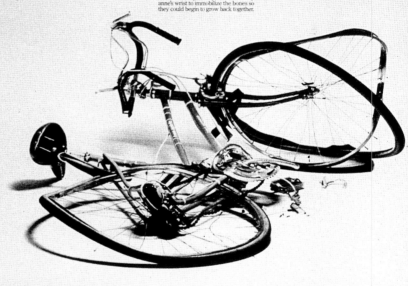

TO GET HIRED THESE DAYS, YOU HAVE TO FILL MORE THAN THE JOB REQUIREMENTS.

Many companies across Ohio are instituting mandatory drug testing procedures, such as urinalysis, for screening job applicants.
Starting Wednesday, Tom Beres will show you what it means when they tell you they want to see a sample of your work. Watch "The Test That Could Mean Your Job," all this week on Channel 3 News at 11.   **CHANNEL3NEWS**

THIS WEEK, FIND OUT HOW CIGARETTE SMOKING CAN AFFECT SEXUAL PERFORMANCE.

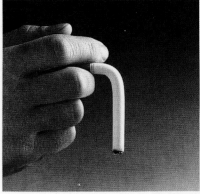

Medical researchers have found a definite connection between cigarette smoking and impotence in men.
Starting Thursday, Eileen Korey will tell you another reason why your loved ones want you to quit smoking. Watch "Smoking & Impotence" on WKYC-TV, Channel 3 News at 11.   **3 NEWS**
Eileen Korey

THANKS TO VIDEO STORES, KIDS HAVE A WHOLE NEW REASON TO CALL TELEVISION THE BOOB TUBE.

Many video stores in this area will rent adult movies to minors—movies that contain explicit sex and violence.
Starting Wednesday, Jill Beach will tell you how these stores are giving the term "boob tube" a whole new meaning. Watch "Sex-'N-Guns To Go" on WKYC-TV, Channel 3 News at 11.   **CHANNEL3NEWS**

7 Silver
Art Director: Don Fibich
Creative Director: Tom Smith
Chuck Withrow
Designer: Don Fibich
Photographer: Ladd Trepal
Martin Reuben
Copywriter: Laura Owen
Agency: Wyse Advertising
Client: WKYC-TV3

LOOK WHAT HAPPENS WHEN YOU PUT THE CUSTOMER FIRST.

J.D. Power & Associates **1987** CUSTOMER SATISFACTION INDEX	J.D. Power & Associates **1988** CUSTOMER SATISFACTION INDEX	J.D. Power & Associates **1989** CUSTOMER SATISFACTION INDEX
1. Acura	1. Acura	1. Acura
2. Honda	2. Mercedes	2. Mercedes
3. Mercedes	3. Honda	3. Honda
4. Toyota	4. Cadillac	4. Toyota
5. Mazda	5. Toyota	5. Cadillac
6. Subaru	6. Lincoln	6. Nissan
7. Cadillac	7. BMW	7. Subaru
8. Nissan	8. Volvo	8. Mazda
8. Jaguar	9. Mazda	8. BMW
10. Mercury	9. Audi	10. Buick
11. BMW	11. Subaru	11. Plymouth
11. Lincoln	12. Nissan	12. Audi
		12. Volvo

Since the Acura Legend and Integra were introduced 3½ years ago, we've had one simple philosophy. Provide the kinds of automobiles and automobile dealers that cater to the needs of the driver, instead of the other way around. Like the old saying goes, putting the customer first. An idea whose time has obviously come again.

For the last three years running, Acura automobiles and Acura dealers have been ranked the most satisfying in America, according to the J.D. Power and Associates Customer Satisfaction Index™ survey of product quality and dealer service. In fact, they've been number one among all automakers every year they've been eligible. And, the people who ranked Acura number one were the people most qualified to judge. The ones who own Acura automobiles.

Which, of course, brings us to yet another old saying...the customer is always right.

For more information or the name of the dealer nearest you, call 1-800-TO-ACURA.

ACURA *Precision crafted performance.*

WHERE IS YOUR CAR PARKED?

ACURA

WE'VE BEEN WORKING ON THIS AD FOR THREE YEARS.

J.D. Power & Associates **1987** CUSTOMER SATISFACTION INDEX	J.D. Power & Associates **1988** CUSTOMER SATISFACTION INDEX	J.D. Power & Associates **1989** CUSTOMER SATISFACTION INDEX
1. Acura	1. Acura	1. Acura
2. Honda	2. Mercedes	2. Mercedes
3. Mercedes	3. Honda	3. Honda
4. Toyota	4. Cadillac	4. Toyota
5. Mazda	5. Toyota	5. Cadillac
6. Subaru	6. Lincoln	6. Nissan
7. Cadillac	7. BMW	7. Subaru
8. Nissan	8. Volvo	8. Mazda
8. Jaguar	9. Mazda	8. BMW
10. Mercury	9. Audi	10. Buick
11. BMW	11. Subaru	11. Plymouth
11. Lincoln	12. Nissan	12. Audi
		12. Volvo

It began in 1987. For the first time in history, a new automobile, in fact, a whole new automobile division, was ranked number one in the prestigious J.D. Power and Associates Customer Satisfaction Index. That automobile was called Acura. And while some were skeptical about this new entry into the luxury automobile segment, the numbers didn't lie.

Over 30,000 Acura automobiles were sold the first year. And when Acura owners were questioned, their answer came back as an overwhelming vote of confidence. The Acura Legend and Integra were indeed, the most satisfying cars in America. In 1988, automotive history repeated itself.

Today, there are over 370,000 Acura automobiles on the road and over 300 dealers nationwide. And as you might have guessed, those cars and dealers have been ranked number one in Customer Satisfaction with product quality and dealer service for the third year in a row. Astonishingly, Acura has been ranked number one among all automakers, both domestic and import, every year that it has been eligible.

To some people, an accomplishment like that would be good cause to celebrate. But, to our way of thinking, this ad still needs work. For more information or the dealer nearest you, call 1-800-TO-ACURA.

ACURA *Precision crafted performance.*

Can you spot the Range Rover in this picture?

Goodbye road. Goodbye traffic. Goodbye 5 m.p.h.

A Range Rover does something far more impressive than get you through a traffic jam in air-conditioned, arm-chaired, stereo-surrounded comfort.

A Range Rover takes you where there are no jams. Because there is no traffic.

Through the woods. Along the beach. Across the desert. Range Rovers, after all, are so extraordinary, they drive for years in places

ordinary cars couldn't drive a quarter of a mile.

So it's not surprising that to many a Range Rover's most luxurious feature isn't its elegant interior, optional sunroof, or the

RANGE ROVER

security of 24 hour roadside assistance.

Its most luxurious feature is its ability to provide an experience a bit more exhilarating than a highway to the suburbs at six p.m.

Why not call 1-800-FINE 4WD for the Range Rover dealer nearest you?

We won't deny that at somewhat above $34,000 a Range Rover is hardly inexpensive.

But after all the time you've spent in trafficlikethis, what could be nicer than going off on your own?

9 Silver

Art Director: Roy Grace
Creative Director: Roy Grace
Diane Rothschild
Photographer: Carl Furuta
Copywriter: Diane Rothschild
Client: Range Rover of North America

WE DESIGN EVERY VOLVO TO LOOK LIKE THIS.

You're looking at a perfect Volvo. A Volvo that performed exactly as our safety engineers designed it to.

Its front and rear ends, for example, collapsed on impact. As a result, much of the crash energy was absorbed instead of being passed on to the passengers.

The car's middle section, however, didn't collapse. That's because the entire passenger compartment is surrounded by Volvo's unique "safety cage." Made of six box section steel pillars, this protective housing is strong enough to support the weight of six Volvos.

But the passengers of this car were also protected in ways you can't see. Because inside are such standard features as a driver's side Supplemental Restraint System, a collapsible steering column and, of course, 3-point seat belts, front and rear.

Every Volvo is designed to help protect its passengers in all these ways. And, as a result, will look remarkably similar to this one after being in the same type of accident.

If you're concerned about safety, you can't find a more beautiful car.

VOLVO
A car you can believe in.

10 Silver

Art Director: Paul Blade
Creative Director: Earl Cavanah
Photographer: James Lindgren
Copywriter: Larry Hampel
Agency: Scali, McCabe, Sloves
Client: Volvo

Many boots are waterproof. Few are water proven.

Of all the tests a bootmaker can use, none is more valuable than the test of time. A test which clearly proves no boot on earth is as warm, dry and comfortable as any in the Timberland Sport Series. Each stands for two decades of leadership in the science of waterproofing. Each goes through a double waterproofing process, which combines advanced silicone-impregnation with the best Gore-Tex fabric bootie construction. And each has our lightweight polyurethane sole for comfort and durability.

Timberland. Still the driest after twenty years in the water.

Boots, shoes, clothing, wind, water, earth and sky.

If you want to walk to heaven, wear a boot that can go through hell.

Proof that the worlds most seaworthy vessels are still built by hand.

11 Silver

Art Director: Brian Fandetti
Creative Director: Paul Silverman
Photographer: Harry DeZitter
Jack Richmond
Agency: Mullen
Client: Timberland Co.

James Clavell. Cardmember since 1967.

*Membership
Has Its Privileges.*

Don't leave home without it.
Call 1-800-THE CARD to apply

Al Hirschfeld. Cardmember since 1959.

*Membership
Has Its Privileges.*

Don't leave home without it.
Call 1-800-THE CARD to apply

Catherine Deneuve. Cardmember since 1978.

*Membership
Has Its Privileges.*

Don't leave home without it.
Call 1-800-THE CARD to apply

12 Silver

Art Director: Parry Merkley
Rick Rabe
Creative Director: Gordon Bowen
Photographer: Annie Leibovitz
Copywriter: Gordon Bowen
Agency: Ogilvy & Mather
Client: American Express

You always come back to the basics.

1959.

1965.

1970.

1973.

1976.

1984.

1987.

1990.

You always come back to the basics.

JIM BEAM

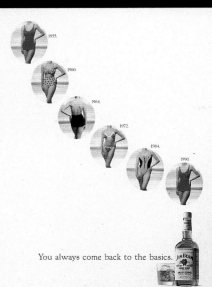

You always come back to the basics.

CHINA, BY WAY OF SHANGRI-LA.

THE PEAKS OF GUILIN RISE ALARMINGLY FROM THE GUANGXI PLAIN, LIKE THE MOUNDS OF BURROWING ANIMALS ABOUT TO SURFACE. "OUR POET ZHANG GU," SAYS YOUR GUIDE, "WROTE that these mountains cross the space from earth to heaven." And for more than a minute, your normally garrulous group falls silent, transfixed. There is only the sound of the wind.

A vacation is not so much a continuous journey as it is a series of moments that you will carry with you and return to for years to come. You never know what

apparently insignificant detail, what tiny thing taken care of just so, will one day be the key to such a memory.

Victoria Harbor, Hong Kong. From the sweep of the Promenade Deck, we look down upon an armada of three-masted junks, quilt-rigged and bobbing like toys in our wake. Astonishingly, pigs and chickens roam their decks. From

an unseen stewpot, a whiff of ginger.

With a gloriously white Royal Viking ship as your base of operations, you will see a China that few other visitors ever uncover.

As the world's most experienced cruise line to The People's Republic, we have been officially designated an "Honored Guest," and accorded special privileges like visitation to Chinese homes, warm welcomes from local officials, and swift, supervised passage for your land excursions.

It is the last nation on earth to continue the manufacture of steam locomotives. Gasping, thunderous, they storm out of the middle distance, casting a dreamy feeling over whatever's going on at the moment.

Our ship is your sanctuary, your home after a busy day. Here you will find the highest crew to passenger ratio in the world. You will find breezy, strollable decks and staterooms worthy of the name. You will dine, in splendid single seating, on the creations of chefs trained at Roger Vergé and Le Nôtre.

Wanlichangcheng, they call it, The Great Wall— 4000 miles long and wide enough to accommodate five horsemen side by side. Once, on this very spot, a network of bonfires warned the emperor of his approaching fate, sealed in the swords of Mongols thousands of miles distant.

The breeze in your hair. High tea at four. Ahead, The Forbidden City.

And so it is that a vacation, in the best sense, can last forever. This is a delicate transaction, however, and one that does not brook compromise. At Royal Viking we know this. We charge a bit more for knowing it. But then, what we are doing may be nothing less than priceless.

Eight trips to China are planned this year. Isn't it time you joined us? For more information and a copy of our colorful 1989 Cruise Atlas, please visit your trusted travel agent or call us at (800) 426-0821.

As always, we look forward to seeing you on board.

ROYAL VIKING LINE

IT IS ONE OF THE WORLD'S GREAT WONDERS. SOON, IT WILL BE MAKING ITS WAY TO THE AMAZON.

A TRULY GREAT SHIP IS SOMETHING OF A DESTINATION IN ITSELF.

Perception.

Reality.

For a new generation of Rolling Stone readers, a mouse is not a furry little animal that processes cheese. The mouse we're talking about processes information. And last year, the mouse population, especially among Rolling Stone readers, was on the rise. Rolling Stone readers purchased more than $657 million worth of personal computer equipment and software during 1988. That ain't cheese. If you want to catch your share of that action, bait your trap in the pages of Rolling Stone.

Rolling Stone

15 Silver

Art Director: Houman Pirdavari
Creative Director: Pat Burnham
Photographer: Rick Dublin
Copywriter: Bill Miller
Agency: Fallon McElligott
Client: Rolling Stone

Sporting Hush Puppies.

Allow us to point out our new look. Soft leather men's casuals and women's Body Shoes—with the Comfort Curve' sole to flex where your foot flexes. In a flush of spring colors.

16 Silver

Art Director: Bob Barrie
Creative Director: Pat Burnham
Designer: Bob Barrie
Photographer: Rick Dublin
Copywriter: Jarl Olsen
Agency: Fallon McElligott
Client: Hush Puppies

For twenty years they've been insulated from snow, oblivious to rain, impervious to competition.

Before the Timberland Company existed, only one kind of boot was truly waterproof. The kind you don't like to wear. Because it's made of something other than leather, something plastic or rubber that doesn't breathe.

Relief came two decades ago, when Timberland craftsmen hand-built a full-grain leather boot that was guaranteed waterproof. And insulated.

It was a concept the world was waiting for. No sooner did our boot hit the stores than it sold out. And today it still sells out, even though imitations abound both here and abroad.

The fact is, copying the look of our classic tan buck boot is far easier than copying the workmanship. The meticulous silicone impregnation of the leather, the four-row nylon stitching, the direct bonding of upper to midsole for a guaranteed waterproof seal, and the unbeatable warmth of Thinsulate® insulation.

You live on an earth that's two-thirds water. Can you afford a lesser boot than ours?

Timberland ⊕

Boots, shoes, clothing, wind, water, / earth and sky.

Boat shoes that have conquered every adverse sailing condition imaginable, including a sea of competition.

The headline on this page isn't something you should accept without substantiation. So let us hasten to provide it.

Timberland boat shoes are stronger because our construction is superior. You will never see one of our soles flapping loose in the breeze, unstitched from its moccasin upper. We eliminate such stitching altogether in favor of permanent bonding, so shoe and sole stay married until the day they die.

And unlike boat shoes of a lesser quality, ours have premium natural leathers that won't crack, impregnable nylon stitching that won't rot, and solid brass eyelets that won't chip.

This year, we're pleased to introduce the high-performance Ultra Boat Shoe, companion to our Super and Classic Boat Shoe. The Ultra combines the grip and stability of a triple density outsole with the comfort and cushioning of a double density midsole. For maximum dryness, the stain-resistant, waterproof leathers have a Hydrofil® lining to wick away moisture.

Water, water, it's everywhere. So is Timberland.

 Timberland ⊕

Boots, shoes, clothing, wind, water, / earth and sky.

There are two things you shouldn't be up the creek without. One of them is a paddle.

The other is a pair of boots from the Timberland Sporting Collection. Because even though we can't keep water out of your boat, we guarantee it won't get through your boots.

Consider the construction of our Super Guide Boot. Comfortable. Dry. Lightweight. Protected by an exclusive Timberland Gore-Tex Leather™ laminate that combines a glove leather lining with a waterproof, breathable Gore-Tex® fabric bootie. The result is a level of comfort and dryness you won't find in any other field boot.

Yet another Super Guide exclusive is a sole of triple density polyurethane permanently bonded to the upper. Compared to boots with traditional rubber soles this lessens weight, adds insulation, expands flexibility and increases slip resistance. Giving you a whole new level of performance.

In fact, every single boot in the Timberland Sporting Collection is built to be warm, dry and comfortable, and the reason is our two-step waterproofing process. Step one is direct bonding of silicone-impregnated waterproof leathers to the sole. Step two is Gore-Tex fabric bootie construction.

Timberland. Not just waterproof. Water-proven.

Timberland ⊕

Boots, shoes, clothing, wind, water, / earth and sky.

Many boots are waterproof. Few are water proven.

Of all the tests a bootmaker can use, none is more valuable than the test of time. A test which clearly proves no boot on earth is as warm, dry and comfortable as any in the Timberland Sport Series. Each stands for two decades of leadership in the science of waterproofing. Each goes through a double waterproofing process, which combines advanced silicone-impregnation with the best Gore-Tex fabric bootie construction. And each has our lightweight polyurethane sole for comfort and durability.

Timberland. Still the driest after twenty years in the water.

Timberland ®

Boots, shoes, clothing, wind, water, earth and sky.

If you want to walk to heaven, wear a boot that can go through hell.

Finally, a collection of hiking boots good enough to be called Timberland. From a company whose products have walked through howling tundras and hellish swamps. In such testing labs we developed standards of performance, comfort and durability that exceed anything most footwear makers have had to know. Standards that shape every millimeter of our new lightweight hikers. From the reinforced nylon stitching of the upper to the bottom of the exclusive Timberland Trail Grip sole. The Timberland hiking collection. Quality of a higher elevation.

Boots, shoes, clothing, wind, water, earth and sky.

Proof that the world's most seaworthy vessels are still built by hand.

In shoe building, as in boat building, two things distinguish the class product from the crass imitation. Quality materials and hand craftsmanship. And our Timberland boat shoes abound in both. You see it in the hand-chosen oil-impregnated leathers that neither crack nor stain nor shrink water. In the hand-fitted, solid brass eyelets. And in the marriage of traditional handsewn construction with technology. Hydrofil linings that wick moisture away from the foot and lightweight triple-density soles that provide comfort and grip.

Timberland. Hands down, the leader.

Boots, shoes, clothing, wind, water, earth and sky.

18 Silver

Art Director: Brian Fandetti
Creative Director: Paul Silverman
Photographer: Harry DeZitter
Jack Richmond
Copywriter: Paul Silverman
Agency: Mullen
Client: Timberland Co

VOGUE IS

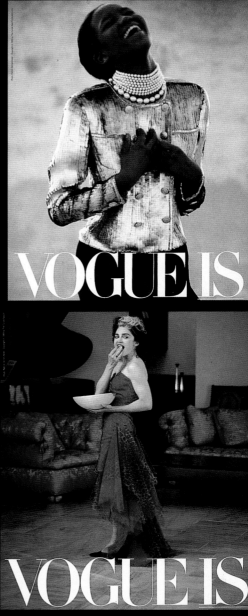

VOGUE IS

VOGUE IS

19 Silver

Art Director: Robert Barthelmes
Creative Director: Rochelle Udell
Photographer: Various
Copywriter: Brenda Cullerton

WE'VE BEEN WORKING ON THIS AD FOR THREE YEARS.

J.D. Power & Associates **1987** CUSTOMER SATISFACTION INDEX	J.D. Power & Associates **1988** CUSTOMER SATISFACTION INDEX	J.D. Power & Associates **1989** CUSTOMER SATISFACTION INDEX
1. Acura	1. Acura	1. Acura
2. Honda	2. Mercedes	2. Mercedes
3. Mercedes	3. Honda	3. Honda
4. Toyota	4. Cadillac	4. Toyota
5. Mazda	5. Toyota	5. Cadillac
6. Subaru	6. Lincoln	6. Nissan
7. Cadillac	7. BMW	7. Subaru
8. Nissan	8. Volvo	8. Mazda
8. Jaguar	9. Mazda	8. BMW
10. Mercury	9. Audi	10. Buick
11. BMW	11. Subaru	11. Plymouth
11. Lincoln	12. Nissan	12. Audi
		12. Volvo

It began in 1987. For the first time in history, a new automobile, in fact, a whole new automobile division, was ranked number one in the prestigious J.D. Power and Associates Customer Satisfaction Index.

That automobile was called Acura. And while some were skeptical about this new entry into the luxury automotive segment, the numbers didn't lie.

Over 70,000 Acura automobiles were sold the first year. And when Acura owners were questioned, their answer came back as an overwhelming vote of confidence. The Acura Legend and Integra were indeed, the most satisfying cars in America. In 1988, automotive history repeated itself.

Today, there are over 370,000 Acura automobiles on the road and over 300 dealers nationwide. And as you might have guessed, those cars and dealers have been ranked number one in Customer Satisfaction with product quality and dealer service for the third year in a row. Astonishingly, Acura has been ranked number one among all automakers, both domestic and import, every year that it has been eligible.

To some people, an accomplishment like that would be good cause to celebrate. But, to our way of thinking, this ad still needs work.

For more information or the dealer nearest you, call 1-800-TO-ACURA.

ACURA *Precision crafted performance.*

J&B Blended Scotch Whisky, 43% Alc. by Vol., Imported by The Paddington Corporation, Ft. Lee, NJ © 1989.

ingle ells,
ingle ells.

The holidays aren't the same without J&B

J&B Scotch Whisky. Blended and bottled in Scotland by Justerini & Brooks, fine wine and spirit merchants since 1749.
To send a gift of J&B anywhere in the U.S., call 1-800-528-6148. Void where prohibited.

Al Hirschfeld.   Cardmember since 1959.

*Membership
Has Its Privileges.*

Don't leave home without it.
Call 1-800-THE CARD to apply.

Tough. Yet sensitive. In addition to muscle, Rhinos have feelings too. Namely, a high-action golden tip that detects the lightest strike. The Rhino rod. ZEBCO

24 Distinctive Merit
Art Director: Roy Grace
Creative Director: Roy Grace
Diane Rothschild
Photographer: Carl Furuta
Copywriter: Diane Rothschild
Client: Range Rover of North America

Lots of people use their Range Rovers just to run down to the corner.

Want to drive where there are no people? No pressures? No pavement? No problem.

With its formidable power and superb engineering, a Range Rover can get you up, over, around or across terrain that would have other 4-wheel drive vehicles waiting for a tow truck.

And what's all the more remarkable is that this same Range Rover is also ideal for such other off-road locales as shopping malls and drive-through banks.

Surprisingly nimble and responsive, the Range Rover is as exceptional on-road as it is off-road.

It out-does a host of luxury cars in posh, polish, and luxury amenities.

It has enough room in back for a refrigerator's worth of food—plus a small refrigerator.

And should you run into anything from a rainstorm to a blizzard, a Range Rover can get you through it with a feeling of comfort and security no ordinary car can approach.

This year, in fact, a Range Rover does that even better. With a new, highly advanced, four-years-in-the developing, anti-lock braking system that many experts consider the most sophisticated in the world.

All in all, there just isn't a car on the road, or off it, as assuredly rugged, as unstintingly luxurious, as eminently practical and as supremely versatile as a Range Rover.

So whether you're interested in the standard, extravagantly appointed Range Rover, or the even more opulent County model, why not call 1-800 FINE 4WD for the name of a dealer near you?

We won't deny that there are considerably less expensive vehicles than a Range Rover.

But then, people don't simply buy Range Rovers just to run down to the corner.

They also buy them to be sure they'll get back.

RANGE ROVER

Catherine Deneuve Cardmember since 1978

Membership Has Its Privileges

Don't leave home without it

25 Distinctive Merit
Art Director: Parry Merkley
Rick Rabe
Creative Director: Gordon Bowen
Photographer: Annie Leibovitz
Copywriter: Gordon Bowen
Agency: Ogilvy & Mather
Client: American Express

26 Distinctive Merit

Art Director: Brian Fandetti
Creative Director: Paul Silverman
Photographer: Gavin Creedon
Copywriter: Paul Silverman
Agency: Mullen
Client: Timberland Co.

For those who accept turbulence as a fact of life.

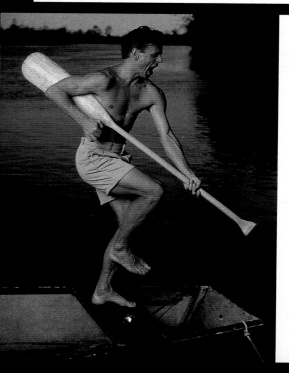

Mikhail Baryshnikov. Cardmember since 1975.

Membership Has Its Privileges.

Don't leave home without it.
Call 1-800-THE CARD to apply.

27 Distinctive Merit

Art Director: Parry Merkley
Rick Rabe
Creative Director: Gordon Bowen
Photographer: Annie Leibovitz
Copywriter: Gordon Bowen
Agency: Ogilvy & Mather
Client: American Express

28 Distinctive Merit

Art Director: Chris Graves
Creative Director: Roy Grace
Diane Rothschild
Copywriter: Craig Demeter
Agency: Roy Grace
Client: Paddington

ingle ells,
ingle ells.

The holidays aren't the same without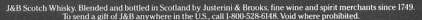

J&B Scotch Whisky. Blended and bottled in Scotland by Justerini & Brooks, fine wine and spirit merchants since 1749.
To send a gift of J&B anywhere in the U.S., call 1-800-528-6148. Void where prohibited.

For twenty years they've been insulated from snow, oblivious to rain, impervious to competition.

Before the Timberland Company existed, only one kind of boot was truly waterproof. The kind you don't like to wear. Because it's made of something other than leather, something plastic or rubber that doesn't breathe.

Relief came two decades ago, when Timberland craftsmen hand-built a full-grain leather boot that was guaranteed waterproof. And insulated.

It was a concept the world was waiting for. No sooner did our boot hit the stores than it sold out. And today it still sells out, even though imitations abound both here and abroad.

The fact is, copying the look of our classic tan buck boot is far easier than copying the workmanship. The meticulous silicone impregnation of the leather, the four-row nylon stitching, the direct bonding of upper to midsole for a guaranteed waterproof seal, and the unbeatable warmth of Thinsulate® insulation.

You live on an earth that's two-thirds water. Can you afford a lesser boot than ours?

Timberland ⊕

Boots, shoes, clothing, wind, water, / earth and sky.

In time, even these shoes will succumb to the sea. But chances are you'll replace the boat first.

The headline on this page isn't something you should accept without substantiation. So let us hasten to provide it.

Timberland boat shoes are stronger because our construction is superior. You will never see one of our soles flapping loose in the breeze, unstitched from its moccasin upper. We eliminate such stitching altogether in favor of permanent bonding, so shoe and sole stay married until the day they die.

And unlike boat shoes of a lesser quality, ours have premium natural leathers that won't crack, impregnable nylon stitching that won't rot, and solid brass eyelets that won't chip.

This year, we're pleased to introduce the high-performance Ultra Boat Shoe, companion to our Super and Classic Boat Shoe. The Ultra combines the grip and stability of a triple density outsole with the comfort and cushioning of a double density midsole. For maximum dryness, the stain-resistant, waterproof leathers have a Hydrofil® lining to wick away moisture.

Water, water, it's everywhere. So is Timberland.

Timberland ⊕

Boots, shoes, clothing, wind, water, / earth and sky.

There are two things you shouldn't be up the creek without. One of them is a paddle.

The other is a pair of boots from the Timberland Sporting Collection. Because even though we can't keep water out of your boat, we guarantee it won't get through your boots.

Consider the construction of our Super Guide Boot. Comfortable. Dry. Lightweight. Protected by an exclusive Timberland Gore-Tex Leather™ laminate that combines a glove leather lining with a waterproof, breathable Gore-Tex® fabric bootie. The result is a level of comfort and dryness you won't find in any other field boot.

Yet another Super Guide exclusive is a sole of triple density polyurethane permanently bonded to the upper. Compared to boots with traditional rubber soles this lessens weight, adds insulation, expands flexibility and increases slip resistance. Giving you a whole new level of performance.

In fact, every single boot in the Timberland Sporting Collection is built to be warm, dry and comfortable, and the reason is our two-step waterproofing process. Step one is direct bonding of silicone-impregnated waterproof leathers to the sole. Step two is Gore-Tex fabric bootie construction.

Timberland. Not just waterproof. Water-proven.

Timberland ⊕

Boots, shoes, clothing, wind, water, / earth and sky.

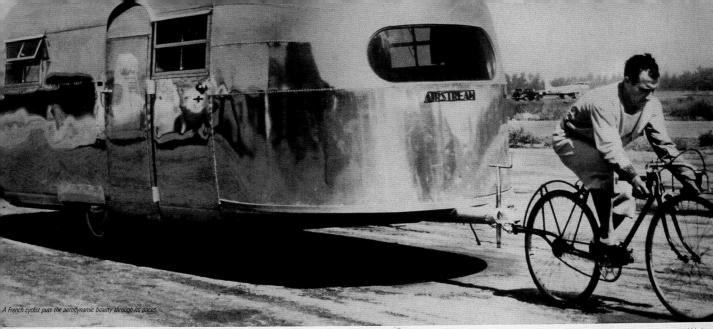

A French cyclist puts the aerodynamic beauty through its paces.

How fuel-efficient is the Airstream?

Way back in the depths of the Depression, our founder Wally Byam happened upon a trailer shape that Airstreamers have since come to know and love.

55 years later, precious little has changed.

Oh, we've added creature comforts all right. Like a deluxe four-burner range. A two-way refrigerator. And almost three dozen other modern-day conveniences.

But our now-familiar fuselage is still honed from the same high-strength, lightweight aluminum. Which, combined with its low center of gravity, means far less vibration. Greater stability in crosswinds. And 30% fewer trips to the gas pump.

(Mileage may vary, depending upon your tow vehicle.)

We'd like to tell you more about our classic trailers, but first you'll need to call: 1 513 596-6111. Or write to Mr. Steve Krivian, 419 W. Pike Street, Jackson Center, OH 45334.

The 1990 Airstream Excella

Dr. H.W. Holman and his wife Thelma have been attached to Airstream trailers just about as long as they've been attached to each other. Over half a century, bless them.

Together, they've lugged their custom made campers across the United States, to Europe, Russia, Africa and Asia. Down ice-encrusted highways, through wind-swept trackless deserts.

And you can bet your beret that they weren't alone.

Owner loyalty like this doesn't surprise us much. After all, our trailers are built for the long haul.

Some 9,000 rivets make sure of that. Along with an exhaustive 96-point quality check on the assembly line. And an unblinking attention to good old Yankee craftsmanship.

A lasting relationship since 1935.

Of course, there may be newer ways to make travel trailers. Faster ones, too. But none that protects your investment better. (Or guarantees happier trails.

We'd like to tell you more about our classic trailers, but first you'll need to call: 1 513 596-6111. Or write to Mr. Steve Krivian, 419 W. Pike Street, Jackson Center, OH 45334.

The 1990 Airstream Excella

The happy campers with their Airstream "Torpedo."

HORNET + 3

July 24, 1969. The Apollo crew is welcomed home.

Shortly after Neil Armstrong, "Buzz" Aldrin and Michael Collins landed on the silver moon, they landed in a silver Airstream.

Had to, you see. Government regulations.

For 17 days, they enjoyed captivity in the climate-controlled coziness of this 35-foot coach.

Savoring real food, prepared in a real kitchen. Stretching out in a cabin furnished with amenities fit for a king.

A lot like our motorhomes today.

Except today, they come with plush carpeted floors and hand-rubbed hickory cabinets. (Our premier model, the 345, is even stocked with a built-in microwave, a color TV and VCR.)

You'd smile too if you had to be quarantined in an Airstream.

Since 1983, Airstream has built Astrovans for NASA's shuttle program. It gives our boys something to look forward to after a hard day in space.

We'd like to tell you more about our classic motorhomes, but first you'll need to call: 1 513 596-6111. Or write to Mr. Steve Krivian, 419 W. Pike Street, Jackson Center, OH 45334.

The 1990 Airstream Motorhome

Perception.

Reality.

For a new generation of Rolling Stone readers, it isn't necessary to munch on magic mushrooms to appreciate contemporary American literature. Rolling Stone readers turn the pages of America's best sellers at the rate of 13 million books a year. If you're looking for a highly educated, discerning audience for your advertising message, you'll get great reviews in the pages of Rolling Stone.

For impact far beyond your size consider our regional éditions.

NATIONAL GEOGRAPHIC

With 30 editions to choose from, no magazine enhances your image more in a single city or worldwide. Before you place another ad, call Joan McCraw, National Advertising Director, at 212-974-1700.

Velvety tree ant magnified 80 times.
Photographer: David Scharf.

Stop 37 million readers in their tracks every month.

The only book more respected than ours doesn't accept advertising.

FROM OCTOBER UNTIL APRIL, THE ROYAL VIKING STAR WILL OFFER FIVE TO ELEVEN - DAY

THIS.

CRUISES TO BARBADOS, WITH CALLS THROUGHOUT THE SUNSWEPT SOUTHERN CARIBBEAN.

FROM OCTOBER UNTIL APRIL, THE ROYAL VIKING STAR OFFERS FIVE TO ELEVEN-DAY CRUISES

PARADISE.

TO BARBADOS, WITH CALLS AT ST. LUCIA, MARTINIQUE AND OTHER CARIBBEAN PORTS.

BEGINNING IN OCTOBER, FIVE TO ELEVEN- DAY CRUISES TO BARBADOS, WITH CALLS

HEAVEN.

THROUGHOUT THE SOUTHERN CARIBBEAN. ABOARD THE ROYAL VIKING STAR.

34 Distinctive Merit

Art Director: Steve Stone
Creative Director: Jeffrey Goodby
Rich Silverstein
Photographer: Jay Maisel
Dan Escobar
Copywriter: David Fowler
Agency: Goodby, Berlin & Silverstein
Client: Royal Viking Line

Some abused children grow up to become famous.

Abused children grow up to become abusing adults. Not in every case, but in too many. Nine out of ten murderers, rapists and drug addicts suffered from physical or emotional abuse as a child. So did the four people pictured above. That's something worth thinking about—even if you don't have kids.

Child Abuse. It hurts all of us.

Citizens for the Prevention of Child Abuse

35 Distinctive Merit

Art Director: John Follis
Creative Director: John Follis
Copywriter: John Follis
Agency: Follis & Verdi, Inc.
Client: Citizens for Prevention
of Child Abuse

36
Art Director: Marcia Gabor
Creative Director: Terry Burris
Designer: Marcia Gabor
Copywriter: Terry Burris
Agency: Conrad, Phillips & Vutech
Client: Bellantoni Bros. Market

37
Art Director: Bob Brihn
Creative Director: Pat Burnham
Designer: Bob Brihn
Photographer: Kerry Peterson
Copywriter: George Gier
Agency: Fallon McElligott
Client: Porsche

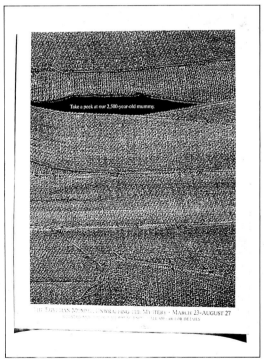

38
Art Director: Bob Brihn
Creative Director: Pat Burnham
Designer: Bob Brihn
Photographer: Kerry Peterson
Copywriter: George Gier
Agency: Fallon McElligott
Client: Porsche

39
Art Director: Dean Narahara
Creative Director: Dick Smith
Designer: Dean Narahara
Copywriter: Laurie Ripplinger
Agency: Taylor, Brown, Smith & Perrault
Client: Houston Museum of Natural Science

Drive Drunk And We'll See You Real Soon.

If you saw drinking and driving from our point of view,
you wouldn't drink and drive.

Goodwine
Funeral Homes
Caring For Families The Way Only A Family Can.

Flat Rock 584-3200
Palestine 586-2067
Robinson 544-2131

40
Art Director: David Straka
Creative Director: Pat Fagan
Copywriter: Pat Fagan
Agency: Keller-Crescent
Client: Goodwine Funeral Homes

It wasn't the sun that burned everybody in Baja.

It was Jack Johnson. The man who drove his V6-powered Nissan Hardbody 4x4 against a whole desert full of V8 trucks in this year's SCORE Baja 1000 race. And won. By over an hour. Hauling off with the 1988 HDRA/SCORE Class 4 championship at the same time. All of which turned November 11th into one of the hottest days of the year for Nissan. While turning the competition extremely red in the face.

Built for the Human Race.

41
Art Director: Richard Bess
Creative Director: Bob Kuperman
Copywriter: Julie Curtis
Agency: Chiat/Day/Mojo
Client: Nissan

With the right oil, this Century could last another ten years.

Whether you drive a Buick Century or a Suzuki Samurai, Amoco LDO is the right oil for your car. That's because LDO meets manufacturers' performance requirements for every car made today. So why not drive over to Amoco and change your oil now? On second thought, if you're not using LDO, you'd better take a cab.

LDO Motor Oil. $15 a case, $1.25 a quart.

Self-service pumps. Open seven days a week.

With so many ways to get pumped up, you'll find that a YMCA membership is a real gas. So join today and start increasing your personal mileage.
Free trial membership during September.

YMCA

42
Art Director: Arty Tan
Creative Director: Pat Burnham
Photographer: Kerry Peterson
Copywriter: Jamie Barrett
Agency: Fallon McElligott
Client: Amoco

43
Art Director: Craig Tanimoto
Creative Director: Jac Coverdale
Designer: Craig Tanimoto
Photographer: Jim Arndt
Copywriter: Joe Alexander
       Jerry Fury
Agency: Clarity, Coverdale, Rueff
Client: Metro-YMCA

44
Art Director: Bob Brihn
Creative Director: Pat Burnham
Designer: Bob Brihn
Photographer: Kerry Peterson
Copywriter: George Gier
Agency: Fallon McElligott
Client: Porsche

45
Art Director: Bob Barrie
Creative Director: Pat Burnham
Designer: Bob Barrie
Copywriter: Jamie Barrett
Agency: Fallon McElligott
Client: Continental Bank

Spend your European vacation in these luxurious accommodations.

Buy a new Porsche from us and we can arrange for you to pick it up in West Germany. Use it to see Europe, then we'll ship it back to you. Come in for details.

PORSCHE

Good (Huff!) luck
to all of our fellow (Puff!)
competitors in today's
(Gulp!) Chicago Sun-Times
(Gasp!) Triathlon.

Continental Bank
Employee Triathlon Team

Use the wrong oil and it won't be a Legend for long.

Whether you drive an Acura Legend or a Pontiac LeMans, Amoco LDO is the right oil for your car. That's because LDO meets manufacturers' performance requirements for every car made today. So why not drive over to Amoco and change your oil now? On second thought, if you're not using LDO, you'd better take a cab.

LDO Motor Oil. $15 a case, $1.25 a quart.

Now if you have an emergency in your 911, you don't have to call 911.

No matter where you are in North America, if you need gas, help or towing just call the number on your roadside assistance card. It's free with any new Porsche. Call or come in for details.

Porsche 24 Hour Road Service.

46
Art Director: Arty Tan
Creative Director: Pat Burnham
Photographer: Kerry Peterson
Copywriter: Jamie Barrett
Agency: Fallon McElligott
Client: Amoco

47
Art Director: Bob Brihn
Creative Director: Pat Burnham
Designer: Bob Brihn
Photographer: Jim Arndt
Copywriter: George Gier
Agency: Fallon McElligott
Client: Porsche

48
Art Director: Arty Tan
Creative Director: Pat Burnham
Copywriter: Jamie Barrett
Agency: Fallon McElligott
Client: Quick Lube

49
Art Director: Arty Tan
Creative Director: Pat Burnham
Photographer: Kerry Peterson
Copywriter: Jamie Barrett
Agency: Fallon McElligott
Client: Quick Lube

Come to Quick Lube and we'll grease your palms.

Get $2 off your next oil change.

In twenty minutes or less, Amoco service technicians will give you a complete oil and lube job. There's no appointment necessary. Plus, with this coupon, you'll get $2 off.

Amoco Quick Lube

We're so good at oil changes, we can do them in the dark.

NOW OPEN UNTIL 10PM

At Amoco Quick Lube, we're open from 7AM to 10 PM. Just stop by at your convenience and our service technicians will give you a complete oil and lube job in twenty minutes or less.

Amoco Quick Lube

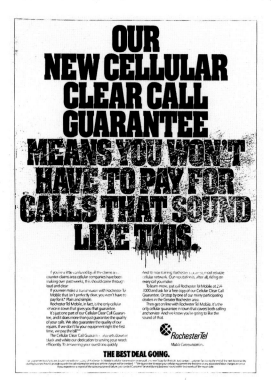

OUR NEW CELLULAR CLEAR CALL GUARANTEE MEANS YOU WON'T HAVE TO PAY FOR CALLS THAT SOUND LIKE THIS.

RochesterTel

THE BEST DEAL GOING.

Make fiber part of every meal.

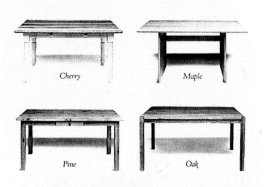

Cherry   Maple

Pine   Oak

Check out our attractive wooden tables on sale for a limited time. With prices starting at $99, you'll never come away with an upset stomach.

HomePlace

50
Art Director: Bob Wisner
Creative Director: Bob MaHarry
　　　　　　　　Sharon Kirk
Designer: Bob Wisner
Illustrator: Bob Wisner
Copywriter: Joel MaHarry
Agency: Hutchins/Young & Rubicam
Client: RTMC

51
Art Director: Bryan Buckley
　　　　　　　Tom DeCerchio
Copywriter: Tom DeCerchio
　　　　　　　Bryan Buckley
Agency: Buckley/DeCerchio
Client: Homeplace

52

Art Director: Larry Jarvis
Ted Gornick
Creative Director: Lloyd Wolfe
Illustrator: Jack Ohman
Copywriter: Rob Rosenthal
Agency: Cole & Weber, Portland
Client: The *Oregonian*

53

Art Director: Chris Graves
Creative Director: Roy Grace
Diane Rothschild
Copywriter: Craig Demeter
Agency: Roy Grace
Client: Paddington

When a politician steps out of line, our man rearranges his face.

How much damage can one man do with his hands? Plenty. If they belong to Jack Ohman, The Oregonian's resident political cartoonist.
Even the slickest political rope-a-dope can't stop his jabs. Then he hits 'em where it hurts: just above that fine line that divides low blow from high comedy.
Be on the lookout for Jack Ohman. And see who gets a facial this week.

Jack Ohman Six Days A Week In Forum. The Oregonian

ingle   ells,
ingle   ells.

The holidays aren't the same without J&B

J&B Scotch Whisky. Blended and bottled in Scotland by Justerini & Brooks, fine wine and spirit merchants since 1749.
To send a gift of J&B anywhere in the U.S., call 1-800-528-6148. Void where prohibited.
J&B Rare Blended Scotch Whisky 43% Alc. by Vol., imported by The Paddington Corporation, N.Y. Inc. Ltd © 1989

With a resale value of 99.43%, this is a true economy car.

You don't buy a new Porsche, you invest in one.
That's because with a resale value of nearly 100%, you'll not only keep your money, you'll get to enjoy it.

PORSCHE

Clean Up Around The House.

GARAGE Sale, turn., much misc. & collect-ibles, $1-$600. 5745 W. Mar

Republic/Gazette Classifieds

54

Art Director: Bob Brihn
Creative Director: Pat Burnham
Designer: Bob Brihn
Photographer: Kerry Peterson
Copywriter: George Gier
Agency: Fallon McElligott
Client: Porsche

55

Art Director: Judy Smith
Creative Director: Chris Poisson
Photographer: Tony Hernandez
Copywriter: Gregg Bergan

56
Art Director: Bryan Buckley
　　　　　Tom DeCerchio
Copywriter: Tom DeCerchio
　　　　　Bryan Buckley
Agency: Buckley/DeCerchio
Client: Homeplace

57
Art Director: Arty Tan
Creative Director: Pat Burnham
Photographer: Kerry Peterson
Copywriter: Jamie Barrett
Agency: Fallon McElligott
Client: Amoco

Come out of the closet.

Check out our attractive pine wardrobes. At only $459, you might have
a hard time believing that we're being straight with you.

HomePlace

Isn't it time Celebrities got a little more attention?

Whether you drive a Chevy Celebrity or a Subaru Brat,
Amoco LDO is the right oil for your car. That's because LDO meets
manufacturers' performance requirements for every car made today.
So why not drive over to Amoco and change your oil now?
On second thought, if you're not using LDO, you'd better take a cab.

LDO Motor Oil. $15 a case, $1.25 a quart.

"EVERYONE NEEDS A HERO. OR AT LEAST A GRILLED CHEESE SANDWICH."

Sherri Krull, Owner.

SGT. PRESTONS
Saloon and Eatery.

221 Cedar Ave. So. at Seven Corners in Minneapolis. 338-6146.

Free rear end alignment.

If your rear end is starting to shimmy and shake, don't sit on it.
Join the YMCA. We also do complete body work and fix spare tires.
Free trial membership during September.

YMCA

58
Art Director: Bob Brihn
Creative Director: Pat Burnham
Copywriter: Jamie Barrett
Agency: Fallon McElligott
Client: Sgt. Preston's

59
Art Director: Craig Tanimoto
Creative Director: Jac Coverdale
Designer: Craig Tanimoto
Photographer: Joe Michl
Copywriter: Joe Alexander
　　　　　Jerry Fury
Agency: Clarity, Coverdale, Rueff
Client: Metro-YMCA

60
Art Director: Arty Tan
Creative Director: Pat Burnham
Copywriter: Jamie Barrett
Agency: Fallon McElligott
Client: Quick Lube

61
Art Director: Ray Fesenmaier
Jessica Welton
Creative Director: Tommy Thompson
Designer: Ray Fesenmaier
Jessica Welton
Photographer: Anthony Sylvestro
Copywriter: Tommy Thompson
Agency: Siddall, Matus & Coughter
Client: Ramada Techworld

You can always count on an Amoco station to give you good directions.

1. Cut out this coupon.
2. Bring it to Amoco Quick Lube.
3. Get $2 off on your oil change.

At Amoco Quick Lube, our service technicians will give you a complete oil and lube job in twenty minutes or less. No appointment necessary.

Expiration date: _____ Not good in conjunction with other Amoco coupon offers.

Avoid the usual Thanksgiving dishes.

Join us instead for our Champagne Thanksgiving Feast. We'll serve you an entire stuffed turkey with giblet gravy, fresh vegetables, homemade rolls, pumpkin, apple or mincemeat pie. And a splendid split of champagne. You can take the leftovers home with you. Or get the entire Thanksgiving meal to go. The price: just $18.95 per person plus tax and gratuity, half-price for children ten and under, 20% off for senior citizens. Serving hours are between 10:30 a.m. and 4:30 p.m. Call 898-9000, ext. 4047 for reservations. And let us do the dishes for you.

RAMADA RENAISSANCE. TECHWORLD

999 9th St. NW, Washington, D.C.

This car comes equipped with central air.

Whether you have the top down or up, you'll be cool no matter how hot it is. Test drive the new 944 S2 Cabriolet today. It's a breath of fresh air. PORSCHE

Expect light, moderate and heavy winds through the weekend.

In fact, powerful performances are forecast from every section of The Minnesota Orchestra for the new season. We have the turbulence of Rachmaninoff. The gentle airs of Mozart and Debussy. The brisk pacing of Beethoven. And much more. All waiting for you weekends from September through May, when you subscribe.

Enjoying the season is a breeze with the many exciting series we offer. Tickets are available for Wednesday, Friday or Saturday evenings at Orchestra Hall. Or, for Thursday or Saturday evenings at the Ordway Music Theatre in St. Paul. And there are plenty of good seats left for the weekend, including our popular Friday night series.

Choices range from five and six concert Mini Series to the 24 concert Imperial Series. With a subscription you can save up to 36% over single ticket prices. And what is more important, you get the richness of experience that comes with repeated attendance, as well as the one-of-a-kind moments that happen only in a live performance.

Best seats go fast, so call 371-5656. And subscribe while conditions are still favorable.

The Minnesota Orchestra 1989/90 Subscription Series.
Edo de Waart, Music Director

62
Art Director: Bob Brihn
Creative Director: Pat Burnham
Designer: Bob Brihn
Photographer: Kerry Peterson
Copywriter: George Gier
Agency: Fallon McElligott
Client: Porsche

63
Art Director: Richard Page
Photographer: Paul Sinkler
Copywriter: Corinne Mitchell
Agency: McCool & Co.
Client: Minnesota Orchestra

64
Art Director: Lisa Rettig-Falcone
Creative Director: Sam Scali
Photographer: Robert Ammirati
Copywriter: Karen Sultz
Agency: Scali, McCabe, Sloves
Client: Perdue

65
Art Director: Craig Tanimoto
　　　　　　Jac Coverdale
Creative Director: Jac Coverdale
Designer: Craig Tanimoto
Copywriter: Joe Alexander
　　　　　　Jerry Fury
Agency: Clarity, Coverdale, Rueff
Client: Metro-YMCA

WHEN YOU BUY THE PERDUE OVEN STUFFER ROASTER,
ASK FOR DOUBLE BAGS.

SAVE $1.00
ON ONE PERDUE OVEN STUFFER ROASTER!

Burn dinner
tonight.

With the food processors at the YMCA, you can get rid of unwanted leftovers. So join today. And start burning food in the gym, instead of the kitchen.
Free trial membership during September.

YMCA

WHERE IS YOUR CAR PARKED?

ACURA

DEPOSITOR'S NAME ON PAGE ONE

FIRST STATEBANK

AT THIS RATE, YOU'LL NEVER GET A HOUSE.

Dreyfus
The right fund at the right time.

66
Art Director: Steve Beaumont
　　　　　　Nan Hutchison
Creative Director: Brent Bouchez
Photographer: Gary McGuire
Copywriter: Brent Bouchez
Agency: Ketchum, Los Angeles
Client: American Honda Motor Corp.

67
Art Director: Leslie Sweet
Creative Director: Tony DeGregorio
Copywriter: Pamela Sullivan
Agency: Levine, Huntley, Schmidt & Beaver
Client: Dreyfus

68
Art Director: John Vitro
Creative Director: Jim Winters
Illustrator: Dugald Stermer
Photographer: Ron Garrison
Copywriter: John Robertson
Agency: Franklin & Associates
Client: San Diego Zoo

69
Art Director: John Vitro
Creative Director: Jim Winters
Photographer: Jim Brandenberg
Copywriter: John Robertson
Agency: Franklin & Associates
Client: San Diego Wild Animal Park

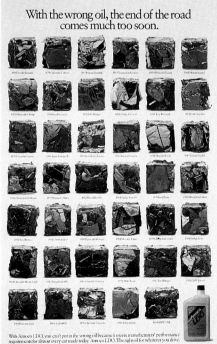

70
Art Director: Arty Tan
Creative Director: Pat Burnham
Photographer: Kerry Peterson
Copywriter: Phil Hanft
Agency: Fallon McElligott
Client: Amoco

71
Art Director: John Vitro
Creative Director: Jim Winters
Photographer: Jim Brandenberg
Copywriter: John Robertson
Agency: Franklin & Associates
Client: San Diego Wild Animal Park

72
Art Director: Mark Hriciga
Creative Director: Jim Durfee
Copywriter: Jerry Della Femina
Agency: Della Femina, McNamee WCRS
Client: Isuzu

74
Art Director: Tracy Wong
Creative Director: Gary Goldsmith
Photographer: Steve Hellerstein
Copywriter: Dean Hacohen
Agency: Goldsmith/Jeffrey
Client: EL AL Israel Airlines

BUSINESS WEEK ADMIRES JOE ISUZU SO MUCH THAT IN THEIR JUNE 12TH ISSUE, THEY "LIED" ABOUT ISUZU'S SALES.

American Isuzu Motors, Inc.
Della Femina, McNamee WCRS, Inc.

ELALIEIE

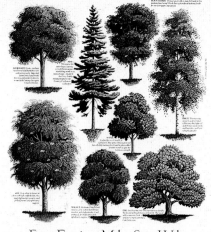

Every Furniture Maker Starts With The Same Material. So Why Do Some Pieces Still Look Better Than Others?

W.L. Landau's
ETHAN ALLEN
We Design The Comforts Of Life

JUNK HAS ALWAYS HAD A PLACE IN OUR COMPANY, JUST NOT IN OUR PORTFOLIO.

Dreyfus
The right fund at the right time.

75
Art Director: Aki Seki
Designer: Aki Seki
Illustrator: Mary Ann Lasher
Copywriter: Augie Cosentino
Agency: Ammirati & Puris Inc.
Client: W.L. Landau's Ethan Allen

76
Art Director: Leslie Sweet
Creative Director: Tony DeGregorio
Designer: Leslie Sweet
Photographer: Cailor/Resnick
Copywriter: Nat Russo
Agency: Levine, Huntley, Schmidt & Beaver
Client: Dreyfus

77
Art Director: Ann Rhodes
Creative Director: Larry Asher
Photographer: Darrell Peterson
Copywriter: Larry Asher
Agency: Borders, Perrin & Norrander
Client: King County Medical Blue Shield

78
Art Director: James Offenhartz
Lee Garfinkel
Photographer: Jeff Zwart
Copywriter: Lee Garfinkel
Agency: Levine, Huntley, Schmidt & Beaver
Client: Subaru of America

79
Art Director: Ernest Neira
Creative Director: Tony DeGregorio
Photographer: Cailor/Resnick
Copywriter: Jerry Confino
Ernest Neira
Agency: Levine, Huntley, Schmidt & Beaver
Client: Dreyfus

80
Art Director: Leslie Sweet
Ernest Neira
Creative Director: Tony DeGregorio
Designer: Leslie Sweet
Ernest Neira
Photographer: Mike Newler
Copywriter: Nat Russo
Agency: Levine, Huntley, Schmidt & Beaver
Client: Dreyfus

81

Art Director: Ronald Rosen
Creative Director: Roy Grace
                  Diane Rothschild
Copywriter: Craig Demeter
Client: Whittle Communications

82

Art Director: Leslie Sweet
Creative Director: Tony DeGregorio
Photographer: William Hines
Copywriter: Nat Russo
Agency: Levine, Huntley, Schmidt & Beaver
Client: Dreyfus

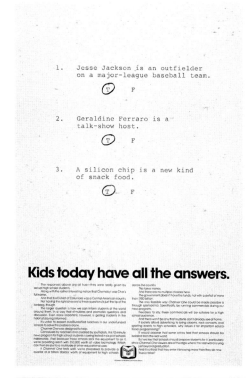

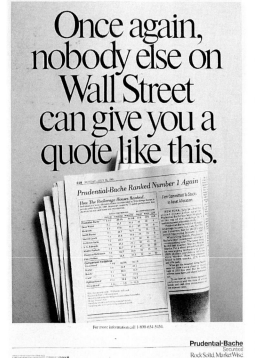

83

Art Director: Paul Jervis
Creative Director: Paul Jervis
Designer: Paul Jervis
Photographer: Dan Barba
Copywriter: Mitchell Wein
Agency: Backer, Spielvogel, Bates
Client: Prudential-Bache

84

Art Director: John Vitro
Creative Director: Jim Winters
Illustrator: Dugald Stermer
Photographer: Ron Garrison
Copywriter: John Robertson
Agency: Franklin & Associates
Client: San Diego Zoo

85
Art Director: John Vitro
Creative Director: Jim Winters
Illustrator: Dugald Stermer
Photographer: Ron Garrison
Copywriter: John Robertson
Agency: Franklin & Associates
Client: San Diego Zoo

86
Art Director: Amy Watt
Creative Director: Paul Silverman
Photographer: Peter Noel
Copywriter: Paul Silverman
Agency: Mullen
Client: Manchester League of Women Voters

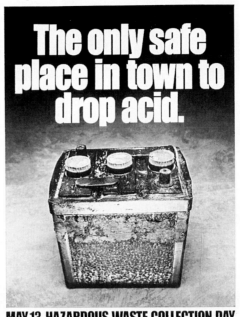

87
Art Director: Cristina Creager
Creative Director: Jim Kingsley
   Brett Robbs
Photographer: Cary Wolinsky
Copywriter: Andy Dumaine
Agency: DDB Needham
Client: National Geographic Society

88
Art Director: Larry Jarvis
Creative Director: Lloyd Wolfe
Photographer: Greg Leno
Copywriter: Rob Rosenthal
Agency: Cole & Weber, Portland
Client: The *Oregonian*

89

Art Director: David Fox
Creative Director: Jac Coverdale
Designer: David Fox
Photographer: Mark LaFavor
Copywriter: Joe Alexander
Agency: Clarity, Coverdale, Rueff
Client: City of Minneapolis Recycling

90

Art Director: Bernie Hogya
Creative Director: Jay Schulberg
Photographer: Jim Arndt
Copywriter: Ronald Wachino
Agency: Bozell
Client: Illinois Power

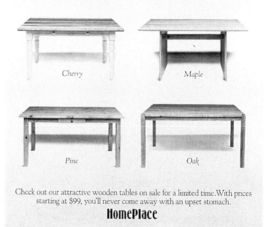

91

Art Director: Ray Redding
Creative Director: Glenn Dady
Mike Malone
Designer: Ray Redding
Bruce Perry
Copywriter: David Culp
Agency: The Richards Group
Client: Bank One

92

Art Director: Bryan Buckley
Tom DeCerchio
Copywriter: Tom DeCerchio
Bryan Buckley
Agency: Buckley/DeCerchio
Client: Homeplace

93
Art Director: Gary Rozanski
Creative Director: Mike Rogers
Photographer: Jim Hall
Copywriter: Mitchell Wein
Agency: DDB Needham Worldwide
Client: Volkswagen

94
Art Director: Bernie Hogya
Creative Director: Jay Schulberg
Copywriter: Ronald Wachino
Agency: Bozell
Client: Illinois Power

The sun you've always wanted.

THIS CHRISTMAS, GIVE A GIFT THAT SOMEONE WILL OPEN UP AND HIDE IN THE ATTIC.

ILLINOIS POWER

The Meadowlands, 1985. The Giants buried the Eagles.

The Meadowlands, 1979. The Giants buried the Falcons.

The Meadowlands, 1975. The Mafia buried Jimmy Hoffa.

Find out exactly where, why and by whom. In our November issue, on sale now.

PLAYBOY

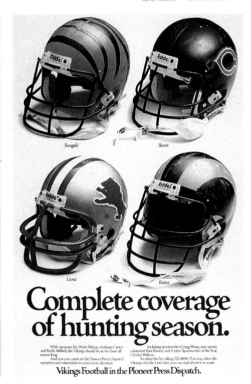

Complete coverage of hunting season.

Vikings Football in the Pioneer Press Dispatch.

95
Art Director: Tod Seisser
　　　　　 Jay Taub
Creative Director: Tod Seisser
　　　　　 Jay Taub
Designer: Tod Seisser
Photographer: Stock
Copywriter: Jay Taub
　　　　　 Tod Seisser
Agency: Keye/Donna/Pearlstein

96
Art Director: Jac Coverdale
Creative Director: Jac Coverdale
Designer: Jac Coverdale
Photographer: Paul Sinkler
Copywriter: Joe Alexander
Agency: Clarity, Coverdale, Rueff
Client: St. Paul Pioneer Press Dispatch

97
Art Director: Kevin Grimsdale
Creative Director: Mike Hughes
Photographer: Wayne Gibson
Copywriter: Ed Cowardin
Agency: The Martin Agency
Client: Bath Plus

98
Art Director: Jac Coverdale
Creative Director: Jac Coverdale
Designer: Jac Coverdale
Photographer: Steve Umland
Copywriter: Joe Alexander
Agency: Clarity, Coverdale, Rueff
Client: St. Paul Pioneer Press Dispatch

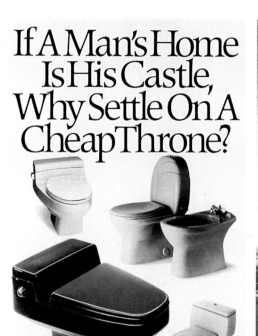

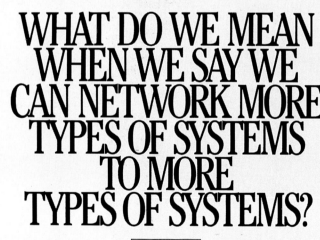

99
Art Director: Mike Moser
Creative Director: Ross Van Dusen
Photographer: Ernie Friedlander
Hunter Freeman
Bob Mizono
Copywriter: David O'Hare
Agency: Chiat/Day/Mojo
Client: 3COM Corp.

100
Art Director: Fred Hammerquist
Creative Director: Rod Kilpatrick
Copywriter: Bob Moore
Agency: Cole & Weber
Client: Safeco

101
Art Director: Ed Evangelista
Creative Director: Ron Berger
Copywriter: Charlie Tercek
Agency: M.V.B.C.S.
Client: Schering Plough

102
Art Director: Gary Yoshida
Creative Director: Larry Postaer
Copywriter: Bob Coburn
Client: American Honda Motor Corp.

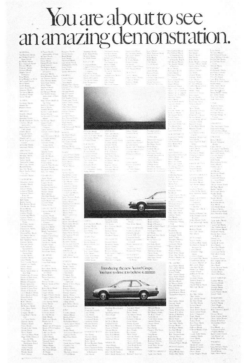

Not actual size.
(Too bad.)

103
Art Director: David Rauch
Creative Director: Ron Louie
Photographer: Larry Sillen
Copywriter: Julie Schireson Ralphs
Agency: DDB Needham Worldwide
Client: Crown Royal

104
Art Director: Don Harbor
Creative Director: Bruce Mansfield
Photographer: Kathy Kemp
Copywriter: Sue Fay
              Bruce Mansfield
Agency: Lawler Ballard
Client: Birmingham *Post-Herald*

105
Art Director: Peggy Fields
Creative Director: Sam Scali
Photographer: Hing-Norton
Copywriter: Barbara Hamilton
Agency: Scali, McCabe, Sloves
Client: Western Union

106
Art Director: Dennis D'Amico
Photographer: Kevin Logan
Copywriter: David Metcalf
Agency: Lowe, Tucker, Metcalf
Client: Volvo Penta

How to get President Bush to read your lips.

Send him a Western Union Telegram telling him exactly how you feel.

Just call 1-800-257-4900, ext. 7713 and tell our operator what you want to say or visit any of our 12,500 locations nationwide. Within minutes a telegram will be on its way from your house to the White House.

We even offer a special rate for telegrams to elected officials, including Senators and Representatives, that won't tax your fiscal budget.

And because Western Union sends telegrams 24 hours a day you can have words with the President any time you want.

Which just goes to show you don't have to be someone special to have influence in the White House.

WESTERN UNION

FISH FOR SALMON, NOT PARTS.

We're using the same bait as last year. Throughout the salmon season we'll have experienced Volvo Diesel dealers, diesel service technicians and an on-site warehouse of genuine Volvo Penta parts and engines in Dillingham. Call George at our warehouse, 907-842-5375, from May 15 to July 31, 1989 for assistance. Good luck on the fishing. If you're powered by Volvo Penta you won't need it on parts.

THE VOLVO PENTA BRISTOL BAY ON-SITE PARTS SERVICE.

Two Hours Ago A Man Applied For A Loan To Buy This Corvette.

Obviously the answer was "yes". Obviously the bank was First Interstate. Because First Interstate is the only bank in town that will process your consumer loan application within two hours. There's no need to even put on your best suit. We'll take your application over the phone and call you back with a response.
The next time you need money, come to First Interstate. We'll put you right back out on the streets.

First Interstate Bank
We go the extra mile for you.

107
Art Director: Clifford Goodenough
Creative Director: Roger Livingston
Photographer: Larry Gilpin
Copywriter: Norah Delaney
Agency: Livingston & Co.
Client: First Interstate Bank of New Mexico

108
Art Director: Chuck Anderson
Creative Director: Jay Schulberg
Copywriter: Judy Johnson
Agency: Bozell
Client: Better Business Bureau NAD

MISLEADING ADS CAN RUN BUT THEY CAN'T HIDE.

Member of Congress
Signature
Address

Name of Advertiser
When Advertising Appeared
Where Advertising Appeared (TV, Magazine, Etc.)

Why You Consider the Advertising Misleading

Mail to: The Director, NAD, 845 Third Avenue, New York, N.Y. 10022

The National Advertising Division of the Council of Better Business Bureaus continues to invite members of Congress to help us identify national advertisers who run misleading or false advertising.

Since 1971, the NAD has resolved more than 2,500 complaints. In over half of the cases, the advertising investigated has been modified or discontinued as a result.

If the NAD fails to achieve a resolution, the case is appealed to the National Advertising Review Board. In almost 20 years of operation, the NARB has never failed to resolve a case.

If you encounter an ad you believe is misleading, send us the information in writing. Your complaint will receive a quick reply and will be handled at no cost to the taxpayer. You will be informed of the results.

Let's continue to work together to protect the public. And to protect advertisers who tell the truth.

THE NATIONAL ADVERTISING DIVISION OF THE COUNCIL OF BETTER BUSINESS BUREAUS

THE BUNK STOPS HERE.

Member of Congress
Signature
Address

Name of Advertiser
When Advertising Appeared
Where Advertising Appeared (TV, Magazine, Etc.)

Why You Consider the Advertising Misleading

Mail to: The Director, NAD, 845 Third Avenue, New York, N.Y. 10022

The National Advertising Division of the Council of Better Business Bureaus is dedicated to helping you prevent the public from false and misleading advertising.

Since 1971, the NAD has resolved more than 2,500 complaints against national advertisers. In over half of the cases, the advertising investigated has been modified or discontinued as a result.

If the NAD fails to achieve a resolution, the case is appealed to the National Advertising Review Board. In almost 20 years of operation, the NARB has never failed to resolve a case.

The NAD invites members of Congress to join us in stopping untruthful advertising. If you have a complaint, send us the information in writing.

Your complaint will receive a quick reply and will be handled at no cost to the taxpayer. You will be informed of the results.

Let's work together to give the public what it deserves—truth, accuracy and no bunk in advertising.

THE NATIONAL ADVERTISING DIVISION OF THE COUNCIL OF BETTER BUSINESS BUREAUS

FREEDOM OF SPEECH DOESN'T MEAN FREEDOM TO LIE.

Member of Congress
Signature
Address

Name of Advertiser
When Advertising Appeared
Where Advertising Appeared (TV, Magazine, Etc.)

Why You Consider the Advertising Misleading

Mail to: The Director, NAD, 845 Third Avenue, New York, N.Y. 10022

Advertising that steps beyond the bounds of truth and accuracy hurts all of us. It misleads the consumer and creates unfair competition for the vast majority of advertisers who play by the rules.

Since 1971, the National Advertising Division of the Council of Better Business Bureaus has resolved more than 2,500 complaints against national advertisers. In over half of the cases, the advertising investigated has been modified or discontinued as a result.

If the NAD fails to achieve a resolution, the case is appealed to the National Advertising Review Board. In almost 20 years of operation, the NARB has never failed to resolve a case.

The NAD invites members of Congress to join us in protecting the public from misleading advertising. If you have a complaint, send us the information in writing. Your complaint will receive a quick reply and will be handled at no cost to the taxpayer. You will be informed of the results.

Let's work together to keep freedom of speech alive and well, and within the bounds that were intended.

THE NATIONAL ADVERTISING DIVISION OF THE COUNCIL OF BETTER BUSINESS BUREAUS

109
Art Director: John C. Jay
Creative Director: John C. Jay
Designer: John C. Jay
Photographer: Lance Stadler
Copywriter: Brian Leitch
Client: Bloomingdale's

110

Art Director: Ronald Rosen
Creative Director: Roy Grace
                  Diane Rothschild
Copywriter: Craig Demeter
Agency: Grace & Rothschild
Client: Whittle Communications

"Dinner's ready!"

For too many students, this is the 6:00 news.

Kids today have all the answers.

1. Jesse Jackson is an outfielder on a major-league baseball team. (T) F

2. Geraldine Ferraro is a talk-show host. (T) F

3. A silicon chip is a new kind of snack food. (T) F

According to many high school textbooks, man will land here one day.

BARRY UNDERSTANDS GREMLINS.

FORD'S TOO. Barry Wilson of Wilson's Auto Repair has been fixing cars for over twenty years. It's a good bet he can fix yours. At a fair price, too. Overhauls, electrical, brakes & shocks, tune-ups, lube & oil changes, air conditioning, transmission, clutch, front wheel drive, 24-hour towing. 271-3579 313 Saturn S. of Kingsley Garland

Barry **WILSON'S** AUTO REPAIR

BARRY OVERSEES CARAVANS.

HONDA'S TOO. Barry Wilson of Wilson's Auto Repair has been fixing cars for over twenty years. It's a good bet he can fix yours. At a fair price, too. Overhauls, electrical, brakes & shocks, tune-ups, lube & oil changes, air conditioning, transmission, clutch, front wheel drive, 24-hour towing. 271-3579 313 Saturn S. of Kingsley Garland

Barry **WILSON'S** AUTO REPAIR

BARRY RACKS UP ZZZ's.

MAZDA'S TOO. Barry Wilson of Wilson's Auto Repair has been fixing cars for over twenty years. It's a good bet he can fix yours. At a fair price, too. Overhauls, electrical, brakes & shocks, tune-ups, lube & oil changes, air conditioning, transmission, clutch, front wheel drive, 24-hour towing. 271-3579 313 Saturn S. of Kingsley Garland

Barry **WILSON'S** AUTO REPAIR

111

Art Director: James Howe
                Steve Stith
Designer: James Howe
            Dirk Mitchell
Copywriter: Dirk Mitchell
Agency: Thompson/Marince
Client: Barry's Auto

112
Art Director: Bob Brihn
Creative Director: Pat Burnham
Designer: Bob Brihn
Photographer: Kerry Peterson
Copywriter: George Gier
Agency: Fallon McElligott
Client: Porsche

Presenting a Porsche for the open minded.

The Porsche 944 S2 Cabriolet. Just try to top this. Come in for a test drive and open it up. **PORSCHE**

This car comes equipped with central air.

Whether you have the top down or up, you'll be cool no matter how hot it is. Test drive the new 944 S2 Cabriolet today. It's a breath of fresh air. **PORSCHE**

Ride it bare back.

Put the top down on the new 944 S2 Cabriolet, start it up and wind it out through all five gears on your favorite stretch of road. This is your moment in the sun. **PORSCHE**

Isn't it time Celebrities got a little more attention?

Whether you drive a Chevy Celebrity or a Subaru Brat, Amoco LDO is the right oil for your car. That's because LDO meets manufacturers' performance requirements for every car made today. So why not drive over to Amoco and change your oil now? On second thought, if you're not using LDO, you'd better take a cab.

LDO Motor Oil. $15 a case, $1.25 a quart.

Use the wrong oil and it won't be a Legend for long.

Whether you drive an Acura Legend or a Pontiac LeMans, Amoco LDO is the right oil for your car. That's because LDO meets manufacturers' performance requirements for every car made today. So why not drive over to Amoco and change your oil now? On second thought, if you're not using LDO, you'd better take a cab.

LDO Motor Oil. $15 a case, $1.25 a quart.

With the right oil, this Century could last another ten years.

Whether you drive a Buick Century or a Suzuki Samurai, Amoco LDO is the right oil for your car. That's because LDO meets manufacturers' performance requirements for every car made today. So why not drive over to Amoco and change your oil now? On second thought, if you're not using LDO, you'd better take a cab.

LDO Motor Oil. $15 a case, $1.25 a quart.

113
Art Director: Arty Tan
Creative Director: Pat Burnham
Photographer: Kerry Peterson
Copywriter: Jamie Barrett
Agency: Fallon McElligott
Client: Amoco

114
Art Director: Gary Goldsmith
　　　　　　　Tracy Wong
Creative Director: Gary Goldsmith
Photographer: Steve Hellerstein
Copywriter: Dean Hacohen
Agency: Goldsmith/Jeffrey
Client: NYNEX Information Resources

115
Art Director: Dan Scarlotto
　　　　　　　Terri Barrett
Creative Director: Tommy Thompson
Photographer: Richard Hoflich
　　　　　　　Anthony Sylvestro
Copywriter: John Schmidt
Agency: Siddall, Matus & Coughter
Client: FCEDA

116

Art Director: Tracy Wong
Gary Goldsmith
Creative Director: Gary Goldsmith
Photographer: Susan Goldman
Steve Hellerstein
Stock
Copywriter: Dean Hacohen
Agency: Goldsmith/Jeffrey
Client: EL AL Israel Airlines

To keep our customers happy, EL AL provides the most nonstop flights to Israel.

The most direct flights to Israel.

The best-trained pilots to Israel.

The best on-time record to Israel.

The best kosher meals to Israel.

Complimentary wine and movies to Israel.

To the man who requested a complete 12-lane bowling alley on board: Please be patient.

At EL AL, we've lowered our New York/Tel Aviv roundtrip fare to $679.

We've lowered our Boston/Tel Aviv fare to $679.

We've lowered our Chicago/Tel Aviv fare to $799.

We've lowered our Miami/Tel Aviv fare to $799.

We've lowered our Los Angeles/Tel Aviv fare to $869.

That's not to say you can't find cheaper ways to Israel.

You may be wondering how for just $849, EL AL can afford to give you roundtrip tickets to London.

Plus a week in a first class hotel.

Plus daily continental breakfasts.

Plus a city tour.

Plus two theatre tickets.

Plus transfers to and from the airport.

Suffice it to say, our accountants are wondering the same thing.

117

Art Director: Richard Martino
Creative Director: Steven Cohen
Copywriter: Shen Henricks
Agency: Martino & Co.

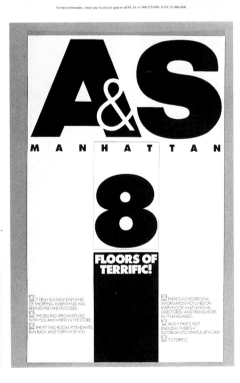

118
Art Director: Jordin Mendelsohn
Creative Director: Jordin Mendelsohn
Copywriter: Perrin Lam
Agency: Mendelsohn/Zien
Client: Acura

BUY A $30,000 AUTOMOBILE BASED ON WHAT A 2 YEAR OLD TELLS YOU.

ACURA INTEGRA SEDAN

ACURA HAS NEVER TAKEN A SECOND TO SATISFY ITS CUSTOMERS.

IT NOW APPEARS THE MOST EXPENSIVE PART MANUFACTURED BY LUXURY CAR COMPANIES IS THE PRICE.

COCAINE. FOR PEOPLE WHO WANT TO EXPERIENCE LIFE IN THE FAST LANE.

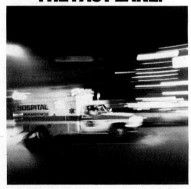

Some people think that cocaine helps them get more out of life.
But what they get are heart attacks, kidney failure, brain damage, or death.
Starting Wednesday, Eileen Korey takes a look at the physical reality of using cocaine in a special report.
Watch "White Death" on Channel 3 News at 11. **CHANNEL 3 NEWS**

THIS SHOW FEATURES THE MOST SOUGHT-AFTER CAST EVER ASSEMBLED.

Weekdays at 5 p.m. on Superior Court, watch criminals come to justice in dramatizations of real courtroom trials. Don't get caught missing it.
Superior Court. Weekdays at 5 P.M.

CHANNEL 3 WKYC

IT'S AMAZING WHAT YOU CAN GET AWAY WITH WHEN YOU HAVE A MASK TO HIDE BEHIND.

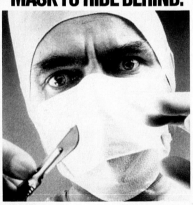

Because professional records are confidential, doctors guilty of malpractice are often able to continue treating patients.
Starting Monday, Eileen Korey will show you how a doctor's mask may protect him more than it does you. Watch "When Doctors Do Wrong," all this week on Channel 3 News at 11. **CHANNEL 3 NEWS**

119
Art Director: Don Fibich
Creative Director: Tom Smith
 Chuck Withrow
Designer: Don Fibich
Photographer: Ladd Trepal
Copywriter: Laura Owen
 Chuck Withrow
Agency: Wyse Advertising
Client: WKYC-TV3

120

Art Director: Bob Brihn
Creative Director: Pat Burnham
Designer: Bob Brihn
Photographer: Rick Dublin
              Jim Arndt
Copywriter: George Gier
Agency: Fallon McElligott
Client: Porsche

It's about as fast as you can go without having to eat airline food.

The all wheel drive system in the 911 Carrera 4 distributes 247 horsepower to the road at once giving it incredible acceleration. Come in for a test drive. And, then fasten your seatbelts.

PORSCHE

How to put a little distance between you and the rest of society.

If you're in the market for a luxury car, you don't have to sacrifice performance. The Porsche 928 has more luxury than you'd expect, plus the kick of 326 horses. Visit us for a closer look.

PORSCHE

Take a 6.9 second test drive.

With 208 horsepower, the Porsche 944 S2 accelerates to 60 mph in a mere 6.9 seconds. Take one for a test drive. You'll fall in love with it very fast.

PORSCHE

"WE WILL SELL NO WINE BEFORE 11:00 AM."

Steve Mularky, Owner.

SGT. PRESTONS
Saloon and Eatery.

Open at 11:00 AM daily. 221 Cedar Ave. So. at Seven Corners. 338-6146.

"AT OUR BAR YOU WON'T FEEL LIKE A PIECE OF MEAT. YOU'LL FEEL LIKE AN ENTIRE SANDWICH."

Keith Henneberg, Chef.

SGT. PRESTONS
Saloon and Eatery.

221 Cedar Ave. So. at Seven Corners in Minneapolis. 338-6146.

"A LOT OF BARS HAVE A HAPPY HOUR. OURS IS ECSTATIC."

Kristen Young, Waitress.

SGT. PRESTONS
Saloon and Eatery.

221 Cedar Ave. So. at Seven Corners in Minneapolis. 338-6146.

121

Art Director: Bob Brihn
Creative Director: Pat Burnham
Designer: Bob Brihn
Copywriter: Jamie Barrett
Agency: Fallon McElligott
Client: Sgt. Preston's

122
Art Director: Clifford Goodenough
Creative Director: Roger Livingston
Photographer: Larry Gilpin
Copywriter: Norah Delaney
Agency: Livingston & Co.
Client: First Interstate Bank of New Mexico

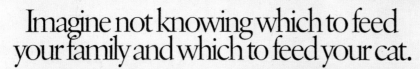

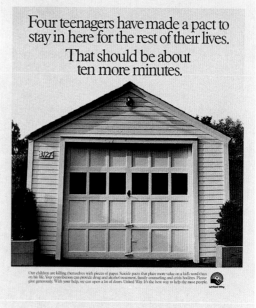

123
Art Director: Mike Sellers
Creative Director: David Terrenoire
Photographer: Tony Pearce
Copywriter: David Terrenoire
Agency: On Your Own Time Advertising
Client: Durham County Literacy Council

124
Art Director: Jeff Tresidder
Creative Director: Bruce Mansfield
Photographer: Rick Dublin
Copywriter: Scott Mackey
Agency: Lawler Ballard
Client: United Way

125
Art Director: Mike Sellers
Creative Director: David Terrenoire
Photographer: Tony Pearce
Copywriter: David Terrenoire
Agency: On Your Own Time Advertising
Client: Durham County Literacy Council

126
Art Director: John Follis
Creative Director: John Follis
Copywriter: John Follis
Agency: Follis & Verdi, Inc.
Client: Citizens for Prevention of Child Abuse

If one out of five adults can't read this sign, where is America headed?

You can read the future in a nation's literacy statistics. If our literacy rate continues to decline, our influence in the world's culture and economy will decline as well. Fortunately, we can still turn this trend around. But it will take your help.

If you know someone who has trouble reading, encourage that person to call us.

If you can give us your time, become a tutor. If you can't give your time, give your financial support. America is now at the crossroads. Which way do you want us to go?

♥ DURHAM COUNTY LITERACY COUNCIL
Call for help. 493-0555.

Some abused children grow up to become famous.

Abused children grow up to become abusing adults. Not in every case, but in too many. Nine out of ten murderers, rapists and drug addicts suffered from physical or emotional abuse as a child. So did the four people pictured above. That's something worth thinking about—even if you don't have kids.

Child Abuse. It hurts all of us.

CLIP & SAVE.

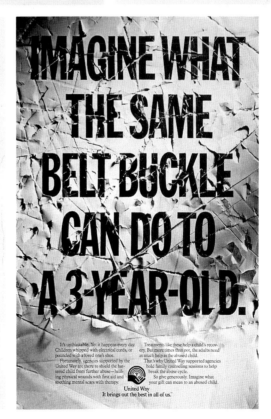

IMAGINE WHAT THE SAME BELT BUCKLE CAN DO TO A 3-YEAR-OLD.

It's unthinkable. Yet it happens every day. Children whipped with electrical cords, or pounded with a loved one's shoe.

Fortunately, agencies supported by the United Way are there to shield the battered child from further abuse—healing physical wounds with first aid and soothing mental scars with therapy.

Treatments like these help a child's recovery. But more times than not, the adults need as much help as the abused child.

That's why United Way supported agencies hold family counseling sessions to help break the abuse cycle.

So give generously. Imagine what your gift can mean to an abused child.

United Way
It brings out the best in all of us.

127
Art Director: Clark Lamm
Creative Director: Rick Gibson
Designer: Clark Lamm
Copywriter: Glen Wachowiak
Agency: Grant & Palombo
Client: Red Cross

128
Art Director: Chuck Finkle
Creative Director: Bob Neuman
Designer: Chuck Finkle
Photographer: Susan Goldman
Copywriter: Jerry Giordano
Client: United Way of Tri-State

129
Art Director: Ron Fisher
                April Norman
Creative Director: Ron Fisher
                Virgil Shutze
Photographer: Glenn Bewley
Copywriter: Ron Fisher
                Ralph McGill
Agency: HutchesonShutze
Client: Atlanta's Table

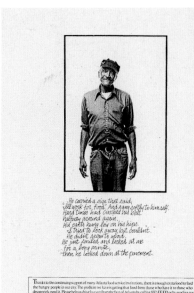

ON SOME NIGHTS IT RESEMBLES SHINING ARMOR.

NOT MANY VOLUNTEER JOBS INCLUDE USE OF THE COMPANY CAR.

WE CAN'T GIVE YOU A SALARY, BUT THAT DOESN'T MEAN YOU WON'T GET PAID.

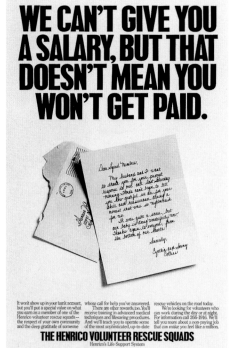

130
Art Director: Jim Brock
Creative Director: Ed Jones
Designer: Jim Brock
Photographer: Pat Edwards
Copywriter: Mac Calhoun
Client: Henrico Volunteer Rescue Squads

131

Art Director: Tom Marcantel
Creative Director: Bob Whitmore
Designer: Tom Marcantel
Photographer: Gordon Myhre
Copywriter: Mike Caughill
Agency: Tampa Art Directors Club
Client: United Way

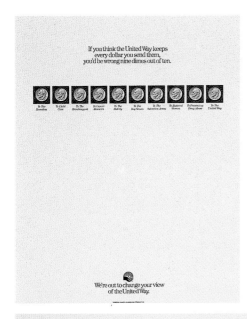

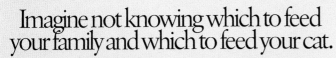

132

Art Director: Mike Sellers
Creative Director: David Terrenoire
Illustrator: Jackie Pittman
Photographer: Tony Pearce
Copywriter: David Terrenoire
Agency: On Your Own Time Advertising
Client: Durham County Literacy Council

THE PRICE OF FREEDOM IS A LOT HIGHER THAN TWO TRAIN TICKETS TO VIENNA.

134
Art Director: Bryan Nimeth
Creative Director: Mark H. Davis
Designer: Bryan Nimeth
Photographer: Charlie Co.
Copywriter: Mark H. Davis
Agency: Marcus Advertising
Client: Cleveland Jewish Federation

CONSIDERING WHAT YOU COULD SPEND ON LIFE'S LUXURIES THIS YEAR, THE NECESSITIES COME PRETTY DARN CHEAP.

LET FREEDOM BRING.

After Years Of Major Exhibits, We Now Present A Miner One.

The Gold Exhibit at The Museum Of Science.

Presenting An Exhibit That's A Lot More Than Just A Flash In The Pan.

The Gold Exhibit at The Museum Of Science.

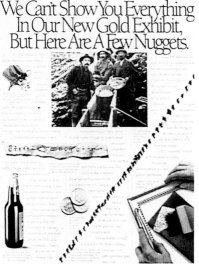

We Can't Show You Everything In Our New Gold Exhibit, But Here Are A Few Nuggets.

The Gold Exhibit at The Museum Of Science.

135
Art Director: R. Smith
　　　　　　K. Allensmith
Creative Director: Ron Lawner
Photographer: Stock
Copywriter: Fred Bertino
Agency: Della Femina, McNamee WCRS
Client: Museum of Science

136
Art Director: Craig Hadorn
Creative Director: Ken Hines
Designer: Craig Hadorn
Photographer: John Hood
Copywriter: Ken Hines
           Linda Whitmire
Agency: Lawler Ballard
Client: United Way

For what it costs to watch a horror story, you could keep a child from living one.

Imagine what it would be like if the terror didn't stop when you turned off the VCR. For hundreds of abused children, it doesn't.

But when you donate as little as $2.00 per week to the United Way, you can help organizations like Family And Children's Service provide intensive short-term counseling for abused children and their families. Or help Richmond Aftercare treat two recovering substance abusers.

Or your money could be used to support more than 80 other good causes.

So please give. Because with your help, all these stories could have happy endings.

 UNITED WAY

This is the only coupon in today's paper that lets you redeem yourself.

1989 UNITED WAY CAMPAIGN
In support of human services provided for our community, I contribute $_____ to United Way.
☐ Payment Enclosed. ☐ Bill Me Quarterly. ☐ Bill Me Annually.
Name _____
Address _____
City _____ State _____
Zip _____ Telephone(___) _____
Signature _____ Title _____
Mail coupon to United Way Services, 1901 Fitzhugh Avenue, P.O. Box 6649, Richmond, VA 23030. Or call (804) 353-2900 for more information.

Sure you can save money with those other coupons, but can you save lives?

Your donation helps provide shelter for homeless families. Meals for the hungry and undernourished. And medical care for the sick who couldn't otherwise afford it.

It helps provide counseling and support services for rape victims. A place for battered women and children to stay. And support for many other worthwhile causes.

And besides that, it makes you feel good. So if you haven't already, please give.

 UNITED WAY

Once a year, the idea of placing a dollar value on human life makes a lot of sense.

When you give to the United Way, your money helps support organizations right here in the Richmond and Tri-Cities area.

Organizations that provide a warm, dry place for homeless families to stay. That conduct daily telephone checks on seniors living alone. Organizations that provide both health and rehabilitative services for patients in their homes. And volunteer rescue squad and ambulance services for those who need help in a hurry.

In fact, your money could help support more than 80 potentially lifesaving services.

So please give. Your contribution really could mean the difference between life and death.

 UNITED WAY

Last Year, This Was Larry Tormey's Thanksgiving Dinner.

This Year, He May Not Be So Lucky.

Thanksgiving is almost here. But for thousands of people in Maryland, it will be just another day without food. Unless you help.

Look for your Bags of Plenty bag inside today's Baltimore Sun. Fill it with non-perishable foods and bring it to your neighborhood Giant store. Provident Bank or a Baltimore City fire station by November 27.

If you can, give cash. We will accept cash contributions until December 5. But that leaves us very little time.

To make a very big difference.

Bags of Plenty

I want to help with cash.
Name _____
Address _____
City _____
State _____ Zip _____
Here's my check for
☐ $100 ☐ $50
☐ $25 ☐ Other _____ Phone _____
Make your check payable to Maryland Food Committee and mail to: Maryland Food Committee, Sunbridge, Calvert Savings & Loan, P.O. Box 1204, Baltimore, MD 21218.

At Thanksgiving, the only thing some people think about is food, food, food.

Bags of Plenty

"Gee, Mom, that turkey smells great. I can have a drumstick, right? And lots of mashed potatoes and stuffing? I'll even eat those yukky peas if I can have tons of whipped cream on my pumpkin pie. And can we please eat soon? 'Cause I'm really hungry."

"Gee, Mom, ~~that turkey smells great. I can have a drumstick, right? And lots of mashed potatoes and stuffing? I'll even eat those yukky peas if I can have tons of whipped cream on my pumpkin pie. And can we please eat soon?~~ 'Cause I'm really hungry."

Please do what you can to help us feed a hungry family.
Chater us at live the time we turn Bags of Plenty

I want to help with cash.

Bags of Plenty

137
Art Director: Sharon Brady
Creative Director: James Dale
Photographer: Steve Longley
Copywriter: Sara Slater
           Sharon Brady
Agency: W.B. Doner
Client: The *Baltimore Sun*

138

Art Director: Debby Lucke
Creative Director: Ron Lawner
Photographer: John Holt
Copywriter: David Abend
Agency: Della Femina, McNamee WCRS
Client: Stanley

139

Art Director: Debby Lucke
Creative Director: Ron Lawner
Photographer: John Holt
Copywriter: Fred Bertino
Agency: Della Femina, McNamee WCRS
Client: Stanley

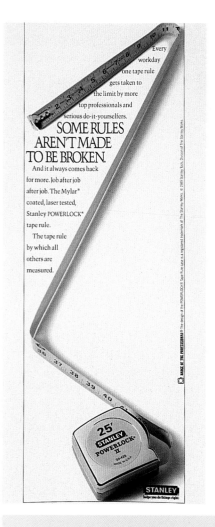

140

Art Director: Bob Brihn
Creative Director: Pat Burnham
Designer: Bob Brihn
Photographer: Jeff Zwart
Copywriter: Bruce Bildsten
Agency: Fallon McElligott
Client: Porsche

141

Art Director: Tom Lichtenheld
Creative Director: Pat Burnham
Designer: Tom Lichtenheld
Copywriter: George Gier
Agency: Fallon McElligott
Client: Time-Life Books

142

Art Director: John Butler
　　　　　　Mike Shine
Creative Director: Bill Hamilton
Designer: Graham Clifford
Photographer: Joe Baraban
Copywriter: Mike Shine
　　　　　　John Butler
Agency: Chiat/Day/Mojo Advertising Inc.
Client: NYNEX Information Resources

143

Art Director: Tom Lichtenheld
Creative Director: Pat Burnham
Designer: Tom Lichtenheld
Photographer: Kent Severson
Copywriter: Jarl Olsen
Agency: Fallon McElligott
Client: Time-Life Books

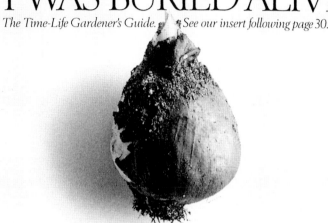

145

Art Director: Bob Barrie
Creative Director: Pat Burnham
Designer: Bob Barrie
Photographer: Stock
Copywriter: Luke Sullivan
Agency: Fallon McElligott
Client: KRIV-TV

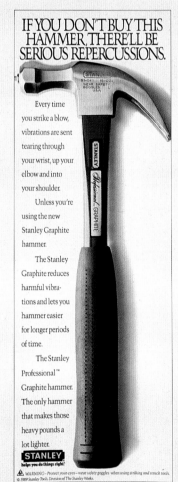

144

Art Director: Debby Lucke
Creative Director: Ron Lawner
Photographer: John Holt
Copywriter: Fred Bertino
Agency: Della Femina, McNamee WCRS
Client: Stanley

146

Art Director: John Butler
Mike Shine
Creative Director: Bill Hamilton
Photographer: Joe Baraban
Copywriter: Mike Shine
John Butler
Agency: Chiat/Day/Mojo Advertising Inc.
Client: NYNEX Information Resources

147

Art Director: Mitch Gordon
Creative Director: Jan Zechman
Designer: Mitch Gordon
Illustrator: Nadav Kander
Copywriter: Jim Carey
Agency: Zechman & Associates
Client: Coastal Properties

148

Art Director: John Butler
Mike Shine
Creative Director: Bill Hamilton
Designer: Graham Clifford
Photographer: Joe Baraban
Copywriter: Mike Shine
John Butler
Agency: Chiat/Day/Mojo Advertising Inc.
Client: NYNEX Information Resources

149

Art Director: Frank Haggerty
Creative Director: Frank Haggerty
Photographer: Jim Marvy
Copywriter: Kerry Casey
Agency: Carmichael Lynch
Client: ZEBCO

150

Art Director: Bryan Lahr
Creative Director: Bryan Lahr
Photographer: Stock
Copywriter: Bryan Lahr
 Patrick Hanlon
Agency: The Lahr Agency
Client: Longhorn Steaks

151

Art Director: Gary Goldsmith
Creative Director: Gary Goldsmith
Photographer: Gilles Larrain
Copywriter: Dean Hacohen
Agency: Goldsmith/Jeffrey
Client: Knoll International

152

Art Director: Houman Pirdavari
Creative Director: Pat Burnham
Photographer: Rick Dublin
Copywriter: Jarl Olsen
Agency: Fallon McElligott
Client: Penn

153

Art Director: Frank Haggerty
Creative Director: Frank Haggerty
Photographer: Jim Marvy
Copywriter: Kerry Casey
Agency: Carmichael Lynch
Client: ZEBCO

154
Art Director: Jim Mochnsky
Creative Director: James Dale
Designer: Jim Mochnsky
Photographer: Stephen John Phillips
Copywriter: Arthur Mitchell
        Jim Mochnsky
Agency: W.B. Doner
Client: The World Wildlife Fund

155
Art Director: Bob Barrie
Creative Director: Pat Burnham
Designer: Bob Barrie
Photographer: Rick Dublin
Copywriter: Jarl Olsen
Agency: Fallon McElligott
Client: Jim Beam

How do you fit five elephants in a box?

First find someone who'll do the killing. Arm him with a machine gun and an axe. Send him off to slaughter elephants. Pay him for the tusks. And ship them away to be carved into bracelets and necklaces.

The African elephant is being driven from the face of the earth for the sake of consumer demand for ivory trinkets. In just 10 years, the population of African elephants has been more than halved. If this rate of killing continues, the African elephant could be extinct in just 25 years. The killers and the people who pay them don't care about elephant deaths. They don't hear the world's outrage. They just want money. They're the people we must stop.

Please join World Wildlife Fund's Elephant Action Campaign. Help us put these killers and the people who finance them out of business. Your donation of $15 or more will help us support increased anti-poaching patrols. And supply equipment to those rangers who are already in the field – desperately trying to stop the senseless slaughter of one of the world's great species.

Time is running out. 143 African elephants are dying every day. So their tusks can be turned into jewelry. You can stop this. Before it's too late. Call 1-800-453-6100 to make a donation.

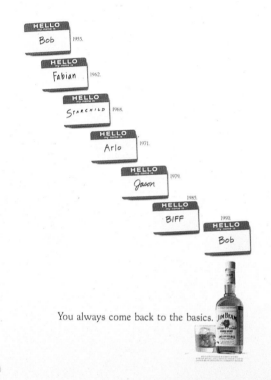

You always come back to the basics. JIM BEAM

With what pen did Sir Arthur Conan Doyle write "The Case Book of Sherlock Holmes"?

◆ PARKER

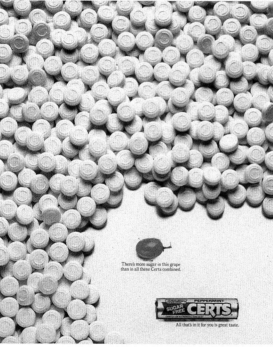

There's more sugar in this grape
than in all these Certs combined.

SUGAR FREE CERTS

All that's in it for you is great taste.

156
Art Director: Dennis D'Amico
Photographer: Kevin Summers
Copywriter: David Metcalf
Agency: Lowe, Tucker, Metcalf
Client: Parker Pen

157
Art Director: Tony Carillo
Creative Director: Mike Robertson
Copywriter: David Oakley
Agency: Young & Rubicam, Inc.
Client: Warner-Lambert Co.

158
Art Director: Tony DeGregorio
Creative Director: Tony DeGregorio
Photographer: Steve Horn
Copywriter: Rochelle Klein
Agency: Levine, Huntley, Schmidt & Beaver
Client: Maidenform

159
Art Director: George Zipparo
Creative Director: Ron Arnold
Photographer: Diane Padys
Copywriter: Carol Turturro
Agency: HDM
Client: Dannon

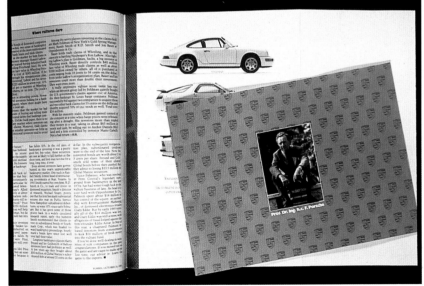

160
Art Director: Earl Cavanah
Creative Director: Sam Scali
Photographer: Jerry Friedman
Copywriter: Larry Cadman
Agency: Scali, McCabe, Sloves
Client: Nikon

161
Art Director: Mark Johnson
Creative Director: Pat Burnham
Photographer: Andreas Burz
Copywriter: John Stingley
Agency: Fallon McElligott
Client: Porsche

162
Art Director: Rob Dalton
Creative Director: Pat Burnham
Photographer: Craig Perman
Copywriter: Jamie Barrett
Agency: Fallon McElligott
Client: Palmer

163
Art Director: Gary Goldsmith
Creative Director: Gary Goldsmith
Copywriter: Tom Churm
                Gary Goldsmith
Agency: Goldsmith/Jeffrey
Client: Everlast Activewear

164
Art Director: Tom Lichtenheld
Creative Director: Pat Burnham
Illustrator: Sharon Werner
Copywriter: Bruce Bildsten
Agency: Fallon McElligott
Client: Azur

165
Art Director: Paul Boley
Creative Director: John Eding
Photographer: Dewitt Jones
Copywriter: Richard Rand
Agency: Leo Burnett Co.
Client: Schenley/Dewars White Label

166
Art Director: Bob Wyatt
Creative Director: John Eding
Photographer: Harry DeZitter
Copywriter: Tom Coleman
Agency: Leo Burnett Co.
Client: Schenley/Dickel

167
Art Director: Mike Hall
Creative Director: Jim Winters
Photographer: Jon Woodward
Copywriter: Bryan Behar
Agency: Franklin & Associates
Client: Ektelon

**YOU MAY FORGET YOU'RE WEARING OUR EYEWEAR.
UNTIL SUDDENLY IT HITS YOU.**

When the game's on the line, the last thing you should be thinking about is your eyewear. That's why Ektelon offers you a comfortable new line of eye protection. With anti-fog lenses, padded nose bridges, absorbent brow bridges and adjustable headstraps. In a variety of styles that let you look as good as you see. Ektelon eyewear. It helps keep your eye off the ball. And your mind on the game.

168
Art Director: Phil Silvestri
Creative Director: Jamie Seltzer
Photographer: Bettman Archive
Copywriter: Rich Roth
Agency: Della Femina, McNamee WCRS
Client: Tott's

169
Art Director: Patty Thompson
Creative Director: Ron Fisher
            Virgil Shutze
Photographer: Charles Jameson
Copywriter: Ralph McGill
Agency: HutchesonShutze
Client: American Forest Council

170
Art Director: Andy Dijak
Creative Director: Lee Clow
Copywriter: Dick Sittig
Agency: Chiat/Day/Mojo Advertising Inc.
Client: Nissan

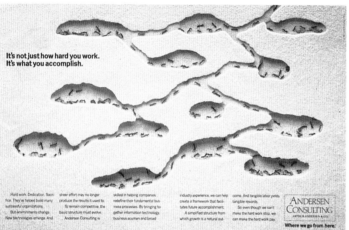

171
Art Director: Mary Ellen Cohen
Creative Director: Cary Lemkowitz
Copywriter: Dick Sinreich
Agency: Young & Rubicam, Inc.
Client: Arthur Andersen Co.

172
Art Director: Phil Silvestri
Creative Director: Jamie Seltzer
Photographer: Bettman Archive
Copywriter: Rich Roth
Agency: Della Femina, McNamee WCRS
Client: Tott's

173
Art Director: Jim Henderson
Creative Director: Lyle Wedemeyer
Photographer: Ron Crofoot
Copywriter: Pete Smith
Agency: Martin/Williams
Client: 3M Co.

174
Art Director: George Zipparo
Creative Director: Ron Arnold
Photographer: Diane Padys
Copywriter: Carol Turturro
Client: Dannon

175
Art Director: Jean Robaire
Creative Director: Jean Robaire
　　　　　　　　　John Stein
Designer: Jean Robaire
Illustrator: Dave McMaken
Photographer: Paul Gersten
Copywriter: John Stein
Agency: Stein, Robaire, Helm
Client: RolandCorp US

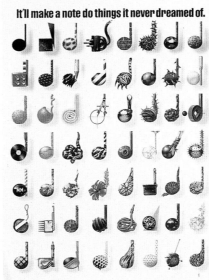

176
Art Director: Jud Smith
Creative Director: Jack Supple
Illustrator: Bill Reynolds
Photographer: Rod Pierce
Copywriter: Kerry Casey
Agency: Carmichael Lynch
Client: Federal Cartridge

177
Art Director: David Page
Creative Director: Jack Supple
Photographer: Dennis Manarchy
Copywriter: Joe Nagy
Agency: Carmichael Lynch
Client: Harley-Davidson

178
Art Director: Susan Hoffman
Creative Director: Dan Wieden
              David Kennedy
Copywriter: Steve Sandoz
Agency: Wieden & Kennedy
Client: Nike

179
Art Director: Roy Grace
Creative Director: Roy Grace
              Diane Rothschild
Illustrator: Roy Grace
Copywriter: Diane Rothschild
Client: Paddington

A SHOE FOR ATHLETES WITH THE WORLD'S SHORTEST ATTENTION SPAN.

J&B neat.

Another sign that you need a Range Rover.

Nobody ever said it **DIETING AGAIN?** was easy, right? But with a little help from Diet Polar, you can watch your weight and indulge yourself at the same time.

180
Art Director: Roy Grace
Creative Director: Roy Grace
              Diane Rothschild
Photographer: Bruno
Copywriter: Diane Rothschild
Client: Range Rover of North America

181
Art Director: Oliver White
Creative Director: Terry MacDonald
              Oliver White
Photographer: Jim Thomas
              Dan Guravich
Copywriter: Terry MacDonald
Client: Polar Corp.

182
Art Director: Roy Grace
Creative Director: Roy Grace
                    Diane Rothschild
Photographer: David McNamara
Copywriter: Diane Rothschild
Client: TVA

183
Art Director: Paul Asao
Creative Director: Jack Supple
Photographer: Aaron Jones
Copywriter: Katie Franson
Agency: Carmichael Lynch
Client: Ecowater Systems

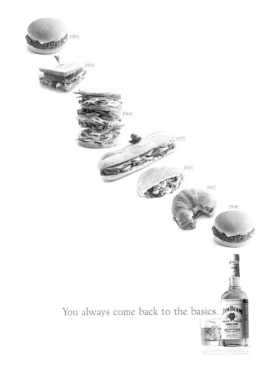

184
Art Director: Bob Barrie
Creative Director: Pat Burnham
Designer: Bob Barrie
Photographer: Kerry Peterson
Copywriter: Jarl Olsen
Agency: Fallon McElligott
Client: Jim Beam

185
Art Director: Bill Shea
Creative Director: Sean Fitzpatrick
Photographer: Douglas Foulke
Copywriter: Rona Oberman
Agency: McCann-Erickson
Client: The Gillette Co.

186
Art Director: Dan Scarlotto
Creative Director: Tommy Thompson
Designer: Dan Scarlotto
Illustrator: Ernest Stubbs
Copywriter: John Schmidt
Agency: Siddall, Matus & Coughter
Client: Kettler & Scott

187
Art Director: Brian Stymest
Creative Director: Sean Fitzpatrick
Photographer: Diane Padys
Copywriter: Charles Mullen
Agency: McCann-Erickson
Client: Wamsutta/Pacific Home Products

188
Art Director: Mark Shap
Creative Director: Malcolm End
Photographer: Eric Michelson
Copywriter: Veronica Nash
Agency: Ogilvy & Mather
Client: Cheeseborough-Ponds

189
Art Director: Gary Rozanski
Photographer: Jeff Zwart
Copywriter: Mitchell Wein
Agency: DDB Needham
Client: Volkswagen

190

Art Director: Ed Evangelista
Creative Director: Ron Berger
Designer: Ed Evangelista
Copywriter: Ron Berger
Agency: M.V.B.C.S.
Client: Windstar Sail Cruise

191

Art Director: Bob Brihn
Creative Director: Pat Burnham
Designer: Bob Brihn
Photographer: Mark LaFavor
Copywriter: Jamie Barrett
Agency: Fallon McElligott
Client: Porsche

THE DIFFERENCE BETWEEN FEELING LIKE A TOURIST WHO HAS INVADED AN ISLAND AND A GUEST WHO HAS BEEN INVITED.

Two Of These And You'll Be Back On Your Feet In No Time.

Public phone. Private moment. Lee jeans.

192

Art Director: Mark Johnson
Creative Director: Pat Burnham
Photographer: Kurt Markus
Copywriter: Bill Miller
Agency: Fallon McElligott
Client: Lee Jeans

THE JACKSON 5.

See Bo cross-train. See Bo cross-train in a shoe with Nike-Air cushioning and plenty of support. See Bo cross-train in the Air Trainer SC. See if you can do everything Bo can do in it.

193

Art Director: Rick McQuiston
Creative Director: Dan Wieden
                      David Kennedy
Copywriter: Jim Riswold
Agency: Wieden & Kennedy
Client: Nike

194
Art Director: John Staffen
Creative Director: Mike Rogers
Photographer: Aaron Jones
Copywriter: Mike Rogers
Agency: DDB Needham
Client: Cigna

195
Art Director: Bill Spewak
Designer: Bill Spewak
Copywriter: Bill Spewak
          John Barker
Agency: Grey Entertainment & Media
Client: ABC Entertainment

The pencil costs 14¢.
The eraser, millions.

Mistakes make products late, more expensive and inferior.
Leaving customers dissatisfied, reputations damaged. Since there
are no quick fixes, only costly ones, what's a business to do?
At the CIGNA Property and Casualty Companies, we have a very
basic goal: Get it right the first time.

Granted, nobody's perfect. But it's surprising how many mistakes can be prevented.

By working to find the best solution, rather than the most expedient one.

Whether we're providing protection for small and medium-size businesses, or meeting the risk management needs of the largest corporations, the benefits are the same: Answers that are fast and accurate. Service that is responsive. Value that is real. And customers who are satisfied. Anything less would be a big mistake.

For more about our business insurance for commercial banks, sponsored by the American Bankers Association, call MarketDyne International, a CIGNA company, at 1-800-523-2710. After all, anyone can pay for lots of pencils. But who can afford all the erasers?

We get paid for results." CIGNA

Based on the true, triumphant story of the rescue that united a Texas town— and all of America.

Imagine a child, trapped 22 feet underground, in a hole exactly this size.

EVERYBODY'S BABY: THE RESCUE OF JESSICA McCLURE

Starring Beau Bridges Patty Duke
ABC Sunday Night Movie 9:00 PM

You always come back to the basics.

The magazine to read from the time you
leave the cradle.

When you're a new arrival into the world of sailing, your first excursions across the bay are as important as your first unaided steps across your parents' kitchen floor. For it's a time to develop new skills, discover your potentials and widen your horizons.

Which is why we publish Sail to instruct, inform and inspire novices, as much as we write it to stimulate performance sailors and engage bluewater cruisers.

It's an editorial commitment exemplified in columns like Learning to Sail, Offshore Racing and Coastwise Cruising. As well as special sections on everything from buying a new boat to commissioning a used one. No other sailing magazine offers so much to help launch you on your way. Which is probably why no other sailing magazine has so much in the way of dedication from its readership. So whether you're leaving the cradle for the first time or the fifty-first, there's only one word you really need to know – Sail.

SAIL

196
Art Director: Bob Barrie
Creative Director: Pat Burnham
Designer: Bob Barrie
Photographer: Rick Dublin
Copywriter: Jarl Olsen
Agency: Fallon McElligott
Client: Jim Beam

197
Art Director: Steve Haesche
Photographer: Christopher Cunningham
Copywriter: Peter Pappas
Agency: Mullen
Client: Sail

198
Art Director: Mike Mazza
Creative Director: Lee Clow
Copywriter: Brian Belefant
Agency: Chiat/Day/Mojo
Client: Nissan

199
Art Director: Bob Barrie
Creative Director: Pat Burnham
Designer: Bob Barrie
Photographer: Robin Moyer
Copywriter: Jamie Barrett
Agency: Fallon McElligott
Client: Federal Express

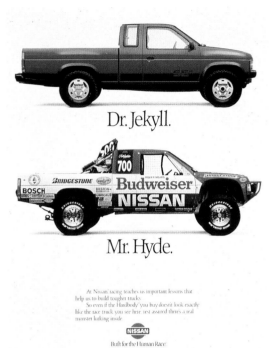

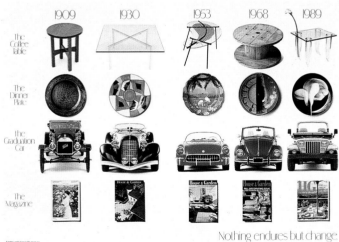

200
Art Director: Donna Weinheim
Creative Director: Donna Weinheim
Photographer: David Langley
Copywriter: Cliff Freeman
　　　　　　　Jane King
Agency: Cliff Freeman & Partners
Client: Conde Nast

201
Art Director: John Vitro
Creative Director: Jim Winters
Photographer: Jim Brandenberg
Copywriter: John Robertson
Agency: Franklin & Associates
Client: San Diego Wild Animal Park

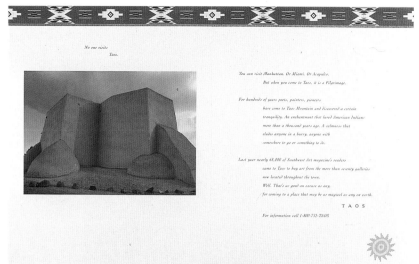

202
Art Director: Steven Sessions
Creative Director: Steven Sessions
Designer: Steven Sessions
Illustrator: Steven Sessions
Copywriter: John Hartmann
Agency: Steven Sessions, Inc.
Client: Southwest Art Magazine

203
Art Director: John Staffen
Creative Director: Mike Rogers
Photographer: Lamb & Hall
Copywriter: Giff Crosby
Agency: DDB Needham
Client: Michelin

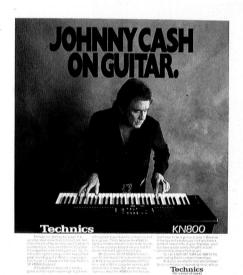

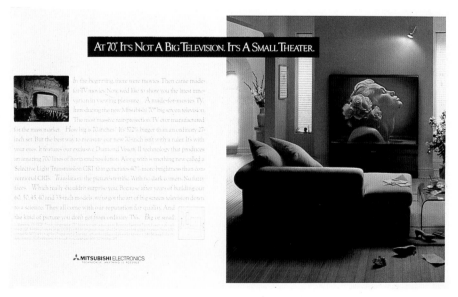

204
Art Director: James Offenhartz
Creative Director: Lee Garfinkel
Photographer: Ken Nahoum
Copywriter: Marian Allen Godwin
Agency: Levine, Huntley, Schmidt & Beaver
Client: Technics

205
Art Director: Rick Boyko
Creative Director: Bob Kuperman
Copywriter: Steve Rabosky
Agency: Chiat/Day/Mojo
Client: Mitsubishi

Big enough to hold a meeting. Fast enough to keep it short.

206
Art Director: Jerry Gentile
Mike Mazza
Creative Director: Bob Kuperman
Copywriter: Jerry Fields
Agency: Chiat/Day/Mojo
Client: Nissan

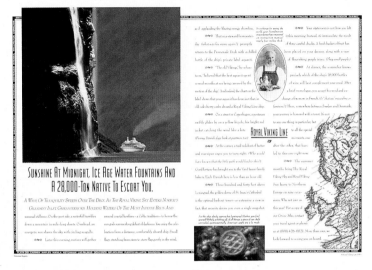

207
Art Director: Jeremy Postaer
Creative Director: Jeffrey Goodby
Rich Silverstein
Photographer: Harvey Lloyd
Hank Benson
Copywriter: Amy Krouse
Agency: Goodby, Berlin & Silverstein
Client: Royal Viking Line

208
Art Director: Larry Martin
Creative Director: Guy Bommarito
Copywriter: Guy Bommarito
Agency: GSD&M Advertising
Client: Texas Department of Commerce

209
Art Director: Steve Stone
Creative Director: Jeffrey Goodby
Rich Silverstein
Photographer: Loren McIntyre
Jay Maisel
Dan Escobar
Copywriter: Rob Bagot
Agency: Goodby, Berlin & Silverstein
Client: Royal Viking Line

210
Art Director: Leslie Sweet
Creative Director: Tony DeGregorio
Designer: Leslie Sweet
Photographer: Cailor/Resnick
Copywriter: Pamela Sullivan
Agency: Levine, Huntley, Schmidt & Beaver
Client: Dreyfus

211
Art Director: Rick Boyko
Creative Director: Steve Rabosky
Copywriter: Rob Feakins
Agency: Chiat/Day/Mojo
Client: Mitsubishi

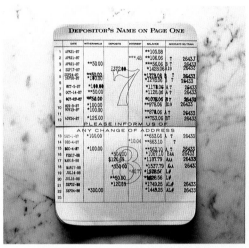

AT THIS RATE, YOU'LL NEVER GET A HOUSE.

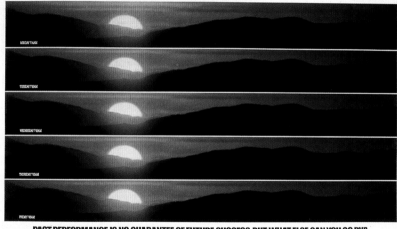

PAST PERFORMANCE IS NO GUARANTEE OF FUTURE SUCCESS. BUT WHAT ELSE CAN YOU GO BY?

THIS IS NOT OUR IDEA OF A COMFORTABLE RETIREMENT.

212
Art Director: Leslie Sweet
Creative Director: Tony DeGregorio
Copywriter: Pamela Sullivan
Agency: Levine, Huntley, Schmidt & Beaver
Client: Dreyfus

213
Art Director: Leslie Sweet
       Sal DeVito
Creative Director: Tony DeGregorio
Designer: Leslie Sweet
Photographer: Cailor/Resnick
Copywriter: Nat Russo
       Sal DeVito
Agency: Levine, Huntley, Schmidt & Beaver
Client: Dreyfus

214

Art Director: Andy Dijak
Creative Director: Lee Clow
Copywriter: Brian Belefant
            Dick Sittig
Agency: Chiat/Day/Mojo
Client: Nissan

215

Art Director: Tim Hannell
Creative Director: Ross Van Dusen
Photographer: Hunter Freeman
Copywriter: Jim Noble
Agency: Chiat/Day/Mojo
Client: Atari Corp.

216

Art Director: Brian Fandetti
Creative Director: Paul Silverman
Photographer: Abe Seltzer
            John Holt
Copywriter: Paul Silverman
Agency: Mullen
Client: Stride Rite Footwear

217

Art Director: Gary Yoshida
Creative Director: Larry Postaer
Copywriter: Bob Coburn
Client: American Honda Motor Corp.

218
Art Director: Roy Grace
Creative Director: Roy Grace
Diane Rothschild
Photographer: Elizabeth Heyert
Copywriter: Diane Rothschild
Client: Century Furniture

219
Art Director: Jud Smith
Creative Director: Jack Supple
Illustrator: Bill Reynolds
Photographer: Rod Pierce
Copywriter: Kerry Casey
Agency: Carmichael Lynch
Client: Federal Cartridge

Why we offer the same sofa in 67 sizes.

Unfortunately, while most sofas come in standard sizes, many spaces don't.
So at Century Furniture we make a full line of Custom Designer
Seating to solve exactly that problem.
Available in a range of styles, each one is lavishly hand-crafted, carefully
finished, and custom made in any length from 54 to 120 inches.
Why not call 1-800-852-5552 for more information,
or for the name of a store selling Century Furniture near you?
After all, even if you're considering a new slant in decorating,
we don't suppose you mean the kind up there.

Century Furniture

If You Buy Ammunition Like A City Boy, You're Going To Shoot Like A City Boy.

FEDERAL

No other *guitar* effects processor lets you PLAY up to *twelve* effects simultaneously.

Send in the clones.

There's a good reason why more cars are looking more and more alike. It's called the Accord.

The Honda Accord has become the benchmark for other car makers. They take it apart. Study it. Take it apart again.

Now while they're busy doing that, we would like to move on to something bigger and better. The new Accord.

The new Accord was redesigned to create a new car. A car attuned to the driver. One that improves the quality of driving.

The NewAccord

220
Art Director: Kevin McCarthy
Creative Director: Jean Robaire
John Stein
Designer: Kevin McCarthy
Photographer: Paul Gersten
Copywriter: Brian Belefant
Agency: Stein, Robaire, Helm
Client: RolandCorp US

221
Art Director: Gary Yoshida
Creative Director: Larry Postaer
Copywriter: Bob Coburn
Client: American Honda Motor Corp.

222
Art Director: Frank Todaro
Creative Director: Earl Cavanah
Photographer: Gil Smith
Copywriter: Rob Slosberg
Agency: Scali, McCabe, Sloves
Client: Volvo

223
Art Director: Houman Pirdavari
Creative Director: Pat Burnham
Photographer: Rick Dublin
Copywriter: Jarl Olsen
Agency: Fallon McElligott
Client: Penn

THE BMW 525i IS SLOWER, LESS ROOMY AND COSTS $10,000 MORE. MAYBE IT'S THE NEW MATH.

We'll spot the dead ball before you will.
Penn tennis balls. You've seen one. You've seen them all.

The Truth Is In The Lie.

432 PRECEPT 1

Worth its wait.

224
Art Director: Jay Shields
Creative Director: Bob Warren
Photographer: Parish Kohanim
Copywriter: Pat Wages
Client: Bridgestone Sports

225
Art Director: Sheri Olmon
Creative Director: Marty Cooke
Photographer: David Bailey
Copywriter: Alan Platt
Agency: Chiat/Day/Mojo Advertising Inc.
Client: American Express Gold Card

226
Art Director: John Doyle
Designer: John Doyle
Photographer: Clint Clemens
Copywriter: Paul Silverman
Agency: Mullen
Client: Timberland Co.

227
Art Director: Leslie Sweet
Creative Director: Tony DeGregorio
Photographer: William Hines
Copywriter: Nat Russo
Agency: Levine, Huntley, Schmidt & Beaver
Client: Dreyfus

228
Art Director: Gary Johns
Creative Director: Gary Johns
Designer: Gary Johns
Photographer: Mark Coppos
Copywriter: Gary Johns
Agency: Gary D. Johns, Inc.
Client: Bissell & Wilhite Co.

229
Art Director: Pam Cunningham
Creative Director: Bob Kuperman
Copywriter: Steve Bassett
Agency: Chiat/Day/Mojo
Client: Nissan

230

Art Director: Laura Della Sala
Creative Director: Bob Kuperman
Copywriter: Rob Feakins
Agency: Chiat/Day/Mojo
Client: Mitsubishi

231

Art Director: Rod Smith
Creative Director: Ron Lawner
Photographer: Myron
Copywriter: Alan Marcus
Agency: Della Femina, McNamee WCRS
Client: Foot-Joy

You left a teapot in a taxi. We replaced it.
You wrecked your rented car. We covered it. You missed your flight. We changed it. You always wanted the perfect traveling companion. Now you've got it.

232

Art Director: Sheri Olmon
Creative Director: Marty Cooke
Photographer: David Bailey
Copywriter: Alan Platt
Agency: Chiat/Day/Mojo Advertising Inc
Client: American Express Gold Card

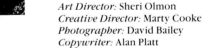

233

Art Director: Jeremy Postaer
Creative Director: Jeffrey Goodby
                    Rich Silverstein
Photographer: Duncan Sim
                Hank Benson
Copywriter: Rob Bagot
Agency: Goodby, Berlin & Silverstein
Client: Royal Viking Line

234
Art Director: Jeanne MacDonald
Creative Director: Bob Kuperman
Photographer: Dan Arsenault
Copywriter: Matt Bogen
Agency: Chiat/Day/Mojo Advertising Inc.
Client: Mitsubishi

235
Art Director: Mark Johnson
Creative Director: Pat Burnham
Photographer: Kurt Markus
Copywriter: Bill Miller
Agency: Fallon McElligott
Client: Lee Jeans

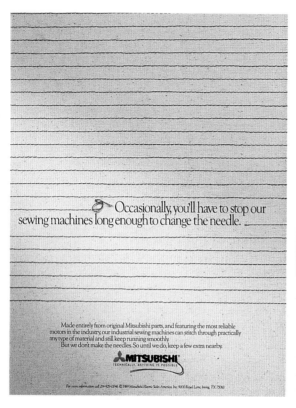

Too much road. Too little time. Six miles from home. Lee jeans.

236
Art Director: Patty Thompson
Creative Director: Ron Fisher
                      Virgil Shutze
Photographer: Charles Jameson
Copywriter: Ralph McGill
Agency: HutchesonShutze
Client: American Forest Council

"BY 1945, AMERICA'S FORESTS WILL BE HISTORY."

237
Art Director: Mark Johnson
Creative Director: Pat Burnham
Photographer: Kurt Markus
Copywriter: Bill Miller
Agency: Fallon McElligott
Client: Lee Jeans

22 years. 3 months. 6 days. Lee jeans.

238
Art Director: Ed Evangelista
Creative Director: Ron Berger
Copywriter: Charlie Tercek
Agency: M.V.B.C.S.
Client: Life Magazine

239
Art Director: Fred Hammerquist
Creative Director: Rod Kilpatrick
Photographer: Bruce Wilson
Copywriter: Bob Moore
Agency: Cole & Weber
Client: Raleigh Bicycles

Is Morton Downey Jr. what television is coming to? Judge for yourself in LIFE's 50-year retrospective of TV.

No matter what's being investigated or who's being interviewed, LIFE's coverage is always the same: emotionally and intellectually involving, and impossible to overlook.

All of which makes something else hard to overlook: the fact that LIFE's ad pages keep increasing. In 1988, they climbed 32%. And for the first quarter of '89, they're up 61%.

It's numbers like these that helped LIFE become one of Adweek's "10 Hottest Magazines of the Year."

LIFE The Power of Pictures

Why The Heat Rides The Chill.

You always come back to the basics. JIM BEAM

You always come back to the basics. JIM BEAM

240
Art Director: Bob Barrie
Creative Director: Pat Burnham
Designer: Bob Barrie
Photographer: Kerry Peterson
Copywriter: Jarl Olsen
Agency: Fallon McElligott
Client: Jim Beam

241
Art Director: Bob Barrie
Creative Director: Pat Burnham
Designer: Bob Barrie
Photographer: Kerry Peterson
Copywriter: Jarl Olsen
Agency: Fallon McElligott
Client: Jim Beam

242
Art Director: Parry Merkley
Creative Director: Gordon Bowen
Photographer: Annie Leibovitz
Copywriter: Gordon Bowen
Agency: Ogilvy & Mather
Client: American Express

243
Art Director: John Doyle
Creative Director: Paul Silverman
Photographer: Clint Clemens
Copywriter: Paul Silverman
Agency: Mullen
Client: Timberland Co.

244
Art Director: John Doyle
Creative Director: Paul Silverman
Photographer: Clint Clemens
Copywriter: Paul Silverman
Agency: Mullen
Client: Timberland Co.

245
Art Director: Tim Delaney
Creative Director: Jim Copacino
Copywriter: Jim Copacino
Agency: Livingston & Co.
Client: Alaska Airlines

246
Art Director: Tim Delaney
Creative Director: Jim Copacino
Copywriter: Jim Copacino
Agency: Livingston & Co.
Client: Alaska Airlines

247

Art Director: Scott Ballew
        Steve Popp
Creative Director: Stan Richards
Photographer: Ka Yeung
        Brian McWeeney
Copywriter: Chris Sekin
        Kevin Swisher
Agency: The Richards Group
Client: Pier 1 Imports

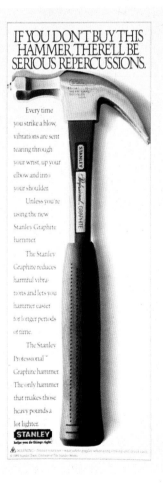

248

Art Director: Debby Lucke
Creative Director: Ron Lawner
Photographer: John Holt
Copywriter: Fred Bertino
Agency: Della Femina, McNamee WCRS
Client: Stanley

249

Art Director: Dan Scarlotto
Creative Director: Tommy Thompson
Designer: Dan Scarlotto
Illustrator: Ben Marshell
        Greg Ragland
        Allen Garns
Copywriter: John Schmidt
Agency: Siddall, Matus & Coughter
Client: Kettler & Scott

250

Art Director: Roy Grace
        Chris Graves
Creative Director: Roy Grace
        Diane Rothschild
Photographer: Bruno
Copywriter: Diane Rothschild
        Craig Demeter
Client: Paddington

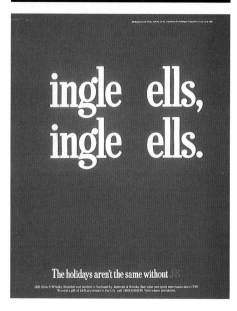

251

Art Director: John Butler
            Mike Shine
Creative Director: Bill Hamilton
Designer: Graham Clifford
Photographer: Joe Baraban
Copywriter: Mike Shine
            John Butler
Agency: Chiat/Day/Mojo Advertising Inc.
Client: NYNEX Information Resources

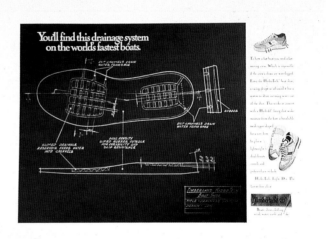

252

Art Director: Brian Fandetti
Creative Director: Paul Silverman
Photographer: Harry DeZitter
            Jack Richmond
Copywriter: Paul Silverman
Agency: Mullen
Client: Timberland Co.

253
Art Director: Brian Stymest
Creative Director: Sean Fitzpatrick
Photographer: Diane Padys
　　　　　　　Charles Purvis
Copywriter: Charles Mullen
Agency: McCann-Erickson
Client: Wamsutta/Pacific Home Products

254
Art Director: Roy Grace
Creative Director: Roy Grace
　　　　　　　　Diane Rothschild
Copywriter: Diane Rothschild
Client: Range Rover of North America

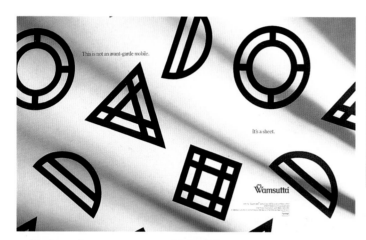

255
Art Director: John Doyle
Designer: John Doyle
Photographer: Clint Clemens
Copywriter: Paul Silverman
Agency: Mullen
Client: Timberland Co.

There are two things you shouldn't be up the creek without. One of them is a paddle.

The other is a pair of boots from the Timberland Sporting Collection. Because even though we can't keep water out of your boat, we guarantee it won't get through your boots.

Consider the construction of our Super Guide Boot. Comfortable. Dry. Lightweight. Protected by an exclusive Timberland Gore-Tex Leather™ laminate that combines a glove leather lining with a waterproof, breathable Gore-Tex® fabric bootie. The result is a level of comfort and dryness you won't find in any other field boot.

Yet another Super Guide exclusive is a sole of triple density polyurethane permanently bonded to the upper. Compared to boots with traditional rubber soles this lessens weight, adds insulation, expands flexibility and increases slip resistance. Giving you a whole new level of performance.

In fact, every single boot in the Timberland Sporting Collection is built to be warm, dry and comfortable, and the reason is our two-step waterproofing process. Step one is direct bonding of silicone-impregnated waterproof leathers to the sole. Step two is Gore-Tex fabric bootie construction.

Timberland. Not just waterproof. Water-proven.

Boots, shoes, clothing, wind, water, / earth and sky.

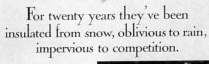

For twenty years they've been insulated from snow, oblivious to rain, impervious to competition.

Before the Timberland Company existed, only one kind of boot was truly waterproof. The kind you don't like to wear. Because it's made of something other than leather, something plastic or rubber that doesn't breathe.

Relief came two decades ago, when Timberland craftsmen hand-built a full-grain leather boot that was guaranteed waterproof. And insulated.

It was a concept the world was waiting for. No sooner did our boot hit the stores than it sold out. And today it still sells out, even though imitations abound both here and abroad.

The fact is, copying the look of our classic tan buck boot is far easier than copying the workmanship. The meticulous silicone impregnation of the leather, the four-row nylon stitching, the direct bonding of upper to midsole for a guaranteed waterproof seal, and the unbeatable warmth of Thinsulate® insulation.

You live on an earth that's two-thirds water. Can you afford a lesser boot than ours?

Boots, shoes, clothing, wind, water, / earth and sky.

In time, even these shoes will succumb to the sea. But chances are you'll replace the boat first.

The headline on this page isn't something you should accept without substantiation. So let us hasten to provide it.

Timberland boat shoes are stronger because our construction is superior. You will never see one of our soles flapping loose in the breeze, unstitched from its moccasin upper. We eliminate such stitching altogether in favor of permanent bonding, so shoe and sole stay married until the day they die.

And unlike boat shoes of a lesser quality, ours have premium natural leathers that won't crack, impregnable nylon stitching that won't rot, and solid brass eyelets that won't chip.

This year, we're pleased to introduce the high-performance Ultra Boat Shoe, companion to our Super and Classic Boat Shoe. The Ultra combines the grip and stability of a triple density outsole with the comfort and cushioning of a double density midsole. For maximum dryness, the stain-resistant, waterproof leathers have a Hydrofil® lining to wick away moisture.

Water, water, it's everywhere. So is Timberland.

Boots, shoes, clothing, wind, water, / earth and sky.

ARE AMERICA'S FORESTS OUT OF THE WOODS?

♠ AMERICAN FOREST COUNCIL
MANAGING THE FUTURE OF AMERICA'S FORESTS

"BY 1945, AMERICA'S FORESTS WILL BE HISTORY."

♠ AMERICAN FOREST COUNCIL
MANAGING THE FUTURE OF AMERICA'S FORESTS

ANOTHER DAY, ANOTHER 6 MILLION TREES.

♠ AMERICAN FOREST COUNCIL
MANAGING THE FUTURE OF AMERICA'S FORESTS

256
Art Director: Patty Thompson
Creative Director: Ron Fisher
Virgil Shutze
Photographer: Charles Jameson
Copywriter: Ralph McGill
Agency: HutchesonShutze
Client: American Forest Council

257
Art Director: Rick Boyko
Creative Director: Bob Kuperman
                     Steve Rabosky
Copywriter: Rob Feakins
              Steve Rabosky
Agency: Chiat/Day/Mojo
Client: Mitsubishi

258
Art Director: Frank Haggerty
Creative Director: Kerry Casey
Photographer: Jim Marvy
Copywriter: Kerry Casey
Agency: Carmichael Lynch
Client: ZEBCO

259
Art Director: Fred Hammerquist
Creative Director: Rod Kilpatrick
Photographer: Rod Photo
Copywriter: Hugh Saffel
Agency: Cole & Weber
Client: K2 Corp.

260
Art Director: Ed Evangelista
Creative Director: Ron Berger
Designer: Ed Evangelista
Copywriter: Ron Berger
Agency: M.V.B.C.S.
Client: Windstar Sail Cruise

Eat your vegetables.

Feed them to your dog.

Be home by 10:30.

A.M.

Don't question authority.

Ignore it.

I see a man and a mule in your future.

261
Art Director: Sharon Occhipinti
Creative Director: Charlie Piccirillo
Photographer: Nancy Ney
         Raymond Meier
         James Koepnick
Copywriter: Doug Raboy
Agency: DDB Needham Worldwide
Client: Colombian Coffee

Some people can't wait for their next coffee break.

The perfect Sunday.

ALL YOU NEED FOR COOL RANCH DRESSING.

ALL YOU NEED FOR CHANGING ATTIRE.

ALL YOU NEED WITH A PAIR OF BLUE JEANS.

ALL STARS. ALL YOU NEED.

262
Art Director: Peter Favat
Photographer: Dwight Olmsted
Copywriter: Don Pogany
Agency: Ingalls, Quinn & Johnson
Client: Converse

263
Art Director: Tom Lichtenheld
Creative Director: Pat Burnham
Illustrator: Sharon Werner
Copywriter: Bruce Bildsten
Agency: Fallon McElligott
Client: Azur

WILD FURNITURE.
WILD MUSIC.
WILD MUSHROOMS.

RESTAURANT · BALLROOM
GAVIIDAE COMMON

BLACK TRUFFLES.
GREEN LENTILS.
PURPLE CHAIRS.

RESTAURANT · BALLROOM
GAVIIDAE COMMON

TOO WEIRD.
TOO NOISY.
TOO DIFFERENT.

RESTAURANT · BALLROOM
GAVIIDAE COMMON

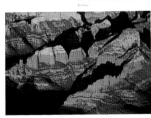

264
Art Director: Steven Sessions
Creative Director: Steven Sessions
Designer: Steven Sessions
Illustrator: Steven Sessions
Copywriter: John Hartmann
Agency: Steven Sessions, Inc.
Client: Southwest Art Magazine

265
Art Director: Rich Silverstein
Photographer: Jay Maisel
Agency: Goodby, Berlin & Silverstein
Client: Royal Viking Line

Spring Ahead! Spring Downtown!

April Showers Bring People Indoors!

You Are About To Go On A Fantastic Adventure. Downtown!

266
Art Director: Stephen Doyle
Creative Director: Stephen Doyle
Photographer: George Hein
Agency: Drenttel Doyle Partners
Client: Olympia & York/World Financial Center

Four day weekend. Fifth day. Lee jeans.

Lee
Easy Rider

Public phone. Private moment. Lee jeans.

Lee
Easy Rider

9 O'clock date. 8:55. Lee jeans.

Lee
Baggy Rider

267

Art Director: Mark Johnson
Creative Director: Pat Burnham
Photographer: Kurt Markus
Copywriter: Bill Miller
Agency: Fallon McElligott
Client: Lee Jeans

HAS YOUR AIRLINE LOST ITS PERSONALITY?

Over the last few years, a lot of bright, spunky west coast airlines have been replaced by a few huge, national carriers. Airlines that are very efficient. Very businesslike. And about as interesting as a tax form.

One airline, however, hasn't lost its identity. Alaska Airlines, the one with the smiling Eskimo on the tail. Hop on an Alaska Airlines flight and you'll still find bright, energetic people who take great pride in doing everything they can to serve their customers. With flair, spirit, and their own individual style. So the next time you're traveling up or down the west coast, fly Alaska Airlines.

And see if our attitude toward flying doesn't change yours.

Alaska Airlines

AT ALASKA AIRLINES, WE BRUSH AFTER EVERY MEAL.

We also dust, sweep, scrub and polish. Whatever it takes to keep our planes neat and tidy.

That's why we not only vacuum the seats, we also vacuum the seat pockets. We don't just sweep our carpets, we regularly steam clean them.

And on a regular basis, we spend 36 worker-hours "deep cleaning" the entire aircraft. Why do we go to all this trouble? Because we know how you feel about messy airplanes. So along with friendlier people, tastier meals and roomier seats, we'll do all we can to make sure you fly in a clean cabin.

Next trip to or from California, the Pacific Northwest, Arizona, Alaska or Mexico, take off on Alaska Airlines. We can promise you a clean getaway.

Alaska Airlines

WHO IN HIS RIGHT MIND EATS AIRLINE FOOD ON THE GROUND?

The Chairman of Alaska Airlines does. So does every other key executive in the company.

It happens during our "officers' lunch"—a twice-weekly meeting where our top managers sink their teeth into important corporate issues. Such as our meal service.

After all, we want to be certain that we're serving our passengers the kind of food that we would want to eat ourselves.

That's why you can look forward to entrees like Chicken Bordelaise and Pasta Alfredo, all prepared with fresh ingredients. And served with crisp green salads and tasty desserts.

So next trip up or down the west coast, or to Mexico, be sure to fly Alaska Airlines.

And try the Chicken Piccata. Our Chairman highly recommends it.

Alaska Airlines

BRUCE KENNEDY
CHAIRMAN

268

Art Director: Tim Delaney
Creative Director: Jim Copacino
Photographer: Hank Benson
Copywriter: Jim Copacino
Agency: Livingston & Co.
Client: Alaska Airlines

269

Art Director: Barbara Simon
Creative Director: Andrew Langer
Copywriter: Ginni Stern
Agency: Lowe Marschalk
Client: Free Press

270

Art Director: Bob Barrie
Creative Director: Pat Burnham
Designer: Bob Barrie
Illustrator: Bob Barrie
Copywriter: Jarl Olsen
Agency: Fallon McElligott
Client: Hush Puppies

271

Art Director: Dean Hanson
Creative Director: Pat Burnham
Photographer: Eric Saulitis
Agency: Fallon McElligott
Client: Eleanor Moore

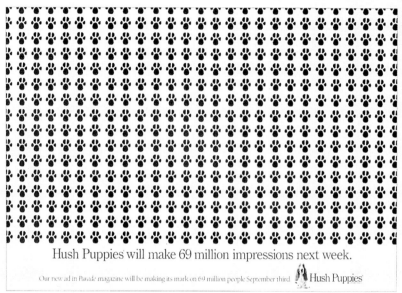

272

Art Director: Paul Asao
Creative Director: Jack Supple
Copywriter: Kerry Casey
Agency: Carmichael Lynch
Client: Blue Fox

273
Art Director: Houman Pirdavari
Creative Director: Pat Burnham
Photographer: Jim Arndt
Copywriter: Bill Miller
Agency: Fallon McElligott
Client: Rolling Stone

274
Art Director: Brian Fandetti
Creative Director: Paul Silverman
Photographer: Harry DeZitter
Copywriter: Paul Silverman
Agency: Mullen
Client: Timberland Co.

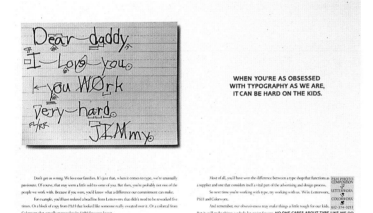

275
Art Director: Bob Brihn
Creative Director: Pat Burnham
Designer: Bob Brihn
Photographer: Rick Dublin
Copywriter: Jamie Barrett
Agency: Fallon McElligott
Client: Letterworx

276
Art Director: Cristina Creager
Creative Director: Jim Kingsley
                    Brett Robbs
Photographer: David Scharf
Copywriter: Andy Dumaine
Agency: DDB Needham
Client: National Geographic Society

277
Art Director: Houman Pirdavari
Creative Director: Pat Burnham
Photographer: Dave Jordano
Copywriter: Jarl Olsen
Agency: Fallon McElligott
Client: Penn

278
Art Director: Jac Coverdale
Creative Director: Jac Coverdale
Designer: Jac Coverdale
Photographer: Tom Connors
Copywriter: Joe Alexander
Agency: Clarity, Coverdale, Rueff
Client: Twin Cities Direct Choice

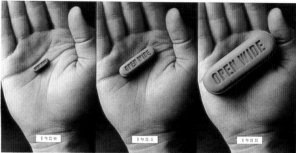

279
Art Director: Jeremy Postaer
Creative Director: Jeffrey Goodby
Rich Silverstein
Photographer: Duncan Sim
Copywriter: Rob Bagot
Agency: Goodby, Berlin & Silverstein
Client: Royal Viking Line

280
Art Director: Jeremy Postaer
Creative Director: Jeffrey Goodby
Rich Silverstein
Photographer: Duncan Sim
Copywriter: Rob Bagot
Agency: Goodby, Berlin & Silverstein
Client: Royal Viking Line

281

Art Director: Mark Ashley
Creative Director: Jim Cole
　　　　　　　　Dick Henderson
Photographer: Parish Kohanim
Copywriter: Ken Lewis
Agency: Cole Henderson Drake, Inc.
Client: Dunlop Tennis

282

Art Director: Adrian Saker
Creative Director: Andy Berlin
Photographer: Gerry Bybee
Copywriter: Jim Anderson
Agency: Goodby, Berlin & Silverstein
Client: Clark's of England

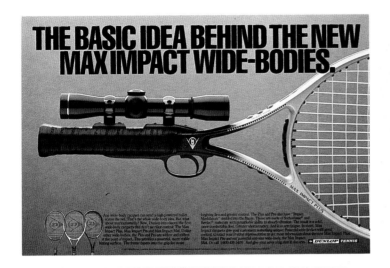

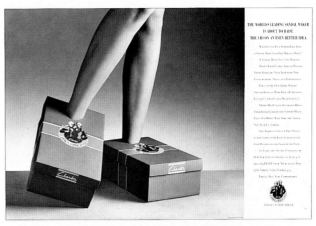

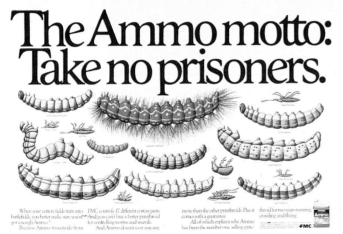

283

Art Director: Shari Hindman
Creative Director: Mike Hughes
Illustrator: Ed Lindlof
Copywriter: Kerry Feuerman
Agency: The Martin Agency
Client: FMC Corp.

284

Art Director: Steve Stein
Creative Director: Jeffrey Goodby
　　　　　　　　Rich Silverstein
Photographer: Jay Maisel
　　　　　　　　Dan Escobar
　　　　　　　　Peter Hendrie
Copywriter: David Fowler
Agency: Goodby, Berlin & Silverstein
Client: Royal Viking Line

285
Art Director: Bob Barrie
Creative Director: Pat Burnham
Designer: Bob Barrie
Photographer: Rick Dublin
Copywriter: Jarl Olsen
Agency: Fallon McElligott
Client: Jim Beam

286
Art Director: Mike Rosen
Creative Director: Gary Goldsmith
Photographer: Nora Scarlet
Copywriter: Mike Rosen
Agency: Goldsmith/Jeffrey
Client: Knoll International

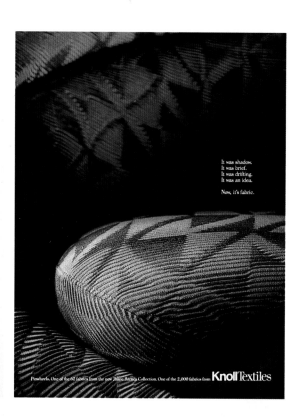

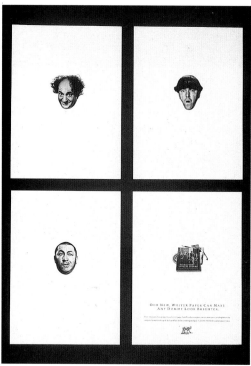

287
Art Director: Dean Hanson
Creative Director: Pat Burnham
Copywriter: Phil Hanft
Agency: Fallon McElligott
Client: Weyerhaeuser

288
Art Director: Bob Brihn
Creative Director: Pat Burnham
Designer: Bob Brihn
Photographer: Rick Dublin
Copywriter: Jamie Barrett
Agency: Fallon McElligott
Client: Letterworx

289
Art Director: Jim Henderson
Creative Director: Lyle Wedemeyer
Photographer: Jim Marvy
Copywriter: Pete Smith
Agency: Martin/Williams
Client: 3M Co.

290
Art Director: Wendy Hansen
Creative Director: Lyle Wedemeyer
Photographer: Rick Dublin
Copywriter: Pete Smith
Agency: Martin/Williams
Client: 3M Co.

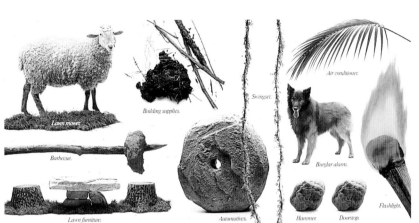

Lawn mower. *Building supplies.* *Swingset.* *Air conditioner.* *Barbecue.* *Burglar alarm.* *Flashlight.* *Lawn furniture.* *Automotives.* *Hammer.* *Doorstop.*

What you'd be selling without new ideas.

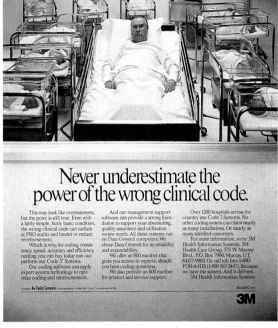

Never underestimate the power of the wrong clinical code.

IF YOU NEED YOUR HEADLINES IN A HURRY,
WE'LL WORK THROUGH LUNCH.

291
Art Director: Bob Brihn
Creative Director: Pat Burnham
Designer: Bob Brihn
Photographer: Rick Dublin
Copywriter: Jamie Barrett
Agency: Fallon McElligott
Client: Letterworx

OUR RUB-DOWNS WILL EVEN
STICK TO TEFLON.

292
Art Director: Bob Brihn
Creative Director: Pat Burnham
Designer: Bob Brihn
Photographer: Rick Dublin
Copywriter: Jamie Barrett
Agency: Fallon McElligott
Client: Letterworx

293
Art Director: James Offenhartz
Creative Director: Lee Garfinkel
Photographer: Ken Nahoum
Copywriter: Marian Allen Godwin
Agency: Levine, Huntley, Schmidt & Beaver
Client: Technics

294
Art Director: Victor Mazzeo
Creative Director: Kathy Kiely
Photographer: Mark Weiss
Copywriter: Joe Sweet
Agency: Pedone & Partners
Client: Cumberland Packing Corp.

I see a man and a mule in your future.

Some people can't wait for their next coffee break.

The perfect Sunday.

295
Art Director: Sharon Occhipinti
Creative Director: Charlie Piccirillo
Photographer: Nancy Ney
              Raymond Meier
              James Koepnick
Copywriter: Doug Raboy
Agency: DDB Needham Worldwide
Client: Colombian Coffee

296
Art Director: Jeff A. Barnes
Creative Director: Jeff A. Barnes
Designer: Jeff A. Barnes
Photographer: Gina Uhlmann
Copywriter: Jeff A. Barnes
Agency: Barnes Design Office
Client: Johnson Industries

297
Art Director: Steve Haesche
Photographer: Christopher Cunningham
Copywriter: Peter Pappas
Agency: Mullen
Client: Sail

298
Art Director: Adrian Saker
Creative Director: Andy Berlin
Photographer: Gerry Bybee
Copywriter: Jim Anderson
Agency: Goodby, Berlin & Silverstein
Client: Clark's of England

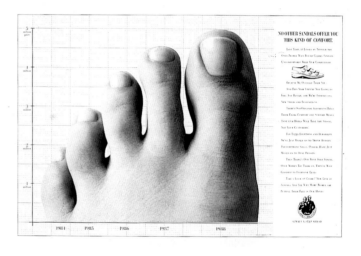

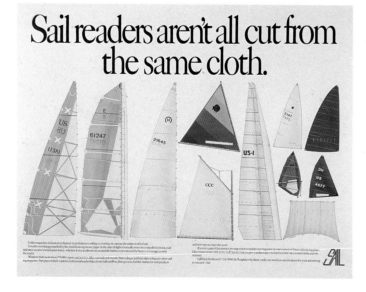

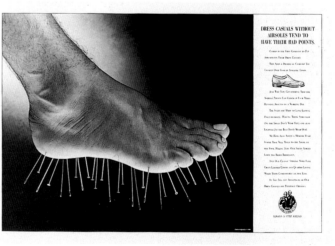

299
Art Director: Glenn Scheuer
Photographer: Blackstar
      Sygma
Copywriter: Dorothy Linder
      Glenn Scheuer
      Murray Klein
Agency: Smith/Greenland, Inc.
Client: Penthouse Magazine

300
Art Director: Timothy Ryan
Photographer: Dan Walsh
Copywriter: Timothy Ryan
      Daisy Scott
      Jord Poster
Agency: Marketplace Consulting
Client: American Express

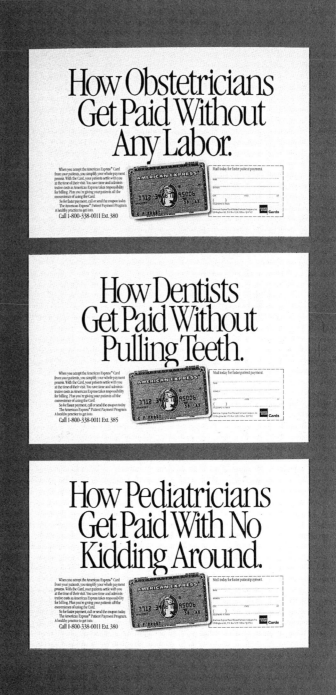

A GREAT LOOKING SHEET OF PAPER
CAN GIVE AEMOST ANY ORGANIZATION
INSTANT CREDIBILITY.

Minimal show-through. Maximum brightness. Sharper contrast. A more substantial feel. These are
the things that make your documents look and feel like important documents. Compare these pages with
your current paper. Or call 1-800-621-0114 for samples to run on your laser printers and copiers.

FIRST CHOICE
FOR IMPORTANT DOCUMENTS

301
Art Director: Dean Hanson
Creative Director: Pat Burnham
Copywriter: Phil Hanft
Agency: Fallon McElligott
Client: Weyerhaeuser

BE CAREFUL.
OUR NEW BUSINESS PAPER CAN MAKE
EVEN BAD IDEAS LOOK GOOD.

Minimal show-through. Maximum brightness. Sharper contrast. A more substantial feel. These are
the things that make your documents look and feel like important documents. Compare these pages with
your current paper. Or call 1-800-621-0114 for samples to run on your laser printers and copiers.

FIRST CHOICE
FOR IMPORTANT DOCUMENTS

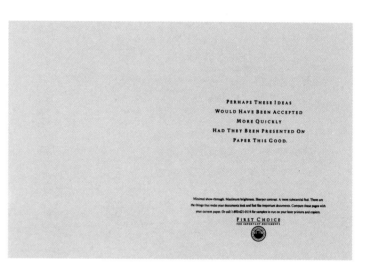

PERHAPS THESE IDEAS
WOULD HAVE BEEN ACCEPTED
MORE QUICKLY
HAD THEY BEEN PRESENTED ON
PAPER THIS GOOD.

Minimal show-through. Maximum brightness. Sharper contrast. A more substantial feel. These are
the things that make your documents look and feel like important documents. Compare these pages with
your current paper. Or call 1-800-621-0114 for samples to run on your laser printers and copiers.

FIRST CHOICE
FOR IMPORTANT DOCUMENTS

Does Your Ground Roast Taste Like Roast Ground?

Get fast relief from high volume headaches.

Taster's Choice. Coffee System

In High Volume, It's A Waste Basket.

Get fast relief from high volume headaches.

Taster's Choice. Coffee System

The Problem With Ground Roast Is The Long ....
....
....
....
....
....
....
.... Delays.

Get fast relief from high volume headaches.

Taster's Choice. Coffee System

302
Art Director: Kevin Beauseigneur
Creative Director: Linda Masterson
Photographer: Dennis Scott
Copywriter: Gary Doyle
Client: Nestle

303
Art Director: Jac Coverdale
Creative Director: Jac Coverdale
Designer: Jac Coverdale
Photographer: Buck Holzemer
Copywriter: Jerry Fury
Agency: Clarity, Coverdale, Rueff
Client: Rolfs

Ever notice that people with money
have a knack for putting it in the right place?

ROLFS.

With over 100 styles of wallets for men and women, Rolfs has all kinds of smart places to put your money.

Who says a financial statement
can only be red or black?

ROLFS.

With colors like these, Rolfs lets you turn your financial statement into a fashion statement.

Maybe if you gave your money a nicer home,
it would stay around longer.

ROLFS.

Rolfs makes over 100 styles of wallets for men and women, so there's bound to be one you'll feel right at home with.

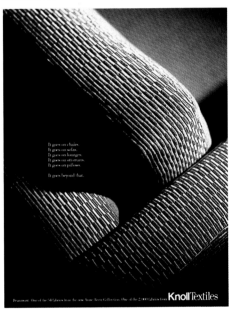

It goes on chairs.
It goes on sofas.
It goes on lounges.
It goes on ottomans.
It goes on pillows.

It goes beyond that.

Beaumont. One of the 54 fabrics from the new Anne Beetz Collection. One of the 2,000 fabrics from **Knoll**Textiles

It was shadow.
It was brief.
It was drifting.
It was an idea.

Now, it's fabric.

Pinwheels. One of the 62 fabrics from the new Jhane Barnes Collection. One of the 2,000 fabrics from **Knoll**Textiles

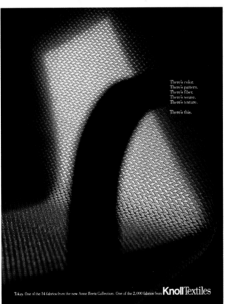

There's color.
There's pattern.
There's fiber.
There's weave.
There's texture.

There's this.

Tokay. One of the 54 fabrics from the new Anne Beetz Collection. One of the 2,000 fabrics from **Knoll**Textiles

304
Art Director: Mike Rosen
Creative Director: Gary Goldsmith
Photographer: Nora Scarlet
Copywriter: Mike Rosen
Agency: Goldsmith/Jeffrey
Client: Knoll International

305
Art Director: Jeff Hopfer
Creative Director: Stan Richards
Designer: Jeff Hopfer
Photographer: Tom Ryan
Copywriter: Marc Harty
Agency: The Richards Group
Client: M/A/R/C

306
Art Director: Bryan Jessee
Steve Popp
Creative Director: Stan Richards
Designer: Bryan Jessee
Photographer: Randy Miller
Copywriter: Glenn Gill
Kevin Swisher
Agency: The Richards Group
Client: Wyndham

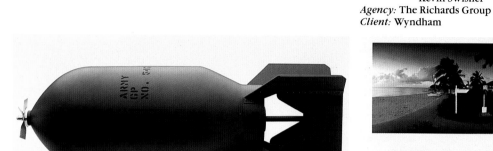

This Year, Packaged Goods Companies Will Produce More Of These Than The Department Of Defense.

Are You Comfortable Traveling Alone Through A Risk-Infested Market?

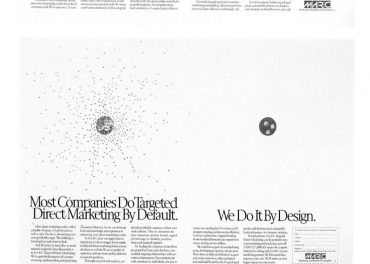

Most Companies Do Targeted Direct Marketing By Default.

We Do It By Design.

ACTION PACKED PEACE AND QUIET.

TO THE SUN WORSHIPER, IT'S NIRVANA.

THE BEST RESERVATION IN ARIZONA.

307

Art Director: Mike Greico
Creative Director: Patrick Cunningham
Illustrator: Brian Saurill
Photographer: Ralph Meycer
Copywriter: Jack Cardone
Agency: NW Ayer
Client: Omni

308

Art Director: Mike Martin
Creative Director: Jim Armstrong
Photographer: Shawn Harper
Copywriter: Jim Armstrong
Agency: Armstrong Creative
Client: Madison Advertising Federation

MEN AND WOMEN NEEDED FOR EXTENSIVE TRAVEL.

NASA
YES)YOU CAN

Make America's future part of your future. Contact NASA.

HE LOVES ME.

HE LOVES ME NOT.

AIDS

In 1981, one American had AIDS.

In 1983, one thousand Americans had AIDS.

In 1989, one million Americans have AIDS.

How fast can you write a check?

AIDS is a big problem. And it just keeps getting bigger.
At Continental Bank, we urge you to support AmFAR, the American Foundation for AIDS Research.
Send your donations to: AmFAR, 1515 Broadway, Suite 3601, New York, NY 10036.

If you don't think animal protection is a battle, consider the weapons we're up against.

309

Art Director: Bob Barrie
Creative Director: Pat Burnham
Designer: Bob Barrie
Copywriter: Jamie Barrett
Agency: Fallon McElligott
Client: Continental Bank

310

Art Director: Margaret McGovern
Creative Director: Edward Boches
Photographer: John Holt
Copywriter: Edward Boches
Agency: Mullen
Client: World Society for Protection of Animals

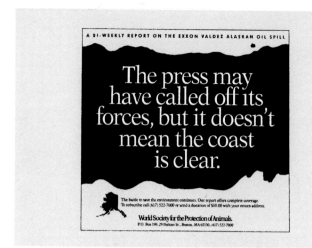

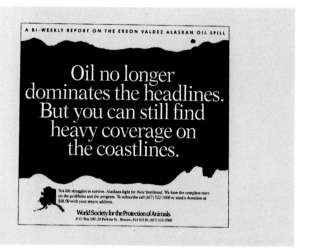

311

Art Director: Margaret McGovern
Creative Director: Edward Boches
Copywriter: Edward Boches
Agency: Mullen
Client: World Society for Protection of Animals

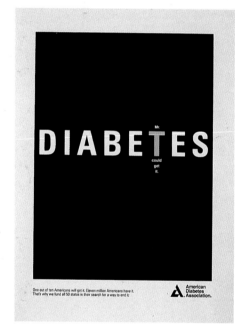

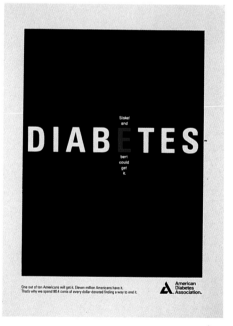

312

Art Director: Mike Rosen
Creative Director: Gary Goldsmith
Copywriter: Gary Goldsmith
　　　　　　 Mike Rosen
Agency: Goldsmith/Jeffrey
Client: American Diabetes Association

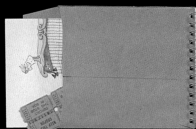

He had pecul
iar ideas

313 Gold

Art Director: Bruce Crocker
Creative Director: Bruce Crocker
Designer: Bruce Crocker
Mark Olson
Illustrator: Deborah Lipman Artists
Copywriter: Holly Anderson
Studio: Crocker Inc., Boston
Client: Deborah Lipman Artist's Rep.

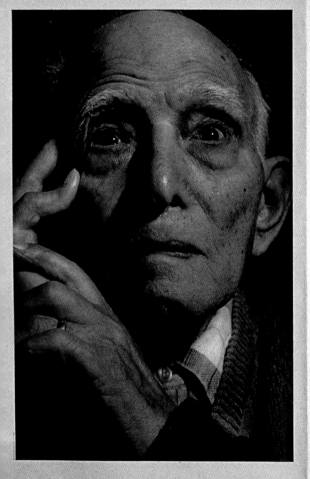
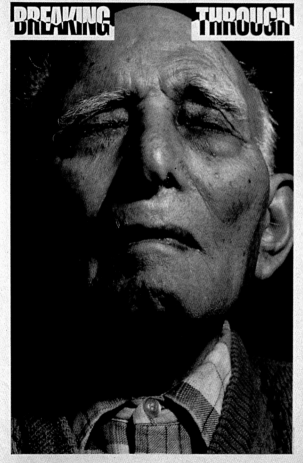

316
Art Director: Terry Koppel
Creative Director: Terry Koppel
Designer: Terry Koppel
Illustrator: Various
Copywriter: Peter Hauck
Studio: Koppel & Scher
Client: Queens Group

317
Art Director: Alyn Carlson-Webster
Creative Director: Jason Grant
Photographer: Photocoloratura
Stock
Copywriter: Marc Braunstein
Agency: Jason Grant Associates
Client: Gant

directions

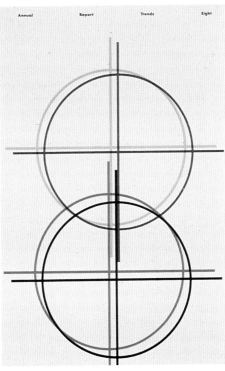

318
Art Director: Sharon Werner
Designer: Sharon Werner
Illustrator: Charles Burns
Sharon Werner
Copywriter: Chuck Carlson
Agency: The Duffy Group
Client: Fox River Paper

319
Art Director: John Cleveland
Creative Director: John Cleveland
Designer: John Cleveland
Copywriter: Rose DeNeve
Studio: Bright & Associates
Client: S.D. Warren Co.

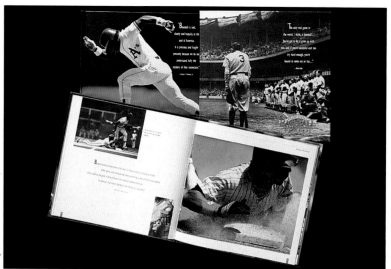

320
Art Director: Jim Shefcik
Creative Director: Andrew Kner
Designer: Jim Shefcik
Photographer: Stock
Copywriter: Caroline Crimmins
Agency: Backer, Spielvogel, Bates
Client: CBS

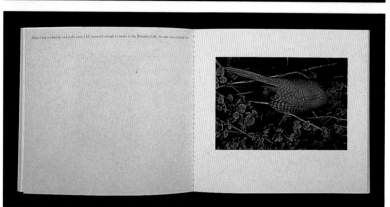

321
Art Director: Doug Wolfe
Creative Director: Doug Wolfe
Designer: Doug Wolfe
Photographer: Louis Bencze
Copywriter: Louis Bencze
Client: Louis Bencze

322
Art Director: Gordon Hochhalter
Creative Director: Gordon Hochhalter
Designer: Dan Larocca
Copywriter: Gordon Hochhalter
Agency: R.R. Donnelley Creative
Client: R.R. Donnelley Computer Documentation

323
Art Director: Jim Shefcik
Creative Director: Andrew Kner
Designer: Jim Shefcik
Photographer: Stock
Copywriter: Gail Duncan
Agency: Backer, Spielvogel, Bates
Client: CBS

324
Art Director: Doug Akagi
Designer: Doug Akagi
        Lenore Bartz
        Kimberly Powell
Client: J. Walter Thompson

325
Art Director: Tom Fowler
Designer: Tom Fowler
        Elizabeth P. Ball
        Karl Maruyama
Photographer: Hans Neleman
Studio: Tom Fowler, Inc.

326
Art Director: Jeffrey Keyton
Creative Director: Leslie Leventman
Designer: Scott Wadler
Photographer: Frederick Lewis
Copywriter: Jake Ehlers
Agency: MTV Networks Creative Services
Client: VH-1

327
Art Director: Alfredo Rossi
        David Thall
Creative Director: Alberto Baccari
Illustrator: Robert Rodriguez
Agency: Armando Testa, Advertising
Client: Time Exchange, Inc.

328
Art Director: Charles S. Anderson
Designer: Charles S. Anderson
　　　　　 Dan Olson
Illustrator: Charles S. Anderson
　　　　　 Randy Dahlk
Copywriter: Lisa Pemrick
Studio: Charles S. Anderson Design
Client: French Paper Co.

329
Art Director: John Bricker
Designer: Cinnie Worthington
Copywriter: Dana Dubbs
Studio: Gensler
Client: Steelcase, Stow & Davis

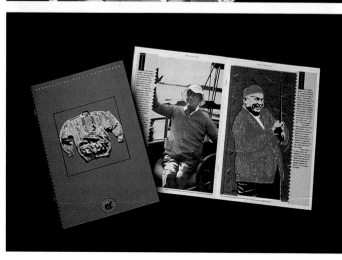

330
Art Director: Arthur Simmons
　　　　　 Richard Gavos
Creative Director: Harry Harrison
Designer: Richard Gavos
Illustrator: Various
Photographer: Various
Copywriter: Harry Harrison
Agency: HarrisonSimmons, Inc.
Client: Hopper Paper Co.

331
Art Director: John Sayles
Designer: John Sayles
Studio: Sayles Graphic Design
Client: Norwest Bank Iowa

332
Art Director: Clive Helfet
Creative Director: Christopher A. Kogler
Designer: Clive Helfet
Producer: Steven Weinstock
Client: Thirteen/WNET

333
Art Director: David Warren
Client: Denver Art Museum

334
Art Director: John Sayles
Designer: Craig Keiran
Studio: Sayles Graphic Design
Client: Iowa Rural Electric Cooperative

335
Art Director: Patrick SooHoo
Creative Director: Harry Kerker
Designer: Katherine Lam
　　　　　Eddie Yip
Studio: Patrick SooHoo Designers
Client: Acapulco Tourism Board

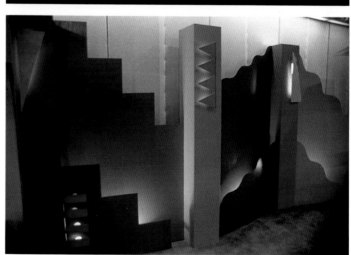

ISSUE 560 • SEPTEMBER 7TH, 1989 • UK £1.90 • $2.50

Rolling Stone

THE CURE

MICK AND KEITH'S
UNEASY TRUCE

The Rolling Stones

PEACE, PART II

FALL'S HOT FASHION

BOBBY BROWN

SOUL II SOUL

0 14023 5 3
01363

He hasn't **CAN** had a big
hit album in years. The other Beatles are
suing him. **PAUL** But with
'Flowers in the Dirt,' his strong new record,
McCARTNEY
and plans for his first world tour in more than
a decade, the **GET** ex-Beatle is
doing his best to toughen up his image and
climb back **BACK?** to the top.

BY JAMES HENKE

As the
Rolling Stones
hit the road
to support their finest
album in a decade,
Keith Richards & Mick Jagger
work to maintain their
delicate
truce

SATIS*f*ACTION?

BY
DAVID FRICKE

PHOTOGRAPHS BY

ALBERT WATSON

LETTERING BY ANITA KARL

PART ONE: THE SHIFT

Most of us have lived our entire lives with the threat of the cold war, the terror of nuclear annihilation. But now, for the first time in memory, peace–not  war–is breaking out around the world. From Moscow to Washington, the old assumptions are falling away, and a new and vastly different era is coming into being. After all the darkness and carnage of the twentieth century, is man finally ready to give up his most catastrophic habit– the urge to make war? BY LAWRENCE WRIGHT

PEACE

PART TWO: LIVING WITHOUT ENEMIES

Gorbachev wasn't just revolutionizing his own society; he was transforming ours as well. Since Stalin's day, the Soviets had played the perfect enemy. The evil Russian bear defined our national purpose and gave us a global mission. But here was Gorbachev declaring peace. Could we look at him and still see the face of the enemy? And what posed the greater threat, having an enemy or not having one? BY LAWRENCE WRIGHT

PEACE

ILLUSTRATIONS BY BRIAN CRONIN

PART THREE: INNER PEACE

Pentagon employees "visualizing" world peace at weekly meditation sessions. Soviet bigwigs soaking in hot tubs, talking peace under a sybaritic California sun. No one looking at the peace movement today can deny the fact that it has turned inward, hooking up with the New Age. Easy enough to mock–but is it so nonsensical to believe that inner peace might be a necessary precondition to outer peace? BY LAWRENCE WRIGHT

PEACE

ILLUSTRATIONS BY BRIAN CRONIN

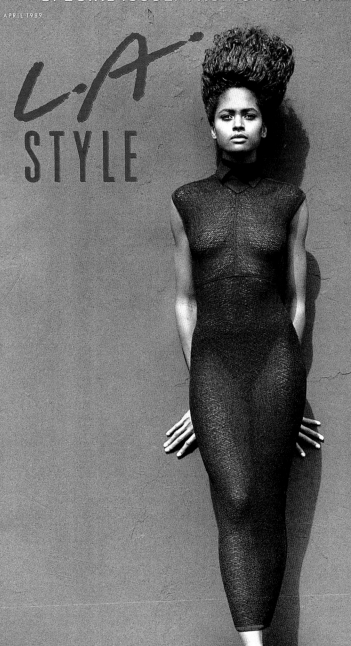

L.A.
STYLE

ISSUE 561 • SEPTEMBER 21st, 1989 • UK £1.90 • $2.95

Rolling Stone

A SPECIAL ISSUE

FANTASTIC FANS

LIVING BLUES MASTERS

MUSICIANS & THEIR MENTORS

THE NEW WOMEN OF ROCK

UNCONVENTIONAL

IN THE 150 YEARS SINCE PHOTOGRAPHY WAS INVENTED, THE PHOTO IMAGE HAS THOROUGHLY INFILTRATED OUR CULTURE. FROM THE BARRAGE OF STILL AND MOVING PICTURES WE CONFRONT DAILY, TO THE MOST ARCANE OF GALLERY FARE, THE RECORDED IMAGE, FOR BETTER OR WORSE, HAS IN LARGE PART SUPPLANTED THE WORD AS THE PRIMARY METHOD OF COMMUNICATION. NOWHERE IS THAT MORE TRUE THAN IN LOS ANGELES, WHERE MANIPULATION OF IMAGE (IN ALL SENSES) IS A CENTRAL ACTIVITY AND A SIGNIFICANT CONTRIBUTION TO THE NATION'S IDENTITY. ⌂ SO IN CELEBRATION OF THE 150TH ANNIVERSARY OF PHOTOGRAPHY AND THE FOURTH ANNIVERSARY OF L.A. STYLE, WE DECIDED TO EXPLORE THE STATE OF PHOTOGRAPHY IN OUR CITY IN 1989. WE ASKED HISTORIAN AND PHOTOGRAPHER MARK JOHNSTONE TO PROVIDE A CHRONICLE OF LOS ANGELES PHOTOGRAPHY, AND GROUNDBREAKING PHOTOGRAPHER ROBERT HEINECKEN OFFERED HIS PERSPECTIVE ON THE ESSENTIAL PHOTOGRAPHIC IMPULSE AND HOW IT ACTUALLY CHANGED SEEING. WE ASKED A GROUP OF PHOTO INSIDERS FOR THEIR COMMENTS ON THE L.A. PHOTO SCENE, AND ASKED NUMEROUS IMPORTANT PHOTOGRAPHERS TO DISPLAY THEIR WORK. AND WE'VE TAKEN A LOOK AT ROBERT SHAPAZIAN'S EXTRAORDINARY COLLECTION OF EARLY AND AVANT-GARDE IM- *Photography* AGES, PROFILED THE BLACK GALLERY, AND ASSEMBLED A PORTFOLIO OF CONTEMPO- IN RARY PHOTOGRAPHS, SOME OF THEM MAKING THEIR DEBUT PUBLIC APPEARANCE IN *L.A.* THESE PAGES, ELSEWHERE IN THE ISSUE, WE OFFER A LOOK AT L.A. PIONEER EDMUND TESKE ("IN CHARACTER"), AT MASTER FRAMER STEVE JOSEFSBERG ("STYLEMAKERS"), AT THE BEST IN EASY-TO-USE CAMERAS ("EQUIPMENT") AND AT MOCA'S GARRY WINOGRAND SHOW ("DATEBOOK"). ⌂ NATURALLY, OUR SELECTION IS REPRESENTATIVE. WE COULD NOT HAVE INCLUDED ALL THE WORTHY ARTISTS IN A BOOK MANY TIMES THE SIZE OF OUR MAGAZINE. ALSO, IT IS FAIR TO POINT OUT THAT WE HAVE APPROACHED THIS PROJECT WITH AT LEAST TWO CURATORIAL PREJUDICES: FIRST, WE DO NOT BELIEVE THAT THE DISTINCTION BETWEEN "ART" AND "PHOTOGRAPHY" MAKES ANY SENSE AT ALL, BUT OUR SELECTION OF PICTURES, PARTICULARLY IN "THE EMERGING IMAGE" PORTFOLIO, LEANS TO WORK THAT REMAINS FIRMLY ROOTED IN PHOTOGRAPHY (RATHER THAN ART THAT MIGHT BEST BE DESCRIBED AS "PHOTO-DERIVED"). SECOND, WHEN THERE WAS A CHOICE TO BE MADE, WE FREQUENTLY ELECTED TO SHOW LESSER-KNOWN WORK OR PHOTOGRAPHS BY LESSER-KNOWN ARTISTS RATHER THAN FAMOUS IMAGES BY WORLD-RENOWNED PHOTOGRAPHERS THAT ARE ROUTINELY USED TO REPRESENT PHOTOGRAPHY IN LOS ANGELES. WE APOLOGIZE IN ADVANCE TO ALL THOSE WHO ARE OFFENDED BY OUR INCLUSIONS AND EXCLUSIONS. —MICHAEL LASSELL AND GARRETT WHITE

PERSPECTIVES

Rod Rav

VISIONS FROM FLATLAND: BLATER HEAP #2, 1986-88, WELDED STEEL, 74 x 42 x 42

THE SOUL OF EAST TEXAS

A land of tall trees and deep roots, where the past still haunts the present.

PHOTOGRAPHY BY
KEITH CARTER

TEXT BY
PRUDENCE MACKINTOSH

WORSHIPER

NEW BETHEL MISSIONARY BAPTIST CHURCH, CHEEK COMMUNITY ›

EARS ARE ATTUNED to the voices of East Texas even though I've lived in the city for twenty years. "I oughta whup the tar outta you," I hear a mother tell her son as I finger the Jacksonville tomatoes at the farmers' market. I linger around the okra, hungrier for the expressions of my childhood than for the produce.

In a doctor's office a man from East Texas tells me about his heart surgery. "I was sure I was sick to where I couldn't hardly get out of bed." He is clearly enjoying the attention that his failing heart has attracted from important city doctors. "I was brought up hard," he explains.

The black woman championing my hair nominations her aunt's life and recent death in one confident sentence: "She did what the Lord gave her to do." I scribble the sentence in the margin of a magazine, tear off the scrap of paper, and put it in my purse.

Perhaps I am making up for the anisotrovies of childhood. With no other frame of reference, I, like most children, regarded the landscape of my childhood as ordinary. In 1956 my sixth-grade class celebrated the end of elementary school with a trip to Dallas, where we took in such extraordinary sights as Goriama, the Health and Science Museum at Fair Park, with its shocking plastic representations of a baby lying there, and

BEECH TREE

HORTON'S MANTEL

MAN WITH BLIND ROOSTER

FAMILY IN GARDEN

MEAGAN

GET ALONG, LITTLE
Doggies

BOOTS ARE A TEXAN'S BEST FRIEND. NO WONDER THEY'RE SO DOGGONE POPULAR. PHOTOGRAPHER WILLIAM WEGMAN AND MODEL FAY RAY PAY TRIBUTE TO THE FOOTWEAR WE WALK, STOMP, WORK, DANCE, LIVE, LOVE, AND KICK UP OUR HEELS IN.

FAY RAY, ONE WELL-HEELED WEIMARANER, WILL DON ANYTHING FOR HER MASTER, PHOTOGRAPHER WILLIAM WEGMAN. TO CAPTURE HIS FAVORITE SUBJECT MODELING A VARIETY OF CLASSIC WESTERN BOOTS, WEGMAN USED ONE OF THE FEW 20-BY-24-INCH POLAROID CAMERAS IN

THE WORLD. PAGE 114: CRUSHED GOATSKIN BOOTS BY LARRY MAHAN ($199), J BAR W WESTERN WEAR (CLEBURNE, DALLAS, FORT WORTH); SPURS BY RANDY BUTTERS ($275), TWO MOONS TRADING COMPANY (DALLAS). PAGE 115: CUSTOM CALFSKIN BOOTS ($525), M. L. LEDDY'S BOOT

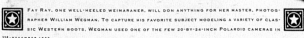

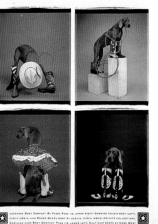

THINLY VEILED

ISSEY MIYAKE'S SHEER LAMÉ BLOUSE

AZZEDINE ALAÏA'S SLEEK DRESS IN STRETCH KNIT

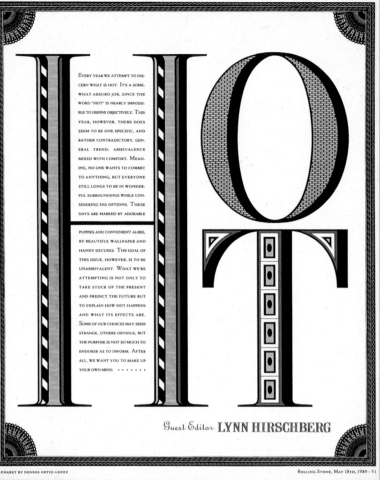

HOT

EVERY YEAR WE ATTEMPT TO DISCERN WHAT IS HOT. IT'S A SOMEWHAT ABSURD JOB, SINCE THE WORD "HOT" IS NEARLY IMPOSSIBLE TO DEFINE OBJECTIVELY. THIS YEAR, HOWEVER, THERE DOES SEEM TO BE ONE SPECIFIC, AND RATHER CONTRADICTORY, GENERAL TREND: AMBIVALENCE MIXED WITH COMFORT. MEANING, NO ONE WANTS TO COMMIT TO ANYTHING, BUT EVERYONE STILL LONGS TO BE IN WONDERFUL SURROUNDINGS WHILE CONSIDERING HIS OPTIONS. THESE DAYS ARE MARKED BY ADORABLE PUPPIES AND CONVENIENT ALIBIS, BY BEAUTIFUL WALLPAPER AND HANDY EXCUSES. THE GOAL OF THIS ISSUE, HOWEVER, IS TO BE UNAMBIVALENT. WHAT WE'RE ATTEMPTING IS NOT ONLY TO TAKE STOCK OF THE PRESENT AND PREDICT THE FUTURE BUT TO EXPLAIN HOW HOT HAPPENS AND WHAT ITS EFFECTS ARE. SOME OF OUR CHOICES MAY SEEM STRANGE, OTHERS OBVIOUS, BUT THE PURPOSE IS NOT SO MUCH TO ENDORSE AS TO INFORM. AFTER ALL, WE WANT YOU TO MAKE UP YOUR OWN MIND. •••••••

Guest Editor **LYNN HIRSCHBERG**

ALPHABET BY DENNIS ORTIZ-LOPEZ

HOT COVER
Inspiring lust in audiences, Sylvester Stallone and gossip columnists alike, starlet Uma Thurman tries to cope with all the attention while keeping her sense of Uma··· *Photographs by* **MATTHEW ROLSTON**

HOT MOOD
These are not the best of times; these are not the worst of times. At the end of the decade, we are turning ambivalent. Maybe.

NOWADAYS, THERE ARE TWO SIDES to every answer. We don't face facts and, hell, simply *decide*. No. That would be too instinctual, too easy, too blithe, too unlike us.

Instead, we consider every alternative and feel complete enthusiasm for none of them. We postpone. We fret. We second-guess. Whether it's a matter of deciding what to have for lunch (a sandwich? a salad?) or how to spend the rest of our lives (duplicitous corporate scumbag in New York? bad lyric poet in Seattle?), neither a wholehearted yes nor an unequivocal no comes naturally. We say maybe. We try to act on both impulses, to be unsentimental romantics, to work uptown but live downtown or vice versa, to have it all, foreclosing no option. As individuals, and even as a nation, we grow faint at the prospect of absolute commitment, whether it's marriage, or military intervention in the third world, or thirty-year fixed-rate mortgages. We find it hard to feel unalloyed pleasure (would you say you love Bette Midler's Disney movies?) or unmitigated disapproval (would you say you hate George Bush?). To most of us, every city, every book, practically every way of life is an interesting place to visit, but we wouldn't want to live there. Would we? Ours is a generation comfortably adrift, bobbing on a sea of ambivalence.

But that's not all bad. Probably.

Ambivalence as a defining sensibility, widespread and full-blown, is something new. There is virtually nothing today about which thoughtful people – especially thoughtful younger people – do not feel mixed emotions. Every hankering, whether it's for a policy (like national health insurance), or a commodity (like microwave ovens), or a performer (like David Letterman), comes with disclaimers, a special codicil of qualifiers or qualms.

This is not to say that one's parents and their parents never second-guessed themselves. Despite the upbeat sheen of the official 1950s, the last generation had its own ambivalents: Jack Lemmon, John Updike, John Cheever and, in his thuggish tavern-philosopher way, Frank Sinatra are all about being of two (or more) minds, about the competing seductions of suburb and city, convention and impulse, the familiar and the new.

But Letterman's discombobulated characters were excrescences. Cheever's and Updike's white-collar Hamlets were mere literary creatures. Until rather recently, television was obliged to depict the official dad – Ward Cleaver, Ozzie Nelson, Mike Brady. Today the only remaining official dad is the president of the United States, and TV's most beloved parents, downscale (*Roseanne*) and up (*thirtysomething*), are liners of no-easy-answers ambivalence. *Thirtysomething* is appealing, one of its creators explains, because its stories are untidy, its characters irresolute. "Ambiguity and ambivalence," he says, "are as much a part of life as resolution." And according to *Newsweek*, the film *Broadcast News* was "the first romantic comedy driven by ambivalence." Tell me I'm smart and attractive, yes, but even better, tell me I'm smart, attractive *and confused*.

In 1962, Tom Hayden drafted the Students for a Democratic Society charter, the so-called Port Huron Statement, which launched the New Left. Its jumping-off point was a collective sense of ambivalence, its signatories people privileged enough to harbor mixed feelings about their privilege. "We are people of this generation," Hayden wrote, "bred in at least modest comfort, housed now in universities, looking uncomfortably at the world we inherit." Because they were very young, and because the injustices were more spectacular and more remediable, the New Lefties coped with ambivalence by plunging into unsubtle political commitment, not (as they would later) by wandering away, jaded and flip. It was simple in the Sixties: Once the world came up to snuff – no more war, no more greed, no more lies – ambivalence would be remedied. And indeed, for most of those who felt it, the thrilling surge of antiwar sentiment was the last moment of absolute certainty about politics.

Today's ambivalence is a post-Vietnam syndrome, civilian shell shock. The war itself was a mess of second thoughts from beginning to end: President Kennedy and Johnson were ambivalent about sending U.S. troops. The war was waged ambivalently by infantrymen ordered to kill and protect the same people by generals ambivalent about strategy and tactics. From 1968 on, the American public was composed not mainly of hawks or doves but of confused, anxious citizens. Even to those who demanded withdrawal, the final spectacle – GIs bashing would-be refugees on the helipad, North Vietnamese tanks rolling through Saigon – was not exactly gladdening. The memorial to Vietnam veterans in Washington, D.C., is a grand, heartbreaking dead end, ambivalence in black granite.

By the time the war ended, a certain "Hey, who cares?" fecklessness had already set in among the young, a rejection of both hippie abandon and conventional so-

Illustration by Etienne Delessert   **BY KURT ANDERSEN**

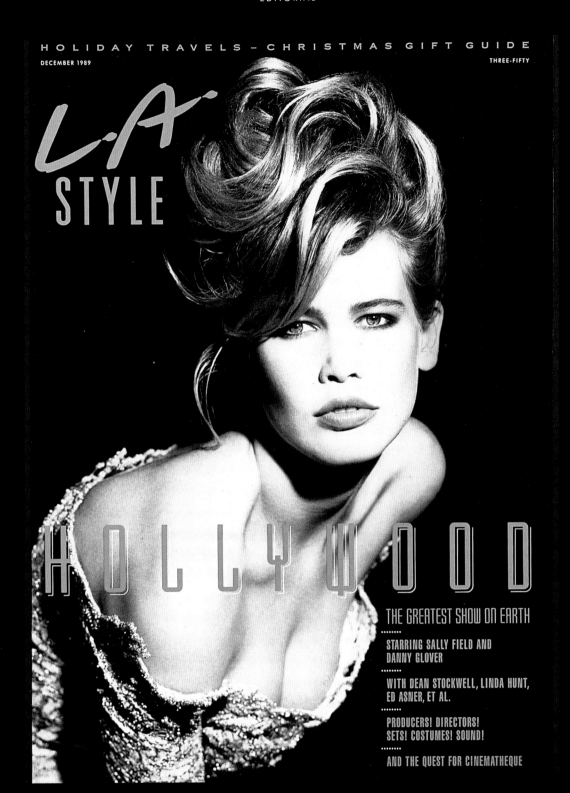

HOLIDAY TRAVELS – CHRISTMAS GIFT GUIDE

DECEMBER 1989   THREE-FIFTY

L.A
STYLE

HOLLYWOOD

THE GREATEST SHOW ON EARTH
·········
STARRING SALLY FIELD AND
DANNY GLOVER
·········
WITH DEAN STOCKWELL, LINDA HUNT,
ED ASNER, ET AL.
·········
PRODUCERS! DIRECTORS!
SETS! COSTUMES! SOUND!
·········
AND THE QUEST FOR CINEMATHEQUE

347 Distinctive Merit
Art Director: Michael Brock
Designer: Michael Brock
Photographer: Herb Ritts
Studio: Michael Brock Design
Client: LA Style

348 Distinctive Merit
Art Director: Fred Woodward
Designer: Fred Woodward
Photographer: Matt Mahurin
Publication: Rolling Stone

PART ONE

Terrorized by her husband's repeated death threats, Renee Linton did everything women are supposed to do to protect themselves under the system. Yet despite her calls for help, her court order of protection, her flights ‹Nowhere to Run› to a shelter for battered women, the system failed to save her.

By Ellen Hopkins

PHOTOGRAPH BY MATT MAHURIN

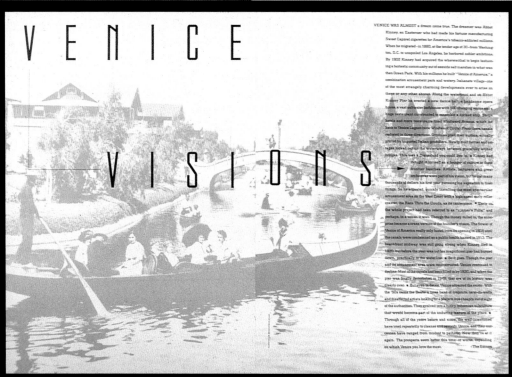

VENICE

VISIONS

VENICE WAS ALMOST a dream come true.

349 Distinctive Merit
Art Director: Michael Brock
Designer: Michael Brock
Studio: Michael Brock Design
Client: LA Style

350 Distinctive Merit
Art Director: Fred Woodward
Designer: Jolene Cuyler
Photographer: Matt Mahurin
Publication: Rolling Stone

THE ROLLING STONE INTERVIEW

Elvis Costello may be thought of as the angry young man of the British New Wave, but as he and his wife, Cait O'Riordan, greet me in the elegant piano bar of the Four Seasons Clift Hotel,

— BY DAVID WILD —

photograph by matt mahurin

351 Distinctive Merit
Art Director: Michael Brock
Designer: Michael Brock
Photographer: Deborah Turbeville
Studio: Michael Brock Design
Client: LA Style

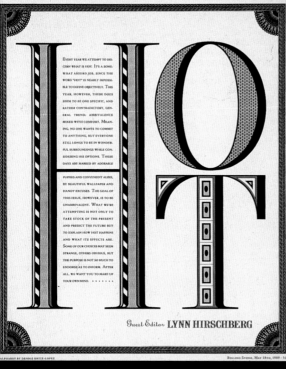

352 Distinctive Merit
Art Director: Fred Woodward
Designer: Fred Woodward
Gail Anderson
Photographer: Matthew Rolston
Publication: Rolling Stone

Photography by
Bret Wills

SAFE AT HOME

This summer in Cooperstown, N.Y., the National Baseball Hall of Fame and Museum celebrates its 50th anniversary as the spiritual home of the game and as the repository of its treasures. From the essential (the Babe's bat) to the eccentric (the Babe's bowling ball), the Hall has it all. Enjoy the tour

MAYS STEPPED HERE: ON MAY 30, 1971, WILLIE MAYS CROSSED THIS PLATE AT CANDLESTICK PARK TO SCORE AN NL-RECORD 1,950TH RUN

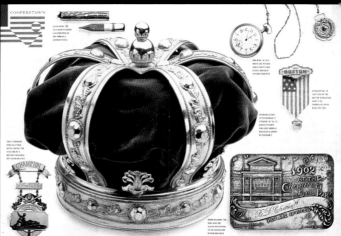

SIDE BY SIDE

PHOTOGRAPHY BY WILLIAM COUPON

In Mexico *"¡Ay, Chihuahua!"* is an expression of amazement and surprise, and for good reason. Chihuahua, Mexico's largest state, is a land of extremes, embracing both the scorching desert that bears its name and the northern Sierra Madre Occidental, a mountain range with the coldest temperatures in Mexico. It is only natural, then, that Chihuahua is also home to two tribes on the extremes of their cultures, the Tarahumara Indians and the German-speaking Altkolonier, or Old Colony Mennonites.

Both groups have agreements with the government that allow them to sidestep two important requirements of Mexican citizenship: education in the Spanish language and mandatory weekend military training for young men. Both groups eschew city life and have settled in the dry triangle created by the towns of Cuauhtémoc, Creel, and Guachóchic. But the similarities between the two tribes halt there.

The Mennonites are an old Anabaptist group whose members migrated from the Alps to the south of Russia in 1789 and fled to Canada in 1874. When the Canadians required them to teach English in their church schools in 1922, the Altkolonier moved to Mexico. As far as historians know, the Tarahumara settled in Chihuahua eons ago, though many of them lived at lower elevations before the tribe's trouble with the Tepehuane and Apache.

Mennonite

Tarahumara

Within fifteen years of their arrival, the Mennonites became Mexico's most productive small farmers. They are the country's leading commercial producers of oats and a white cheese called *queso Chihuahua*, a fundamental in dishes like *queso fundido* and *quesadillas*. Part of the Mennonite success is owed to technology; they use tractors because tractors facilitate working, but for transportation they prefer horse-drawn wagons because cars, they say, facilitate sinning.

In their own language, the Tarahumara call themselves Rarámuri, or "foot runners," because their ancestors had little need for bows and arrows; they ran down game on foot. They have never concerned themselves with productivity or technology. They use nineteenth-century implements and draft animals to eke out a subsistence based on corn and squash.

The Tarahumara are as indefatigably festive as the Mennonites are austere. They devote a significant portion of their corn harvest to making *tesgüino* (corn beer) and about one hundred days a year to drinking it and recovering from hangovers.

Despite these apparent differences, the Mennonites and the Tarahumara have a deep spiritual affinity. Passionate about their chosen ways of life, both have found in Chihuahua a place where they can be free of the pressures of the modern world. — DICK J. REAVIS

I*n the mountains and deserts of northern Indians live bound by timeless traditions.*

Mexico, Mennonite farmers and Tarahumara They couldn't be more different—or more alike.

E*ven as children, the Mennonites and Tarahumara inhabit separate worlds. There is little interaction between them, since each group speaks its own language, not Spanish.*

B*oth the Tarahumara and the Mennonites have been granted exemptions from military service and schooling in Spanish. Centuries after the conquest of Mexico, they remain unassimilated.*

A*s colorful as the Mennonites are plain, the festive Tarahumara love flamboyant clothes and strong drink. Much of their corn harvest goes to the production of a home brew called* tesgüino.

Turning their   backs to the world, the Tarahumara long ago took to the hills to escape hostile tribes.

THE MANY RECENT sightings of Elvis Presley have led to a new and illuminating line of inquiry: If Elvis is able to make appearances after his death, shouldn't he have been able to show up before his birth? ～ He is, after all, the King. ～ Exhaustive research has uncovered a wealth of evidence previously ignored by scholars who were distracted by events of lesser significance. ～ Skeptics may choose to pooh-pooh the Peruvian mountain carvings – visible only by aircraft – in the shape of a teddy bear. They may dismiss as coincidence the fact that Inca priests of the period wore chains

Lascaux, France (left): The birth of rock. Not by any means the last time the King will be criticized by Neanderthals. Carvings tell of a benevolent stranger who came out of nowhere, defeated the clan's enemies with martial arts and gave everybody a free bone. Easter Island (right): The audience at the National Geographic Society began to cough and wheeze uncomfortably when forced to confront this picture. Some members of the Memphis Mafia have commented on Elvis's big head.

IN SEARCH of HISTORIC ELVIS

BY ALAN D. MAISLEN · ILLUSTRATIONS BY ANITA KUNZ

around their necks. ～ The open-minded Elvisologist (as opposed to the Presliquarian, with his amateur faddism) can only sigh with tolerance. ～ Naysayers cannot so easily abrogate the Rouen tapestry that depicts the martyrdom of Saint Joan of Arc. The figure in the background was assumed to be a Burgundian bishop, chiefly because of his high-collared, gold-sequined robe and the fact that he seems to be sneering at Saint Joan. Embroidered along the bottom: *Je veux un morceau d'amour brûlant.* Loose translation: "I want a hunk, a hunk of burning love." ～ Compelling evidence of Elvisitation may be seen in any of a thousand Asian jungles, from Cambodia to Japan. There it is commonplace to find great, ornate decaying temples. Should it surprise anyone that, for untold millennia, these were sites where thousands of worshipers swooned before the imposing centerpiece: a giant statue of a man weighing over 500 pounds? ～ And is it mere happenstance that these are the same cultures in which originated the art of painting on black velvet? ～ Why hasn't this proof come to light sooner? A deliberate conspiracy to suppress it? The motive? Scientific ego, unwilling to give credit to the munificent contributions of the preternatural Presley. The most blatant example? The 1900 diaries of Walter Reed, the so-called father of the

cure for yellow fever. He describes his first patient: "Hands: shaking. Knees: weak. Can't seem to stand on own two feet. Lips: hot (like volcano). Patient delirious. Acts wildly, as if he were a bug. Question: Why is he all shook up?" ～ Is it not curious that, weeks later, Reed should "discover" the cause of yellow fever to be a mosquito? And how peculiar that he should find it in Cuba, a land renowned for its "fuzzy trees." ～ Only Elvis's characteristic modesty prevented him from taking credit for his many cross-cultural contributions, and even doubters agree it's a good thing Colonel Parker never contemplated the T-shirt rights. ～ Should you embrace my theory, prepare to suffer the indignities inflicted on all who hold unpopular beliefs; for truly, the unwashed masses have yet to learn the golden rule: Don't be cruel. In fact, this author has been hounded into virtual seclusion, not unlike the post-Vegas Presley. ～ Nevertheless, I have followed my dream and discovered a promising new course of study. Anybody's grandmother can claim to have seen Elvis sucking down a grape Slurpy at the local Bob's Big Boy years after his "death." Few, however, have bothered to look for the very real appearances of Elvis in inappropriate places while he was still alive. ～ Just who was that shadowy pompadoured figure lurking on the Grassy Knoll? ～ I'll never tell.

by JOHN WEST   photography by DAVE G. HOUSER

Q "DOES ANYONE HERE REMEMBER HOWARD CARTER'S DISCOVERY of King Tut's tomb?" our guide asked as we walked into the Valley of the Kings, across the Nile and west of the city of Luxor, where the lion-colored Theban Hills lie like a clenched fist in the dust. "Of course!" muttered the retired doctor at my shoulder, "it was only sixty-six years ago," and he was off like a shot to join the line waiting to see the smallest, least rewarding and most cramped excavation among the 62 tombs known to exist here—that of King Tutankhamen.

Sixty-six years ago seems as current as your next breath in this land of the Old. If we date our civilization from the Renaissance, Egypt has existed ten times as long; if we count our years from the birth of Christ, the Sphinx was already older than Christianity is now. Spend a few weeks along the Nile and what comes to mind is death and the magnificent opening verse in Ecclesiastes: "The earth abideth for ever. . . and there is no new thing under the sun."

Take, for instance, the most aggressive touts on the planet, who pounce on you at the Pyramids or here, 400 miles south of Cairo, the way mosquitos pounce on bathers in a swamp. Earlier in the day, the spry octogenarian doctor and I had set out from Luxor for the west riverbank and the tombs in a narrow-awninged ferry launch with a clattering motor like a tractor engine, chugging creakily and patiently on across the sprawling surface of the Nile back into the furthest sunstruck silences of antiquity.

The insistent pleas and opened palms instantly begin to nibble at your attention and follow you through every turn, even through car windows, like some siege of piranhas, the unblinking, beseeching stares regarding you calmly, at once unhoping and ravenous. Then comes the entrepreneur, a famished-looking youth with a dull yellow pallor like a nicotine stain and wet black eyes. He captures your attention with scraps of gaiety and jokes snatched up at random over years from fleeing Americans:

THE NILE

"What's up doc? Everything copacetic? All A-OK? Mister! Monsieur! You know what is a camel with no hump? Make a guess, mister. You couldn't guess? Hubert Humphrey! See? Hump-free. You don't like jokes? Maybe you like to be serious all the time." Wrong. What I liked to be was up the road with the doctor, who had rented a bicycle that ran better than a new policeman. After while, crocodile.

There's nothing new about this. Tourists have flocked to Egypt for 3,000 years, and from the beginning, natives have had a reputation as sarcastic fast-talkers—"witty and ready in abuse," wrote Seneca. However, I could not imagine any one of them telling a worse joke than Hump-free. I was on a two-week tour of Egypt, traveling from Cairo all the way up to Abu Simbel near the Sudanese border and working my way back on a three-day boat trip on the Nile from Aswan to Luxor through the most intense concentration of tombs, temples, treasures, mystic art and ruins in the world.

Cairo was like entering some living many-layered Troy—some old massive millstone still thick with the intermingled pulps and chaff of its slow immense gristings through 4,000 years: Alexander, the Caesars, Napoléon, Europeans. In the seethe of its streets, 14 million people dwelt, most as close to dust as lizards. Five hundred thousand alone lived in a huge necropolis, the "city of the dead" that stretched along Cairo's eastern edge. Down an interminable succession of narrow alleys, I glimpsed milling tunnels of trade in hot tea, tin pots, cabbages and tallow-white chicken carcasses as I sat in a traffic jam so infinite and tangled it brought to mind the Amazonian jungle. The noise was stultifying, the horn being the one part of the estimated one million cabs, 2,300 buses and 780,000 cars that works. Once moving, my driver drove with

ABU SIMBEL, A TEMPLE
DEDICATED TO PHARAOH
RAMSES II, BY THE
SUDANESE BORDER
ABOVE; THE GRAND AND
IMPOSING NILE, RIGHT.

66

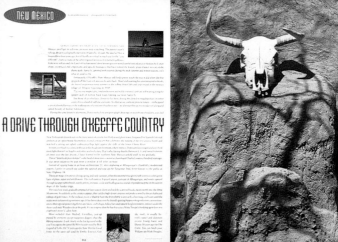

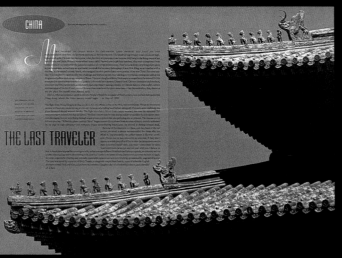

CHINA

THE LAST TRAVELER

NEW MEXICO

A DRIVE THROUGH O'KEEFFE COUNTRY

356 Distinctive Merit
Art Director: Michael Brock
Designer: Michael Brock
Photographer: Various
Studio: Michael Brock Design
Client: LA Style

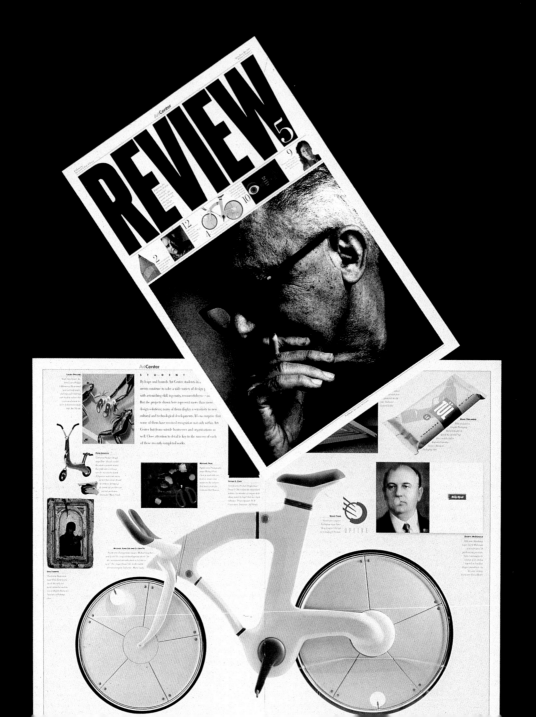

359 Distinctive Merit
Art Director: Kit Hinrichs
Designer: Kit Hinrichs
Terri Driscoll
Illustrator: Benoit Jacques
Photographer: Steven A. Heller
Rick Eskite
Studio: Pentagram
Client: Art Center College of Design

360
Art Director: Michael Grossman
Designer: Michael Grossman
Illustrator: Philip Burke
Publication: Village Voice

361
Art Director: Nicki Kalish
Creative Director: Tom Bodkin
Designer: Nicki Kalish
Illustrator: Jim Ludtke
Publication: The *New York Times*

362
Art Director: Lynn Phelps
Designer: Lynn Phelps
Illustrator: Theo Rudnak
Publication: Minnesota Guide

363
Art Director: Lynn Phelps
Designer: Lynn Phelps
Illustrator: Seymour Chwast
Publication: Minnesota Guide

364
Art Director: Francesca Messina
Creative Director: Tom Bodkin
Designer: Francesca Messina
Illustrator: Terry Allen
Publication: The *New York Times*

365
Art Director: Lynn Phelps
Designer: Lynn Phelps
Illustrator: Guy Billout
Publication: Minnesota Guide

366
Art Director: Lucy Bartholomay
Designer: Lucy Bartholomay
Illustrator: John Sibbick
Publication: The *Boston Globe*

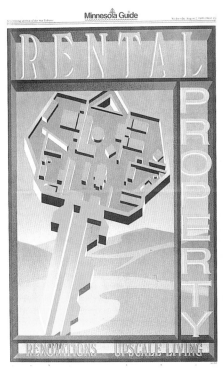

367
Art Director: Lynn Phelps
Designer: Lynn Phelps
Illustrator: Peter Lindman
Photographer: Peter Lindman
Publication: Minnesota Guide

368
Art Director: Lynn Phelps
Designer: Lynn Phelps
Illustrator: Laura Smith
Publication: Minnesota Guide

369
Art Director: Lucy Bartholomay
Designer: Lucy Bartholomay
Illustrator: Tim Carroll
     John Hersey
     Etienne Delessert
     Maira Kalman
     Sheldon Greenberg
     J. W. Stewart
Publication: The *Boston Globe*

370
Art Director: JoEllen Murphy
Illustrator: Tim Lewis
Publication: The *Washington Post*

371
Art Director: Ed Kohorst
Designer: Ed Kohorst
Illustrator: Carol Zuber
Publication: The *Dallas Morning News*

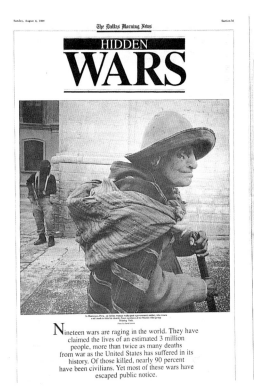

The Dallas Morning News

HIDDEN
WARS

Nineteen wars are raging in the world. They have claimed the lives of an estimated 3 million people, more than twice as many deaths from war as the United States has suffered in its history. Of those killed, nearly 90 percent have been civilians. Yet most of these wars have escaped public notice.

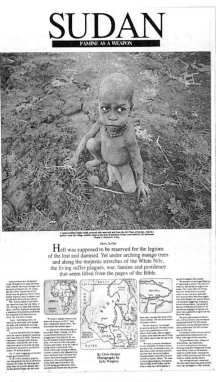

SUDAN
FAMINE AS A WEAPON

Hell was supposed to be reserved for the legions of the lost and damned. Yet under arching mango trees and along the majestic stretches of the White Nile, the living suffer plagues, war, famine and pestilence that seem lifted from the pages of the Bible.

By Chris Hedges
Photography by
Judy Walgren

COLOMBIA & PERU

Musicians symbolize both the past and future of Cuba. They exist today for the tourists that Havana hopes will return, bringing with them desperately needed dollars. Bars and cabarets that once were heavily frequented by Americans are beginning to fill up again—with Argentinians, Canadians, and Europeans.

Like other teen-agers, Cuban students form friendships, listen to music, and go to parties. Their schooling, however, includes military training, and rifles go along with pencils and notebooks.

The drum of Cuba comes from the drum of Africa, and for some people the spirits that inhabit them are the same. Drum music remains a call to worship rather than a call to dance, although both occur. A drummer might play jazz one night and ceremonial music the next. In each tradition, the sounds connect the people with one another and with the spirits of Africa in the New World.

Cuba is an amalgam of Latin and African cultures, overlaid with 30 years of strident Marxism—a culture isolated not only by its unique political path but also by the sea that surrounds it. It is a one-party state, and the economy is inefficient and indebted. But Cuba is not cut from the dour mold of typical communist countries. While the symbols of Marxism might dominate the landscape, the popular culture retains an easygoing Caribbean flavor.

The Boston Globe Magazine
MAY 14 1989

Cuba

PHOTOGRAPHY
BY KEITH JENKINS

The island nation

372
Art Director: Lucy Bartholomay
Designer: Lucy Bartholomay
Photographer: Keith Jenkins
Publication: The *Boston Globe*

373
Art Director: Scott Menchin
Creative Director: Scott Menchin
Designer: Scott Menchin
Photographer: Timothy Greenfield-Sanders
Publication: 7 Days

374
Art Director: Michael Brock
Designer: Michael Brock
Photographer: Herb Ritts
Studio: Michael Brock Design
Client: LA Style

375
Art Director: Ronda Kass
Creative Director: Everett Halvorsen
Publication: Forbes

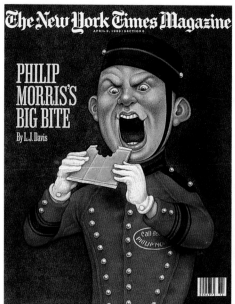

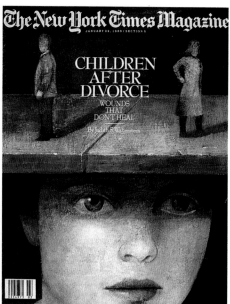

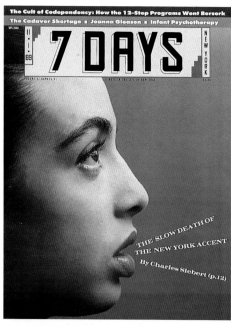

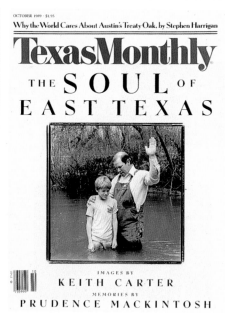

376
Art Director: Janet Froelich
Designer: Janet Froelich
Illustrator: Anita Kunz
Publication: The *New York Times*

377
Art Director: Janet Froelich
Designer: Janet Froelich
Illustrator: Wiktor Sadowski
Publication: The *New York Times*

378
Art Director: D. J. Stout
Designer: D. J. Stout
Photographer: Keith Carter
Publication: Texas Monthly

379

Art Director: Scott Menchin
Creative Director: Scott Menchin
Designer: Scott Menchin
Photographer: William Duke
Publication: 7 Days

380

Art Director: Fred Woodward
Photographer: William Coupon
Publication: Rolling Stone

381

Art Director: Fred Woodward
Designer: Jolene Cuyler
Illustrator: Sue Coe
Publication: Rolling Stone

382

Art Director: Mary Workman
Designer: Timothy W. Brown
Photographer: Chip Simons
Publication: Tennessee Illustrated

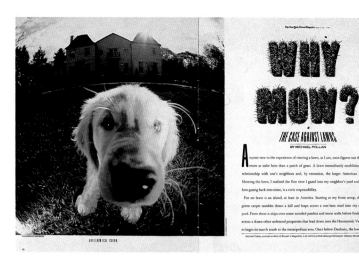

383
Art Director: Janet Froelich
Photo Editor: Kathy Ryan
Designer: Justine Strasberg
Photographer: Chip Simons
Illustrator: Kam Mak
Publication: The *New York Times*

384
Art Director: Janet Froelich
Photo Editor: Kathy Ryan
Designer: Richard Samperi
Photographer: James Nachtwey
Publication: The *New York Times*

385
Art Director: Robert Best
David Walters
Designer: Robert Best
David Walters
Mary Ann Salvato
Copywriter: Pete Hamill
Publication: Premiere

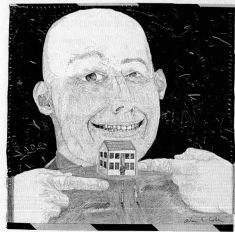

386
Art Director: Jane Palecek
Designer: Jane Palecek
Illustrator: Alan Cober
Publication: Hippocrates Magazine

GARBO
TALKS
(a little)

387

Art Director: Tom Bentkowski
Designer: Nora Sheehan
Publication: Life Magazine

Instead of the skid row regulars who sell their
● blood plasma, a doctor sees the new poor: ●
● single mothers, artists, the guy next door. ●

PHOTOGRAPHS BY KEN WILKES

388

Art Director: Jane Palecek
Designer: Jane Palecek
Photographer: Ken Wilkes
Publication: Hippocrates Magazine

389

Art Director: Tom Bentkowski
Designer: Nora Sheehan
Photographer: Timothy White
Publication: Life Magazine

BODY
And
SOUL
INTERACT IN WAYS WE ARE ONLY
BEGINNING TO UNDERSTAND

BY KEITH C. WATSON

390

Art Director: Mark Geer
Designer: Mark Geer
Illustrator: Gary Kelley
Copywriter: Keith Watson
Studio: Geer Design, Inc.
Client: Memorial Care Systems

TATTOO YOU

391
Art Director: Olivia Badrutt-Giron
Photographer: Tyen
Publication: Elle

392
Art Director: Robert Best
David Walters
Designer: Robert Best
Photographer: Karen Kuehn
Publication: Premiere

393
Art Director: Robert Best
David Walters
Designer: Robert Best
David Walters
Mary Ann Salvato
Copywriter: Peter Biskind
Publication: Premiere

394
Art Director: Robert Best
David Walters
Designer: Mary Ann Salvato
Photographer: Miche Del Sol
Copywriter: Stacy Title
Publication: Premiere

395
Art Director: Robert Best
David Walters
Designer: Robert Best
David Walters
Illustrator: Gary Halgren
Copywriter: Jack Barth
Trey Ellis
Publication: Premiere

396
Art Director: Robert Best
David Walters
Designer: Robert Best
David Walters
Mary Ann Salvato
Photographer: Terry O'Neill
Copywriter: Phoebe Hoban
Publication: Premiere

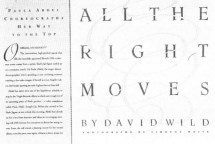

397
Art Director: Fred Woodward
Designer: Debra Bishop
Illustrator: Tom Curry
Publication: Rolling Stone

398
Art Director: Fred Woodward
Designer: Debra Bishop
Photographer: Timothy White
Publication: Rolling Stone

399

Art Director: Robert Best
      David Walters
Designer: Robert Best
      David Walters
      Mary Ann Salvato
Illustrator: Kam Mak
Copywriter: Jon Bowermaster
Publication: Premiere

400

Art Director: Robert Best
      David Walters
Designer: Robert Best
      David Walters
      Mary Ann Salvato
Illustrator: Daniel Torres
Copywriter: Rex Reed
Publication: Premiere

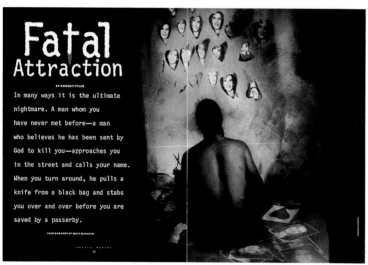

401

Art Director: Doug Renfro
Creative Director: Jim Darilek
Designer: Doug Renfro
Photographer: Matt Mahurin
Publication: Special Report: Personalities

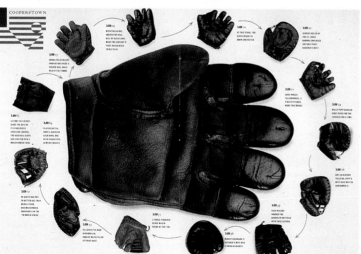

402

Art Director: Steven Hoffman
Designer: Darrin Perry
Photographer: Bret Wills
Publication: Sports Illustrated

403
Art Director: Fred Woodward
Designer: Gail Anderson
Photographer: Deborah Feingold
Publication: Rolling Stone

404
Art Director: Janet Froelich
Designer: Nancy Harris
Illustrator: Douglas Smith
Publication: The *New York Times*

405
Art Director: Janet Froelich
Designer: Janet Froelich
Illustrator: Matt Mahurin
Publication: The *New York Times*

406
Art Director: Mary Workman
Designer: Timothy W. Brown
Illustrator: Steven Madson
Publication: Tennessee Illustrated

407

Art Director: Robert Best
David Walters
Designer: Mary Ann Salvato
Photographer: Terry O'Neill
Publication: Premiere

408

Art Director: Robert Best
David Walters
Designer: Robert Best
David Walters
Mary Ann Salvato
Photographer: Terry O'Neill
Copywriter: Edmund White
Publication: Premiere

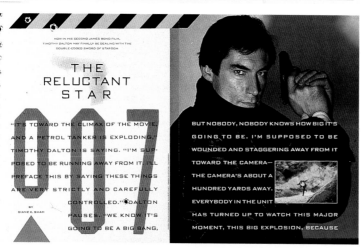

409

Art Director: Robert Best
David Walters
Designer: Robert Best
Photographer: Douglas Kirkland
Copywriter: Diane K. Shaw
Publication: Premiere

410

Art Director: Robert Best
David Walters
Designer: Robert Best
David Walters
Mary Ann Salvato
Photographer: Kobal Collection
Copywriter: Howard Gensler
Publication: Premiere

411

Art Director: D. J. Stout
Designer: D. J. Stout
Photographer: William Coupon
Publication: Texas Monthly

412

Art Director: Tom Bentkowski
Designer: Nora Sheehan
Photographer: Bettina Rheims
Steven Meisel
Publication: Life Magazine

SIDE BY SIDE

PHOTOGRAPHY BY WILLIAM COUPON

In the mountains and deserts of northern Indians live bound by timeless traditions.

Mexico, Mennonite farmers and Tarahumara They couldn't be more different—or more alike.

OOH-LA-LA! THE BRA

MODERN FEMALE

413
Art Director: Andrew Gray
Creative Director: Stephen Doyle
Photographer: Kei Ogata
　　　　　　　Raymond Meier
Agency: Drenttel Doyle Partners
Client: In Fashion

414
Art Director: Randy L. Dunbar
Photographer: Carin Riley
　　　　　　　David Riley
Publication: Home Magazine

Am
I
Blue?

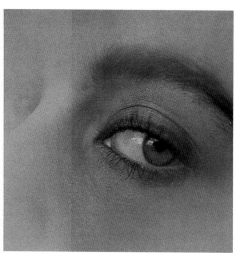

Am I Blue?

Everyone is blue now and then. But this season the blues take on a colorful mood with a brand new attitude. Gone are the days of kitschy, suburban blues and harsh color applied for shock effect. Today's blue makeup is applied with a light touch for a look that's soft, moody and romantic. "Anyone can wear blue," says makeup artist Michele Yoyski. "It's the conventional color for eyes and, blended properly, can be worn on lips and cheeks, too. But it has to be used with care." It's the rebirth of the blues—sensuous and subtle.

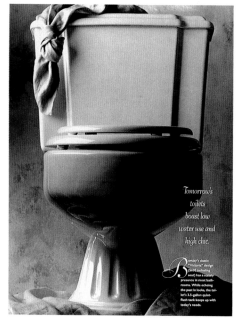

Tomorrow's toilets boast low water use and high chic.

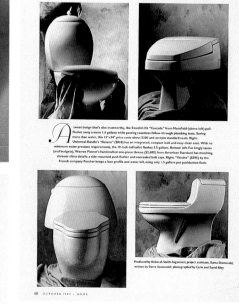

Am
I
Blue?

PORTRAITS IN PORCELAIN
A gallery of new toilet designs from discreet to divine

415
Art Director: Diana LaGuardia
Designer: Chris Gangi
Photographer: Helmut Newton
Publication: Conde Nast Traveler

416
Art Director: Tuan Dao
Creative Director: Mary Russell
Designer: Tuan Dao
Photographer: Jeremy Stitger
Publication: Taxi Magazine

HELMUT NEWTON re-creates in the
Tuscan spa town of Montecatini Terme
the forbidden romantic drama of his youth,
and we mark your card for a visit

The Burning Secret

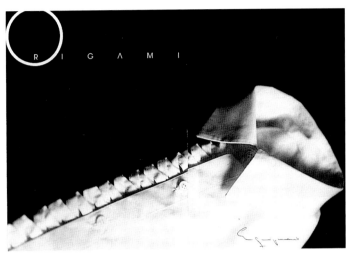

417

Art Director: D. J. Stout
Designer: D. J. Stout
Illustrator: Ian Pollock
　　　　　Philip Burke
　　　　　Anita Kunz
Publication: Texas Monthly

418

Art Director: Diana LaGuardia
Designer: Chris Gangi
Photographer: Helmut Newton
Publication: Conde Nast Traveler

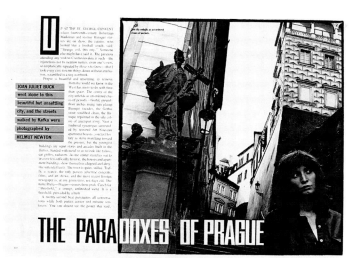

THE MYTHIC RISE OF BILLY DON MOYERS

MOYERS AS SIR LANCELOT

Illustration by Ian Pollock

THE PARADOXES OF PRAGUE

MOYERS AS ODYSSEUS

Illustration by Philip Burke

MOYERS AS ROBIN HOOD

Illustration by Anita Kunz

419
Art Director: Tom Bentkowski
Designer: Nora Sheehan
Publication: *Life* Magazine

420
Art Director: Tom Bentkowski
Designer: Nora Sheehan
Photographer: Mary Ellen Mark
Publication: *Life* Magazine

421

Art Director: Roberto Burroni
                Karen Wells Verlander
Creative Director: Regis Pagniez
Photographer: Edouard Sicot
Publication: Elle Decor Magazine

422

Art Director: D. J. Stout
Designer: D. J. Stout
Photographer: Danny Turner
Publication: Texas Monthly

Washington's
premier chef goes
shopping

BATTERIE
DE
CUISINE

A
BRUSH
WITH
LIFE

PHOTOGRAPHY BY DANNY TURNER

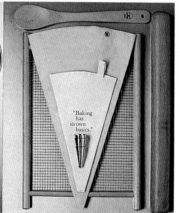

"Baking has its own basics."

Jean-Louis Palladin
chooses nothing
but the best

423
Art Director: D. J. Stout
Designer: D. J. Stout
Photographer: Matt Mahurin
Publication: Texas Monthly

424
Art Director: D. J. Stout
Designer: D. J. Stout
Photographer: Doug Milner
Publication: Texas Monthly

ABORTION STREET

At a nondescript office building in Dallas, two sides wage endless war over an unresolvable question.

by Mimi Swartz

PHOTOGRAPHS BY MATT MAHURIN

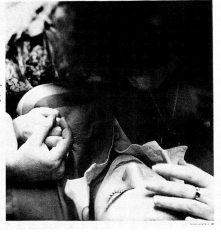

"I'M A NAZI UNTIL DEATH"

TO THE UGLY QUESTION
OF WHY LIFE IS UNFAIR,
THE SKINHEADS OF DAL-
LAS HAVE AN UGLIER
ANSWER. BY ROD DAVIS

425
Art Director: D. J. Stout
Designer: D. J. Stout
Photographer: Kurt Markus
Publication: Texas Monthly

426
Art Director: D. J. Stout
Designer: D. J. Stout
Illustrator: Richard Mantel
  Braldt Bralds
  Etienne Delessert
  Marshall Arisman
  Alex Murawski
Publication: Texas Monthly

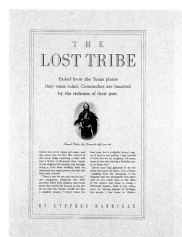

THE
LOST TRIBE

Exiled from the Texas plains
they once ruled, Comanches are haunted
by the richness of their past.

BY STEPHEN HARRIGAN

ANCESTRAL GROUND

THE CLASSIC FACE

STANDING FIRM ON MOTHER EARTH

MODERN TIMES

FACING FORWARD, FACING BACK

COWBOY SONGS

FIVE CLASSICS FROM THE

OPEN RANGE AS YOU'VE NEVER

SEEN THEM BEFORE.

Little Joe, the Wrangler

A Home on the Range

The Strawberry Roan

The Dying Cowboy

Whoopee Ti Yi Yo,
Git Along, Little Dogies

427
Art Director: Steven Hoffman
Designer: Craig Gartner
Publication: Sports Illustrated

428
Art Director: D. J. Stout
Designer: D. J. Stout
Photographer: Sally Gall
Publication: Texas Monthly

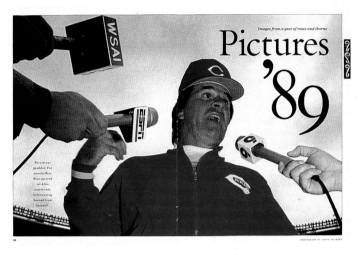

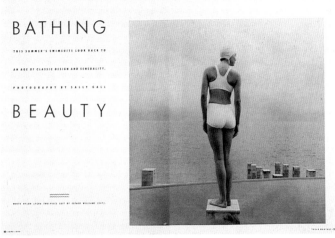

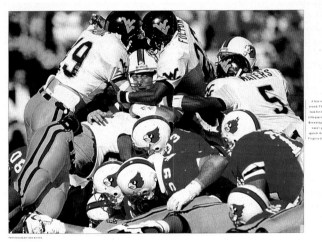

429
Art Director: Steven Hoffman
Designer: Craig Gartner
Photographer: Gregory Heisler
Publication: Sports Illustrated

430
Art Director: Tom Bentkowski
Designer: Nora Sheehan
Publication: Life Magazine

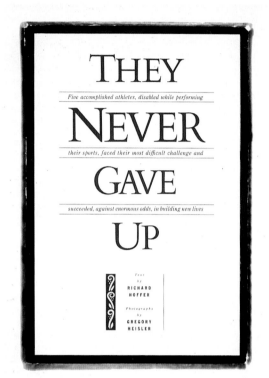

THEY
Five accomplished athletes, disabled while performing
NEVER
their sports, faced their most difficult challenge and
GAVE
succeeded, against enormous odds, in building new lives
UP

Text
by
RICHARD
HOFFER

Photographs
by
GREGORY
HEISLER

CLASSICS
THE 1939

HOLLYWOOD
WAS
NEVER BETTER

Another shift at the Dream Factory: James Stewart and Jean Arthur make their way to the set of *Mr. Smith Goes to Washington,* a golden oldie from the golden year.

25

431

Art Director: Albert Chiang
Photographer: Frans Lanting
Publication: Islands Magazine

432

Art Director: Michael Brock
Designer: Michael Brock
Photographer: Stuart Watson
Studio: Michael Brock Design
Client: LA Style

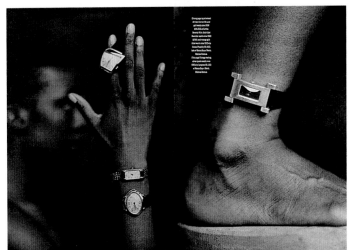

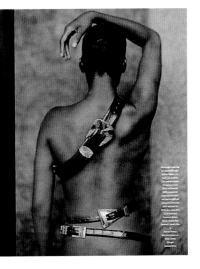

433
Art Director: Mary Workman
Designer: Timothy W. Brown
Photographer: Russell Monk
Publication: Tennessee Illustrated

434
Art Director: Diana LaGuardia
Designer: Catherine Caldwell
    Chris Gangi
    Audrey Razgaitis
Illustrator: Various
Photographer: Various
Publication: Conde Nast Traveler

THE HOMELESS
In Their Own Words

HOMELESSNESS. A word on the tips of so many tongues. The social issue of the '80s. ■ I took the photos on the following pages in the summer and late fall of 1988. They exist not because I had any great desire to help the homeless but because I was asked. It was another assignment. ■ When my friends discovered that I was going to meet "the homeless," they looked at me with concerned eyes, as if I were the one who might need support in the face of danger. ■ I expected these people to be indignant and angry. Yet I was amazed at how gentle and trusting most of them were. They listened to my spiel about how these photographs might help them. Some listened with naïveté in their eyes and others with indifference, and some asked, "What good will they do for me?" ■ When I took their pictures, I asked them to write a message for Tennesseans to read. Their stories poured out to me, a stranger. ■ Few resisted or shunned me. Maybe they were too beaten down by a society they can't figure out. Maybe they just had nothing to lose. ■ This story hasn't changed my life. Yes, it has dispelled some myths and eradicated some fears. But I am still like most people, capricious with charity. Some days I dig into my pockets and make eye contact, and some days I don't. We get too caught up in our own lives. ■ The plight of the homeless will be with us forever. Sure, they need more shelters, more soup kitchens, more aid. But you can't help everyone. Some people don't want to be helped; they themselves don't even know why.
—R. M.

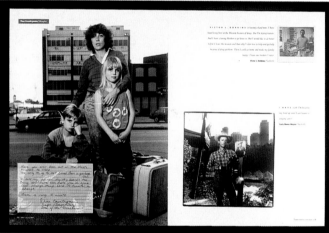

435
Art Director: Paul Davis
Designer: Risa Zaitschek
Illustrator: Various
Photographer: Various
Client: Wigwag Magazine Co., Inc.

436
Art Director: Fred Woodward
Publication: Rolling Stone

437
Art Director: D. J. Stout
Designer: D. J. Stout
Publication: Texas Monthly

PART ONE

Terrorized by her husband's repeated death threats, Renee Linton did everything women are supposed to do to protect themselves under the system. Yet despite her calls for help, her court order of protection, her flights ‹Nowhere to Run› to a shelter for battered women, the system failed to save her.

By Ellen Hopkins

PHOTOGRAPH BY MATT MAHURIN

HOLY ART!

THE "REVEREND HOWARD FINSTER" IS SPREADING GOD'S WORD AS FAST AS HE CAN PAINT, AND FOR GALLERY GOERS AND ROCK STARS ALIKE, SEEING IS BELIEVING BY DAVID HANDELMAN

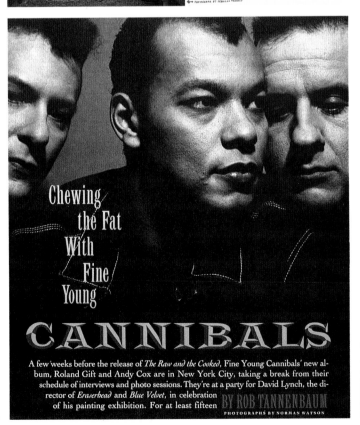

Chewing the Fat With Fine Young

CANNIBALS

A few weeks before the release of *The Raw and the Cooked*, Fine Young Cannibals' new album, Roland Gift and Andy Cox are in New York City, taking a break from their schedule of interviews and photo sessions. They're at a party for David Lynch, the director of *Eraserhead* and *Blue Velvet*, in celebration of his painting exhibition. For at least fifteen

BY ROB TANNENBAUM
PHOTOGRAPHS BY NORMAN WATSON

DECEMBER 1989 · $1.95

All-American Crooks: What Went Wrong at Dallas' Carter High

Texas Monthly

Wild Forever

A Sneak Preview of Big Bend Ranch, Texas' Rugged New Parkland

BY STEPHEN HARRIGAN · PHOTOGRAPHY BY MARK KLETT

THE ALL-

ONCE THEY WERE FOOTBALL

HEROES, BOUND FOR GLORY.

NOW THEY ARE FELONS,

AMERICAN

BOUND FOR PRISON. HERE

IS WHAT WENT WRONG

AT DALLAS' CARTER HIGH.

CROOKS

BY DANA RUBIN

ILLUSTRATION BY MATT MAHURIN

A Fool and his Money

I'VE TAKEN A PERSONAL FINANCE COURSE, SET UP A HOUSEHOLD BUDGET, AND KEPT MY 1972 VOLKSWAGEN. SO HOW COME I'M ALWAYS BROKE?

BY LAWRENCE WRIGHT

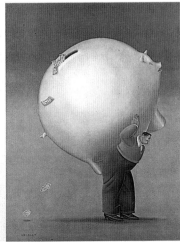

438
Art Director: Diana LaGuardia
Designer: Chris Gangi
        Audrey Razgaitis
Illustrator: Various
Photographer: Various
Publication: Conde Nast Traveler

439
Art Director: Fred Woodward
Publication: Rolling Stone

"I don't need this shit!" says *USA Today* gossip columnist Jeannie Williams. It's the morning of May 19th, and Williams has just seen the breakfast press screening of *Do the Right Thing* at the Cannes film festival. Tonight, the film will have its black-tie, red-carpet gala première at the Palais des Festivals, on the Côte d'Azur beach, where it will be competing with films from around the world for the coveted Palm d'Or prize. This morning, the more modest Palais press-confer-

Director Spike Lee's 'Do the Right Thing' Takes a Provocative Look at Race Relations By David Handelman

PART ONE: THE SHIFT Most of us have lived our entire lives with the threat of the cold war, the terror of nuclear annihilation. But now, for the first time in memory, peace–not war–is breaking out around the world. From Moscow to Washington, the old assumptions are falling away, and a new and vastly different era is coming into being. After all the darkness and carnage of the twentieth century, is man finally ready to give up his most catastrophic habit– the urge to make war? BY LAWRENCE WRIGHT

PEACE

440
Art Director: Shoshanna Sommer
Creative Director: Dan Barron
Designer: Shoshanna Sommer
Illustrator: Philippe Weisbecker
Publication: Art Direction

441
Art Director: Scott Menchin
Creative Director: Scott Menchin
Designer: Scott Menchin
Photographer: Susan Schelling
Publication: How

442
Art Director: Claude Skelton
Designer: Claude Skelton
Illustrator: Anthony Russo
Publication: Warfield's

OF COUNSEL
By Chris Scheuble

THE MARYLAND COURTS ARE CLOGGED WITH THOUSANDS OF

ASBESTOS CASES—MORE THAN IN ALL BUT THREE STATES IN

THE COUNTRY. IN FACT, IF THERE WILL BE A WAY OUT OF THE JAM,

PLAINTIFF SUPERLAWYER PETER ANGELOS WILL DECIDE IT.

BREATHING ROOM

It's one of those hot, humid August days in Baltimore, and the air conditioning
is barely cooling the musty air inside the city courthouse on Calvert Street.
This is usually a quiet time of year, with many judges and lawyers out of town,
cooling off at the beach. But today, a number of attorneys have cut short their
vacations and returned to Baltimore. Along with scores of other members of
the bar, they've pushed their way into Courtroom 556, a cavernous,
mahogany-paneled chamber that is often used for ceremonial gatherings.

443
Art Director: Claude Skelton
Designer: Claude Skelton
Photographer: C. Paul Haynes
Publication: Warfield's

THE CEO
By Tom Ichniowski

Fairchild's End

DOWN THE STAIRS FROM THE SPARE,
modern lobby of Fairchild Industries' headquarters

in northern Virginia is a mini-museum that contains remembrances of the company's past.

Deserted near the end of a summer weekday, the place silently recounts Fairchild's

decades in aviation, from the Roaring Twenties to the Space Age. At the foot of the stairs

is a terra cotta bust, larger than life-size, of Sherman Mills Fairchild, whose pioneering

aviation camera launched the company in 1920. Behind the silent gaze of the founder and

longtime chairman, several exhibits chronicle notable developments in Fairchild's

history. Nearby is a display devoted to the *Stars and Stripes,* the Fairchild-built aircraft

that traveled with Admiral Richard Byrd to the South Pole and was the first plane to fly

444
Art Director: Claude Skelton
Designer: Claude Skelton
Photographer: Tom Wolff
Publication: Warfield's

THE FIRST TIME JIM BROOKS SAW THE COLOSSUS OF MEMPHIS, THE COM-

MANDING, 27-FOOT RENDERING IN GRANITE OF RAMSES II, IT LAY COL-

LAPSED AND BROKEN IN A TANGLE OF WEEDS IN MEMPHIS, EGYPT, AWAITING

A COSTLY RECONSTRUCTION JOB. AS WITH MANY OTHER MONUMENTS, ARTI-

FACTS, AND STATUES IN A TREASURE-LADEN COUNTRY EAGER TO FUND

TECHNOLOGICAL ADVANCEMENTS, THE RESTORATION OF RAMSES'

COLOSSUS WAS PLACED ON HOLD. IT WAS 1967, AND BROOKS WAS IN EGYPT

TO DO GEOLOGICAL SURVEY WORK ON THE QATTARA DEPRESSION, AN AREA

ROUGHLY THE SIZE OF SWITZERLAND. EGYPTIAN GOVERNMENT OFFICIALS

HOPED THE DEPRESSION COULD BE FLOODED WITH WATER CHANNELED

FROM THE MEDITERRANEAN SEA AND USED AS A SOURCE OF HYDRO-

ELECTRIC POWER. IN 1986, GEOLOGIST BROOKS WAS AGAIN IN EGYPT, BUT

ON BUSINESS OF A DIFFERENT NATURE. THIS TIME, THE QATTARA DEPRES-

SION PROJECT WAS ON HOLD, BUT THE COLOSSUS OF MEMPHIS HAND-

SOMELY RESTORED THROUGH AN INGENIOUS COMBINATION OF POWDERED

GRANITE, CONCRETE, STEEL RODS, AND AMERICAN MONEY, WAS UP FROM

OUT OF EGYPT

FOR NEARLY THREE DECADES, SMU RESEARCHERS HAVE JOURNEYED
TO EGYPT TO PROBE AND PRESERVE THE LEGACY OF AN ANCIENT
CIVILIZATION. THIS YEAR, THE SMU-EGYPT CONNECTION HELPED
BRING THE TREASURES OF RAMSES THE GREAT TO DALLAS.

BY JEAN MAZA

445
Art Director: David Lerch
Designer: David Lerch
Illustrator: David Lerch
Studio: Peterson & Co.
Client: Southern Methodist University

446

Art Director: Kit Hinrichs
Designer: Kit Hinrichs
      Belle How
Illustrator: Seymour Chwast
Copywriter: Connie Hinckley
Studio: Pentagram
Client: Pacific Telesis

447

Art Director: Kit Hinrichs
Designer: Kit Hinrichs
      Sandra McHenry
Illustrator: Melissa Grimes
      Jack Unruh
Copywriter: Peterson Skolnick & Dodge
Studio: Pentagram
Client: Royal Viking Line

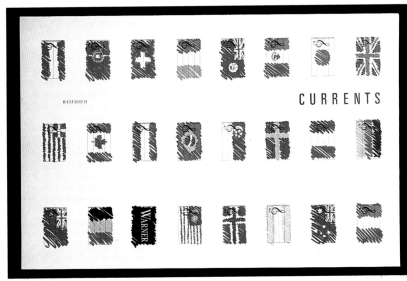

448

Art Director: Peter Harrison
      Harold Burch
Designer: Harold Burch
Illustrator: Harold Burch
      Tim Lewis
      David Suter
Photographer: Scott Morgan
Studio: Pentagram Design
Client: Warner Communications Inc.

449

Art Director: Peter Harrison
  Harold Burch
Designer: Harold Burch
Illustrator: Neil Shigley
  David Suter
  Harold Burch
  Tim Lewis
Studio: Pentagram Design
Client: Warner Communications Inc.

450

Art Director: Peter Good
Designer: Peter Good
Copywriter: Guthrie Sayen
Studio: Peter Good Graphic Design
Client: Wadsworth Atheneum

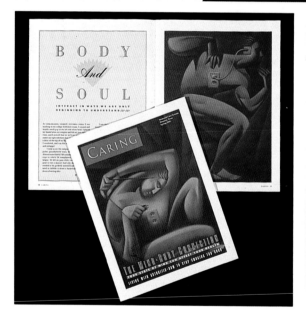

451

Art Director: Mark Geer
Creative Director: Karen Kephart
Designer: Mark Geer
  Tad Griffin
  Brandee Delaney
Illustrator: Gary Kelley
Photographer: Mike Hallaway
Studio: Geer Design, Inc.
Client: Memorial Care Systems

452

Art Director: Kit Hinrichs
Designer: Kit Hinrichs
  Sandra McHenry
Illustrator: Melissa Grimes
Copywriter: Peterson Skolnick & Dodge
Studio: Pentagram
Client: Royal Viking Line

453

Art Director: Peter Harrison
Harold Burch
Designer: Harold Burch
Christina Freyss
Illustrator: Chris Gall
Photographer: Geof Kern
Josef Astor
Studio: Pentagram Design
Client: Chase Manhattan Bank

454

Art Director: Kit Hinrichs
Designer: Kit Hinrichs
Terri Driscoll
Illustrator: Regan Dunnick
Copywriter: Peterson Skolnick & Dodge
Studio: Pentagram
Client: Royal Viking Line

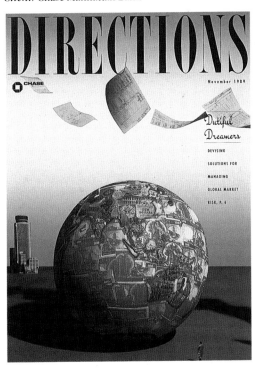

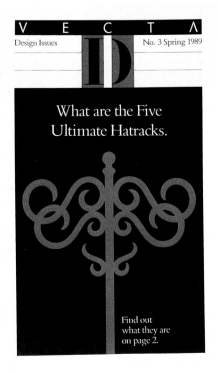

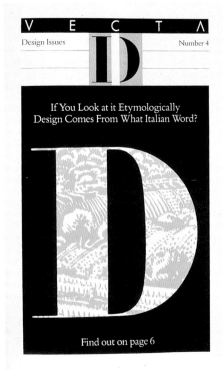

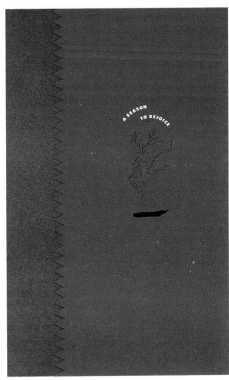

455

Art Director: Milton Glaser
Creative Director: Milton Glaser
Designer: Suzanne Zumpano
Illustrator: Milton Glaser
Copywriter: Eva Doman Bruck
Agency: Milton Glaser, Inc.
Client: Vecta

456
Art Director: Milton Glaser
Creative Director: Milton Glaser
Designer: Suzanne Zumpano
Agency: Milton Glaser, Inc.
Client: The Rockefeller Center Club

457
Art Director: Mark Feldman
Lakshmi Narayan-Burns
Creative Director: Nancy Tait
Designer: Various
Copywriter: Mary Ellen Sullivan
Cindy Rippa
Agency: Creative Services Group
Client: Evangelical Health Systems

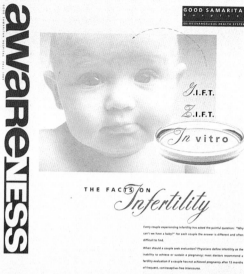

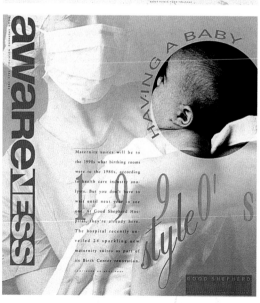

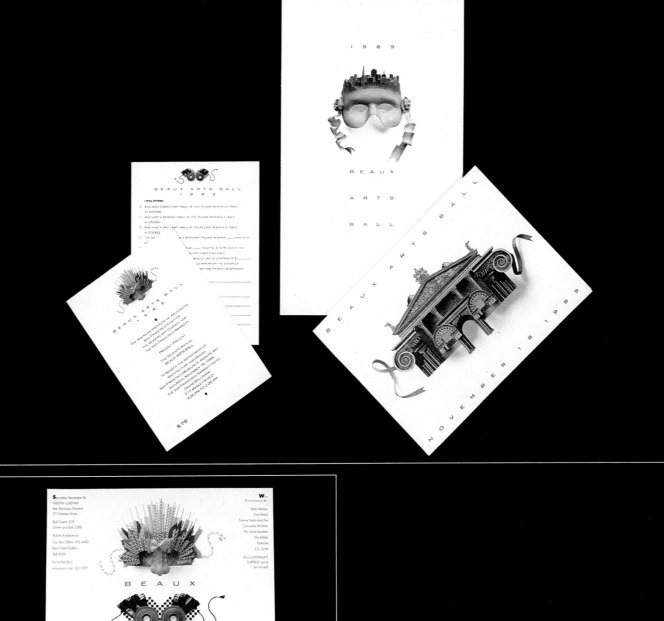

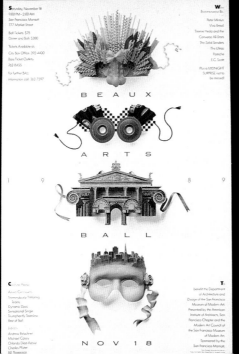

Art Director: Dick Lemmon
Creative Director: Jan Zechman
Designer: Dick Lemmon
Client: Illinois Film Office

FILM

PULL THE FIRST RIPE TOMATO, WARM FROM THE SUN, OFF THE VINE. THROW SALT AND PEPPER ON IT, AND MUNCH. NOW, THAT'S CELEBRATION. SAME GOES FOR AUGUST CORN. AND BROTHER YOU'VE GOT YOURSELF A MEAL. AND

every juicy tomato and sweet corn August, towards the last two weeks, our family would saunter off from Nashville to Lawrenceburg, Tennessee for the annual family wing-ding. All sixty plus of us.

When younger, I always wondered, while wandering the rural roads, about other families that were doing the same, joining in the celebration of reunion. Oddly enough, I noticed around the town square a caravan of over twenty vehicles, all alien looking, older dumpier cars and a few trucks. All, I mean all, of these vehicles had mud flaps with those jewel-like reflectors, like it was their trademark, their link to each other. They were loaded down with families, and I guessed, they too were reuniting, then I learned it was the season for the gypsies.

We'd stay for a week and normally pounce wherever there was a bed, a couch,

a hideaway somewhere. There were seven different houses packing in our families. Seven overlapping families: brothers, sisters, aunties, uncles. Dogs, cats, rabbits, parakeets, puppies, and a pet squirrel.

If you could hold a utensil, you'd be assigned to cook. I learned a lot that way. We all took turns. We called it the cousin system, there was no particular order. My aunt Dotty took charge and yelled commands on whose turn it was to help in the mess hall, which was a different kitchen each day. Dinner started at four in the afternoon and went on until the sun shut its bright light off. Evening activities were chit-chat and cards for the "older's", dances at the Elk's Club for the "younger's" (to Eric Desseffort's Band-of-Reknown) and double features. When I found that I was favoring more the activity around home base, I knew then I was starting to become an "older."

SWEET AUGUST CORN - ON - THE - COB

FAMILY REUNION PICNIC

AN ARMSTRONG FAMILY REUNION picnic was held on Saturday, August 21st by Mr. and Mrs. Alfred T. Armstrong at their home in Petersville, Kentucky. The occasion honored nephew Peter Morris (home on leave) and niece, Miss Katherine S. Parks, back from Owensboro, Kentucky. Pictured above are (left to right) Mrs. Thomas A. Armstrong, Mr. and Mrs. Alfred T. Armstrong, Mrs. Eugene W. Smith, Mrs. Luke Watson, Miss Mamie Phillips, Miss Parks, Mr. Morris and Mrs. John Rogers. The young gentlemen in front are (left to right) Luke Watson, Jr., younger brother John, and Nelson Armstrong.

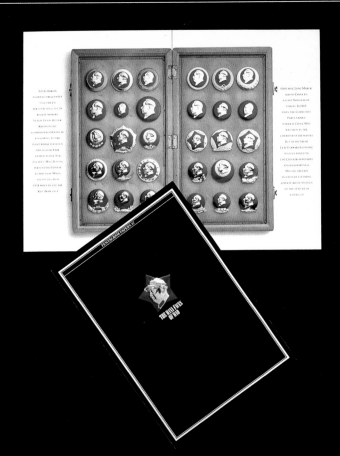

464 Distinctive Merit

Art Director: James Cross
Designer: James Cross
Yee-Ping Cho
Illustrator: Various
Photographer: Various
Copywriter: Jane Arnold
Maxwell Arnold
Studio: Cross Associates, A Siegel & Gale Co.
Client: Simpson Paper Co.

466 Distinctive Merit
Art Director: Jeff Larson
Scott Johnson
Designer: Scott Johnson
Jeff Larson
Agency: Larson Design Associates
Client: Larson Design Associates

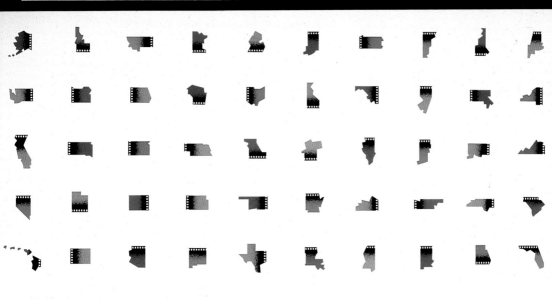

U S A   F I L M   F E S T I V A L   X I X

467 Distinctive Merit
Art Director: Kenny Garrison
Creative Director: Kenny Garrison
Designer: Kenny Garrison
Studio: Richards Brock Miller Mitchell & Assoc.
Client: USA Film Festival/Dallas

469
Art Director: Barbara Vick
Designer: Barbara Vick
Illustrator: Miro Salazar
Copywriter: Linda Peterson
Agency: SBG Partners
Client: Capital Guaranty

470
Art Director: Bill Tomlinson
Creative Director: Bill Tomlinson
Designer: Bill Tomlinson
Illustrator: Jon Ellis
Copywriter: Cathleen Toomey
          Mark Melton
Studio: Tomlinson Advertising Design
Client: Timberland Co.

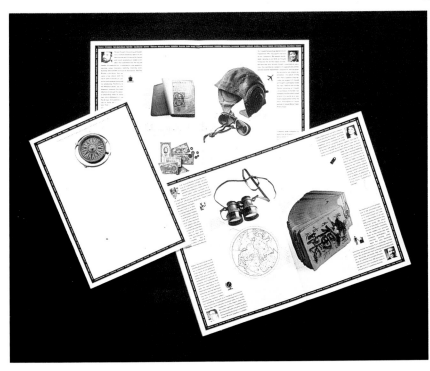

471
Art Director: John Van Dyke
Creative Director: John Van Dyke
Designer: John Van Dyke
Photographer: Cliff Fiess
Copywriter: Rick Moss
Agency: Van Dyke Co.
Client: Expeditors International

472
Art Director: Peter Harrison
          Harold Burch
Designer: Harold Burch
          Peter Harrison
Illustrator: Gene Greif
Copywriter: John Berendt
          Warner Communications
Studio: Pentagram Design
Client: Warner Communications Inc.

473
Art Director: Kit Hinrichs
Designer: Kit Hinrichs
　　　　　　Belle How
Copywriter: Valoree Dowell
Studio: Pentagram
Client: Immunex Corp.

474
Art Director: Brian Boyd
Designer: Brian Boyd
Illustrator: John Craig
Photographer: Robert Latorre
Copywriter: Kevin Orlin Johnson
Studio: Richards Brock Miller Mitchell & Assoc.
Client: Chili's, Inc.

475
Art Director: Dale Lamson
Creative Director: Dale Lamson
Designer: Dale Lamson
Photographer: Greg Grosse
Copywriter: Dale Lamson
Studio: Lamson Design

476
Art Director: Lynn Bernick
　　　　　　Doug May
Designer: Lynn Bernick
Photographer: Various
Copywriter: Lisa Cobb
Studio: May & Co.
Client: Cobb & Friend

477
Art Director: Tjody Overson
Illustrator: Various
Copywriter: Mike Gibbs
Agency: McCool & Co.
Client: Weyerhaeuser

478
Art Director: Larry Brooks
Kosh
Designer: Larry Brooks
Kosh
Illustrator: Larry Brooks
Kosh
Copywriter: John Timpane
Studio: Kosh/Brooks
Client: Champion International

479
Art Director: Charles S. Anderson
Dan Olson
Designer: Charles S. Anderson
Dan Olson
Illustrator: Randy Dahlk
Copywriter: Lisa Pemrick
Studio: Charles S. Anderson Design
Client: French Paper Co.

480
Art Director: Charles S. Anderson
Dan Olson
Designer: Charles S. Anderson
Dan Olson
Photographer: Various
Copywriter: Jon Anderson
Studio: Charles S. Anderson Design
Client: Goldsmith, Aigo & Co.

481
Art Director: Andrée Cordella
Creative Director: Andrée Cordella
Designer: Andrée Cordella
Illustrator: Rob Howard
    Andrew Berry
Photographer: Geoffrey Stein
Copywriter: Andrée Cordella
Studio: Cordella Design
Client: Gilbert Paper Co.

482
Art Director: Kevin Prejean
Creative Director: Willie Baronet
Designer: Kevin Prejean
Illustrator: Lynn Rowe Reed
Copywriter: Poppy Sundeen
Agency: Knape&Knape
Client: HCA Medical Center of Plano

483
Art Director: Leslee Avchen
    Laurie Jacobi
Designer: Leslee Avchen
    Laurie Jacobi
Photographer: Terry Heffernan
Copywriter: Cynthia Zwirn
Studio: Avchen & Jacobi, Inc.
Client: Consolidated Papers, Inc.

484
Art Director: John Sayles
Illustrator: John Sayles
Copywriter: LeAnn Koerner
Studio: Sayles Graphic Design
Client: Professional Match Consultants

485
Art Director: Charles S. Anderson
Designer: Charles S. Anderson
Photographer: Gary McCoy
Copywriter: Chuck Carlson
Studio: The Duffy Group
Client: Dorsey & Whitney

486
Art Director: Charles S. Anderson
Designer: Charles S. Anderson
Dan Olson
Photographer: James Williams
Copywriter: Lisa Pemrick
Studio: Charles S. Anderson Design
Client: Pantone, Inc.

487
Art Director: Brent Croxton
Creative Director: Bob Manley
Designer: Brent Croxton
Illustrator: Brian Cronin
Copywriter: Craig Walker
Agency: Altman & Manley
Client: Group Health Plan

488
Art Director: Joe Duffy
Designer: Joe Duffy
Haley Johnson
Illustrator: Jan Evans
Lynn Schulte
Photographer: Jeff Zwart
Copywriter: Chuck Carlson
Studio: The Duffy Group
Client: Porsche

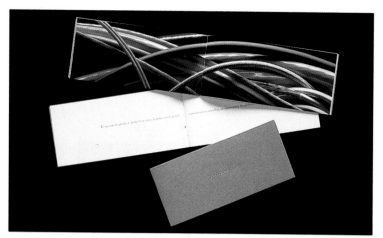

489
Art Director: John Van Dyke
Creative Director: John Van Dyke
Designer: John Van Dyke
Photographer: Doug Evans
Copywriter: Brian McKenna
Agency: Van Dyke Co.
Client: The Northern Group

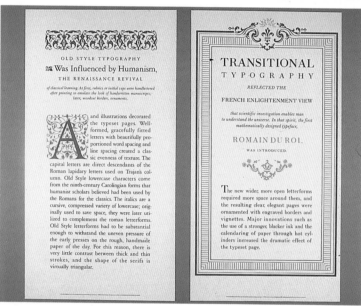

490
Art Director: Leah Toby Hoffmitz
Creative Director: Leah Toby Hoffmitz
Designer: Terry Irwin
    Leah Toby Hoffmitz
Copywriter: Leah Toby Hoffmitz
    Shawn Woodyard
Studio: Letterform Design
Client: Characters & Color

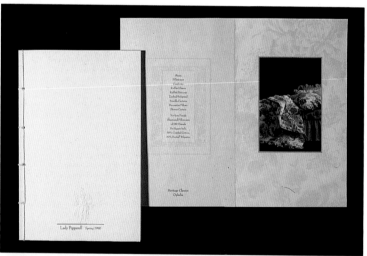

491
Art Director: Jean McCartney
Creative Director: Bryan Dixon
Designer: Jean McCartney
Photographer: Steven Randazzo
Client: West Point Pepperell

492
Art Director: Andrew Gray
Creative Director: Thomas Kluepfel
Photographer: George Hein
Agency: Drenttel Doyle Partners
Client: Arrow Co.

493
Art Director: Vic Cevoli
Creative Director: Vic Cevoli
Designer: John Avery
Photographer: Clint Clemens
Copywriter: Neill Ray
Agency: Hill, Holliday
Client: Nissan Infiniti

494
Art Director: Tyler Smith
Creative Director: Tyler Smith
Designer: Tyler Smith
Photographer: George Petrakes
Copywriter: Steve Battista
Studio: Tyler Smith
Client: Fox River Paper

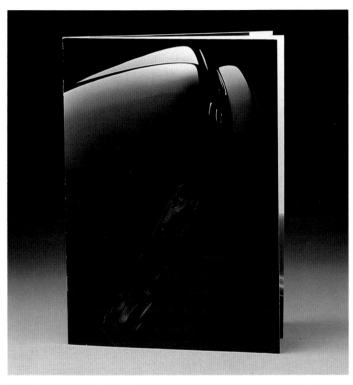

495
Art Director: Jerry Takigawa
Creative Director: Jerry Takigawa
Designer: Jerry Takigawa
LeAnn Hansen
Photographer: Batista Moon Studio
Westlight
Copywriter: Gay Machado
Studio: Jerry Takigawa Design
Client: Metricom Inc.

496
Art Director: Jack Byrne
Creative Director: Jack Byrne
Designer: Jack Byrne
Photographer: Symore Mednick
Copywriter: Phil Yadinsky
Studio: Design Resource, Inc.
Client: Design Resource, Inc.

497

Art Director: Karen Kornblum
Creative Director: Kevin Maginnis
Designer: Karen Kornblum
Photographer: Various
Copywriter: Bobbe Kendall
Client: Siemens Medical Systems

498

Art Director: Sharon Werner
Designer: Sharon Werner
Illustrator: Sharon Werner
Photographer: James Williams
Copywriter: Chuck Carlson
Studio: The Duffy Group
Client: D'Amico Cucina

499

Art Director: Martin Stevers
Designer: Martin Stevers
Illustrator: Jennifer Hewitson
Photographer: Dave Harrison
Copywriter: Ken Alfrey
Studio: Grayson
Client: The Baldwin Co.

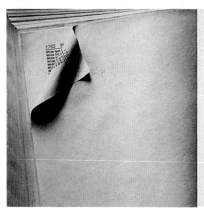

500

Art Director: Janet Odgis
Creative Director: Janet Odgis
Designer: Janet Odgis
      Elizabeth Bakacs
      Richard Manville
Illustrator: Various
Photographer: Various
Copywriter: Paul Rosenthal
Client: Champion International

501
Art Director: Sharon Werner
Designer: Sharon Werner
Illustrator: Charles Burns
Copywriter: Chuck Carlson
Studio: The Duffy Group
Client: Fox River Paper

502
Art Director: Janis Koy
Designer: Janis Koy
　　　　　Michelle Freisenhahn
Photographer: Bob Cardellino
　　　　　Jim Keller
Client: Bexar County Hospital District Auxiliary

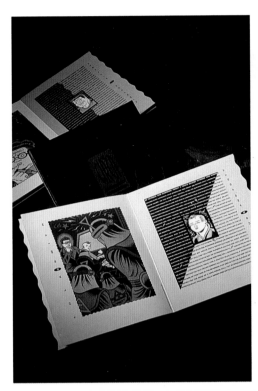

503
Art Director: Tom Schifanella
Creative Director: Robin Shepherd
Copywriter: Amanda Townsend
Studio: Robin Shepherd Studios

504
Art Director: Kit Hinrichs
Designer: Susie Leversee
Copywriter: Jeff Atlas
Studio: Pentagram
Client: Aspen Skiing Co.

505

Art Director: Andrea Kelley
Creative Director: Paul Pruneau
Designer: Andrea Kelley
Photographer: Bill Gallery
Copywriter: Brad Londy
Agency: Apple Communications Design
Client: Apple Computer Inc.

506

Art Director: Terry Koppel
Creative Director: Terry Koppel
Designer: Terry Koppel
Illustrator: Various
Copywriter: Peter Hauck
Studio: Koppel & Scher
Client: Queens Group

507

Art Director: Emil Micha
Designer: Elliot Schneider
Illustrator: Roy Weiman
Copywriter: Charles Decker

508

Art Director: Amy Watt
                Ann Dakis
                Margaret McGovern
Creative Director: Paul Silverman
Photographer: John Holt
                Eric Meola
Copywriter: Peter Pappas
Agency: Mullen
Client: Timberland Co.

509

Art Director: David Edelstein
                Lanny French
                Rick Jost
Photographer: Nick Vacarro
Copywriter: David N. Meyer II
Agency: Edelstein Associates
Client: Generra Sportswear

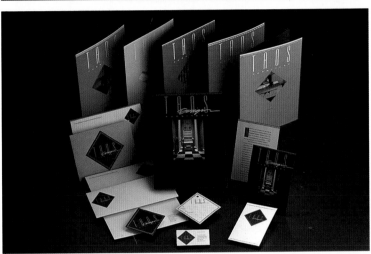

510

Art Director: Rick Vaughn
Creative Director: Rick Vaughn
Designer: Rick Vaughn
Photographer: Robert Reck
Copywriter: Richard Kuhn
Studio: Vaughn/Wedeen Creative
Client: Taos Furniture

511

Art Director: David Edelstein
                Lanny French
                Rick Jost
                Eric Haggard
Photographer: Veronica Simm
Copywriter: David N. Meyer II
Agency: Edelstein Associates
Client: Generra Sportswear

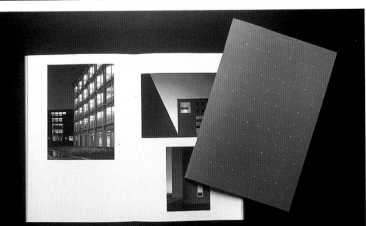

512

Art Director: Lowell Williams
Creative Director: Lowell Williams
Designer: Lana Rigsby
Illustrator: Andy Dearwater
Photographer: Nick Merrick
Copywriter: JoAnn Stone
Studio: Lowell Williams Design Inc.
Client: Maguire Thomas Partners

513
Art Director: Scott Mires
Designer: Scott Mires
Illustrator: Gerry Bustamante
Copywriter: Barry Boyt
Agency: Mires Design
Client: First Capital Life

514
Art Director: Vic Cevoli
Creative Director: Vic Cevoli
Designer: John Avery
Photographer: Clint Clemens
Copywriter: Neill Ray
Agency: Hill, Holliday
Client: Nissan Infiniti

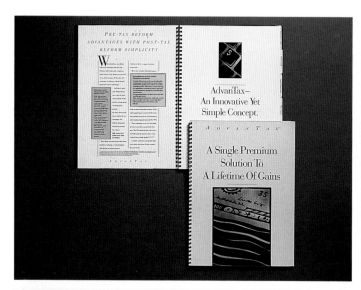

515
Art Director: Doreen Caldera
Designer: Doreen Caldera
        Bart Welch
        Paul Caldera
        Dave Kottler
Copywriter: Leslie Johnson
Photographer: Rodney Rascona
        Dugald Bremner

516
Art Director: James Sebastian
        John Plunkett
Designer: John Plunkett
        Thomas Schneider
        David Reiss
Photographer: Neil Selkirk
        Jody Dole
Client: The L•S Collection

517
Art Director: Bob Dennard
Creative Director: Bob Dennard
Designer: Chuck Johnson
          Art Garcia
          Brad Wines
Illustrator: Various
Photographer: Various
Agency: Dennard Creative, Inc.
Client: Herring Marathon Group

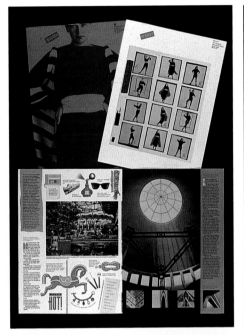

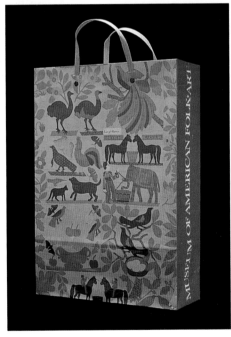

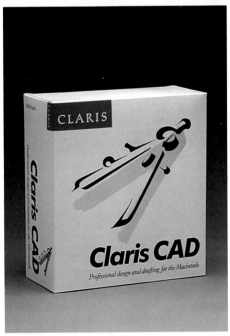

518
Art Director: John Warwicker
Studio: Vivid ID
Client: CBS Records

519
Art Director: Faye H. Eng
          Anthony T. Yee
Designer: Faye H. Eng
          Anthony T. Yee
Photographer: Schecter Lee
Studio: Eng & Yee Designs, Inc.
Client: Museum of American Folk Art

520
Art Director: Marty Neumeier
Designer: Marty Neumeier
          Chris Chu
Illustrator: Chris Chu
          Curtis Wong
Copywriter: Marty Neumeier
          Desiree LaGrone
Studio: Neumeier Design Team
Client: Claris Corp.

521
Art Director: Jennifer Morla
Designer: Jennifer Morla
   Marianne Mitten
Illustrator: Jennifer Morla
   Marianne Mitten
Client: Spectrum Foods

522
Art Director: Charles S. Anderson
   Dan Olson
Designer: Charles S. Anderson
   Dan Olson
Illustrator: Charles S. Anderson
   Dan Olson
Photographer: James Williams
Studio: Charles S. Anderson Design
Client: Aravis Distilleries

523
Art Director: Charles S. Anderson
   Dan Olson
Designer: Charles S. Anderson
   Dan Olson
Illustrator: Charles S. Anderson
   Dan Olson
Photographer: James Williams
Studio: Charles S. Anderson Design
Client: Aravis Distilleries

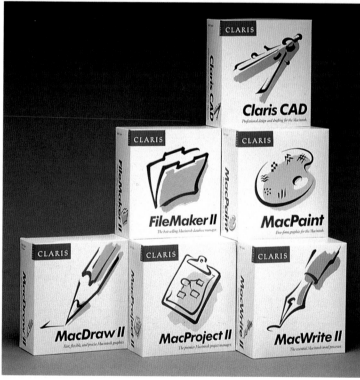

524
Art Director: Marty Neumeier
Designer: Marty Neumeier
   Chris Chu
Illustrator: Chris Chu
   Curtis Wong
Copywriter: Marty Neumeier
   Desiree LaGrone
Studio: Neumeier Design Team
Client: Claris Corp.

525
Art Director: Charles S. Anderson
   Dan Olson
Designer: Charles S. Anderson
   Dan Olson
Illustrator: Charles S. Anderson
   Dan Olson
Photographer: James Williams
Studio: Charles S. Anderson Design
Client: Aravis Distilleries

526
Art Director: Edward Walter
Carrie Berman
Designer: Carrie Berman
Illustrator: Jack J. Mortensbak
Carrie Berman
Studio: Edward Walter Design
Client: PC Magazine

527
Art Director: Lanny Sommese
Creative Director: Lanny Sommese
Designer: Lanny Sommese
Illustrator: Lanny Sommese
Agency: Lanny Sommese Design
Client: Penn State Department of Architecture

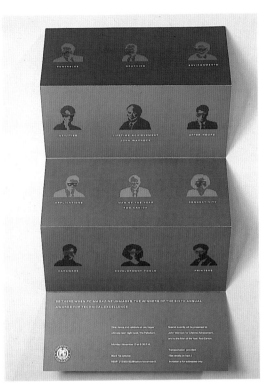

528
Art Director: Ron Sullivan
Creative Director: Ron Sullivan
Mark Perkins
Designer: Jon Flaming
Illustrator: Steven Guarnaccia
Jon Flaming
Copywriter: Mark Perkins
Studio: Sullivan Perkins
Client: Dallas Society of Visual Comm.

529
Art Director: Linda Decker
Creative Director: Andrew Kner
Designer: Linda Decker
Illustrator: John Alcorn
Copywriter: CBS
Agency: Backer, Spielvogel, Bates
Client: CBS

530

Art Director: Jack Anderson
Creative Director: Jack Anderson
Designer: Jack Anderson
　　　　　David Bates
Photographer: Jim Laser
Copywriter: Basho
Agency: Hornall Anderson Design Works
Client: Jim Laser

531

Art Director: Jack Anderson
Creative Director: Jack Anderson
Designer: Jack Anderson
　　　　　David Bates
Photographer: Jim Laser
Copywriter: Louis Kahn
Agency: Hornall Anderson Design Works
Client: Jim Laser

532

Art Director: E. D. Corra
　　　　　　Cynthia Kerby
Designer: E. D. Corra
　　　　　Cynthia Kerby
Photographer: Peter Rosenbaum
Copywriter: Cynthia Kerby
　　　　　　E. D. Corra
Studio: Two Ideas
Client: Unique Printers & Lithographers

533
Art Director: Michael R. Orr
Designer: Michael R. Orr
Client: Corning Inc.

534
Art Director: Seymour Chwast
Designer: Greg Simpson
Agency: The Pushpin Group
Client: Solo Editions, Inc.

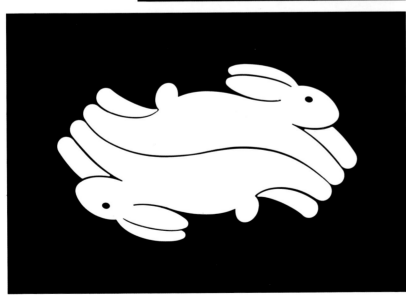

535
Art Director: Michael McGinn
             Takaaki Matsumoto
Designer: Michael McGinn
Illustrator: Jack Tom
Studio: M Plus M Inc.
Client: Rebo Research, Inc.

536
Art Director: Woody Pirtle
Designer: Woody Pirtle
Studio: Pentagram Design
Client: Fox River Paper

537
Art Director: James A. Stygar
Creative Director: James A. Stygar
Designer: James A. Stygar
Agency: Stygar Group, Inc.
Client: Micro Magnetic, Inc.

538
Art Director: Thom Smith
 Gregg Frederickson
Designer: Gregg Frederickson
Illustrator: Gregg Frederickson
Studio: Smith Group
Client: Ted Nelson Co.

539
Art Director: Thom Marchionna
Creative Director: Thom Marchionna
Designer: Thom Marchionna
Agency: The Town Criers
Client: Cass Street Optometric Center

540
Art Director: Mark Steele
            Randy Presson
Designer: Mark Steele
Studio: Steele/Presson
Client: Advantage Marketing

541
Art Director: Lee-Anne Setterington
Creative Director: Marc Gobé
Designer: Lee-Anne Setterington
Studio: Cato Gobé
Client: Sergio

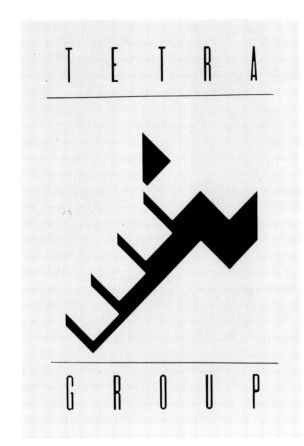

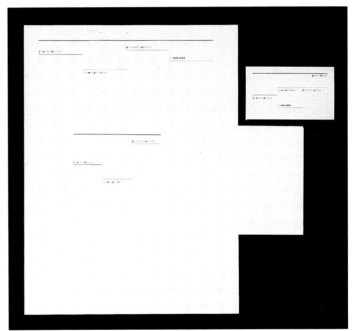

542
Art Director: Jon Anders Bjornson
Creative Director: Jon Anders Bjornson
Designer: Jon Anders Bjornson
Studio: Jon Anders Bjornson Design
Client: Jon Anders Bjornson Design

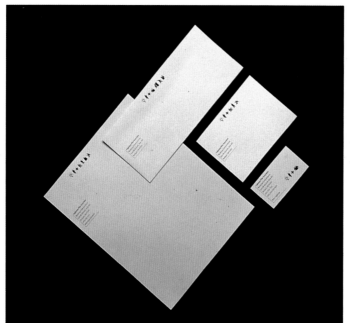

543
Art Director: Thom Smith
Designer: Thom Smith
            Gregg Frederickson
Illustrator: Gregg Frederickson
Studio: Smith Group
Client: Robert Lightman

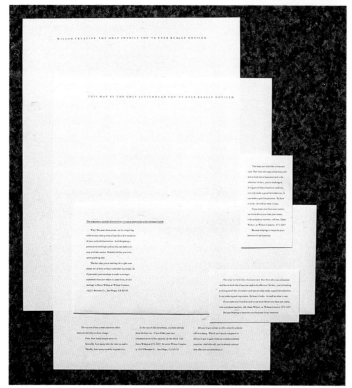

544
Art Director: Daniel C. Wilson
Creative Director: Daniel C. Wilson
Designer: Daniel C. Wilson
Copywriter: Cam Davis
Agency: Wilson Creative Services
Client: Wilson Creative Services

545
Art Director: Ward Pennebaker
Designer: Ward Pennebaker
Studio: Pennebaker Design
Client: Vine Arts Mapping Co.

546
Art Director: Minoru Morita
Designer: Minoru Morita

547
Art Director: Don Trousdell
Designer: Don Trousdell

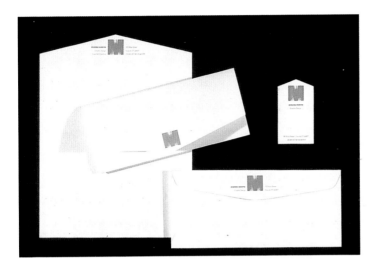

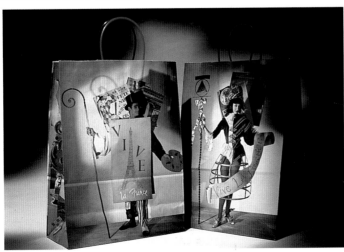

548
Art Director: Robert Valentine
Designer: Robert Valentine
Photographer: Geof Kern
Copywriter: Amie Valentine

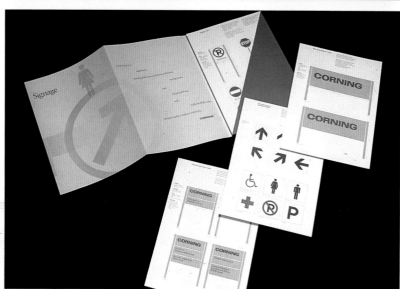

549
Art Director: Frederick Murrell
Designer: Frederick Murrell
Douglas Harp
William Lucas
Illustrator: William Lucas
Copywriter: David Bellin
Rhonda Morton

550
Art Director: Fabrizio La Rocca
Creative Director: Vignelli Associates
Designer: Frank Fasano
Illustrator: David Linroth, Inc.
Karl Tanner
Photographer: Various
Publication: Fodor's Travel Publications, Inc.

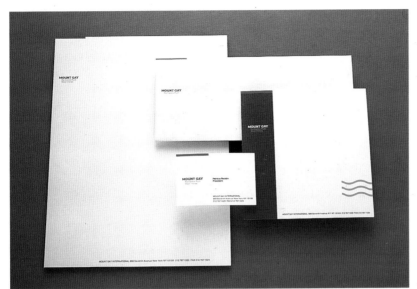

551
Art Director: Linda Pierro
Designer: Linda Pierro
Studio: Fountainhead Productions
Client: Mount Gay International

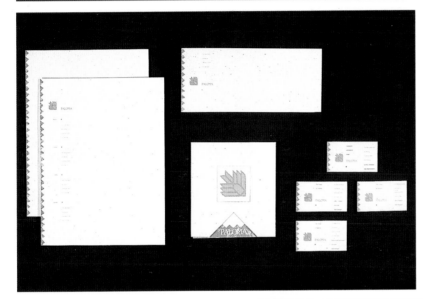

552
Art Director: Martin Stevers
Designer: Martin Stevers
Illustrator: Jennifer Hewitson
Photographer: Dave Harrison
Copywriter: Ken Alfrey
Studio: Grayson
Client: The Baldwin Co.

553
Art Director: Woody Pirtle
Designer: Woody Pirtle
Agency: Pentagram Design
Client: Crossroads Films

554
Art Director: Keith Bright
Designer: Wilson Ong
Agency: Bright & Associates
Client: Andresen Typographics

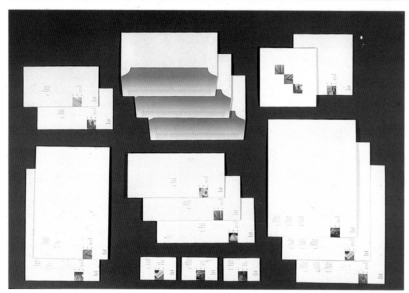

555
Art Director: Martin Stevers
Designer: Martin Stevers
            Catherine Rainbolt
Studio: Grayson
Client: RGC

556
Art Director: Sharon Werner
Designer: Sharon Werner
Illustrator: Charles Burns
              Sharon Werner
Copywriter: Chuck Carlson
Studio: The Duffy Group
Client: Fox River Paper

C A R R O T

AN IMPORTANT SOURCE OF VITAMIN A.

SOW SEEDS IN LOOSE, WELL-DRAINED SOIL

TO ENCOURAGE GOOD ROOT DEVELOPMENT.

FULL GROWTH IS OBTAINED IN 75 TO 90 DAYS.

PULL UP A SNAPPY SPRING TERM SCHEDULE.

BYU REGISTRATION DEADLINE — APRIL 15.

R A D I S H

GROWS BEST IN COOL BUT SUNNY
WEATHER. PLANT SEEDS ONE-HALF INCH
DEEP. THIN SEEDLINGS TO ONE INCH
APART, AND HARVEST IN ABOUT 24 DAYS.
RELISH A SAVORY SPRING TERM SCHEDULE.
COMPLETE YOUR REGISTRATION TODAY.

R E D   B E E T

RICH IN IRON, THIS HEARTY BIENNIAL
WAS FIRST CULTIVATED FOR ITS LEAFY
TOP. EASY TO GROW, BUT PREFERS COOL
WEATHER. SOW SEEDS ONE-HALF INCH DEEP.
DON'T BE A DEADBEET. MAIL FEES NOW.
SUMMER TERM TUITION DEADLINE—JUNE 7.

557 Gold

Art Director: McRay Magleby
Creative Director: McRay Magleby
Designer: McRay Magleby
Copywriter: Norman Darais
Studio: BYU Graphics

DROP OUT OF SCHOOL AND YOU CAN STILL GET A JOB ON WALL STREET.

© 1989 BURGER KING CORPORATION

NOURISH YOUR MIND.
— STAY IN SCHOOL —

DROP OUT OF SCHOOL AND YOU'LL STILL HAVE TO GO TO WORK IN A SUIT.

DROP OUT OF SCHOOL AND YOU COULD COME OUT SMELLING LIKE A ROSE.

SO WHAT. DID SHE EVER WIN A HOMBURG?

Announcing The 9th Annual Homburg Awards ⋅ Sponsored By The Advertising Club Of San Diego

YEAH. BUT DID HE EVER WIN A HOMBURG?

Announcing The 9th Annual Homburg Awards ⋅ Sponsored By The Advertising Club Of San Diego

IMPRESSIVE. BUT DID SHE EVER WIN A HOMBURG?

Announcing The 9th Annual Homburg Awards ⋅ Sponsored By The Advertising Club Of San Diego

Handy packets of spirulina and natural energizers. For when you need a lift.

Handy packets of spirulina and natural energizers. For those demanding sports.

Handy packets of Spirulina and natural energizers. Stamina for the big event.

Unclogs major arteries.

Porsche 911 Carrera

(Dealer Name)

Some women will never talk to anyone about being abused.

L.A. BATTERING HOTLINE (213) 392-8381

Art Director: Wendy Hansen
Creative Director: Lyle Wedemeyer
Photographer: Kerry Peterson
Copywriter: Lyle Wedemeyer
Agency: Martin/Williams
Client: Minnesota Department of Health

Art Director: Wendy Hansen
Creative Director: Lyle Wedemeyer
Photographer: Rick Dublin
Copywriter: Lyle Wedemeyer
Agency: Martin/Williams
Client: Minnesota Department of Health

565 Distinctive Merit
Art Director: Jon Lee
Marty Weiss
Creative Director: Bill Hamilton
Photographer: Mark Weiss
Copywriter: Paula Dombrow
Robin Raj
Agency: Chiat/Day/Mojo Advertising Inc.
Client: NYNEX Information Resources

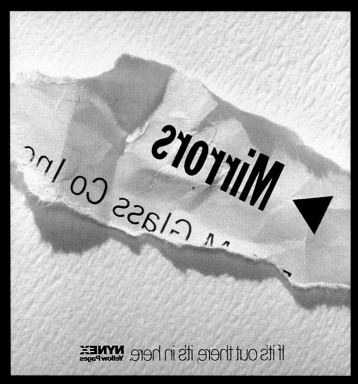

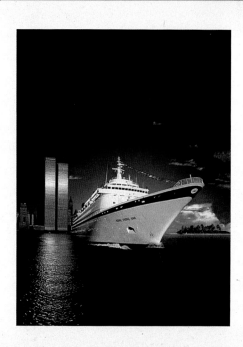

566 Distinctive Merit
Art Director: Rich Silverstein
Creative Director: Jeffrey Goodby
Rich Silverstein
Designer: Betsy Zimmermann
Photographer: Jay Maisel
Copywriter: David Fowler
Agency: Goodby, Berlin & Silverstein
Client: Royal Viking Line

567 Distinctive Merit
Art Director: Jon Lee
Marty Weiss
Creative Director: Bill Hamilton
Photographer: Mark Weiss
Copywriter: Paula Dombrow
Robin Raj
Agency: Chiat/Day/Mojo Advertising Inc.
Client: NYNEX Information Resources

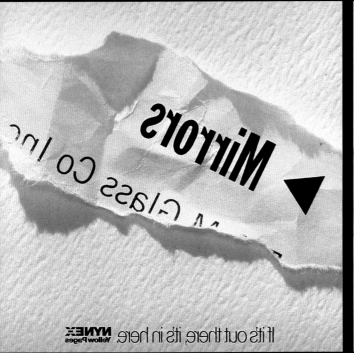

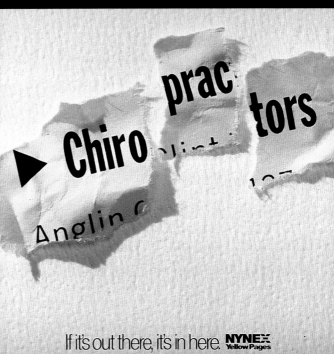

BRECHT'S "DRUMS IN THE NIGHT"
OHIO THEATRE 66 WOOSTER STREET SOHO NYC
NOV 23 - DEC 3 TUESDAY - SUNDAY AT 8.00 PM
$10 (STUDENTS & SENIORS $6) RES: (212) 924 0415
THANKSGIVING PERFORMANCE AND FEAST $26 ($15)
CHAMPAGNE BENEFIT PERFORMANCE (THURSDAY NOV 30) $25
TEXT TRANSLATION BY WILLIAM E SMITH AND RALPH MANHEIM
TINY MYTHIC THEATRE COMPANY   AN EQUITY APPROVED SHOWCASE

TINY MYTHIC THEATRE COMPANY
KRISTIN AMES FRANCINE ZERFAS KRISTIN MARTING
TIM MANER WITH DAVID BEACH* BRIAN BENDLIN LOREN KIDD
DANIEL BLACKMAN CALVIN CHURCHMAN MARTY FINKELSTEIN
CINDY DORREL GEORGE FEASTER* DAVID MAIER JOHN MILLER
JAMES FERGUSON ABIGAIL GAMPEL RICHARD MORTIMER*
NOAH GARDINER STEVEN CHESLIK-DEMEYER JENI STERNBERG
*APPEARS COURTESY OF THE ACTORS' EQUITY ASSOCIATION

A GERMAN COMEDY

568 Distinctive Merit
Art Director: Nick Cohen
Copywriter: Ty Montague
Agency: Chiat/Day/Mojo Advertising Inc.
Client: Pointed Stick Theater

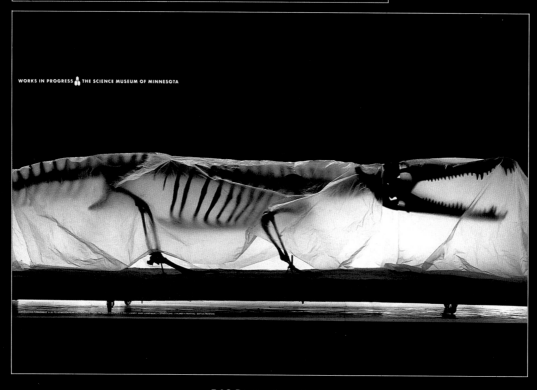

WORKS IN PROGRESS ⚗ THE SCIENCE MUSEUM OF MINNESOTA

569 Distinctive Merit
Art Director: David Steinlicht
Creative Director: Mark Odegard
Designer: David Steinlicht
Photographer: Mark Luinenburg
Client: Minnesota Science Museum

570 Distinctive Merit
Art Director: McRay Magleby
Creative Director: McRay Magleby
Designer: McRay Magleby
Copywriter: Norman Darais
Studio: BYU Graphics

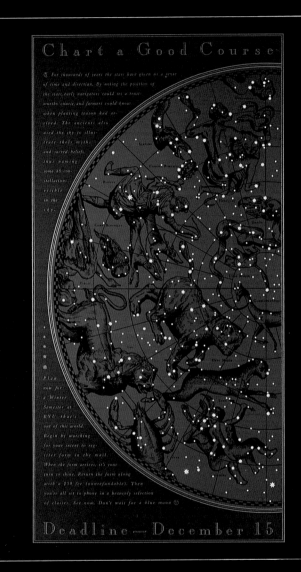

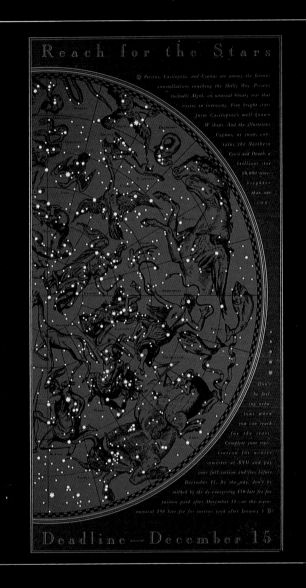

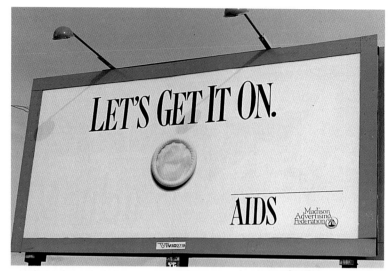

571
Art Director: Mike Martin
Creative Director: Jim Armstrong
Photographer: Shawn Harper
Copywriter: Jim Armstrong
Agency: Armstrong Creative
Client: Madison Advertising Federation

572
Art Director: David Meador
Creative Director: David Hale
Copywriter: Alison Grant

573
Art Director: Mark Johnson
Photographer: Jeff Zwart
Copywriter: Tom McElligott
Agency: Fallon McElligott
Client: Porsche

574
Art Director: Jeff Weekley
Creative Director: John Armistead
Illustrator: Stan Watts
Copywriter: Pieter Dreiband
Agency: DMB&B

575
Art Director: Vickery Eckhoff
Creative Director: Vickery Eckhoff
Copywriter: Vickery Eckhoff
Client: Friends of Animals

576
Art Director: Mike Martin
Creative Director: Jim Armstrong
Photographer: Shawn Harper
Copywriter: Jim Armstrong
Agency: Armstrong Creative
Client: Madison Advertising Federation

577
Art Director: Gretchen van der Grinten
Janet Boye
Photographer: Davies & Starr
Copywriter: Sarah Person
Agency: Conran's Habitat

578
Art Director: Mark Johnson
Creative Director: Tom McElligott
Photographer: Jeff Zwart
Copywriter: Tom McElligott
Agency: Fallon McElligott
Client: Porsche

579
Art Director: Silas H. Rhodes
Creative Director: Silas H. Rhodes
Designer: Tony Palladino
Illustrator: Tony Palladino
Copywriter: Dee Ito
Studio: School of Visual Arts Press
Client: School of Visual Arts

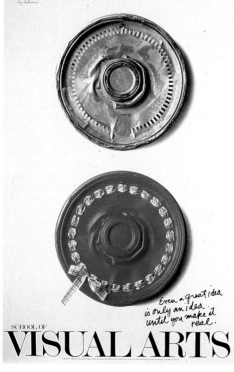

580
Art Director: Peter Favat
Designer: Don Pogany
       Peter Favat
Photographer: Dwight Olmsted
Copywriter: Don Pogany
Agency: Ingalls, Quinn & Johnson
Client: Institute of Contemporary Art

581
Art Director: Raul Pina
Creative Director: Jamie Seltzer
Photographer: Jim Galante
Copywriter: David Bernstein
Client: New York Mets

582
Art Director: Joe DelVecchio
Creative Director: John Morrison
Sharon Vanderslice
Copywriter: Sharon Vanderslice
Agency: Della Femina, McNamee WCRS
Client: Pan Am

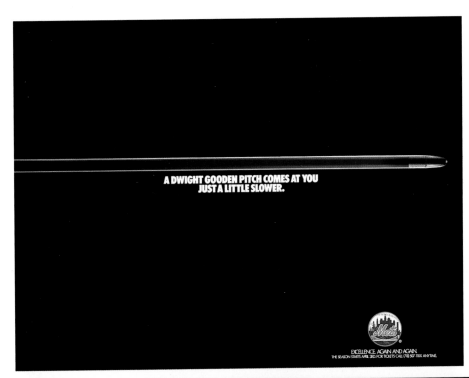

583
Art Director: Raul Pina
Creative Director: Jamie Seltzer
Copywriter: David Bernstein
Agency: Della Femina, McNamee WCRS
Client: New York Mets

584
Art Director: Steve Sweitzer
Designer: Steve Sweitzer
Photographer: Ben Saltzman
Copywriter: Jarl Olsen
Agency: Fallon McElligott
Client: Ben Saltzman

585
Art Director: David Fox
Creative Director: Jac Coverdale
Designer: David Fox
Photographer: Mark LaFavor
Copywriter: Joe Alexander
Agency: Clarity, Coverdale, Rueff
Client: City of Minneapolis Recycling

586
Art Director: David Fox
Creative Director: Jac Coverdale
Designer: David Fox
Photographer: Mark LaFavor
Copywriter: Joe Alexander
Agency: Clarity, Coverdale, Rueff
Client: City of Minneapolis Recycling

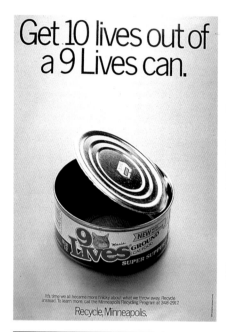

588
Art Director: Jon Lee
　　　　　　Marty Weiss
Creative Director: Bill Hamilton
Photographer: Mark Weiss
Copywriter: Paula Dombrow
　　　　　　Robin Raj
Agency: Chiat/Day/Mojo Advertising Inc.
Client: NYNEX Information Resources

587
Art Director: David Fox
Creative Director: Jac Coverdale
Designer: David Fox
Photographer: Mark LaFavor
Copywriter: Joe Alexander
Agency: Clarity, Coverdale, Rueff
Client: City of Minneapolis Recycling

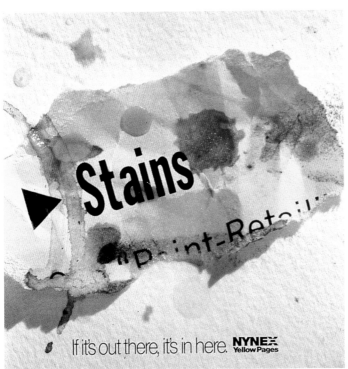

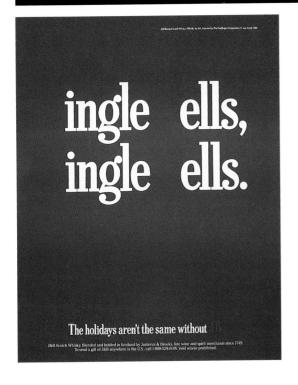

589
Art Director: Jon Lee
　　　　　　　Marty Weiss
Creative Director: Bill Hamilton
Photographer: Mark Weiss
Copywriter: Paula Dombrow
　　　　　　Robin Raj
Agency: Chiat/Day/Mojo Advertising Inc.
Client: NYNEX Information Resources

590
Art Director: Jon Lee
　　　　　　　Marty Weiss
Creative Director: Bill Hamilton
Photographer: Mark Weiss
Copywriter: Paula Dombrow
　　　　　　Robin Raj
Agency: Chiat/Day/Mojo Advertising Inc.
Client: NYNEX Information Resources

591
Art Director: Jon Lee
　　　　　　　Marty Weiss
Creative Director: Bill Hamilton
Photographer: Mark Weiss
Copywriter: Paula Dombrow
　　　　　　Robin Raj
Agency: Chiat/Day/Mojo Advertising Inc.
Client: NYNEX Information Resources

592
Art Director: Chris Graves
Creative Director: Roy Grace
　　　　　　　　　Diane Rothschild
Copywriter: David Corr
Client: Paddington

593
Art Director: Richard Ostroff
Creative Director: Allan Beaver
           Lee Garfinkel
Photographer: Cailor/Resnick
Copywriter: Amy Borkowsky
Agency: Levine, Huntley, Schmidt & Beaver
Client: Ad Council

594
Art Director: Leslie Sweet
          Ernest Neira
Creative Director: Tony DeGregorio
Designer: Leslie Sweet
        Ernest Neira
Photographer: Mike Newler
Copywriter: Nat Russo
Agency: Levine, Huntley, Schmidt & Beaver
Client: Dreyfus

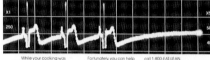

595
Art Director: Jon Lee
        Marty Weiss
Creative Director: Bill Hamilton
Photographer: Mark Weiss
Copywriter: Paula Dombrow
        Robin Raj
Agency: Chiat/Day/Mojo Advertising Inc.
Client: NYNEX Information Resources

596
Art Director: Alain Briere
Creative Director: John Morrison
　　　　　　　　Sharon Vanderslice
Copywriter: Sharon Vanderslice
Agency: Della Femina, McNamee WCRS
Client: Pan Am

597
Art Director: Raul Pina
Creative Director: Jamie Seltzer
Copywriter: David Bernstein
Agency: Della Femina, McNamee WCRS
Client: New York Mets

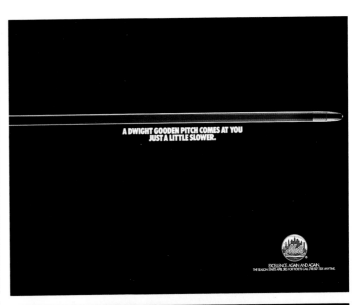

598
Art Director: Don Miller
Photographer: Stock
Copywriter: Don Miller
Agency: After Midnight Advertising
Client: Friends of Animals

599
Art Director: John Doyle
Creative Director: Edward Boches
      John Doyle
Photographer: Clint Clemens
Copywriter: Edward Boches
Agency: Mullen
Client: World Society for Protection of Animals

600
Art Director: Deborah Hepler
Creative Director: John Barrett
Designer: Deborah Giorno-Rivello
Illustrator: Bob Schenker
Copywriter: Deborah Giorno-Rivello
Client: Clement Communications, Inc.

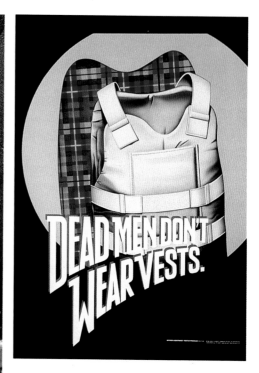

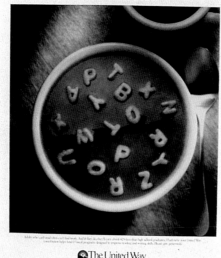

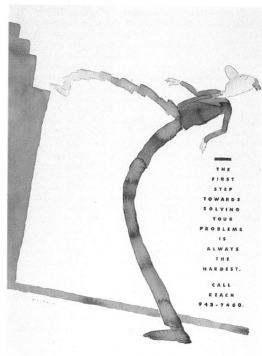

601
Art Director: Bill Winchester
Creative Director: George Halvorson
Photographer: Mark LaFavor
Copywriter: Joe Milla
Agency: CME
Client: United Way

602
Art Director: Lisa Bennett
Creative Director: Steve Nubie
Designer: R. O. Blechman
Illustrator: R. O. Blechman
Copywriter: Bill Cokas
Studio: R. O. Blechman, Inc.
Client: Reach

603
Art Director: Bill Winchester
Creative Director: George Halvorson
Photographer: Tom Berthiaume
　　　　　　　　Mark LaFavor
Copywriter: Joe Milla
Agency: CME
Client: United Way

He's already lived through one great depression. Old age shouldn't be another.

The United Way

Ignore a problem and it can only get bigger.

The United Way

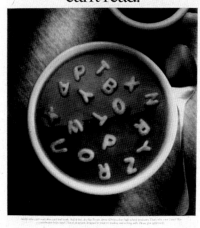

What a job application looks like to someone who can't read.

The United Way

WHY GIVE WHEN HER FATHER WILL TAKE CARE OF HER.

PLEASE GIVE YOUR FAIR SHARE TO THE UNITED WAY

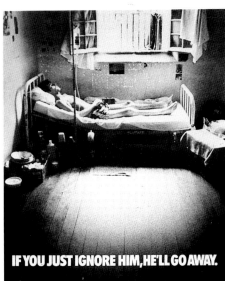

IF YOU JUST IGNORE HIM, HE'LL GO AWAY.

PLEASE GIVE YOUR FAIR SHARE TO THE UNITED WAY

SOME PEOPLE JUST CAN'T SAY NO TO DRUGS.

PLEASE GIVE YOUR FAIR SHARE TO THE UNITED WAY

604
Art Director: Kate Corr
Creative Director: Dave Clark
　　　　　　　　Charlie Breen
Photographer: Hans Neleman
　　　　　　　　Wide World Stock
Copywriter: Hilary Smith
Agency: Backer, Spielvogel, Bates

605
Art Director: Mickey Paxton
Creative Director: Jay Schulberg
Photographer: Nancy Moran
Copywriter: Mike Wilson
Agency: Bozell
Client: United Way

606
Art Director: Matt Myers
Creative Director: Jim Copacino
Copywriter: Jim Copacino
Agency: Livingston & Co.
Client: Alaska Airlines

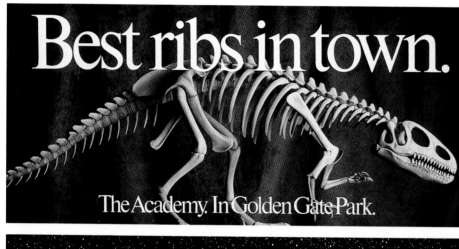

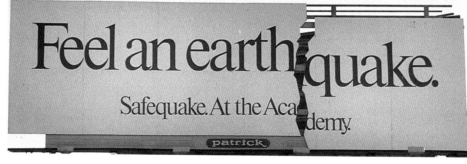

607
Art Director: Nick Cohen
Copywriter: Graham Turner
Agency: Chiat/Day/Mojo Advertising Inc.
Client: Pointed Stick Theater

608
Art Director: Kevin Lory Mote
Creative Director: Jim Anderson
Copywriter: Kevin Lory Mote
          Diana Hickerson
Agency: GSD&M Advertising
Client: The *Wall Street Journal*

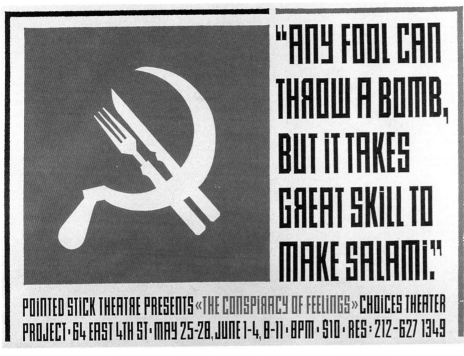

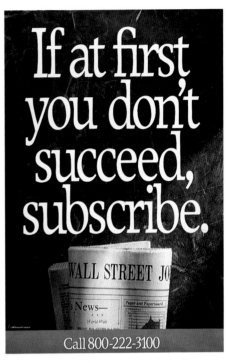

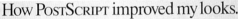

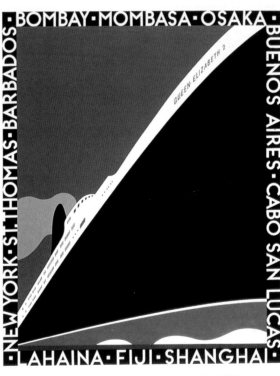

609
Art Director: Marty Neumeier
Designer: Marty Neumeier
          Chris Chu
Illustrator: Chris Chu
          Les Chibana
Copywriter: Marty Neumeier
Studio: Neumeier Design Team
Client: Adobe Systems Inc.

610
Art Director: Michael Schwab
Designer: Michael Schwab
Illustrator: Michael Schwab
Studio: Michael Schwab Design
Client: Bella Blue

611
Art Director: Mark Geer
Designer: Mark Geer
   Morgan Bomar
Copywriter: Pat Byers
Agency: Boswell Byers
Client: Decorative Center Houston

612
Art Director: Jerry McDaniel
Creative Director: Nina Krammer
Designer: Jerry McDaniel
Illustrator: Jerry McDaniel
Agency: Nike Communications
Client: Mouton-Cadet

613
Art Director: Alyn Carlson-Webster
Creative Director: Jason Grant
Photographer: Photocoloratura
   Stock
Copywriter: Marc Braunstein
Agency: Jason Grant Associates
Client: Gant

614
Art Director: Olga Kaljakin
Creative Director: Tony Seiniger
   Mike Kaiser
Photographer: Merrick Morton
Agency: Seiniger Advertising
Client: Tri-Star/Columbia Pictures

615
Art Director: Michael Prieve
Creative Director: Dan Wieden
                   David Kennedy
Copywriter: Jim Riswold
Agency: Wieden & Kennedy
Client: Nike

616
Art Director: Bob Brihn
Creative Director: Pat Burnham
Designer: Bob Brihn
Photographer: Rick Dublin
Copywriter: Jarl Olsen
Agency: Fallon McElligott
Client: Power Pac

617
Art Director: Pam Cunningham
Creative Director: Lee Clow
Agency: Chiat/Day/Mojo
Client: Nissan

618
Art Director: Warren Eakins
Creative Director: Dan Wieden
                   David Kennedy
Agency: Wieden & Kennedy
Client: Nike

619

Art Director: Matt Canzano
Creative Director: Joe Sciarrotta
                    Tenney Fairchild
Illustrator: Douglas Fraser
Copywriter: Dave Merhar
Agency: J. Walter Thompson
Client: Miller Brewing Co.

620

Art Director: Paul Davis
Illustrator: Paul Davis
Client: New York Shakespeare Festival

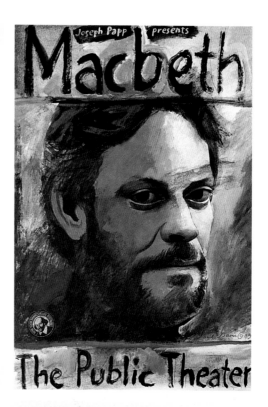

621

Art Director: Rob Biro
Creative Director: Cindy L. Hauser
Designer: Rob Biro
Photographer: Ron Derhacopian
Agency: B.D. Fox & Friends, Inc.
Client: Twentieth Century Fox TV

622

Art Director: Tim Fisher
                Chris Robb
Photographer: Lee Crum
Copywriter: Tim Fisher
              Chris Robb
Agency: Carmichael Lynch

623
Art Director: Lowell Williams
Creative Director: Lowell Williams
Designer: Lowell Williams
　　　　　Andy Dearwater
Illustrator: Andy Dearwater
Copywriter: JoAnn Stone
Studio: Lowell Williams Design Inc.
Client: Hedrich Blessing

624
Art Director: Milton Glaser
Designer: Milton Glaser
Agency: Milton Glaser, Inc.
Client: The Society of Newspaper Design

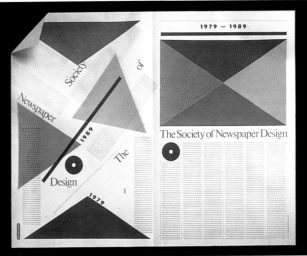

625
Art Director: Onofrio Paccione
Creative Director: Onofrio Paccione
Designer: Onofrio Paccione
Photographer: Onofrio Paccione
Studio: Paccione Photography
Client: Type Directors Club

626
Art Director: Charles S. Anderson
　　　　　Dan Olson
Designer: Charles S. Anderson
　　　　　Dan Olson
Illustrator: Charles S. Anderson
　　　　　Randy Dahlk
Studio: Charles S. Anderson Design
Client: French Paper Co.

627
Art Director: Charles S. Anderson
Designer: Charles S. Anderson
Illustrator: Japanese Menko Cards
Studio: Charles S. Anderson Design
Client: Ginza Graphic Gallery

628
Art Director: Charles S. Anderson
Designer: Charles S. Anderson
      Dan Olson
Illustrator: Charles S. Anderson
      Randy Dahlk
Copywriter: Lisa Pemrick
Studio: Charles S. Anderson Design
Client: Charles S. Anderson Design

629
Art Director: Charles S. Anderson
      Dan Olson
Designer: Charles S. Anderson
      Dan Olson
Studio: Charles S. Anderson Design
Client: Minneapolis College of Art & Design

630
Art Director: McRay Magleby
Creative Director: McRay Magleby
Designer: McRay Magleby
Copywriter: Norman Darais
Studio: BYU Graphics

631
Art Director: Don Sibley
Designer: Don Sibley
Illustrator: Don Sibley
Agency: Dancie Ware, Houston
Studio: Sibley/Peteet Design
Client: Galveston Park Board of Trustees

632
Art Director: Jane Kasstrin
　　　　　David Sterling
Creative Director: Jane Kasstrin
　　　　　David Sterling
Designer: Jane Kasstrin
　　　　　David Sterling
Photographer: Geoff Spear
Studio: Doublespace
Client: American Express Publishing Corp.

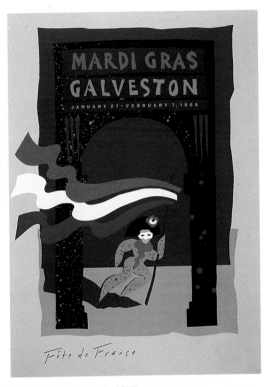

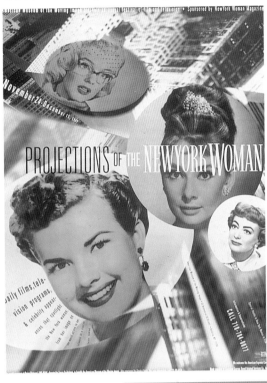

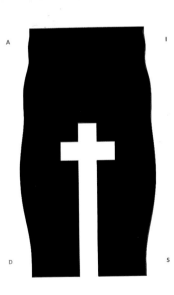

633
Art Director: Neal Posener
Designer: Neal Posener
Illustrator: John Jinks
Agency: Russek Advertising
Client: Playwright Horizons

634
Art Director: McRay Magleby
Creative Director: McRay Magleby
Designer: McRay Magleby
Copywriter: Norman Darais
Agency: BYU Graphics

635
Art Director: Rex Peteet
Designer: Rex Peteet
Illustrator: John Evans
Studio: Sibley/Peteet Design
Client: Sibley/Peteet Design

636
Art Director: Fred Woodward
Designer: Fred Woodward
           Gail Anderson

637
Art Director: Linda Sullivan
Designer: Linda Sullivan
Studio: BYU Graphics
Client: BYU

638
Art Director: Charles S. Anderson
Designer: Charles S. Anderson
Illustrator: Charles S. Anderson
            Lynn Schulte
Studio: The Duffy Group
Client: STA Chicago

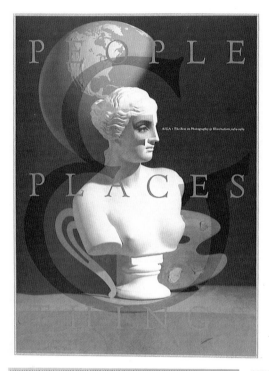

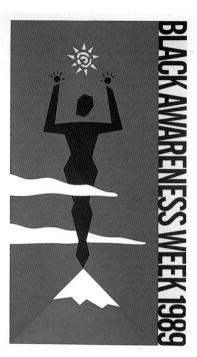

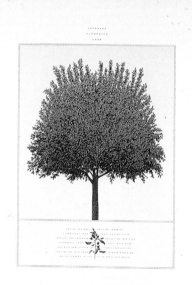

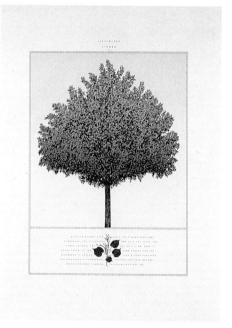

639
Art Director: Don Weller
Creative Director: Don Weller
Designer: Don Weller
Illustrator: Don Weller
Copywriter: Don Weller
Studio: The Weller Institute
Client: TDCTJHTBIPC

640
Art Director: McRay Magleby
Creative Director: McRay Magleby
Designer: McRay Magleby
Copywriter: Norman Darais
Studio: BYU Graphics

641

Art Director: Charles S. Anderson
Designer: Charles S. Anderson
Illustrator: Charles S. Anderson
                Lynn Schulte
Studio: The Duffy Group
Client: French Paper Co.

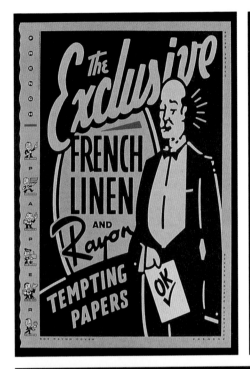

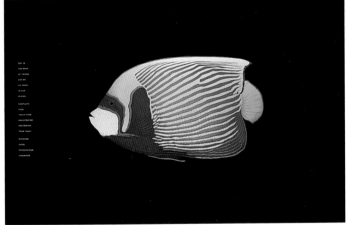

642

Art Director: McRay Magleby
Creative Director: McRay Magleby
Designer: McRay Magleby
Copywriter: Norman Darais
Studio: BYU Graphics

Public phone. Private moment. Lee jeans.

643
Art Director: Mark Johnson
Creative Director: Pat Burnham
Photographer: Kurt Markus
Copywriter: Bill Miller
Agency: Fallon McElligott
Client: Lee Jeans

Four day weekend. Fifth day. Lee jeans.

9 O'clock date. 8:55. Lee jeans.

You always come back to the basics. JIM BEAM

You always come back to the basics. JIM BEAM

You always come back to the basics. JIM BEAM

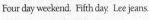

644
Art Director: Bob Barrie
Creative Director: Pat Burnham
Designer: Bob Barrie
Photographer: Rick Dublin
                Kerry Peterson
Copywriter: Jarl Olsen
Agency: Fallon McElligott
Client: Jim Beam

BOOKS & JACKETS

645 Silver

Art Director: Fred Woodward
Designer: Fred Woodward
Photographer: Various
Publication: Simon and Schuster

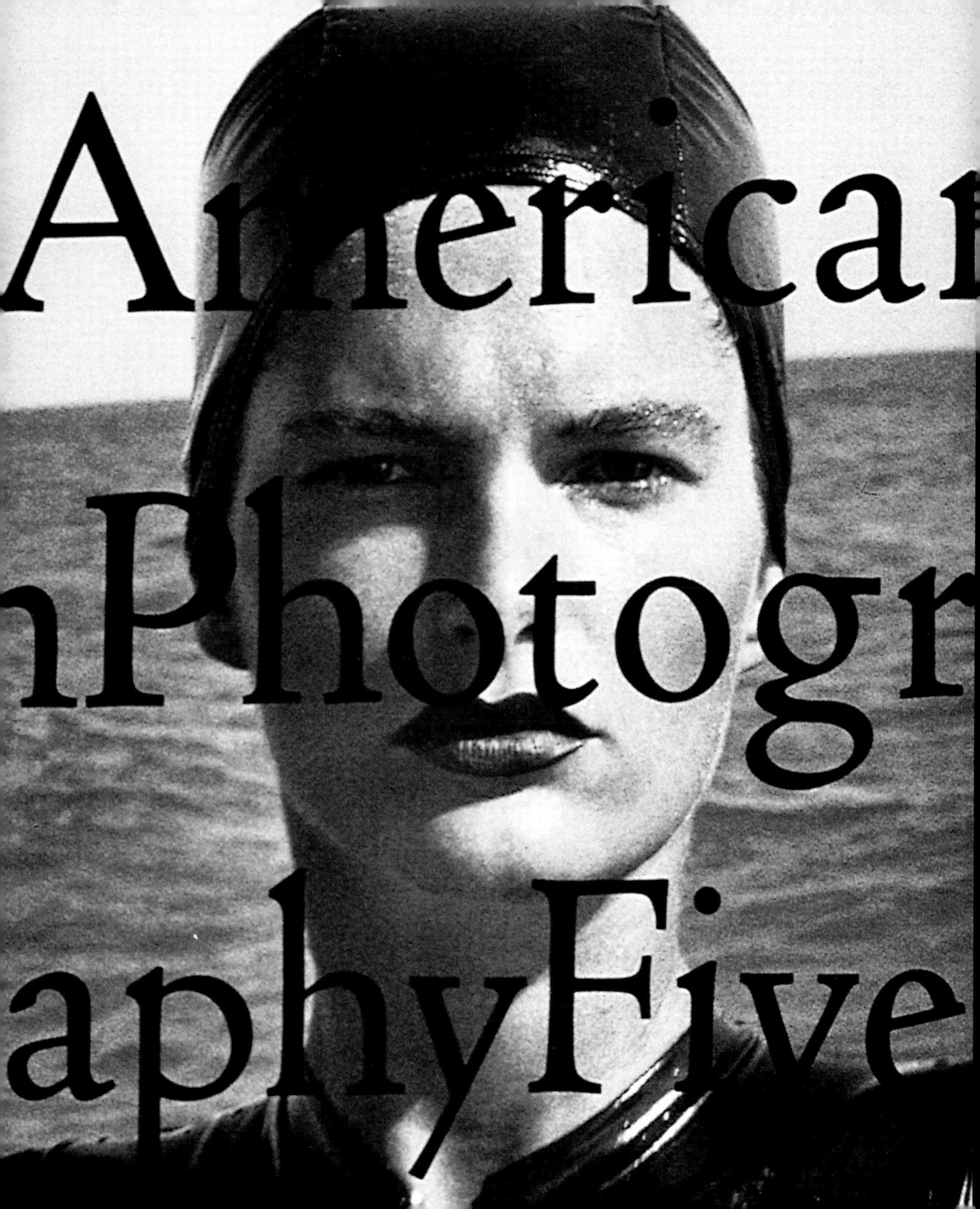

American

Photogr

aphyFive

ROLLINGSTONE

THE PHOTOGRAPHS

648
Art Director: Richard Eckersley
Studio: Nebraska University Press
Client: Nebraska University Press

649
Art Director: Samuel Antupit
Designer: Ray Konai

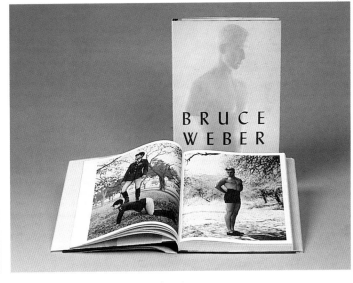

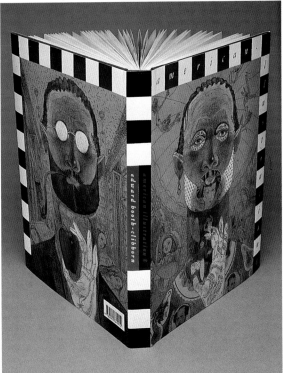

650
Art Director: Woody Pirtle
Illustrator: Jack Unruh
Studio: Pentagram Design
Client: American Illustration

651
Art Director: John Cheim
Designer: John Cheim

652

Art Director: Greg Samata
              Pat Samata
Designer: Greg Samata
              Pat Samata
Illustrator: Paul Thompson
Copywriter: Steve Huggins
Client: Samata Associates

653

Art Director: Diane Jaroch
Designer: Diane Jaroch
Illustrator: Various
Copywriter: Roger Remington
              Barbara Hodik
Studio: The MIT Press Design Department
Client: The MIT Press

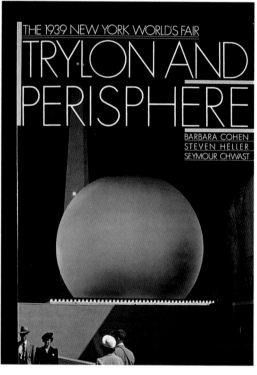

654

Art Director: Nancy Garruba
Designer: Nancy Garruba
Client: Blue House Press

655

Art Director: Samuel Antupit
Creative Director: Seymour Chwast
Designer: Seymour Chwast
              Roxanne Slimak
Photographer: Reven Wurman
Studio: The Pushpin Group
Client: Harry N. Abrams, Inc.

656
Art Director: Jennifer Barry
Designer: Jennifer Barry
          Charles Tyrone
Photographer: Various
Copywriter: David DeVoss
Client: Collins Publishers

657
Art Director: Don McQuiston
Creative Director: Don McQuiston
Designer: Don McQuiston
Photographer: John Oldenkamp
          Cynthia Sabransky
Agency: McQuiston & Partners
Publication: Chronicle Books

658
Art Director: Paula Scher
Creative Director: Paula Scher
Designer: Paula Scher
Illustrator: Various
Photographer: Various
Studio: Koppel & Scher
Client: Avon Books

659
Art Director: James Wageman
Designer: James Wageman
Publication: Abbeville Press, Inc.

660
Art Director: Jackie Merri Meyer
Creative Director: Jackie Merri Meyer
Designer: Charles S. Anderson
Client: Warner Books

661
Art Director: Neil Stuart
Designer: Neil Stuart
Illustrator: Chris Gall
Client: Viking Penguin

662
Art Director: Neil Stuart
Designer: Neil Stuart
Illustrator: Raphael & Bolognese
Client: Viking Penguin

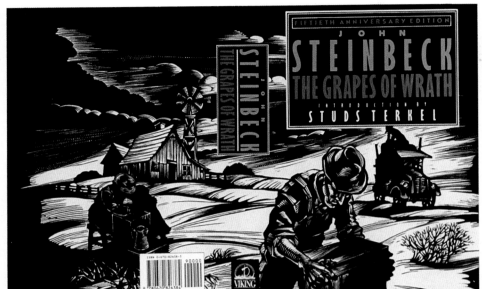

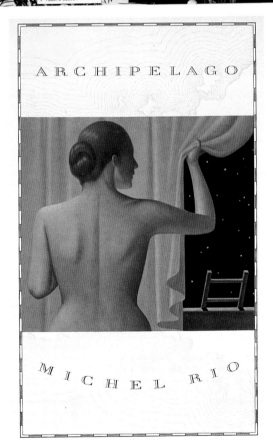

663
Art Director: Louise Fili
Designer: Louise Fili
Illustrator: Robert Goldstrom
Client: Pantheon Books

664
Art Director: Susan Mitchell
Designer: Marc J. Cohen
Photographer: Edward S. Ross

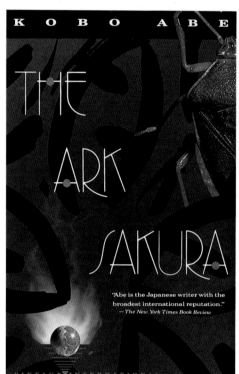

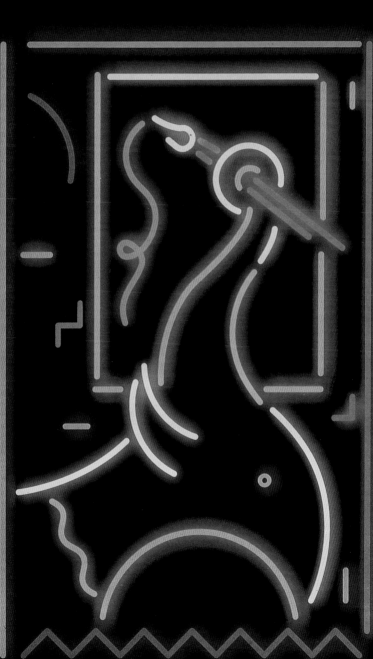

Zoo visitors, please remember: ugly animals like being looked at, too.

When you take a look at some of our not-exactly-what-you'd-call-cuddly animals here at the Zoo, always try to remember one thing.

Ugliness is in the eye of the beholder.

Please keep this in mind when you first behold the warthog.

The bat is one of the most misunderstood mammals. Nature needs fruit bats to help pollinate plants.

The warthog may look a little odd to you. But, in nature, almost everything has its purpose.

Take those lumpy bumps on the sides of a warthog's head (it's not called a warthog for nothing, you know). They protect the warthog as it digs up the ground

Don't think of it as a large nose. Think of it as a small air filter and heater.

looking for tasty roots.

And they also protect the males when they bang their heads together to compete for a female.

The warthog also has a stringy, scraggly tail that sticks up in the air when it runs. Some people think that it acts like a little flag to the other warthogs running behind in the tall grasses.

So you see?

Ugly to you, maybe. Very useful to a warthog.

WARTHOG
Weight: up to 200lbs.
Length: 5' Height: 28"at shoulder
Tusks: Upper pair can curl upward
to 12" or more in length.

After you've seen all you want to see of the warthog, walk over to Hoof and Horn Mesa and look for an animal called the Russian saiga (you can't miss it, just look for a big nose).

In Siberia where the saiga lives, it's bitter cold in the winter and very dusty in the summer. When the saiga breathes, the large nose works as a heater and air filter.

TWO-HEADED SKINK

If you're a skink's enemy, you're never really sure which end to attack first.

Over on the other side of the Zoo, stop by Reptile Mesa where we have the tortoises and alligators. And check out the two-headed skink.

So named because its back end looks like its front end, and vice versa.

In the wild, this tends to confuse a skink's enemy, at least long enough for the skink to get both of its ends out of there.

Why don't you come and see some of these things for yourself?

When you find out why some animals are different-looking, maybe you'll start looking at them a little differently.

*What big eyes a gecko has.
All the better to see you with at night, my dear.*

And then you'll feel the way we do. That there's really no such thing as an ugly animal.

Although the warthog comes very, very close.

Just when you thought you'd seen everything.
The San Diego Zoo

An amazing thing happens when you put animals in a natural setting. They act natural.

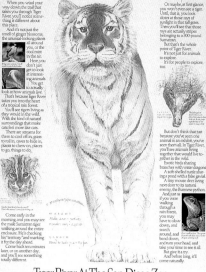

When you wind your way down the trail that takes you through Tiger River, you'll notice something is different about this place.

And it's not just the smell of ginger blossoms, the unusual-looking plants all around you, or the cool mist in the air.

Here you don't just get to look at interesting animals. You get to actually look at how animals live.

That's because Tiger River takes you into the heart of a tropical rain forest.

You'll see tigers living as they would in the wild. With the kind of natural surroundings that make cats feel more like cats.

There are streams for them to cool off in, grass to roll in, caves to hide in, plants to chew on, places to go, things to do.

Come early in the morning, and you may see the male Sumatran tiger walking around the entire enclosure. He's checking his "territory" and marking it for the day ahead.

Come back ten minutes later, or on another day, and you'll see something totally different.

Or maybe, at first glance, you won't even see a tiger. Until, that is, you look closer at those rays of sunlight in that tall grass. Then you'll see that those rays are actually stripes belonging to a 300-pound Sumatran.

But that's the whole point of Tiger River. It's not just for animals to explore. It's for people to explore, too.

But don't think that just because you've seen one animal in an exhibit, you've seen them all. In Tiger River, you'll see animals living together that would live together in the wild.

Exotic birds sharing branches with water dragons.

A soft-shelled turtle sharing a pond with a false gavial.

A tiny mouse deer living next door to its natural enemy, the Burmese python.

And just as if you were walking through a rain forest, you may have to slow down, and search around, and bend down, and turn your head, and take your time to see it all.

But give it a try. And before long, it'll come naturally.

Tiger River At The San Diego Zoo
Just when you thought you'd seen everything.

Pygmy hippos. Isn't that like saying jumbo shrimp?

Is this some sort of zoo-keeper joke?

How can there be such a thing as a pygmy hippo?

Well, as you walk out the exit of Tiger River, take a look at the enclosure right in front of you.

Then you go. It's a mini-hippo, all right.

The elephant shrew has a nose like an elephant. But it's nowhere near that size.

The pygmy hippo, even when fully grown, is about one-eighth the size of the river hippo.

The best time to see them (we've got two, a lovely couple) is early in the morning, after they've had breakfast.

They're most active then, and maybe you'll see them doing laps in their pool. (Sometimes they cheat and walk along the bottom. Wouldn't you, if you were a hippo?)

Some of the most interesting animals at the Zoo are on the small side.

If you can call a hippo small.

Over in the Children's Zoo, you can see the lesser panda.

Much smaller than the giant panda we're all familiar with, the lesser panda is about the size of a raccoon. In fact, it's actually related to the raccoon, with a masked face to prove it.

You know, we try not to play favorites here, but we

have to admit the lesser panda is right up there on the list of the cutest animals at the Zoo.

Speaking of small and cute, don't forget to see the new baby tiger in the Children's Zoo Nursery.

Then, when you leave the Children's Zoo, walk over to the Klauber-Shaw Reptile House and look for the poison arrow frogs. They're small—the drawing on this page is about actual size—but these little fellas are big-time dangerous.

They secrete a poison that's so powerful, natives in South America use it on the tips of their arrows.

Well, we still haven't mentioned the dwarf mongoose, the pygmy chimp, the mouse deer or the dwarf crocodile. You won't want to miss those. But enough small talk for now.

Come on out to the Zoo, and take a look at all kinds of animals. Big. Small. And in-between.

There's always something amazing to see, just when you thought you'd seen everything.

Small wonder, isn't it?

Just when you thought you'd seen everything.
The San Diego Zoo

THE MANY RECENT sightings of Elvis Presley have led to a new and illuminating line of inquiry: If Elvis is able to make appearances after his death, shouldn't he have been able to show up before his birth? ◠ He is, after all, the King. ◠ Exhaustive research has uncovered a wealth of evidence previously ignored by scholars who were distracted by events of lesser significance. ◠ Skeptics may choose to pooh-pooh the Peruvian mountain carvings – visible only by aircraft – in the shape of a teddy bear. They may dismiss as coincidence the fact that Inca priests of the period wore chains

Lausaux, France (left): The birth of rock. Not by any means the last time the King was criticized by Neanderthals. Carvings tell of a benevolent stranger who came out of nowhere, defeated the clan's enemies with martial arts and gave everybody a free home. Easter Island (right): The audience at the National Geographic Society began to cough and wheeze uncomfortably when forced to confront this picture. Some members of the Memphis Mafia have commented on Elvis's big head.

IN SEARCH of HISTORIC ELVIS

BY ALAN D. MAISLEN · ILLUSTRATIONS BY ANITA KUNZ

---

around their necks. ◠ The open-minded Elvisiologist (as opposed to the Preslisquarian, with his amateur faddism) can only sigh with tolerance. ◠ Naysayers cannot so easily abrogate the Rouen tapestry that depicts the martyrdom of Saint Joan of Arc. The figure in the background-was assumed to be a Burgundian bishop, chiefly because of his high-collared, gold-sequined robe and the fact that he seems to be sneering at Saint Joan. Embroidered along the bottom: Je veux un morceau d'amour brûlant. Loose translation: "I want a hunk, a hunk of burning love." ◠ Compelling evidence of Elvisitation may be seen in any of a thousand Asian jungles, from Cambodia to Japan. There it is commonplace to find great, ornate decaying temples. Should it surprise anyone that, for untold millenniums, these were sites where thousands of worshipers swooned before the imposing centerpiece: a giant statue of a man weighing over 300 pounds? ◠ And is it mere happenstance that these are the same cultures in which originated the art of painting on black velvet? ◠ Why hasn't this proof come to light sooner? A deliberate conspiracy to suppress it? The motive? Scientific ego, unwilling to give credit to the manifest contributions of the preternatural Presley. The most blatant example? The 1900 diaries of Walter Reed, the so-called father of

Region, Saigon (left): Just another Holy Joe? Seventy Iended the original version of much-bootlegged Living Last Sound Sessions circa 1810. Cabinaku, the inventors of rock by the medical age-old cleansing ritual, trated whose refreshingly remedies in the edifying reof the Orbon Surky, is safe known from the Vatican Library). Torre the devil he deserves, committing attempting in combination the Shroud of Turin entirely snotted up their clothing. Why? Look what their society, baking princes invaded? Napoleon reliable, Ireland.

cure for yellow fever. He describes his first patient: "Hands: shaking. Knees: weak. Can't seem to stand on own two feet. Lips: hot (like volcano). Patient delirious. Acts wildly, as if he were a hog. Question: Why is he all shook up?" ◠ Is it not curious that, weeks later, Reed should "discover" the cause of yellow fever to be a mosquito? And how peculiar that he should find it in Cuba, a land renowned for its "heavy trees." ◠ Only Elvis's characteristic modesty prevented him from taking credit for his many cross-cultural contributions, and even doubters agree it's a good thing Colonel Parker never contemplated the T-shirt rights. ◠ Should you embrace my theory, prepare to suffer the indignities inflicted on all who hold unpopular beliefs; for truly, the unwashed masses have yet to learn the golden rule: Don't be cruel. In fact, this author has been hounded into virtual seclusion, not unlike the post-Vegas Presley. ◠ Nevertheless, I have followed my dream and discovered a promising new course of study. Anybody's grandmother can claim to have seen Elvis sucking down a grape Slurpy at the local Bob's Big Boy years after his "death." Few, however, have bothered to look for the very real appearances of Elvis in inappropriate places while he was still alive. ◠ Just who was that shadowy pompadoured figure lurking on the Grassy Knoll? ◠ I'll never tell.

Should you embrace my theory, prepare to suffer the indignities inflicted on all who hold for the masses have yet to learn the golden rule: Don't be cruel.

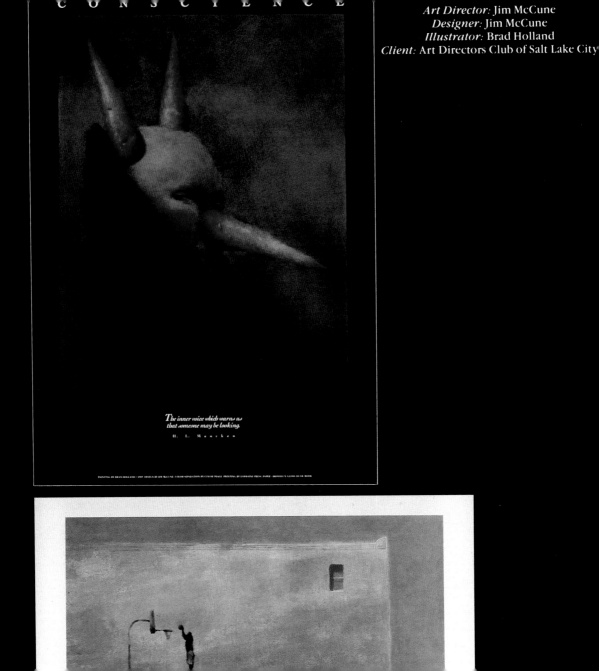

Art Director: Jim McCune
Designer: Jim McCune
Illustrator: Brad Holland
Client: Art Directors Club of Salt Lake City

GARLIC.

Garlic plants average 24" to 36" in height.

References to garlic date back thousands of years. Homer mentions it in the Odyssey & poets & writers through the ages have discussed its curative power.

Individual cloves are used as seed for new crop plantings.

Bulbs range in size from 1½" to 3" in diameter.

BASIC EARLY GARLIC
LE 4050

PART TWO: LIVING WITHOUT ENEMIES

Gorbachev wasn't just revolutionizing his own society; he was transforming ours as well. Since Stalin's day, the Soviets had played the perfect enemy. The evil Russian bear defined our national purpose and gave us a global mission. But here was Gorbachev declaring peace. Could we look at him and still see the face of the enemy? And what posed the greater threat, having an enemy or not having one? BY LAWRENCE WRIGHT

PEACE

ILLUSTRATIONS BY BRIAN CRONIN

HBO honchos are plotting America's first nonstop
comedy channel. MTV hopes to outwit them
with HA! TV. But can they keep the laughs coming?

EVERYBODY THINKS IT'S A REALLY GREAT JOKE, maybe the best one they've come up with so far. The only trouble is that the joke takes two months to set up.

Here's the idea: When HBO's Comedy Channel – the first all-day, all-night, all-the-time cable comedy station – begins broadcasting November 1st, it would have an official mascot: Happy the Duck. He'd show up in all the advertising and promotion, he'd be part of the logo (THE COMEDY CHANNEL – HONK!), he'd be personified on air as a guy dressed up in a duck suit. He'd be cute.

Too cute.

Actually, he'd be your worst nightmare, the kind of comedy cliché you might fear from such a twenty-four-hour station – only one step up from beetle-browed, big-nosed Groucho glasses.

So: All of the Comedy Channel hosts would hate Happy the Duck. They'd get annoyed whenever he turned up on their shows. Over time it would become clear that the official mascot was not working out. The guy in the duck suit would skulk around in the background, not even bothering to put on his duck head. He'd have audible telephone arguments about his contract with his agent. He'd be Happy the Disaffected Duck. Then one day he'd just be gone, another victim of show business.

So, with eighty-six days before the station's launch – a countdown has begun in the office – the Comedy Channel staff hasn't definitively decided whether or not to go with Happy the Duck. Well, Eddie Gorodetsky, the beefy, affable thirty-two-year-old head writer, is

Illustration by Lane Smith

ROLLING STONE

GOLDEN DELICIOUS

·

PENTHOUSE LETTERS
ART COLLECTOR'S
SPECIAL EDITION

ILLUSTRATIONS BY BLAIR DRAWSON

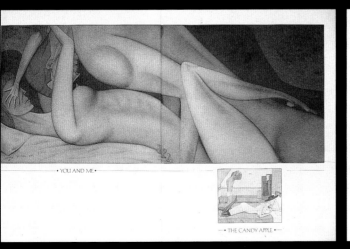

· YOU AND ME ·

· THE CANDY APPLE ·

· HEAVY BREATHING ·   · OPERA NIGHT ·

672 Distinctive Merit

Art Director: Danielle Gallo
Creative Director: Frank DeVino

THE HA-HA HORIZON

Carbon-dating comedy does not reveal when the first funny lady emerged from the dark sea of Victorian morality, but it was no later than 1926—the year Mae West waded ashore with her Broadway play *Sex*. A brick-house Venus, West was busty, lusty, and hilarious. Her jokes, timed with a roll of hip and eye, crashed like breakers on a stick-in-the-mud society. Roiling the waters could be dangerous; West's career almost sank when Hollywood's Hays office censored her films in the mid-'30s. But West survived; she knew the ropes, if not the limits. All the early female comics did. As these pioneers in a man's world knew, street smarts had to be masked with buffoonery.

Once consigned to the freak show, funny ladies now play the big top. They host talk shows: Oprah Winfrey finds humor in the angst of cellulite and broken hearts. They endorse products: belligerent accordionist Judy Tenuta uses her put-down "Pigs!" to plug Dr Pepper. Now women outside the entertainment industry are expressing their wit. Even den-mother-to-the-nation Barbara Bush gets into the act. "I mean, look at me," she exclaimed to *The New York Times* in all her sensibly shod frumpiness. The gales of laughter that greet her are those of solidarity. For as the world becomes a woman's, so does the right to poke fun at it.

ROBERT RISKO

47

Lucy Ricardo may have been the national nitwit in the 1950s, but her creator, Lucille Ball, was nobody's fool. As Empress of Comedy, her reign was long (it spanned more than two decades) and fruitful (with husband Desi Arnaz, she built the profitable Desilu Inc.). Her kingdom tottered in the 1970s when it became clear that humor based on an addlepated hausfrau no longer worked—perhaps because most of the audience did; why go after "Ba-Ba-Lu" when the boardroom beckoned? Ball's last TV series, launched in 1986, vanished in eight weeks. Last April, death robbed her of the chance to make a comeback. Yet her legacy of 30-minute sitcoms, now rerun around the planet, ensures that in the gag-eat-gag humor biz, Ball still triumphs.

71

674
Art Director: Dan Larocca
Creative Director: Gordon Hochhalter
Illustrator: Braldt Bralds
Agency: O'Grady
Client: R.R. Donnelley & Sons

675
Art Director: David Bartels
Illustrator: Braldt Bralds
Agency: Bartels & Carstens
Client: St. Louis Zoo

676
Art Director: Pedro Tabernero
Illustrator: Brad Holland
Studio: Pandora
Client: Expo-92

677
Art Director: Don Weller
Creative Director: Don Weller
Designer: Don Weller
Illustrator: Don Weller
Copywriter: Don Weller
Studio: The Weller Institute
Client: Graphic Comm. Society in Oklahoma

678
Art Director: Christopher Johnson
Creative Director: Stephen Doyle
Illustrator: Etienne Delessert
Agency: Drenttel Doyle Partners
Client: Olympia & York/World Financial Center

679
Art Director: Abby Merrill
Designer: Gerard Huerta
Illustrator: Roger Huyssen
Studio: 2H Studio
Client: Society of Illustrators

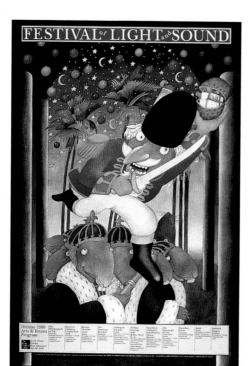

680
Art Director: Chris North
Creative Director: Chris North
　　　　　　　　Braldt Bralds
Illustrator: Braldt Bralds
Copywriter: Christopher Robin
Studio: River City Studio
Client: Kansas Art Directors Club

681
Art Director: Peter Galperin
Creative Director: Peter Galperin
Illustrator: Chris Gall
Agency: Middleberg & Associates
Client: Royce Carlin Hotel

682
Art Director: Mike Scricco
Designer: Mike Scricco
Illustrator: Brad Holland
Client: Art Directors Club of Connecticut

683
Art Director: Dugald Stermer
Designer: Dugald Stermer
Illustrator: Dugald Stermer
Client: Perry's

A FAIR OF THE HEART

MAHAFFEY THEATER

684
Art Director: George Halvorson
Creative Director: George Halvorson
Illustrator: Dan Craig
Agency: CME
Client: United Way

685
Art Director: Susan T. Baldassare
Creative Director: Valerie K. Newton
Designer: Susan T. Baldassare
Illustrator: Susan T. Baldassare
Copywriter: Valerie K. Newton
Client: Bay Area Civic Opera

It's Getting Awfully Crowded In There.

686
Art Director: Helen Lindberg
Creative Director: Art Broughton
Illustrator: Nicholas Wilton
Copywriter: Bob Dorfman
Brad Londy
Agency: TFB/BBDO
Client: Businessland

Decisions, Decisions, Decisions.

Need A Hand?

687
Art Director: Bill Freeland
Designer: Seymour Chwast
James McMullan
Milton Glaser
Illustrator: Seymour Chwast
James McMullan
Milton Glaser
Copywriter: Bill Freeland

688
Art Director: Janet Froelich
Designer: Janet Froelich
Illustrator: Matt Mahurin
Publication: The *New York Times*

689
Art Director: Mary Workman
Designer: Timothy W. Brown
Illustrator: Gwyn Stramler
Copywriter: David Hunter
Publication: Tennessee Illustrated

WILLIE HORTON AND ME

BY ANTHONY WALTON

HARD-WON MIDDLE-CLASS CREDENTIALS DON'T COUNT, THE AUTHOR FINDS. WHAT COUNTS, STILL, IS HIS FACE, AND IT'S BLACK.

TIME PIECES

Dark Mystery
Who are the Melungeons, and where did they come from?

—*David Hunter*

THE HISTORY OF ROCK & ROLL

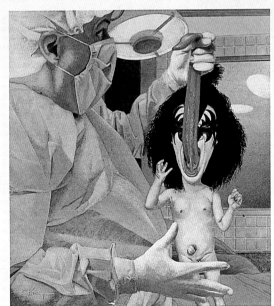

Kiss the Baby: The Birth of Gene Simmons
BY C.F. PAYNE

RECORDINGS

Tracy Chapman at the 'Crossroads'

★★★½
CROSSROADS
Tracy Chapman
Elektra

By Fred Goodman

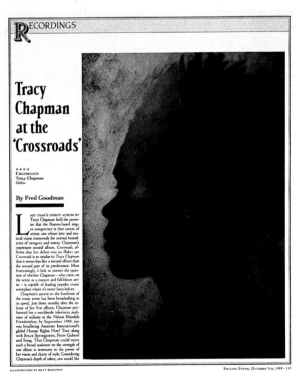

ILLUSTRATION BY MATT MAHURIN   ROLLING STONE, OCTOBER 7TH, 1989 · 135

690
Art Director: Fred Woodward
Illustrator: C. F. Payne
Publication: Rolling Stone

691
Art Director: Fred Woodward
Illustrator: Matt Mahurin
Publication: Rolling Stone

692
Art Director: Fred Woodward
Designer: Jolene Cuyler
Illustrator: Sue Coe
Publication: Rolling Stone

693
Art Director: Mary Workman
Designer: Timothy W. Brown
Illustrator: Alan Cober
Copywriter: Madison Smartt Bell
Publication: Tennessee Illustrated

694
Art Director: Mary Workman
Designer: Timothy W. Brown
Illustrator: Paul Cox
Copywriter: Carolyn Gray
Publication: Tennessee Illustrated

695
Art Director: Richard Bleiweiss
Creative Director: Frank DeVino
Designer: Richard Bleiweiss
Illustrator: Gottfried Helnwein

696

Art Director: Fred Woodward
Illustrator: Anita Kunz
Publication: Rolling Stone

697

Art Director: Mary Workman
Designer: Pamela Smith
Illustrator: Bill Russell
Copywriter: David Hunter
Publication: Tennessee Illustrated

THE HISTORY OF ROCK & ROLL

Talkin' Bout an Evolution
BY ANITA KUNZ

CONSCIENCE OF A COP

698

Art Director: Marilu Lopez
Illustrator: Anthony Russo
Copywriter: Kate White
Publication: Child Magazine

THE LOVE TRIANGLE

when a child gets a crush on a parent

when hollywood *came to* natchitoches, louisiana

699

Art Director: Robert Best
    David Walters
Designer: Robert Best
    David Walters
    Mary Ann Salvato
Illustrator: Daniel Torres
Copywriter: Rex Reed
Publication: Premiere

700
Art Director: Michael B. Marcum
Creative Director: Jim Darilek
Designer: Michael Taylor
Illustrator: Joseph Salina
Publication: Special Report: On Sports

701
Art Director: D. J. Stout
Creative Director: Fred Woodward
Designer: D. J. Stout
Illustrator: Braldt Bralds
Publication: Texas Monthly

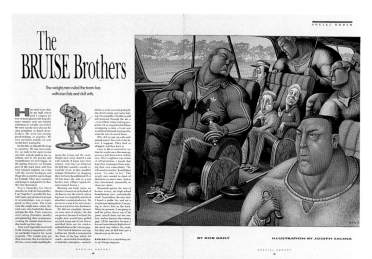

702
Art Director: Janet Froelich
Designer: Janet Froelich
Illustrator: Wiktor Sadowski
Publication: The *New York Times*

703
Art Director: Fred Woodward
Illustrator: Blair Drawson
Publication: Rolling Stone

704
Art Director: Fred Woodward
Illustrator: Philip Burke
Publication: Rolling Stone

705
Art Director: Susan Overstreet
Illustrator: Lane Smith
Publication: Personnel Journal

706
Art Director: Fred Woodward
Illustrator: Thomas Woodruff
Client: Rolling Stone

707
Art Director: Fred Woodward
Designer: Debra Bishop
Illustrator: Tom Curry
Publication: Rolling Stone

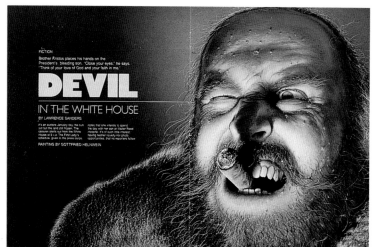

708
Art Director: Richard Bleiweiss
Creative Director: Frank DeVino
Designer: Richard Bleiweiss
Illustrator: Gottfried Helnwein

709
Art Director: Tom Stabler
Kerig Pope
Illustrator: Brad Holland
Copywriter: Norman Mailer
Publication: Playboy

710
Art Director: Melissa Brown
Designer: Melissa Brown
Illustrator: Mark Penberthy
Publication: Sun Magazine

711
Art Director: Richard Bleiweiss
Creative Director: Frank DeVino
Designer: Richard Bleiweiss
Illustrator: Gottfried Helnwein

712
Art Director: Mary Workman
Designer: Timothy W. Brown
Illustrator: Sean Earley
Copywriter: Carolyn Gray
Publication: Tennessee Illustrated

713
Art Director: Dwayne Flinchum
Creative Director: Frank DeVino
Illustrator: Brad Holland

714
Art Director: Kerig Pope
Illustrator: Everett Peck
Studio: Richard W. Salzman
Publication: Playboy

715

Art Director: Janet Froelich
Designer: Janet Froelich
Illustrator: Wiktor Sadowski
Publication: The *New York Times*

716

Art Director: Mark Fredrickson
Illustrator: Brad Holland
Client: Digital

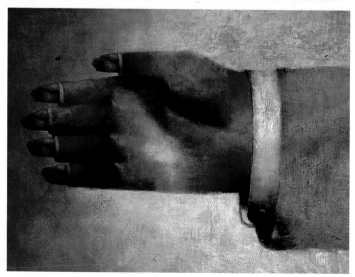

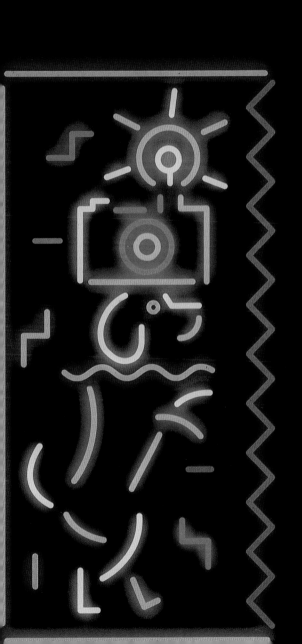

LIVING LEGENDS

BY ANTHONY DeCURTIS

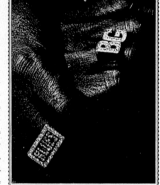

*I*t would be nearly impossible to overestimate the importance of the blues in the formation of rock & roll, but the legendary figures of that seminal music still rarely get the opportunity to step out of the shadows of the artists they have influenced and stand alone on their own formidable terms. In this photo gallery, seven major forces in the blues come forward.

Guitarists B.B. King and Albert King – the first a player of breathtaking sweetness and delicacy, the second a blazing virtuoso – and their musical heir Buddy Guy shaped the music of an entire generation of players, including Eric Clapton, Stevie Ray Vaughan and the late Mike Bloomfield. One of the most significant songwriters in the history of the blues, Willie Dixon penned a cache of classic tunes – among them, "You Shook Me," "Back Door Man," "I Can't Quit You Baby," "(I'm Your) Hoochie Coochie Man" and "I Just Want to Make Love to You" – that provided crucial early material for Jeff Beck, Led Zeppelin, the Rolling Stones and the Doors.

John Lee Hooker's insidious, sexually charged boogie – epitomized in songs like "Boogie Chillun," "Boom Boom," "Dimples" and "I'm in the Mood" – fired up everyone from the Animals and Van Morrison to Bruce Springsteen and Bonnie Raitt.

The fingers of guitarist Buddy Guy

Bo Diddley's propulsive, staccato beat drove songs like "I'm a Man," "Mona" and "Who Do You Love?" and provided a central link between the blues and rock & roll. Junior Wells, the wailing harmonica man best known for his insouciant version of "Messin' With the Kid," was a staple on the Chess Records studio scene, in Chicago. For more than two decades, Wells, as part of a one-two punch with Buddy Guy, has led one of the most active touring blues bands in the country.

Along with the music they created, however, these bluesmen are the product of a world and of a time that has all but disappeared. The photographs that appear on these pages are meant to honor that heritage as well.

"I had two things to choose from," says the seventy-two-year-old John Lee Hooker, whose father was a sharecropper. "One was to stay there with the horses and cows and pigs and work on the farm and go to school and *not* be a musician. I felt from a kid up that wasn't my bag. I was gonna be a musician. I was different from any of the rest of the kids. I was *completely* different."

As a young black person deep in the segregated South in the early [Cont. on 99]

PHOTOGRAPHS BY ALBERT WATSON

717 Gold

Art Director: Fred Woodward
Photo Editor: Laurie Kratochvil
Photographer: Albert Watson
Publication: Rolling Stone

Timberland. Where the elements of design are the elements themselves.

We Timberland people have never built a shoe unless we could build it better than any and all competitors. Which tells you something about the elements that make up our new women's collection. Glove-soft chamois and full-grain leathers, all of a quality virtually unseen in women's footwear. Genuine Timberland handsewn moccasin construction. And a panorama of colors inspired by the environments in which these shoes come alive. The bluffs of Antigua, the coves of the Mediterranean, the valleys of Italy.

A palette of wind, water, earth and sky.

Boots, shoes, clothing, wind, water, earth and sky.

Sporting Hush Puppies.

Allow us to point out our new look. Soft leather men's casuals and women's Body Shoes—with the Comfort Curve sole to flex where your foot flexes. In a flush of spring colors.

Remember when there was more grease in your hair than under the hood?

≋ **National** Car Rental. *Florida Funwheels*

One ride and you'll understand why most rocket scientists are German.

OKTOBER

SO MO DI MI DO FR SA SO MO DI MI DO FR SA SO MO DI MI DO FR SA SO MO DI MI DO FR SA SO MO DI

1 2 3 4 5 6 7 8 9 10 11 12 13 14 15 16 17 18 19 20 21 22 23 24 25 26 27 28 29 30 31

JUNI

1 2 3 4 5 6 7 8 9 10 11 12 13 14 15 16 17 18 19 20 21 22 23 24 25 26 27 28 29 30

JANUAR

1 2 3 4 5 6 7 8 9 10 11 12 13 14 15 16 17 18 19 20 21 22 23 24 25 26 27 28 29 30 31

Compromise is for politicians.

MARC HAUSER

MARC HAUSER

MARC HAUSER

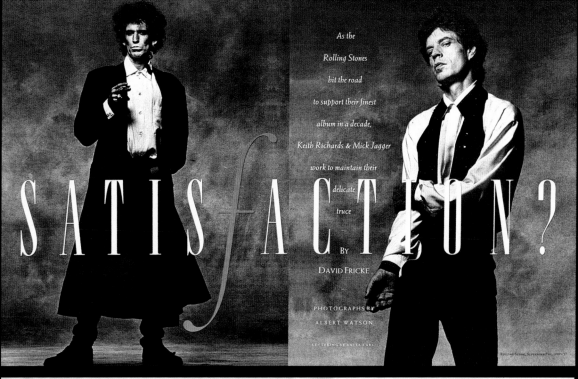

SATIS*f*ACTION?

As the
Rolling Stones
hit the road
to support their finest
album in a decade,
Keith Richards & Mick Jagger
work to maintain their
delicate
truce

BY
DAVID FRICKE

PHOTOGRAPHS BY
ALBERT WATSON

GREENWICH, CONN.

WHY MOW?

THE CASE AGAINST LAWNS

BY MICHAEL POLLAN

Anyone new to the experience of owning a lawn, as I am, soon figures out that there is more at stake here than a patch of grass. A lawn immediately establishes a certain relationship with one's neighbors and, by extension, the larger American landscape. Mowing the lawn, I realized the first time I gazed into my neighbor's yard and imagined him gazing back into mine, is a civic responsibility.

For no lawn is an island, at least in America. Starting at my front stoop, this scruffy green carpet tumbles down a hill and leaps across a one-lane road into my neighbor's yard. From there it skips over some wooded patches and stone walls before finding its way across a dozen other unfenced properties that lead down into the Housatonic Valley, there to begin its march south to the metropolitan area. Once below Danbury, the lawn — now

Michael Pollan, executive editor of Harper's Magazine, is at work on a book about gardening for Atlantic Monthly Press

RIVER BLINDNESS

CONQUERING AN ANCIENT SCOURGE

By Erik Eckholm

RIVER BLINDNESS

CONQUERING AN ANCIENT SCOURGE

By Erik Eckholm

PHOTOGRAPHS BY EUGENE RICHARDS

729 Distinctive Merit

Art Director: Janet Froelich
Photo Editor: Kathy Ryan
Designer: Janet Froelich
Justine Strasberg
Photographer: Eugene Richards
Publication: The *New York Times*
Magazine

TIMELESS VENICE

PHOTO ESSAY BY MICHAEL O'NEILL

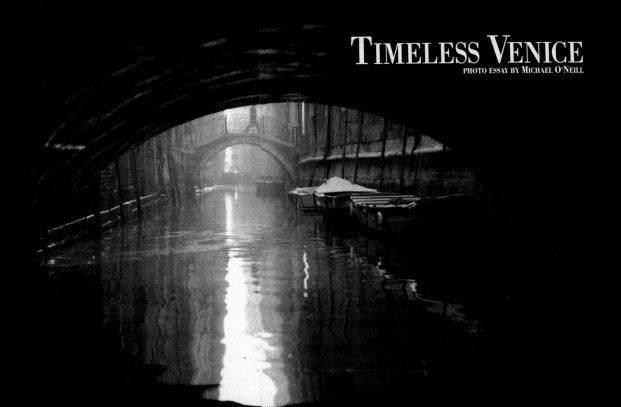

731
Art Director: Bruce Pope
Photographer: Hank Benson

732
Art Director: Jim Mochnsky
Creative Director: James Dale
Designer: Jim Mochnsky
Photographer: Stephen John Phillips
Agency: W.B. Doner
Client: The Maryland Ballet

733
Art Director: Jim Mochnsky
Creative Director: James Dale
Designer: Jim Mochnsky
Photographer: Stephen John Phillips
Agency: W.B. Doner
Client: The Maryland Ballet

734
Art Director: John Butler
Mike Shine
Photographer: Joe Baraban
Copywriter: Tom DeCerchio
Agency: Chiat/Day/Mojo
Client: National Car Rental

735
Art Director: Bob Wyatt
Creative Director: John Eding
Photographer: Harry DeZitter
Copywriter: Tom Coleman
Agency: Leo Burnett Co.
Client: Schenley/Dickel

736
Art Director: David Jenkins
Designer: David Jenkins
Photographer: Arthur Meyerson
Copywriter: Jerry Cronin
Agency: Wieden & Kennedy
Client: Nike

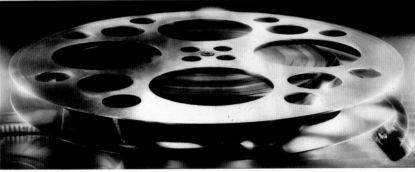

737
Art Director: Jim Robinson
Creative Director: Jim Robinson
Designer: Jim Robinson
Photographer: Nick Vedros
Studio: Jim Robinson Studio
Client: Merchant Ivory Productions

738
Art Director: John Doyle
Designer: John Doyle
Photographer: Clint Clemens
Copywriter: Paul Silverman
Agency: Mullen
Client: Timberland Co.

739
Art Director: Kristine Pallas
Creative Director: Kristine Pallas
                                John Mattingly
Photographer: Aaron Jones
Copywriter: John Mattingly
Agency: Pallas Advertising
Client: Seabourn Cruise Line

740
Art Director: Margie Adkins
Designer: Margie Adkins
Photographer: Arthur Meyerson
Client: T.C.U.
            Fort Worth Society of Creative Comm.

741
Art Director: Margie Adkins
Designer: Margie Adkins
Photographer: Arthur Meyerson
Client: Cockrell Printing

742
Art Director: Mark Johnson
Creative Director: Pat Burnham
Photographer: Kurt Markus
Copywriter: Bill Miller
Agency: Fallon McElligott
Client: Lee Jeans

743
Art Director: Mark Johnson
Creative Director: Pat Burnham
Photographer: Kurt Markus
Copywriter: Bill Miller
Agency: Fallon McElligott
Client: Lee Jeans

21 years. 3 months. 6 days. Lee jeans.

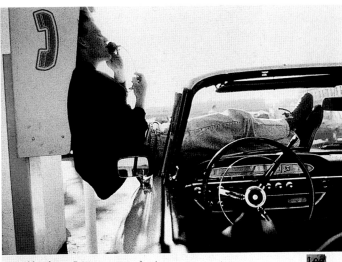

Public phone. Private moment. Lee jeans.

744
Art Director: Andre Nel
Creative Director: Dave Henke
Photographer: Jeff Schewe
Copywriter: Dave Henke
Agency: DMB&B St. Louis
Client: Anheuser-Busch

745
Art Director: Jeff Jones
Creative Director: Kevin Lynch
Photographer: Marvy!
Copywriter: Kevin Lynch
Agency: Lynch, Jarvis, Jones
Client: Catholic Education Marketing Initiative

746
Art Director: Jim Mochnsky
Creative Director: James Dale
Designer: Jim Mochnsky
Photographer: Stephen John Phillips
Agency: W.B. Doner
Client: The Maryland Ballet

747
Art Director: Sharon White
Bob Packert
Photographer: Sharon White
Bob Packert

DECISIONS

WHICH ROUTE LEADS TO
YOUR OPTIMUM
INVESTMENT POLICY?

Issue

Number

Four

Kidder, Peabody

748
Art Director: Miles Abernethy
Creative Director: Barry Shepard
Photographer: Rick Rusing
Agency: SHR Communications
Client: Kidder, Peabody

749

Art Director: Art Lahr
Creative Director: Art Lahr
Photographer: Taran Z
Client: Marriott Corp.

750

Art Director: Ann Schwiebinger
Photographer: Stephen Wilkes
Studio: Nike Design
Client: Nike

751

Art Director: Steve Moscowitz
Nick Vedros
John Muller
Photographer: Nick Vedros
Agency: Hutchins/Young & Rubicam
Muller & Co.
Studio: Vedros & Associates
Client: Vedros & Associates

 Four day weekend. Fifth day. Lee jeans.

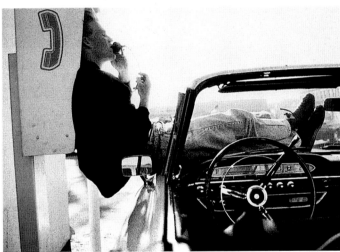

Public phone. Private moment. Lee jeans.

9 O'clock date. 8:55. Lee jeans.

752

Art Director: Mark Johnson
Creative Director: Pat Burnham
Photographer: Kurt Markus
Copywriter: Bill Miller
Agency: Fallon McElligott
Client: Lee Jeans

753

Art Director: Houman Pirdavari
Creative Director: Pat Burnham
Photographer: Dave Jordano
Copywriter: Bruce Bildsten
Agency: Fallon McElligott
Client: Timex

Suitable for dinner. The Timex Carriage Collection.

Grace under pressure. The Timex Carriage Collection.

Just wash and wear. The Timex Carriage Collection.

The right fragrance can bring a room to life.

The right fragrance can bring a room to life.

The right fragrance can bring a room to life.

754

Art Director: Tom Lichtenheld
Creative Director: Pat Burnham
Designer: Tom Lichtenheld
Photographer: Laurie Rubin
                Kerry Peterson
Copywriter: Jamie Barrett
Agency: Fallon McElligott

755
Art Director: John Butler
Mike Shine
Photographer: Joe Baraban
Copywriter: Mike Shine
John Butler
Agency: Chiat/Day/Mojo
Client: NYNEX Boaters Directory

756
Art Director: Bill Heuglin
Creative Director: Bill Heuglin
Photographer: Rick Rusing
Copywriter: Laura Kennedy
Agency: Stone & Adler
Client: Navistar International Transportation

▶ **Pizza Delivery**

Can't get away for a bite to eat? With a complete yellow pages section, the NYNEX Boaters Directory is the perfect guide to help you make the most of your time at sea.

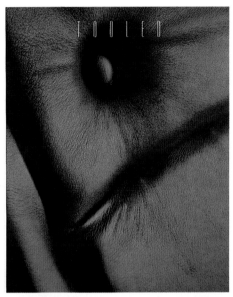

▶ **Cameras**

With everything from boating tips to a complete marine yellow pages, the NYNEX Boaters Directory can prepare you for nearly anything that pops up on a day at sea.

▶ **Boat Cleaning**

With a complete assortment of boating goods and services, the NYNEX Boaters Directory is the only guide you'll need for keeping your poop deck shipshape.

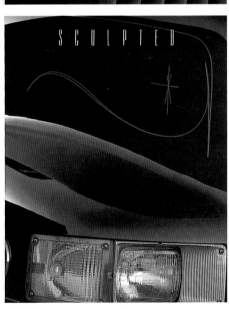

757

Art Director: Mark Danzig
Designer: Mark Danzig
Photographer: Brigitte LaCombe
Publication: The *Washington Post Magazine*

758

Art Director: Mary K. Baumann
Designer: Mary K. Baumann
Photographer: Dennis Marsico
Client: American Express Publishing Corp.
Publication: Favorite Places

759

Art Director: Janet Froelich
Photo Editor: Kathy Ryan
Designer: Janet Froelich
       Justine Strasberg
Photographer: Eugene Richards
Publication: The *New York Times Magazine*

760

Art Director: Michael B. Marcum
Creative Director: Jim Darilek
Designer: Victoria Vaccarello
Photographer: Brian Smale
Agency: Whittle Communications
Publication: Special Report: On Sports

761
Art Director: Mary Workman
Designer: Timothy W. Brown
Photographer: Chip Simons
Publication: Tennessee Illustrated

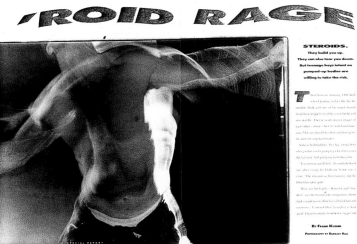

762
Art Director: Michael B. Marcum
Creative Director: Jim Darilek
Designer: James K. Bixby
Photographer: Barnaby Hall
Publication: Special Report: Health

763
Art Director: Robert Best
David Walters
Designer: Robert Best
David Walters
Mary Ann Salvato
Photographer: Mark Hanauer
Copywriter: Chris Connely
Publication: Premiere

764
Art Director: Mark Danzig
Designer: Mark Danzig
Photographer: Tom Wolff
Publication: The *Washington Post Magazine*

JESSE JACKSON

Entered race October 10, 1987 · Campaign ended July 20, 1988 (with formal nomination of Michael Dukakis)

April 23, 1987 Austin, Texas

In the years between his first campaign and his second, his role in the politics of America had dramatically changed. Once a rank outsider, he had moved rather smoothly to a place inside his party, largely accepted if not always warmly welcomed by its hierarchy. Moreover, where he had once been largely dependent on the support of black Americans to sustain his pursuit, he had managed to construct a genuine rainbow coalition. It was a remarkable transition that, from time to time, seemed to surprise even him. There was very little change, if any at all, in the marvelous electricity of his public performances—and they always had that—inspired, perhaps, but practiced as well. He seemed less frivolous in 1988 than in his previous incarnation, less inclined to deal casually with serious matters, more willing to consider the long-term impact of what he was saying or doing. Yet, there was still an improvisational magic to his presence, a chemical charisma in the connection he made with his audiences—the sparkle in his eyes with or without the television lights, the earnest eagerness in his voice, the overwhelming inner dignity of one man spreading outward, lending that dignity to others.

April 22, 1987 Austin, Texas

October 26, 1988 Sioux Falls, South Dakota

October 25, 1988 Columbus, Ohio

CHOOSE ME
PORTRAITS OF A PRESIDENTIAL RACE

ARTHUR GRACE

FOREWORD BY SAM DONALDSON · TEXT BY JIM WOOTEN

765
Art Director: Pam Castaldi
Photographer: Arthur Grace
Agency: Carol Judy Leslie
Client: New England University Press

766
Art Director: Suez Kehl
Designer: Cinda Rose
            Glover S. Johns III
Publication: NGS Traveler

767
Art Director: Mary Workman
Designer: Timothy W. Brown
Photographer: Russell Monk
Publication: Tennessee Illustrated

768
Art Director: Fred Woodward
Photo Editor: Laurie Kratochvil
Photographer: Mark Seliger
Publication: Rolling Stone

769
Art Director: Fred Woodward
Photo Editor: Laurie Kratochvil
Photographer: Herb Ritts
Publication: Rolling Stone

Victories of the Spirit

IN ST. LOUIS, 3,500 ATHLETES OVER 55 GO FOR THE GOLD.

PHOTOGRAPHS BY MARY ELLEN MARK

770

Art Director: Janet Froelich
Photo Editor: Kathy Ryan
Designer: JoDee Stringham
Photographer: Mary Ellen Mark
Publication: The *New York Times Magazine*

EAST BERLIN DIARY

BY CHRISTOPH HEIN

'THIS IS OUR ONE CHANCE
— OUR FIRST AND LAST,' THE AUTHOR SAYS.
'IF WE FAIL, WE WILL BE DEVOURED
BY McDONALD'S.'

RIGHT
NOW,
NOTHING
IS FINAL;
GUESSES
ARE
FUTILE;
EVENTS
ARE
MOVING
TOO
FAST.

771

Art Director: Janet Froelich
Photo Editor: Kathy Ryan
Designer: Kandy Uttreil
Photographer: James Nachtwey
Publication: The *New York Times*

772

Art Director: Ken Newbaker
Designer: Ken Newbaker
Photographer: Nelson Bakerman
Publication: Philadelphia Magazine

Obscure Objects of Desire

Why would someone collect lost baby shoes? Or mangled pennies, or lunch boxes, or knobs? Is it strange? Is it neurotic? Is it art?

For every person who collects something normal, like stamps or Lladró or coins, there's someone else who collects something weird. Something that wouldn't come immediately to mind. Like doodles left on notepads at a stationery store. Or all the rocks you ever kicked home. Or bellybutton lint.

Some of these obsessions are photographed on the next seven pages. They're part of a collection of collections amassed by Richard Torchia, who has lured into public light the very private rituals of some 60 Philadelphians in order to create an exhibit titled "Fieldworks: Collecting as Folklore." It's all on display this month at the Levy Gallery at Moore College of Art—even though Torchia is sure it's not art, and it may not even be folklore. Nonetheless, in some ways it seems

like art. It's creative, it's human, and it's universal yet personal. "It's that inscription of the personal onto the mundane that interests me," Torchia says. A search for meaning in the most meaningless of objects.

Yeah, OK. But nobody's taking this *too* seriously, including the collectors. Mostly, they talk about how it's fun. How your friends want so badly to add to your collection. And how, when you gather a large number of any one type of object, something happens. Patterns emerge. "You put enough dog teeth together," says Torchia, "and at some point it's visually compelling." —*Laurence R. Stains*

OPPOSITE PAGE: These are some of the 50-odd lost shoes collected by Gary Gorton, a professor of finance at the Wharton School. Size is crucial: If it's bigger than seven or eight inches, he won't pick it up. "I just happened to pick up the first one."

PHOTOGRAPHS BY NELSON BAKERMAN

ABOVE: Architect Charles Evers has a collection of about 75 miniatures of international monuments. Most were given to him by friends. His favorite is a tiny St. Peter's Basilica, including the piazza, shrunk into all of two inches. "It's vicarious. These are places I've never been, buildings I'll never design."

BELOW: Alan J. Klawans collects old steamship postcards. "It's a nostalgic look at a bygone era," he says. These ships were the Love Boats of their time, taking people on a daylong excursion for 70 cents and giving them a seafood dinner for 30 cents more. "I must have a couple of hundred postcards by now"—and each one takes him far away from his modern life in Willow Grove.

BELOW: Even though they started including asymmetrical objects years ago, Eric and Allison Olds still call it their "Symmetrical Black Rubber Object Collection" because it's so much fun to say. It's also fun to jump out of your car and snap up one of these things by the roadside while other drivers wonder what the hell is so important. They have close to 400 of these things now, mainly because everyone, including Eric's grandparents, keeps coming up with more.

"There was always some sort of character about a glove lying in the street that would make me want to look at it."

A couple of years ago, Kurt Madison picked up his first lost glove. Now he has about 200. And he doesn't pick up every one he sees: "There has to be some sort of gesture to it."

30 seconds
SFX: Music
ANNCR: Every Saturday night in the city of New York, you can experience many things that are the best of their kind in all the world. Now one of them is a cruise line.
Royal Viking to Bermuda.

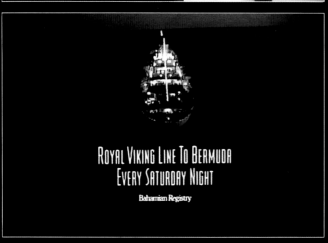

ROYAL VIKING LINE TO BERMUDA
EVERY SATURDAY NIGHT

Bahamian Registry

773 Gold

Art Director: Rich Silverstein
Steve Diamant
Creative Director: Andy Berlin
Photographer: Michael Duff
Copywriter: Andy Berlin
Jeffrey Goodby
Producer: Elizabeth O'Toole
Director: Stan Schofield
Studio: Sandbank & Partners

RT GALLERY
0 seconds
FX: Music
O: You have to drive it to believe it. The new Accord.

MISSING LINK

60 seconds

STUDENT: O.K. Earl, let's call it a night. Thank you. You're welcome

STUDENT VO: Despite being wonderful companions over the past semester...my subject group scored below average in all responses They showed poor communications skills...no understanding of tools and their uses...a complete lack of organization and no decision making abilities. In conclusion... if I can't find some missing link that will unlock the barrier between us   this project...will be cancelled.

STUDENT Thank you!

STUDENT & CHIMP (sign language): You're welcome.

BIKE MESSENGER
30 seconds
SFX: Jazz music
BIKE MESSENGER: You think Bo Jackson's the only guy who
can do this stuff?

776 Gold
Art Director: David Jenkins
Warren Eakins
Creative Director: Dan Wieden
David Kennedy
Copywriter: Steve Sandoz
Jim Riswold
Agency: Wieden & Kennedy
Client: Nike

30 seconds
VO: Ever get the feeling that some airlines aren't too concerned about the little things? Before you get on an Alaska Airlines plane, we make sure...everything is ship-shape, inside and out.

777 Gold

Art Director: Tim Delaney
Creative Director: Jim Copacino
Producer: Cindy Henderson
Director: Joe Sedelmaier
Agency: Livingston & Co.
Client: Alaska Airlines

BABY

45 seconds

SFX: Baby gurgling; music

VO: Nobody's better in cold than All Temperature Cheer.

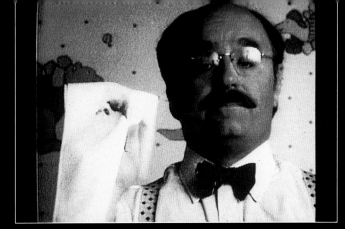

778 Gold

Art Director: Burint Ramany
Creative Director: Gerry Miller
Copywriter: Burint Ramany
Producer: Glant Cohen
Director: Leroy Koetz
Agency: Leo Burnett Co.
Client: Proctor & Gamble

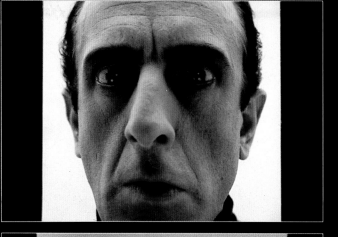

PSYCHIC
60 seconds
SFX: Eerie background music
VO: Timex. It takes a lickin' and keeps on tickin

779 Silver

Art Director: Houman Pirdavari
Creative Director: Pat Burnham
Copywriter: Bruce Bildsten
Producer: Char Loving
Director: Roger Woodburn
Agency: Fallon McElligott
Client: Timex

BO DIDDLEY

60 seconds
SFX: Bo Diddley music
GIBSON: Bo knows baseball.
EVERETT: Bo knows football.
SFX: Music continues
JORDAN: Bo knows basketball, too.
SFX: Music continues
MCENROE: Bo knows tennis?
BENOIT: Bo knows running.
GRETZKY: No.
7-11 TEAM: Bo knows cycling.
WEIGHTLIFTERS: Bo knows weights.
SFX: Music continues
DIDDLEY: Bo, you don't know diddley.

780 Silver
Art Director: David Jenkins
Creative Director: Dan Wieden
David Kennedy
Copywriter: Jim Riswold
Agency: Wieden & Kennedy
Client: Nike

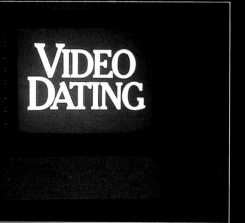

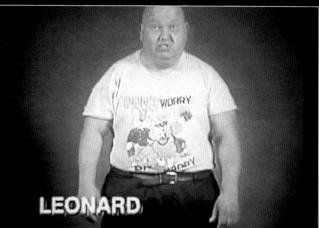

VIDEO DATING

60 seconds

GREGOR: I want a woman who likes to hunt...what do I mean by a woman who likes to hunt...

SFX: Zap

LEONARD: Hi girls my name is Lenny Tepper and I'm looking for a nice girl...

GREGOR: A woman who likes to hunt in the mountains...hunt in the plains...

SFX: Zap

JONATHAN: I am successful, I'm rich and I'm good looking... rich, good looking and successful.

SFX: Zap

GREGOR: Hunt in the mountains with a gun...

SFX: Zap

MAN: I don't do drugs...Ummm Ok I take Lithium.

LEONARD: I want a woman that is hot--Wow...Whooo...

ANNCR: When life is rough, laugh it off with the new Comedy Channel. 24 hours a day, we're there when you need us.

LEONARD: Hi girls it's me Lenny Tepper again...

781 Silver

Art Director: Donna Weinheim
John Colquhoun
Creative Director: Donna Weinheim
Copywriter: Jeff Alphin
Jane King
Rick LeMoine
Cliff Freeman
Agency: Cliff Freeman & Partners
Client: Home Box Office/Comedy Channel

CHANGE OF HEART

60 seconds
MOM: How are things at work, dear?
ABBY: OK. They want me to use a computer.
DAD: A computer? You?
ABBY: I mean, what do I need a computer for? I'm not an
accountant....I figure, what? I've been in this business 11
years, right? Why do I need one now? I've done fine without
one....Can you imagine me working on a computer?
FRIEND: They figure if you can use one, then anybody can
use one.
VO: Macintosh has the power to change your mind about
computers. The power to be your best.
ABBY: So, I was wrong.

782 Silver
Art Director: Susan Westre
Creative Director: Steve Hayden
Copywriter: Chris Wall
Producer: Bob Belton
Pat Walsh
Director: Joe Pytka
Studio: Pytka Productions
Client: Apple Computer Inc.

GLASNOST

60 seconds
(Spoken in Russian)
SFX: Music
FATHER: Noise! Noise! You call that music?
FRIEND: Hey, Dude! Totally awesome day!
VO: (in English) Not very long ago, America introduced Pepsi to the Soviet Union.
LADY: Look! What's this craziness?
FATHER: Look at you! Do you have to dress like that?
VO: (in English) …And while it may be just a coincidence…a lot of refreshing changes have taken place ever since.
FRIEND: Yo! Mickey!
FATHER: Don't you have any normal friends? Kids!
VO: (in English) Pepsi. A generation ahead.
WIFE: Yuri…come on, lighten up.

783 Silver

Art Director: Richard Sabean
Rich Martel
Creative Director: Al Merrin
Copywriter: Michael Patti
Director: Rick Levine
Leslie Dektor
Studio: Rick Levine Productions
Petermann-Dektor

TAXI DRIVER

60 seconds

ANNCR: To understand Asia, you have to understand its
customs, its mysteries, its people. You have to know what
makes a good impression, and what offends. For over 40 years
we've been learning about Asia. So in addition to nearly 90
nonstops weekly, with service from over 200 US cities, and
Worldperks, the best frequent flyer program in the sky, we can
give you something no other US airline can.

The knowledge, information and insight that comes after 40
years of helping people do business in Asia.

Please stand by.

We wanted to show you the NYNEX
Business to Business Yellow Pages.

We are looking for a copy
not in use at his time.

GHT
seconds
NGER: In the fading light,
A cold blue haze.
Gay laughter, sad cries--
These mark our days.
The touch, the feel, the fabric of our lives.
The touch, the feel, the fabric of our lives.

ANIMALS
30 seconds
ANNCR: If you think this looks ridiculous, remember...
smoking is just as unnatural for you as it is for them.

788 Distinctive Merit

Art Director: Bob Barrie
Creative Director: Pat Burnham
Copywriter: Jarl Olsen
Producer: Char Loving
Director: Rick Dublin
Agency: Fallon McElligott
Client: Hush Puppies

789 Distinctive Merit

Art Director: Bob Barrie
Creative Director: Pat Burnham
Copywriter: Jarl Olsen
Producer: Char Loving
Director: Rick Dublin
Agency: Fallon McElligott
Client: Hush Puppies

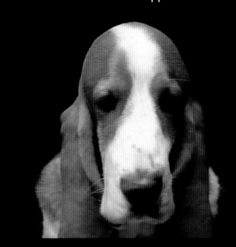

Art Director: Jeff York
Creative Director: Tenney Fairchild
Joe Sciarrotta
Copywriter: Ann O'Phelan
Producer: Carol Faron
Director: Victor Haboush
Agency: J. Walter Thompson
Client: Quaker Oats Co.

SARGE

30 seconds
SFX: Drums
SARGE: What's the meal I hate to miss?
TROOPS: Kibbles 'N Bits 'N Bits 'N Bits!
SARGE: Variety--I can't resist.
TROOPS: Kibbles 'N Bits 'N Bits 'N Bits!
SARGE: Crunchy, chewy--I insist.
TROOPS: Kibbles 'N Bits 'N Bits 'N Bits!
SARGE: My dog food goes like this!
TROOPS: Kibbles 'N Bits 'N Bits 'N Bits!
SARGE: Crunchy!
TROOPS: Chewy!
SARGE: Fall in!
TROOPS: Chow down!
SFX: Music
SARGE: For variety, you should enlist!
TROOPS: Kibbles 'N Bits 'N Bits 'N Bits!

791 Distinctive Merit
Art Director: Susan Wood
Creative Director: Al Merrin
Glenn Miller
Copywriter: Glenn Miller
Producer: Barbara Mullins
Lisa Steinman
Director: Joe Pytka
Studio: Pytka Productions
Client: GE Corporate

EXCUSES
30 seconds
WOMAN 1: I have to cancel.
WOMAN 2: I keep cancelling.
WOMAN 4: Why do you keep putting it off?
WOMAN 5: Mother, I'm not…
VO: GE's breast cancer detection system.
WOMAN 6: I keep meaning to.
WOMAN 7: Did you go?
WOMAN 8: I'm too busy. I'm too busy.
VO: It can help detect tumors too tiny to be felt.
WOMAN 9: I have such a busy week. I'm going next week.
WOMAN 10: I can't find the time.
WOMAN 12: When?
VO: It can increase the survival rate to 91%.
WOMAN 14: Next week.
WOMAN 15: Oh, I can't next week.
WOMAN 16: As soon as I can find the time, I'll go.
VO: But there's one thing GE can't do. We can't make you go.
WOMAN 17: It's nothing to worry about. I just couldn't go.

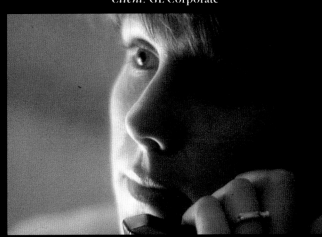

Art Director: Michael Prieve
Creative Director: Dan Wieden
David Kennedy
Copywriter: Jim Riswold
Producer: Patti Greaney
Bill Davenport
Director: Bob Giraldi
Agency: Wieden & Kennedy
Client: Nike

Art Director: Burint Ramany
Creative Director: Gerry Miller
Copywriter: Burint Ramany
Producer: Glant Cohen
Director: Leroy Koetz
Agency: Leo Burnett Co.
Client: Proctor & Gamble

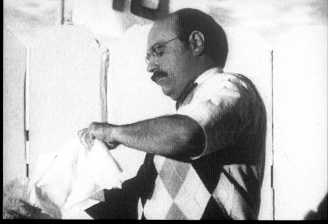

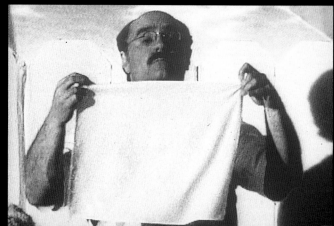

SLAM DUNK
30 seconds
SFX: Music

19TH HOLE
45 seconds
SFX: Scottish bagpipe music
VO: Nobody's better in cold than All Temperature Cheer.

796 Distinctive Merit

Art Director: John Scott MacDaniels
Creative Director: John Scott MacDaniels
Copywriter: Walt Kramer
Producer: Deborah Newman-Cooke
Director: Haskell Wexler
Hobby Morrison
Agency: MacDaniels, Henry & Sproul
Client: Caltrans/Amtrak

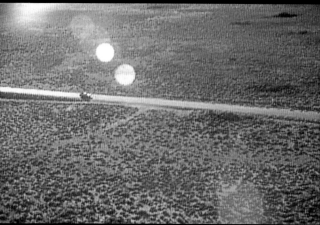

WYOMING

60 seconds
UNCLE HARLIN: Oh no, I think the engine's knocking.
MARSHA: It's Barney's drums.
GARNER: You just keep trying to drive, Uncle Harlin.
ANNCR: Amtrak presents the Carsby family, hoping they're still on the road somewhere between Bakersfield and the Bay Area.
MARSHA/BARNEY: Whooaa!
UNCLE HARLIN: What happened to the clutch?
GARNER: It's an automatic transmission.
MARSHA: How many motels have we stayed in so far?…If we were on Amtrak, we'd be at our destination….We'd be relaxed, saved on gas…
GARNER: Yeah, but they weren't all bad motels.
UNCLE HARLIN: I liked that last one we stayed at….They allow pets.
MARSHA: How do you know that, Uncle Harlin?
UNCLE HARLIN: They gave me this wolverine.
ANNCR: There is a safe and a sane and a certain way to travel the San Joaquin.
MARSHA: We usually see an Amtrak San Joaquin at this time.
UNCLE HARLIN: Oh, look at the sign…"Welcome to Wyoming."

797 Distinctive Merit

Art Director: Gary Goldsmith
Creative Director: Gary Goldsmith
Copywriter: Tom Churm
Gary Goldsmith
Producer: Trisha Caruso
Valerie Edwards
Client: Everlast Activewear

STOPWATCH

15 seconds
SFX: Stopwatch ticking
VO: In the United States, every 10 seconds, another piece of
designer clothing goes out of style.
SFX: Woman screams

TESTING 1-2-3

60 seconds

WOMAN 1: Can I get on there soon?

WOMAN 2: After me.

KEN: Do you think I can get on here soon?

MAN 1: Yeah, give me a minute, man.

ED: You've been staring out there all day. What are you doing?

JOHN: Testing.

ED: Testing what?

JOHN: Computers. I'm trying to figure out which computer is the most powerful.

ED: Well, that's easy. The one with the most memory… megahertz…MIPS…you know.

JOHN: No, I don't think so. I think the most powerful computer is the one that people actually use.

GIRL: Hi, Ken.

KEN: Hey.

VO: Macintosh has the power to change the way you look at computers. The power to be your best.

ED: That's not really a fair comparison. People like using the Mac.

799 Distinctive Merit

Art Director: Matt Smith
Creative Director: Ross Van Dusen
Copywriter: David O'Hare
Producer: Harvey Greenberg
Jan Ushijima
Director: Gary Weis
Agency: Chiat/Day/Mojo
Client: Rainier Dry Beer

REAL PEOPLE & BEER

30 seconds
GUY 1: Okay, real people and beer.
GUY 2: Yeah, real people are cool.
GUY 1: All right, I love this. Nice couple.
GUY 2: Aw, that's nice….Looks like that girl that dumped you…
GUY 1: Thanks for the memory. Whoa! stereo. Hello, boys.
GUY 2: Hey, get the guy on the bike.
GUY 1: Okay, I got him. I got him.
GUY 2: Wait a minute. He's coming back.
GUY 1: Who?
GUY 2: The guy on the bike. See him? Can you get him? Oh, oh…
GUY 1: Let's go.
GUY 2: No, let's get him.
GUY 1: Come on, get out of here.
GUY 2: Did you get the beer in the shot?
GUY 1: Yeah, yeah, yeah, give me the beer.
GUY 2: Come on, he's gaining on us.
GUY 1: Give me the beer.
GUY 2: Pretty cool, huh?

Copywriter: Chris Wall
Producer: Bob Belton
Pat Walsh
Director: Joe Pytka
Studio: Pytka Productions
Client: Apple Computer Inc.

THE NEW TEACHER

60 seconds

PRINCIPAL: Looks like we got a new teacher. Miss Kassman?

SECRETARY: Miss Kassman.

BROTHER: Amy, I hear your new teacher's real mean.

MISS KASSMAN: Good morning, everybody.

CLASS: Good morning!

DOUG: New teachers have to be tough so you're scared of 'em.

MISS KASSMAN: Did you bring your pictures?

CLASS: Yes!

MISS KASSMAN: Amy, would you come up here and bring your picture with you, please?

SFX: Commotion among the students

PRINCIPAL: I'd better check on Miss Kassman.

SFX: More commotion

ANNCR: There's a special power that can bring students and teachers closer together. The power to be your best.

BROTHER: Whoa, that's cool! Hey, how's your new teacher?

AMY: Oh, she's OK.

801

Art Director: Kathy Strall
Eddie Snyder
Creative Director: Eddie Snyder
Copywriter: Dave Nelson
Producer: Eddie Snyder
Director: Lance Russell
Agency: Group 243
Client: The Athlete's Foot

802

Art Director: Mary Mentzer
Creative Director: Dave Bradley
Copywriter: Joel Mitchell
Director: Jim Beresford
Studio: Bajus Jones
Client: First Minnesota

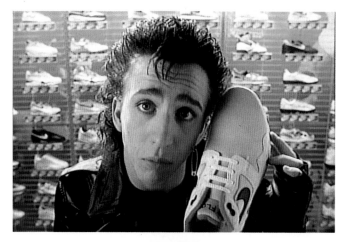

BASIC BLACK
15 seconds
TEEN IN BLACK: Got these Nike's in black? Black? Got 'em in black? Black? Got any blacker?

SENIORS
15 seconds
MAN: I borrowed $200 to take her on a honeymoon to Colorado Springs.
SHE: Borrowed from me.
MAN: From her. Ah…cause I was flat broke.
SHE: You see who's the money manager.
VO: First Minnesota. Taking the family into account.

803

Art Director: Pam Conboy
Creative Director: Lyle Wedemeyer
Copywriter: Emily Scott
Producer: Dain Rodwell
Director: John Kump Zurik
Agency: Martin/Williams
Client: Snyder's Drug Stores

804

Art Director: Gary Goldsmith
Creative Director: Gary Goldsmith
Copywriter: Tom Churm
Gary Goldsmith
Producer: Trisha Caruso
Valerie Edwards

HAIRDO

15 seconds
SFX: '50s music on the radio
SHE: La, la, la…
VO: Out of hair spray? Snyder's has 28 brands of hair spray.
SFX: Deflating sounds

COUNTDOWN

15 seconds
SFX: Bongs
VO: This commercial will last 15 seconds. About as long as most fashion trends.

805

Art Director: Pam Conboy
Creative Director: Lyle Wedemeyer
Copywriter: Emily Scott
Producer: Dain Rodwell
Director: John Kump Zurik
Agency: Martin/Williams
Client: Snyder's Drug Stores

806

Art Director: Larry Jarvis
Creative Director: Lloyd Wolfe
Copywriter: Rob Rosenthal
Agency: Cole & Weber, Portland
Client: The *Oregonian*

SLAPPING

15 seconds
SFX: Slapping sounds
VO: Out of mosquito repellant? Snyder's has 11 different kinds of protective sprays and lotions.

JACK OHMAN

15 seconds
SFX: Scratching of pen on paper
VO: When a politician steps out of line…
SFX: Scratching stops abruptly
VO: …our man rearranges his face. Jack Ohman. Tomorrow in The *Oregonian*.

807

Art Director: Bob Barrie
Creative Director: Pat Burnham
Copywriter: Jarl Olsen
Producer: Char Loving
Director: Rick Dublin
Agency: Fallon McElligott
Client: Hush Puppies

808

Art Director: Bob Barrie
Creative Director: Pat Burnham
Copywriter: Jarl Olsen
Producer: Char Loving
Director: Rick Dublin
Agency: Fallon McElligott
Client: Hush Puppies

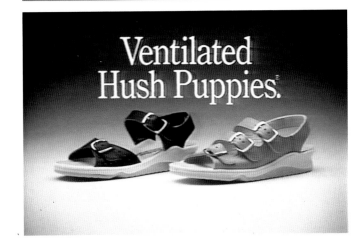

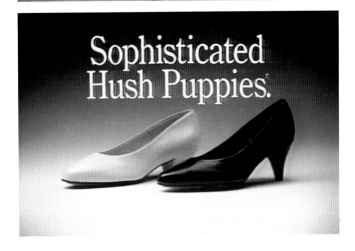

VENTILATED HUSH PUPPIES

15 seconds
SFX: Urban street sounds; rumbling of train

SOPHISTICATED HUSH PUPPIES

15 seconds
SFX: Bottle opening; gurgling sound; dog lapping

809
Art Director: David Fox
Creative Director: Bill Hamilton
Copywriter: Marty Cooke
Producer: Tom Harbeck
　　　　　Lee Weiss
Agency: Chiat/Day/Mojo Advertising Inc.
Client: NYNEX Information Resources

810
Art Director: Steve Juliusson
Creative Director: Tom McConnaughy
Designer: Steve Juliusson
Copywriter: Jim Schmidt
Producer: Clark Dodsworth
Director: Dennis Manarchy
Agency: McConnaughy, Barocci, Brown
Client: Illinois Department of Tourism

SWEEPSTAKES
30 seconds
SFX: Barbecue party sounds
VO 1: Hey, Bob. Nice apron. How ya been?
CHEF: Not bad, not bad. How do you like your steak?
VO 1: Medium, Bob. Medium.
CHEF: Oooops! Hey, Marv. Glad you could make it. How do you like your steak?
VO 2: Well-done, Bob. Burn it.
CHEF: Comin' right up. Ooops!
VO 3: Bob, make mine rare.
CHEF: You got it. Ooooops!
SFX: Sweeping
ANNCR: It's the NYNEX Yellow Pages Sweepstakes. We'll be calling thousands of people to play. So be prepared. The Grand Prize is $25,000.

NO COMMERCIALS
30 seconds
SFX: Frogs croaking; owl hooting; geese honking; crickets chirping; loon calling

811
Art Director: Matt Fischer
Creative Director: John Ferrell
Copywriter: Andrew Landorf
Producer: Joy Luettich
Director: Peter Smillie
Agency: Hill, Holliday
Client: Irish Tourist Board

812
Art Director: John Butler
　　　　　　 Mike Shine
Creative Director: Bill Hamilton
Designer: Graham Clifford
Copywriter: Mike Shine
　　　　　　 John Butler
Producer: Kathi Calef
Agency: Chiat/Day/Mojo Advertising Inc.
Client: Grandy's

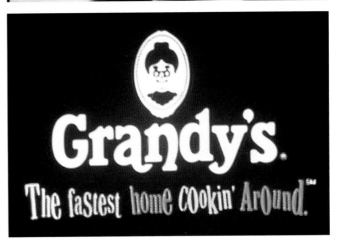

STORYTELLERS

30 seconds
VO: They were called the Seanchai. They spread the legend of
St. Patrick driving out the snakes, of St. Brendan discovering America,
and of Grace O'Malley who beheaded her five husbands…or did she?
So visit Ireland and listen well for there's still a bit of the Seanchai
in all of us.
Ireland. The ancient birthplace of good times.

ALAN PLATT

30 seconds
VO: Grandy's presents the biggest chickens of all time. In 1956, Alan
Platt broke his wife's crystal vase and blamed it on the dog.
GROUP VO: Chicken!
VO: In 1968, Charlie Bidwell took his date to the drive-in, and actually
watched the movie.
GROUP VO: Chicken!
VO: Now Grandy's is offering their big ten-piece Chicken Family Pack.
With mashed potatoes, vegetable and rolls. We'd like to ask $49.99, but
we'll settle for $9.99.
GROUP VO: Chicken!
VO: Grandy's. The fastest home cooking around.

813
Art Director: Sheri Olmon
Creative Director: Bill Hamilton
Copywriter: Alan Platt
Producer: Andrew Chinich
Agency: Chiat/Day/Mojo Advertising Inc.
Client: American Express Gold Card

814
Art Director: John Butler
Mike Shine
Creative Director: Bill Hamilton
Designer: Graham Clifford
Copywriter: Mike Shine
John Butler
Producer: Kathi Calef
Agency: Chiat/Day/Mojo Advertising Inc.
Client: Grandy's

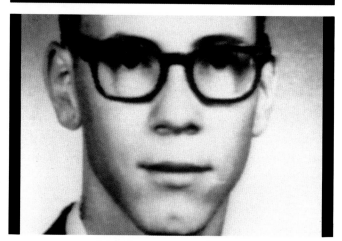

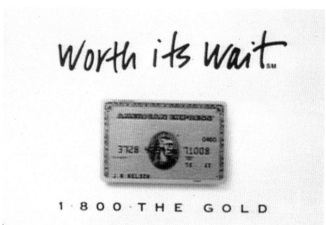

HAT
30 seconds
VO: Bogart. You always told me he was the coolest. Gene Kelly was the smoothest. Sellers was the funniest. Sydney Greenstreet was the meanest. But John Wayne always had the best hat. Happy birthday, Dad. Hope it fits.
The American Express Gold Card.

DAVID WEINER
30 seconds
VO: Grandy's presents the biggest chickens of all time. In 1966, David Weiner was afraid to ask Gwen Lipsky to the prom. She went with his friend Milton instead.
GROUP VO: Chicken!
VO: In 1972, Blake Olson said nothing when his neighbor ran over his petunias with a lawn mower.
GROUP VO: Chicken!
VO: Now Grandy's is offering their big ten-piece Chicken Family Pack. With mashed potatoes, vegetable and rolls. We'd like to ask $49.99, but we'll settle for $9.99.
GROUP VO: Chicken!
VO: Grandy's. The fastest home cooking around.

815

Art Director: Marc Donnenfeld
Creative Director: Andrew Langer
Copywriter: Marc Wolf
Producer: Kathy Tieman
Director: Michael Schrom
Agency: Lowe Marschalk
Client: A-1 Steak Sauce

816

Art Director: Ernie Cox
Copywriter: Jim Doherty
Producer: Bob Carney
Director: Jack Churchill
Agency: NW Ayer
Client: Outboard Marine Corp.

DONE

30 seconds
SFX: Music
VO: A1, it's how steak is done.

CRIB

30 seconds
VO: Studies have shown, it can be determined almost from birth, who's right for an Evinrude outboard motor.
Evinrude owners are born, not made.

817

Art Director: Tony DeGregorio
Creative Director: Tony DeGregorio
Copywriter: Rochelle Klein
Producer: Vera Samama
Director: Paul Giraud
Studio: HSI Productions
Client: Maidenform

818

Art Director: Kristine Pallas
Creative Director: Kristine Pallas
                John Mattingly
Copywriter: John Mattingly
Director: Steve Steigman
Agency: Pallas Advertising
Client: Vipont

BALCONY

30 seconds
VO: It couldn't have happened at a better time. Maidenform. Buy two, get one free.

BEAST

30 seconds
PRESENTER: To demonstrate the new Kick The Habit gradual smoking withdrawal system, we're comparing nicotine to the grasp of a beast. But with the Kick The Habit Level 1 Filter, your nicotine intake is reduced. You'll feel more like this. In a week switch to Level 2. The grasp of nicotine is reduced even more. Week 3? Level 3. Now you're ready to quit. And the monkey's off your back. Kick The Habit. The gradual smoking withdrawal system.

819

Art Director: Phil Triolo
Creative Director: Art Mellor
Robert Greenbaum
Copywriter: Jimmy Siegel
Robert Greenbaum
Producer: Regina Ebel
Director: Rick Levine
Studio: Rick Levine Productions
Client: Federal Express

820

Art Director: Matt Fischer
Creative Director: John Ferrell
Copywriter: Gary Cohen
Producer: Joy Luettich
Director: Peter Smillie
Agency: Hill, Holliday
Client: Irish Tourist Board

MEDITERRANEAN STORM

30 seconds
VO: How to get your package through a Mediterranean storm....Most Federal Express overseas employees are from overseas. So they not only know the local customs regulations, they know the local customs...
FEDERAL EXPRESS EMPLOYEE: ...Per favore...
VO: ...and that helps your package sail right through.
FEDERAL EXPRESS EMPLOYEE: ...Grazie!
VO: Because when delivering in Rome, it helps to be a Roman. Federal Express. The best way to ship it over here is now the best way to ship it over there.

FRIENDS

30 seconds
VO: It is said in the course of a lifetime you make only one or two true friends. We know where you just might find a third.
Ireland. The ancient birthplace of good times.

821

Art Director: Gary Goldsmith
Creative Director: Gary Goldsmith
Copywriter: Dean Hacohen
Producer: Trisha Caruso
Valerie Edwards
Director: Henry Sandbank

822

Art Director: Michael Prieve
Creative Director: Dan Wieden
David Kennedy
Copywriter: Jim Riswold
Producer: Roberta Grubman
Bill Davenport
Director: Bob Giraldi
Agency: Wieden & Kennedy
Client: Nike

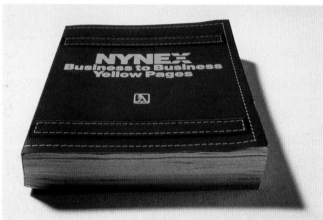

LUNCHTIME
30 seconds
This commercial has no dialogue.

FORCE
30 seconds
SFX: Music

823

Art Director: Andy Dijak
　　　　　　Mike Mazza
Creative Director: Bob Kuperman
Copywriter: Dick Sittig
Producer: Richard O'Neill

824

Art Director: Andy Dijak
　　　　　　Mike Mazza
Creative Director: Lee Clow
Copywriter: Brian Belefant
Producer: Michael Paradise
Director: Leslie Dektor

IF I HAD A 240SX

30 seconds
240SX DREAMER: If I had a Nissan 240SX…it would be a red coupe.—
Wait! A silver fastback. And I'd go for a spin up Route 7, the twisty
part. Just me and Astro…no, Amy. Heck, Christie Brinkley! Wow!
Yeah, me and Christie…in my silver—no, red 240SX…driving into
the sunset.

WE LEARN FROM RACING

30 seconds
SFX: Music
ANNCR: To Nissan, a truck race is nothing more than a learning
experience. It's just another day spent working out the bugs in a new
suspension. Tweaking an engine to get more horsepower. Or figuring
out which chassis design can withstand the most stress. Oh, sure,
we've won a couple hundred races—including the championship at the
last Baja 1000. But the fact is, as long as we learn something, we don't
really care if we win.
Yeah, right.

825

Art Director: Pam Cunningham
Andy Dijak
Creative Director: Lee Clow
Copywriter: Steve Bassett
Producer: Richard O'Neill
Director: Michael Werk

826

Art Director: Ed Maslow
Creative Director: Charlie Meismer
Art Mellor
Ed Maslow
Copywriter: Zoe Heighington
Producer: Barbara Mullins
Director: Fred Petermann
Studio: Fred Petermann
Client: Federal Express

ME AND MY SHADOW

30 seconds
SONG: "Me and My Shadow"
SINGER: Me and my shadow, strolling down the avenue.
Me and my shadow…
ANNCR: The Nissan 240SX. There's never been a sports car quite like it. Except for this one. The 240SX Coupe. For a great selection and a great deal, see your nearest Nissan dealer now.

CHANGING ITS STRIPES

30 seconds
VO: In this package is over 40 years of experience in overseas shipping, and access to more air routes worldwide. Because Flying Tigers has changed its stripes and merged with Federal Express to form the largest all-cargo airline in the world.

827
Art Director: Michael Smith
Creative Director: Bob Kuperman
Copywriter: Jerry Fields
Producer: Vicki Blucher
Director: Maxine Tabak

828
Art Director: Pam Cunningham
Creative Director: Bob Kuperman
Copywriter: Steve Bassett
Producer: Richard O'Neill
Director: John St. Clair

RECIPES

30 seconds
SFX: Lighthearted music
VO: No matter what your favorite recipe, it'll always turn out better if you start from scratch. Introducing Dep Everyday Shampoo. Expressly created to gently wash away styling buildup.

Z CLEAN SHEET

30 seconds
SFX: Loud banging
ANNCR: This is where we started—a clean sheet of paper. No boundaries. No rules. No preconceived ideas. Just desire to build the best sports car in the world. A car for one driver in a thousand. The car destined to leave its mark.
SFX: Loud banging
ANNCR: The new Z. From Nissan.

829
Art Director: Michael Smith
Creative Director: Bob Kuperman
Copywriter: Sam Avery
Producer: Vicki Blucher
Director: Mark Coppos

830
Art Director: Angela Dunkle
Creative Director: Bob Kuperman
Copywriter: Dion Hughes

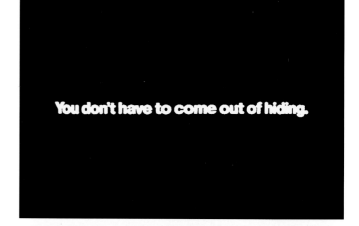

FRAMES
30 seconds
ANNCR: Some people can be very choosy.
WOMAN OC: No. No, no, no.
ANNCR: So to make sure all our customers find what they want…at
EyeMasters we carry over 1,500 frames.
WOMAN OC: No. No.
ANNCR: You'll also get…
WOMAN OC: Yes.
ANNCR: Our honest opinion. EyeMasters. We treat you like a person.
Not a prescription.

ELVIS
30 seconds
This commercial has no dialogue.

831
Art Director: Rick Boyko
Creative Director: Bob Kuperman
Copywriter: Steve Rabosky
Producer: Brianne Howard
Director: Dennis Manarchy

832
Art Director: Woody Swain
Creative Director: Eric Weber
Copywriter: Andrew Landorf
Producer: Diane Flynn
Director: Jeff Gorman
Agency: Young & Rubicam, Inc.
Client: United States Postal Service

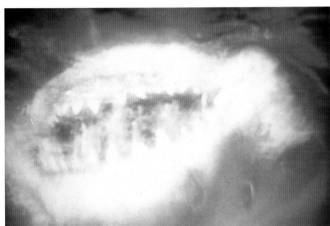

SMALL SCREENS

30 seconds
ANNCR: If you're not watching movies on the Mitsubishi Big Screen television, you're not seeing them the way they were meant to be seen. Introducing the world's first 70 inch TV. At 70 inches, it's not a big television; it's a small theater.

DINOSAURS

30 seconds
MAN: Wait stop! Wait stop! Stop! Stop! Wait stop! Wait wait stop! Don't you know they're coming! Wait stop!
DRIVER: Look out!
MAN: Doesn't anyone…believe me?
POLICE OFFICER: You hear that fellows, dinosaurs are coming to this town.
WOMAN: They're already here.
SFX: Dramatic music
VO: Dinosaur stamps…they're exciting. They're history. They're at your post office now.
MAN: Now do you believe me?

833

Art Director: Dan Weeks
Copywriter: Scott Eirinberg
Producer: Ray Lyle
Director: Jeff Gorman
Studio: Johns & Gorman Films
Client: Sears

834

Art Director: John Cenatiempo
Creative Director: Barry Biederman
Copywriter: Barry Biederman
Producer: Lisa Bifulco
Director: Chris Nolan
Agency: Biederman, Kelly & Shaffer
Client: Tri-State Cadillac Dealers Assoc.

BRANDS

30 seconds
COWBOY #1: Zenith…Braun…Sony…RCA…
SFX: Cattle mooing
VO: At Sears, we've rounded up over 1,000 brands. So now you can get top name brands at great low prices. And we're adding more everyday.
COWBOY #1: …Smith-Corona…
COWBOY #2: Yeah, where is that Smith-Corona, anyhow?
STEER: MOOOOOOOooooooooo…

COMMUTER

30 seconds
COMMUTER: Don't need a lift, Jack…there's my wife in our Lincoln Continental. Ahhh! You're not Doris. And this isn't my car—it's a Taurus. I'm sorry!
VO: It's funny, how much *alike* Ford cars look these days.
COMMUTER: Doris!…Oh, wait…this isn't my car, either--it's a Topaz!!
VO: By contrast, the 1990 Cadillacs are luxuriously, unmistakably Cadillacs.
COMMUTER: Doris…!!Doris…!!Ohhh, not Doris.
VO: See your Cadillac Tri-Statesman…now!

835

Art Director: Raul Pina
Creative Director: Jamie Seltzer
Copywriter: Rich Roth
Producer: Peter Yahr
Director: Carroll Ballard
Agency: Della Femina, McNamee WCRS
Client: Dow

836

Art Director: Mike Mazza
Creative Director: Bob Kuperman
Copywriter: Dick Sittig
Producer: Jack Harrower
Director: John Marles
Agency: Chiat/Day/Mojo
Client: Nissan Motor Corp.

TUNDRA

30 seconds
VO: Today, there's a better way to protect food from the freezing cold. Freezloc, a plastic freezer wrap with special cling strips that seal tighter against freezer burn than any other wrap, to protect your food from the ravages of freezing cold, until the day it's needed. Tough, thick, Freezloc with cling strips for more protection against freezer burn.

4 X 4 DREAMER

30 seconds
4x4 DREAMER: My dream car would be…a truck. A Nissan Hardbody. I'd race in Baja. Whoa, wait a minute, make that the mountains. With nobody around 'cept my girlfriend…and a pizza…and my boss…. Somebody's got to wash the truck.

837

Art Director: Mark Decena
Creative Director: Tom Molitor
Copywriter: David Munroe
Producer: Gale Gortney
Agency: Saatchi & Saatchi DFS/Pacific
Client: U.S. West

This guy walks into a diner and orders the special.

"Which one from the chalkboard would you like?"

GUY IN A DINER

30 seconds
SFX: Diner ambiance
VO: 25 million Americans can't read a dinner menu. U S WEST DIRECT volunteers teach literacy classes to show them what they're missing.

838

Art Director: Andy Dijak
⠀⠀⠀⠀⠀⠀⠀⠀⠀⠀⠀Mike Mazza
Creative Director: Bob Kuperman
Copywriter: Dick Sittig
Producer: Richard O'Neill
Agency: Chiat/Day/Mojo
Client: Nissan Motor Corp.

IF I HAD A 240SX

30 seconds
240SX DREAMER: If I had a Nissan 240SX…I'd get a red coupe.—No! A silver fastback. And I'd go for a spin up Route 7, the twisty part. Just me and Elvis…maybe Mark. Heck, why not Ken Wahl! Yeah, me and Ken…in my silver--no, red 240SX…driving into the sunset.

839
Art Director: Bob Tabor
Creative Director: Bill Chororos
Copywriter: Roger Feuerman
Producer: Bailey Weiss
Director: Jim Lee
Agency: Backer, Spielvogel, Bates
Client: Best Foods

840
Art Director: Phillip Squier
Creative Director: Scott Montgomery
Ken Sakoda
Designer: Phillip Squier
Copywriter: Michael McKay
Producer: Glenn Miller
Agency: Salvati Montgomery Sakoda
Client: Valley National Bank

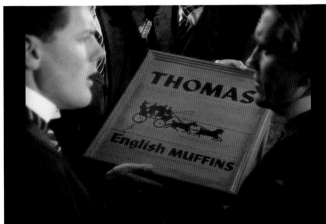

UNIVERSITY

30 seconds
STUDENT'S VOICE: None of us will forget that morning. I joined my
chums as I too was jolted by the news. Mr. Thomas had moved his
bakeshop to America. No more would we have his English muffins,
with nooks and crannies and melted butter, to sustain us through our
dreary day. University without nooks and crannies?! It was yet another
cross for England to bear.
Thomas' English Muffins. For over a hundred years, England's
breakfast tradition in America's hands.

PHOENIX SUNS

30 seconds
SFX: Droning noise
VO: To the hearing impaired, watching the news can be a confusing
experience. Reading lips and interpreting what they see isn't enough.
That's why we at Valley Bank are proud to sponsor channel 12's closed
captioned news.
SFX: Droning stops
VO: Because we understand how important it is for everyone to get the
whole story.

841

Art Director: Tim Delaney
Creative Director: Roger Livingston
Copywriter: Jim Copacino
Producer: Cindy Henderson
Director: Joe Sedelmaier
Agency: Livingston & Co.
Client: Alaska Airlines

842

Art Director: Earl Cavanah
Creative Director: Sam Scali
Copywriter: Larry Cadman
Producer: Sue Chiafullo
Director: Eli Noyes
Agency: Scali, McCabe, Sloves
Client: Nikon

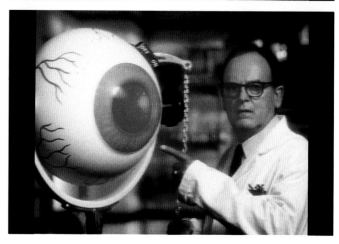

BEEMER

30 seconds
ASSISTANT: That's him, huh, company's top salesman?
CHAUFFEUR: Numero Uno, they say he can sell snow in a snowstorm.
ASSISTANT: A real personality.
CHAUFFEUR: The guy is a dynamo.
VO: Even the most important, dynamic executive can feel downright unimportant…
EXECUTIVE: Miss, oh, miss…
VO: …on a bad flight.
ASSISTANT: Looks like he's been working non-stop.
CHAUFFEUR: He never lets up, that's why he's making the big bucks.
VO: Next trip fly Alaska Airlines. We try to treat everybody like they're somebody.

RED-EYE ROCK

30 seconds
MUSIC: Queen's ''We will rock you''
SFX: Boom…boom…clap. Boom…boom…clap.
CHORUS: Down with, down with Red-eye.
SFX: Boom…boom…clap.
CHORUS: Down with, down with Red-eye.
SFX: Boom…boom…clap. Boom…boom…clap.
CHORUS: Down with, down with Red-eye.
SFX: Boom…boom…clap. Boom…
VO: In response…to popular demand, we proudly introduce the Nikon Teletouch 300. A totally automatic…dual lens camera…that significantly reduces…Red-eye.
SFX: Applause

843

Art Director: Simon Bowden
Creative Director: Earl Cavanah
Copywriter: Debbie Kasher
            Bernie Phillips
Producer: Dane Johnson
Director: Tom Higgins
Agency: Scali, McCabe, Sloves
Client: Volvo

844

Art Director: Bob Tabor
Creative Director: Bill Chororos
Copywriter: Roger Feuerman
Producer: Bailey Weiss
Agency: Backer, Spielvogel, Bates
Client: Best Foods

BUMPER CARS

30 seconds
ANNCR: Every Volvo is equipped with energy-absorbing front and rear crumple zones, rigid steel bars to protect you from side intrusion, and a steel safety cage for all-round protection, which is something you should think about seriously on a ride in the real world.

BRIGADIER

30 seconds
BRIGADIER'S VOICE: It was with great honor that I led a tribute to the town baker, Mr. Thomas. I didn't know the man, but he had been the maker of our marvelous muffins, with nooks and crannies, English to the core. I saluted him now that he had gone off to America. I didn't know the man. But I knew his muffins.
Thomas' English Muffins. For over a hundred years, England's breakfast tradition in American hands.

845

Art Director: Dean Hanson
Creative Director: Pat Burnham
Copywriter: Phil Hanft
Producer: Judy Carter Brink
Director: Henry Sandbank
Agency: Fallon McElligott
Client: Federal Express

846

Art Director: Jim Baldwin
Creative Director: Ray Redding
　　　　　　　　Thomas Hripko
Copywriter: David Longfield
Director: Bob Einstein

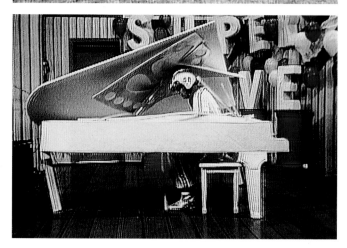

SIMULATOR

30 seconds
PILOT: Tokyo Tower, Tokyo Tower, Flight 101…request permission to land.
VO: Someday…every international air express company will have it all. 24-hour customer service…advanced tracking systems…
CO-PILOT: Whoa.
VO: …and their own fleet of planes flying to Europe, Canada and Japan.
PILOT: Touchdown!
VO: Just like Federal Express.
PILOT: Alright…
VO: But until then the others will just have to pretend.
PILOT: Nice lightning.
VO: Worldwide Service from Federal Express.

SUPER DAVE—HIGHLIGHTS #1

30 seconds
MIKE: PARTNERS Health Plan presents the greatest stunts of Super Dave Osborne.
SFX: Crowd cheers
MIKE: Sensational.
SUPER: Well, thank you, Michael. But, you know, I would not have the confidence to do these stunts without PARTNERS Health Plan.
MIKE: PARTNERS Health Plan.
SUPER: What are you, a parrot? I just said that.
MIKE: Of course you did. PARTNERS Health Plan of Arizona. If it works for Super Dave, it'll work for you.

847

Art Director: Grant Richards
　　　　　　 Carl Warner
Creative Director: Stan Richards
Copywriter: David Longfield
Producer: Lisa Dee
Director: Steve Tobin
Client: Pier 1 Imports

848

Art Director: Tom Lichtenheld
Creative Director: Pat Burnham
Copywriter: Phil Hanft
Director: Buck Holzemer
Agency: Fallon McElligott
Client: Amoco

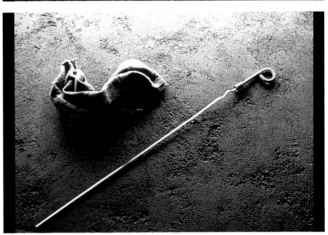

YOU NEVER KNOW

30 seconds
MUSIC: "Hungry Town" by Australian band Big Pig

DIPSTICK

30 seconds
VO: Now that Amoco LDO…meets manufacturer's performance requirements for every car made today…any dipstick can use it. Amoco LDO. Any dipstick can use it.

849

Art Director: Bill Kreigbaum
Tom Gilmore
Jeff Hopfer
Copywriter: Mike Renfro
Mike Malone
Producer: Lisa Dee
Director: Jeff Bednarz
Studio: Bednarz Films
Client: Metroplex Cadillac Group

850

Art Director: Frank Haggerty
Creative Director: Jack Supple
Copywriter: Kerry Casey
Producer: Jack Steinmann
Director: Tim Francisco
Agency: Carmichael Lynch
Studio: C & H Productions
Client: Rapala

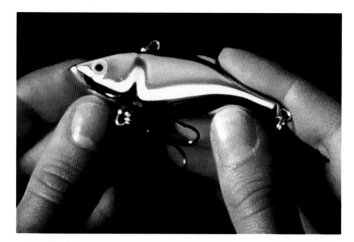

THRILL IS GONE

30 seconds
MUSIC: "Thrill is gone"
ANNCR: If the thought of yet another expensive European car, with yet another sparkling interior doesn't thrill you, take heart. The 1989 Cadillac Seville STS is here. Take one for a thrilling road test.

DISAPPEAR

30 seconds
SFX: Crickets chirping
ANNCR: Introducing the Rattl'n Rap. With the sound no fish can resist.
SFX: Rattle

851

Art Director: Tom Lichtenheld
Creative Director: Pat Burnham
Copywriter: Bruce Bildsten
Producer: Char Loving
Director: Rick Dublin
Agency: Fallon McElligott
Client: Hyponex

852

Art Director: Pat Burnham
Creative Director: Pat Burnham
Copywriter: Jarl Olsen
Director: Jim Lund
Agency: Fallon McElligott
Client: Knox Kitchen Center

FIRE ANTS

30 seconds
SFX: Thud!
Thud! Thud!
Thud! Thud! Thud!
Thud! Thud! Thud! Thud! Thud! Thud! Thud! Thud! Thud! Thud!
Thud!
VO: The Hyponex Fire Ant Extinguisher.
Guaranteed to kill an entire fire ant mound…in just one step.

KITCHEN

30 seconds
SFX: Crickets; click; man crawling; liquid pouring; click; crickets

853

Art Director: Dean Hanson
Creative Director: Pat Burnham
Copywriter: Bruce Bildsten
Producer: Char Loving
Director: Lol Creme
　　　　　 Kevin Godley
Agency: Fallon McElligott
Client: First Tennessee Banks

854

Art Director: Bill Oberlander
Creative Director: Ron Arnold
Copywriter: Craig Demeter

HANDSHAKE

30 seconds

VO: It used to be, getting a loan took little more than a firm handshake. Well, some banks have made it more complicated than that. But at First Tennessee Bank, with our easy telephone loan applications…we're making things simple again.

FLIP CARD MAN

30 seconds

MAN: All Mita makes are great copiers. Which may be why nearly 9 out of 10 people who own them, love them. I know I do. I don't worry about coming out too dark, too light, crumpled, or not coming out at all. In fact, I always look 100%. Sometimes even 151%. At Mita, all we make are great copiers.

855

Art Director: Steve Stone
Creative Director: Jeffrey Goodby
                    Rich Silverstein
Photographer: Don Peterman
Copywriter: David Fowler
Producer: Debbie King
Director: Jon Francis
Studio: Jon Francis Films

856

Art Director: Eric David
Creative Director: Peter Cornish
Copywriter: Eric David
                Peter Cornish
Producer: Pat Raftery
Director: Lenny Hirschfield

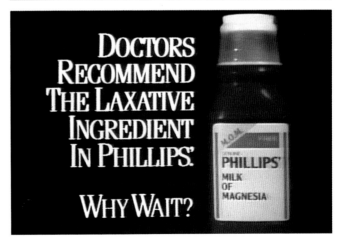

WHAT ELSE

30 seconds
WILL: What else can we do? We've got closing stocks every day…isn't that enough? We've got the Weekend Section on Friday, before the weekend. Wasn't that a big idea? Eh, I guess it wasn't big enough. We've got the Neighborhood Report…what else is there? What?! What more can we do to make this darn paper great?

WHY WAIT

30 seconds
SFX: Music builds throughout; musical hits

857

Art Director: Andy Vucinich
Creative Director: Jon Hyde
Copywriter: Paul Cuneo
Producer: Ann Johnston
Director: David Simpson
Agency: J. Walter Thompson, San Francisco
Client: Kaiser Permanente

858

Art Director: Don Schneider
Creative Director: Ted Sann
　　　　　　　　　　Rick Meyer
　　　　　　　　　　Len McCarron
Copywriter: Jonathon Mandell
Producer: Sally Smith
Director: Leslie Dektor
Studio: Petermann-Dektor
Client: Dupont

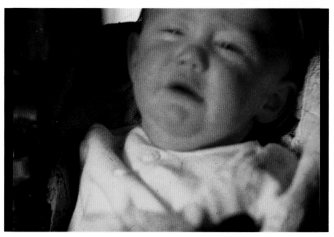

SALUTE

30 seconds
SFX: Piano music
VO: To friends…and families. To those full of history and hard work. To those who have just arrived and those who have been around a bit longer. A salute…to the proud people of Baltimore. From Kaiser Permanente. The people who are proud to be taking care of you.

HOT WORK

30 seconds
SFX: Roar of flames; fireman breathing; sirens
ANNCR: To protect the lives of firefighters, DuPont developed a remarkable fire-resistant fiber for their clothing called Nomex. But perhaps even more remarkable is how it protects those who never even wear it. At DuPont we make things that make a difference.
SFX: Baby crying
ANNCR: Better things for better living.

859

Art Director: Don Easdon
Creative Director: Don Easdon
Bill Heater
Copywriter: Bill Heater
Producer: Mary Ellen Argentieri
Director: Larry Robbins
Agency: Hill, Holliday
Client: Nissan Infiniti

860

Art Director: Amy Levitan
Creative Director: Jack Mariucci
Bob Mackall
Copywriter: Deborah Connolly
Producer: Lora Nelson
Director: Peter Cherry
Agency: DDB Needham Worldwide
Client: Colombian Coffee

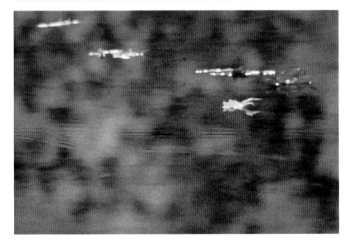

FLOATING LEAVES

30 seconds
VO: From the days of the gilded coach, the concept of luxury in a
luxury car has suggested costly indulgence and material abundance.
But in Japan centuries ago, and today still where true luxury is a spare,
natural idea, and beauty, a close personal experience, there is a
different concept of luxury. Infiniti.

GALLERY

30 seconds
MAN 1: …classical language.
SFX: People mumbling and talking
MAN 2: …Oh yes, yes.
WOMAN 1: Yes, yes humanist admiration.
HOST: Coffee is served.
MAN 2: …yes, indeed they're rich.
HOST: *Colombian* Coffee.
WOMAN 2: Excuse me.
MAN 2: Excuse me.
WOMAN 1: Excuse me.
ANNCR: 100% Colombian Coffee. Hand-picked by Juan Valdez. The
richest coffee in the world.

861

Art Director: Len McCarron
Creative Director: Ted Sann
Copywriter: Rick Meyer
Producer: Linda Horn
Director: Steve Horn
Client: Dupont

862

Art Director: Don Easdon
Creative Director: Don Easdon
Bill Heater
Copywriter: Bill Heater
Producer: Mary Ellen Argentieri
Director: Larry Robbins
Agency: Hill, Holliday
Client: Nissan Infiniti

MARY BRODIE

30 seconds
VO: Mary Brodie won't feel the tiny lump in her breast for another two years. But she'll discover it tomorrow after her first mammogram. Thanks in part to a new x-ray film created by DuPont. That makes it safer to start mammography early. And for Mary early detection means a two year head start on the rest of her life. At DuPont we make the things that make a difference.

WATER ON ROCK

30 seconds
VO: You don't see it, you feel it. You're part of it. You control it. And it is part of you. The Power.
The Q45 luxury sedan from Infiniti.

863

Art Director: Clem McCarthy
Creative Director: Ralph Ammirati
Copywriter: Bill McCullum
Producer: Linda Horn
Director: Steve Horn
Client: B.M.W. of North America

864

Art Director: Don Easdon
Creative Director: Don Easdon
  Bill Heater
Copywriter: Bill Heater
Producer: Mary Ellen Argentieri
Director: Larry Robbins
Agency: Hill, Holliday
Client: Nissan Infiniti

RUGBY

30 seconds
PLAYERS: Oh, we had a little party down in Berkeley,
  There was very little, very little grace.
  Oh, we had a little party down in Berkeley,
  and we had to carry Harry from the place.
  For the Old Blues,
  For the Old Blues, then we start to cry.
  We often do or die.
  For the Old Blues, For the Old Blues,
  For the Old.Blues...
VO: The B.M.W. three series is why some enthusiasts are more
enthusiastic than others.
PLAYERS: Yea, Yea.

MISTY TREE

30 seconds
VO: We've paid so much money for so long maybe the time has come
for sanely priced luxury cars and a new set of luxury values, not based
on what you can afford to pay but on what's reasonable to expect in
terms of performance and comfort. That's a new concept in luxury
cars. It's called Infiniti.

865

Art Director: John Sapienza
Creative Director: Bruce Lee
Copywriter: Tom Hansen
Producer: Den Vadies
Director: Klaus Lucka
Agency: Leo Burnett Co.
Client: Allstate

866

Art Director: Bob Brihn
                Mark Johnson
Creative Director: Pat Burnham
Copywriter: George Gier
Agency: Fallon McElligott
Client: Porsche

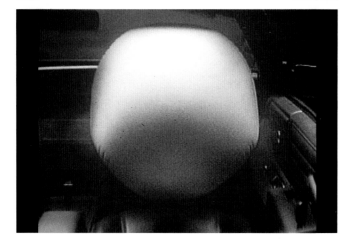

TRUCK

30 seconds
MAN VO: I should be dead. Last year as I was driving home…I
approached a hill. I saw something more frightening than…anything I
have ever seen. I tried to get out of its way. It was too late. I had a head-
on crash…with a 28,000 pound truck. I'm still alive today…because of
an airbag in my car.
VO: Allstate supports airbags because they save lives and lower
insurance costs.

DRIVING SCHOOL

30 seconds
MUSIC: Alice Cooper's "School's Out"
VO: What could be more exciting than two days of high performance
racing school? The drive home.

867

Art Director: Houman Pirdavari
Creative Director: Pat Burnham
Copywriter: Bruce Bildsten
Producer: Char Loving
Director: Roger Woodburn
Agency: Fallon McElligott
Client: Timex

868

Art Director: Brent Ladd
Copywriter: Carl Laflamme
Director: Bruce Braden
Client: The *Dallas Morning News*

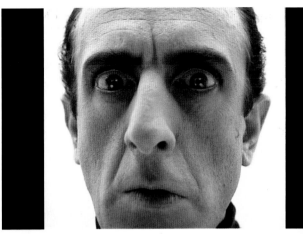

PSYCHIC

30 seconds
SFX: Eerie background music
VO: Timex. It takes a lickin' and keeps on tickin'.

MAGIC TYPEWRITER

30 seconds
SFX: Horses galloping; tennis ball volleying back and forth; basketball dribbling; football players hitting each other; typewriter followed by a buzzer; crowd cheer

869

Art Director: Bryan Buckley
Tom DeCerchio
Copywriter: Tom DeCerchio
Bryan Buckley
Director: Rob Lopes
Agency: Buckley/DeCerchio
Client: Homeplace

870

Art Director: Sal DeVito
Creative Director: Lee Garfinkel
Copywriter: Lee Garfinkel
Producer: Rachel Novak
Director: Carlton Chase
Agency: Levine, Huntley, Schmidt & Beaver
Client: Beneficial

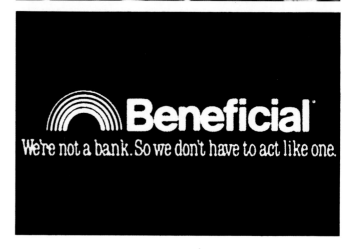

IN THE DARK

30 seconds
SFX: Footsteps, then the sound of a glass table crashing; more footsteps, then shouting; a burst of light and fizzing electronical noises; man yelling, then the crash of a fish tank and water gurgling

QADDAFI

30 seconds
ANNCR: Over the years, U.S. banks have loaned $20 million to people like this. $5.7 billion to people like this. $3 billion to people like this. But for 75 years, we've always believed it was more important to loan money to people like this.
Beneficial. We're not a bank. So we don't have to act like one.

871

Art Director: Bob Meagher
Creative Director: Mike Hughes
Copywriter: Kerry Feuerman
Producer: Morty Baran
Director: Dan Hainey
Agency: The Martin Agency
Client: Residence Inn

872

Art Director: Lisa Bennett
Creative Director: Steve Nubie
Copywriter: Bill Cokas
Producer: Mike Diedrich
Director: Matthew Meshekoff
Agency: Leo Burnett Co.
Client: Heinz

HOUSE TRAILER

30 seconds
SFX: Music
VO: When traveling on business, there are two ways to get a full kitchen, fireplace and a large, comfortable living room…the other way is to stay at a Residence Inn.
Residence Inn. People who travel for a living, live here.

MOUTHFUL

30 seconds
VO: We're still trying to make our Heinz Home Style Gravy just like your own homemade.
JERRY: Mmglbhpb.
ROO: He said, "Nice try."
VO: We made it with real beef and beef juices, so it tastes just like yours.
JERRY: MMMmmphmbl!
ROO: He feels that while the taste and overall quality are good, there is still work to be done.
JERRY: MHuh?
VO: And we season and simmer and stir it 'til it's just like homemade.
JERRY: MM-MM…mmglphb!
ROO: He said, "It's close."
VO: Heinz Homestyle Gravy. So close to homemade.

873

Art Director: Marty McDonald
Creative Director: James Dale
Copywriter: John Parlato
James Dale
Jim Lansbury
Director: John Parlato
John Saag
Client: Baltimore Symphony Orchestra

874

Art Director: John Butler
Mike Shine
Creative Director: Bill Hamilton
Copywriter: Mike Shine
John Butler
Producer: Steve Amato
Trish Reeves
Agency: Chiat/Day/Mojo Advertising Inc.
Client: Soho Natural Sodas

TEAM

30 seconds
MAN 1: I think they're one of the best teams playing today.
WOMAN: I just love their uniforms.
MAN 2: Great stadium, no rain delays.
MUSICIAN: We're feeling good, we're looking good, we're playing good.
FRANK ROBINSON: We could never play like that.
MUSIC: Beethoven's 5th Symphony
ANNCR: The Baltimore Symphony Orchestra. Baltimore's other major league team. For tickets, call 783-8000.
MAN 1: They don't chew tobacco, they don't spit, and they're very polite.

NATURAL/ARTIFICIAL 1

30 seconds
SFX: Zydeco music

875

Art Director: Bob Watson
Creative Director: Allen Klein
Copywriter: Tom Johnston
Producer: Glant Cohen
        Angelo Antonucci
Director: George Gootsan
        Buck Holzemer
Agency: Leo Burnett Co.
Client: Tropicana Twister

876

Art Director: Art Webb
Creative Director: Frank Merriam
Copywriter: Steve Landrum
Director: Mike Caporale
Studio: Caporale
Client: Upper Midwest Marketing

LEERY

30 seconds
MAN VO: Sounds strange to me.
WOMAN VO: Me too.
MAN VO: Us both.
ANNCR: Why are people leery of Tropicana Twister?
MAN VO: It violates the order of nature.
ANNCR: Tropicana Twister. Deliciously tempting flavor combinations Mother Nature never imagined.
GUY VO: The imagination is a dangerous thing.
ANNCR: Captivating flavors like Orange Passionfruit.
MOM VO: Passionfruit?
ANNCR: Tropicana Twister. Flavors Mother Nature never intended. But should've.
MAN VO: It's more excitement than decent people need.

BUCKET

30 seconds
SFX: Footsteps
VO: This is the lure that won last year's National Walleye Championship. A lure so powerful…
SFX: Splash
VO: …it catches fish in places…you'd swear fish don't exist.

877

Art Director: John Butler
Mike Shine
Creative Director: Bill Hamilton
Copywriter: Mike Shine
John Butler
Producer: Steve Amato
Trish Reeves
Agency: Chiat/Day/Mojo Advertising Inc.
Client: Soho Natural Sodas

NATURAL/ARTIFICIAL 3
30 seconds
SFX: Zydeco music

878

Art Director: Dave Nathanson
Creative Director: Bill Hamilton
Copywriter: Ken Sandbank
Producer: Steve Amato
Agency: Chiat/Day/Mojo Advertising Inc.
Client: Bissell

VACUUMING EVERYTHING
30 seconds
VO: What if, instead of really cleaning all the things that got dirty, you simply vacuumed them? Absurd? You would never do that, right? Except when it comes to your carpet. Vacuuming may make carpets look clean, but the Bissell steam cleaner gets deep-down dirt that a vacuum never will. The compact, easy-to-use, Bissell steam cleaner. The best way to get the most out of your carpets.

879

Art Director: David Jenkins
Creative Director: Dan Wieden
David Kennedy
Copywriter: Jerry Cronin
Agency: Wieden & Kennedy
Client: Nike

880

Art Director: Steve Fong
Creative Director: Ross Van Dusen
Copywriter: Dave Woodside
Producer: Harvey Greenberg
Jan Ushijima
Director: Jeff Gorman
Agency: Chiat/Day/Mojo
Client: Worlds of Wonder

HIGH PLAINS

30 seconds
SFX: Piano music
WOMAN: There are clubs you can't belong to…neighborhoods
you can't live in…schools you can't get into…but the roads are
always open.

YOU CAN RUN

30 seconds
SFX: Music; beeping
KID VO: Introducing Hide N' Sneak
MOM: Boys!
KID: Ahhh!…Ahhhh!
KID VO: Hide N' Sneak. You can run, but you can't hide!

881

Art Director: Susan Hoffman
Creative Director: Dan Wieden
                                    David Kennedy
Copywriter: Steve Sandoz
Agency: Wieden & Kennedy
Client: Nike

882

Art Director: Sal DeVito
Creative Director: Lee Garfinkel
Copywriter: Lee Garfinkel
Producer: Rachel Novak
Agency: Levine, Huntley, Schmidt & Beaver
Client: Beneficial

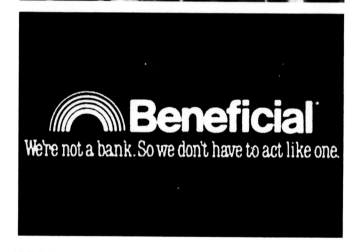

JUST FACE IT/KIDS

30 seconds
SFX: Music
SINGER: Just kick it.
    Just bounce it.
SFX: Kids screaming
SINGER: Just zap it.
    Just flip it.
    Just rock it.
    Just face it.

FOUR LEADERS

30 seconds
ANNCR: Banks don't give everyone who applies for a loan a hard time. He got loans for $20 million. They were kind enough to loan him $600 million. And he borrowed $5.7 billion. We think something is wrong when it's easier for someone like him to get a loan than it is for you. Beneficial. We're not a bank, so we don't have to act like one.

883

Art Director: John D'Asto
Creative Director: Jan Zechman
Copywriter: Barton Landsman
Producer: Jan Jolivette
　　　　　　Renee Raab
Director: David Wild
Studio: Highlight Commercials
Client: Mindscape, Inc.

884

Art Director: Len Fink
Creative Director: Bill Hamilton
Copywriter: Peter Levathes
Producer: Steve Amato
Agency: Chiat/Day/Mojo Advertising Inc.
Client: New England Apple Products

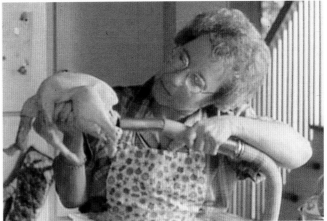

PAPERBOY

30 seconds
VO: Warning: Such behavior is irresponsible, immature and very
foolish. We recommend you try it at home. Paperboy from Mindscape.
For your Nintendo Entertainment System.

THIRST DETECTOR

30 seconds
VO 1: Juice?
VO 2: Veryfine. The Veryfinest.

885

Art Director: Steve Fong
Creative Director: Bill Hamilton
Copywriter: Glenn Porter
Producer: Carey Zeiser
　　　　Lee Weiss
Agency: Chiat/Day/Mojo Advertising Inc.
Client: Reebok International Ltd.

886

Art Director: John D'Asto
Creative Director: Jan Zechman
Copywriter: Jim Carey
Producer: Laurie Berger
Director: Robert Black
Studio: Travisano, Digiacamo
Client: State of Illinois

PUMP

30 seconds
ALTERNATING SPEAKERS: This is your Pump.
Push this little thing here…
And you just pump.
Pump.
Pump.
You know how to do that, don't you?
Five or six pumps.
I'd say fifteen pumps.
Twenty to twenty-five times.
Seventy pumps will do it.
You know, I'm also going to use this to intimidate people.
These things in here, I don't know what they're called.
Airbags.
When you want to release, there is a little button back here that you
just push down and you can hear the air…
…leaving the pump.
I think we're on to something.
VO: Pump it up.

MARTIANS

30 seconds
BARBER: Here in Spring Grove we are often visited by Martians.
VO: There are over 1000 festivals in Illinois.
BARBER: They're purple in color, like eggplant, and real nice.
VO: So get out and join the fun.
BARBER: But don't bark at their tentacles. That gets 'em riled. Why Fifi
here (gesturing toward cat), she used to be a dog.
VO: Just watch out for the storytelling contest down in Spring Grove.
BARBER: A German shepherd.

887

Art Director: Brent Ladd
Creative Director: Gary Brahl
Copywriter: Clay Hudson
Producer: Steve Gilbert
Agency: GSD&M Advertising
Client: Coors Brewing Co.

888

Art Director: Lori Brown
Creative Director: Guy Bommarito
Copywriter: David Smith
Producer: Dorothy Taylor
Agency: GSD&M Advertising
Client: Southwest Airlines

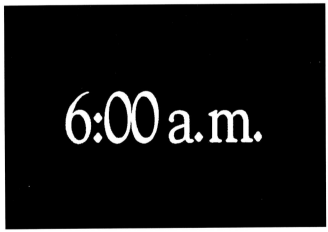

BIRTHDAY

30 seconds
SPOKESMAN: Hey, party timers, I got some special birthday party tips for ya from Extra Gold Draft. First, don't forget the Extra Gold. More beer taste, extra smooth. Ask for an Extra. Another tip—when you make a wish…make it a *wish*—yes, yes—no!
ANNCR: When you want more beer, ask for an Extra.
TOM: Come here—whoaaa…

SKIP

30 seconds
SFX: Scratchy record playing Lefty Frizzell tune
ANNCR: Flying to Los Angeles on business?
SINGER: If you've got the money,
    I've got the time…(record gets stuck)
    I've got the time…
    I've got the time…
    I've got the time…
    I've got the time…
    I've got the time…
SFX: Music fades out
VO: With 18 flights a day to Los Angeles International Airport, flying Southwest Airlines is like having your own company plane.

889

Art Director: Don Fibich
Copywriter: Chuck Withrow
Producer: Ann Russo
　　　　Roseanne Lowe
　　　　Celeste Sciortino
Director: Kenny Mirman
Agency: Wyse Advertising
Client: Cleveland Zoo

FACES

30 seconds
SFX: Music
VO; One of the most beautiful things about faces like these…is the look they'll bring to a face like this.
The Cleveland Metroparks Zoo. It's wild.

890

Art Director: Richard Crispo
　　　　Mark Erwin
　　　　Jon Reeder
Copywriter: Brent Bouchez
　　　　Hillary Jordan
　　　　Rob Siltanen
Producer: Ben Grylewicz
Director: Brent Thomas
Agency: Ketchum, Los Angeles

COMPANY CAR

30 seconds
SHE: Well, what did he say?
HE: He said, Kirkwood…
BOSS: You're smart, you're aggressive, you're…
HE: Brilliant, creative, aggressive, brilliant…
SHE: He said all that, did he?
HE: Well, something to that effect.
SHE: C'mon, c'mon, c'mon, what else?
HE: Stock. Sign-on bonus. Company car. Of course I'm going to turn it down.
SHE: The job?
HE: The car.
VO: The Legend Sedan from Acura. Number one in customer satisfaction three years in a row.

891

Art Director: Warren Eakins
Creative Director: Dan Wieden
David Kennedy
Copywriter: Steve Sandoz
Agency: Wieden & Kennedy
Client: Nike

BIKE MESSENGER
30 seconds
SFX: Jazz music
BIKE MESSENGER: You think Bo Jackson's the only guy who can do this stuff?

892

Art Director: Steve Beaumont
Creative Director: Brent Bouchez
Copywriter: Brent Bouchez
Producer: Ben Grylewicz
Director: Caleb Deschanel
Agency: Ketchum, Los Angeles
Client: American Honda Motor Corp.

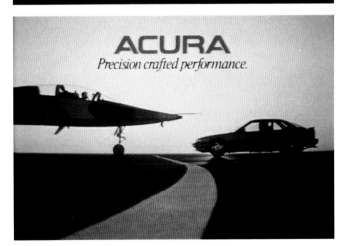

JET
30 seconds
VO: The anti-lock brakes on the 1990 Acura Integra were inspired by those used to stop jet aircraft. And while you might expect to find such technology on a multi-million dollar airplane, you might not expect to find it on an automobile that costs…considerably less.

893

Art Director: Jac Coverdale
Creative Director: Jac Coverdale
Designer: Jac Coverdale
Copywriter: Jerry Fury
Producer: Kate O'Toole
Agency: Clarity, Coverdale, Rueff
Client: United Recovery Center

894

Art Director: Michael Vitiello
Creative Director: Lee Garfinkel
Copywriter: Lee Garfinkel
Producer: Bob Nelson
Director: Henry Sandbank
Agency: Levine, Huntley, Schmidt & Beaver
Client: Subaru of America

HIT BOTTOM

30 seconds
ANNCR: Most people with a drinking problem have to hit bottom before they'll get help for themselves. To help someone you care about before they hit bottom, call United Recovery Center for a free consultation.

BARN

30 seconds
ANNCR: The old grey Subaru ain't what she used to be. Introducing the larger, more powerful Subaru Legacy.

895

Art Director: Susan Westre
Creative Director: Steve Hayden
Copywriter: Chris Wall
Producer: Bob Belton
         Pat Walsh
Director: Joe Pytka
Studio: Pytka Productions
Client: Apple Computer Inc.

TESTING 1-2-3

60 seconds
WOMAN 1: Can I get on there soon?
WOMAN 2: After me.
KEN: Do you think I can get on here soon?
MAN 1: Yeah, give me a minute, man.
ED: You've been staring out there all day. What are you doing?
JOHN: Testing.
ED: Testing what?
JOHN: Computers. I'm trying to figure out which computer is the most powerful.
ED: Well, that's easy. The one with the most memory…megahertz…MIPS…you know.
JOHN: No, I don't think so. I think the most powerful computer is the one that people actually use.
GIRL: Hi, Ken.
KEN: Hey.
VO: Macintosh has the power to change the way you look at computers. The power to be your best.
ED: That's not really a fair comparison. People like using the Mac.

896

Art Director: Mark Haumersen
Creative Director: Lyle Wedemeyer
Copywriter: Lyle Wedemeyer
Director: Michael McNamara
Agency: Martin/Williams
Client: On Mark Group

WAITING

60 seconds
ANNCR: For all those people who have ever waited for someone…and particularly for those who have ever waited for someone to come home from the hospital…St. Francis Hospital has these words of comfort. Through the advanced technology of our Pittsburgh Laser Center, we've helped thousands of patients recover more quickly and with less complications after surgery…for procedures ranging from opthamology to general surgery. All of which means less waiting for the people doing the waiting. If you or someone you know needs surgery, call the Pittsburgh Laser Center at 1-800-648-8877 for a free brochure or to arrange a consultation.
The Pittsburgh Laser Center at St. Francis. Enlightened medicine that's making the wait a little easier.

897

Art Director: Doug Bartow
Creative Director: Doug Bartow
Designer: Doug Bartow
Producer: Bruce Allen
Director: Claude Mougin
Agency: Grey
Client: Bloomingdale's

VIVE LA FRANCE

60 seconds
(Spoken in French)
SHE: I've heard enough.
HE: It's truly horrible.
SHE: Who cares what you think?
HE: You think it's nice? It's an insult to 18th century architecture.
SHE: No, you don't understand at all.
MOM: Let's go Celeste, hurry up. We're going to the museum, we'll see the Mona Lisa in a great big chateau.
LITTLE GIRL: Yes, I'm coming.
MOM: Come on, what are you doing? Stop dreaming. Hurry…
HE: I would say Egyptian
SHE: Very American
HE: French
SHE: Hollywood, very French
VO: (in English) Vive La France. Bloomingdale's celebration of what's new, what's important, what's very French. It's the legendary chic of Paris' great designers working in pure wool. Vive La France at Bloomingdale's. It's like no other store in the world.

898

Art Director: Susan Westre
Creative Director: Steve Hayden
Copywriter: Chris Wall
Producer: Bob Belton
　　　　　　Pat Walsh
Director: Joe Pytka
Studio: Pytka Productions
Client: Apple Computer Inc.

THE NEW TEACHER

60 seconds
PRINCIPAL: Looks like we got a new teacher. Miss Kassman?
SECRETARY: Miss Kassman.
BROTHER: Amy, I hear your new teacher's real mean.
MISS KASSMAN: Good morning, everybody.
CLASS: Good morning!
DOUG: New teachers have to be tough so you're scared of 'em.
MISS KASSMAN: Did you bring your pictures?
CLASS: Yes!
MISS KASSMAN: Amy, would you come up here and bring your picture with you, please?
SFX: Commotion among the students
PRINCIPAL: I'd better check on Miss Kassman.
SFX: More commotion
ANNCR: There's a special power that can bring students and teachers closer together. The power to be your best.
BROTHER: Whoa, that's cool! Hey, how's your new teacher?
AMY: Oh, she's OK.

899

Art Director: Don Easdon
Creative Director: Don Easdon
                   Bill Heater
Copywriter: Bill Heater
Producer: Mary Ellen Argentieri
Director: Joe Pytka
Agency: Hill, Holliday
Client: Nissan Infiniti

RELATIVE IMPORTANCE OF STUFF

60 seconds
WISE OLD MAN: I have a friend…he's not successful and he hasn't accomplished everything he wants to accomplish…but, he's on his way. He's a fisherman, he loves fishing. He does this. What do you call that?
CALLOW YOUTH: Fly fishing?
WISE OLD MAN: That's exactly right. That's his luxury, he's a fly fisherman. He calls it his one luxury. What's your luxury?
CALLOW YOUTH: I don't think of luxury like that. Luxury is a big house, a boat, a luxury car, clothes.
WISE OLD MAN: Luxury is something expensive then? Is that right?
CALLOW YOUTH: Well…that's what they say. I mean…yeah, I think that's luxury. A mink coat is luxury.
WISE OLD MAN: Well, let me ask you this. Which is more of a luxury? Something expensive or something that gives you satisfaction?

900

Art Director: Mike Mazza
Creative Director: Bob Kuperman
Copywriter: Dick Sittig
Producer: Richard O'Neill
Director: Mike Mazza

TURBO Z DREAMER

60 seconds
TURBO Z DREAMER: So I'm havin' this dream—I'm in a Turbo Z…and these guys are after me…but they can't catch me…so they get a car… but they can't catch me…so they get a plane…just as they're about to catch me--the…twin…turbos…kick…in.
SFX: Jet engine

901

Art Director: Susan Westre
Creative Director: Steve Hayden
Copywriter: Chris Wall
Producer: Bob Belton
          Pat Walsh
Director: Joe Pytka
Studio: Pytka Productions
Client: Apple Computer Inc.

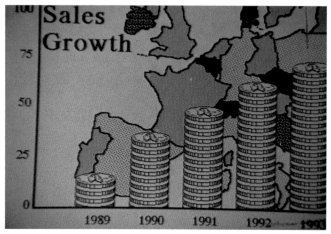

HIT THE ROAD, MAC

60 seconds
SFX: Music; French announcements over airport public address
PHILLIPE MICHEL: Ah, no.
AIDE: (in French) I have the tickets, sir.
PHILLIPE MICHEL: (in Italian) I speak 7 languages, but I can't understand this!
VO: Introducing the first portable computer you already know how to use.
PHILLIPE MICHEL: Excuse me, ah, it's my computer. I seem to be having trouble. I know nothing about computers.
CINDY: I'm sorry. I don't know anything about computers either.

902

Art Director: Rich Silverstein
          Steve Diamant
Creative Director: Andy Berlin
Photographer: Michael Duff
Copywriter: Andy Berlin
          Jeffrey Goodby
Producer: Elizabeth O'Toole
Director: Stan Schofield
Studio: Sandbank & Partners

SATURDAY NIGHT

60 seconds
SFX: Music
ANNCR: Every Saturday night in the city of New York, you can experience many things that are the best of their kind in all the world. Now one of them is a cruise line.

903

Art Director: Leslie Caldwell
Creative Director: Mike Koelker
Copywriter: Mike Koelker
Producer: Steve Neely
Director: Leslie Dektor
Agency: Foote, Cone & Belding

CHICAGO

60 seconds
SFX: Music
VO: The city.
JAZZ MAN: I don't know where it comes from ya know, jus' as long as
it keeps coming, right?
YOUNG MUSICIAN: This is my bass note and this is my treble, what am
I suppose to do?
JAZZ MAN: How old are you?
KID: 15.
JAZZ MAN: Wow?!

904

Art Director: Susan Westre
Creative Director: Steve Hayden
Copywriter: Chris Wall
Producer: Bob Belton
　　　　　Pat Walsh
Director: Joe Pytka
Studio: Pytka Productions
Client: Apple Computer Inc.

ENTREPRENEUR

60 seconds
EX-BOSS: I told Greg he was crazy to start his own business. He won't
have our resources. He won't have our computers…
ANNIE: Good morning, Greg!
GREG: Good morning, Annie.
GUY AT DESK: Sure, it's a lot of space for one guy. He says he's
planning to grow.
WORKER: This noise bothering you, pal?
GREG: No problem, thanks.
EX-BOSS: He won't have our, uh, graphics department, he won't…
EX-ASSOCIATE: He won't have our bureaucracy.
TOM: I heard Greg Clancey went independent.
BOB: Wish I had his guts.
EXEC 2: Who are these guys anyway?
EXEC 3: Greg's the creative guy. Clancey's just a bean counter.
VO: Macintosh has the power to make you independent. The power to
be your best.
WORKER: How come you got so much space?
GREG: I'm an optimist.

905

Art Director: Richard Sabean
Creative Director: Ted Sann
      Michael Patti
      Richard Sabean
Copywriter: Michael Patti
Producer: Gene Lofaro
Director: Terrence Donovan
Studio: Terrence Donovan Ltd.
Client: Pepsi Cola

SIMPLY IRRESISTIBLE

60 seconds
ROBERT PALMER: How can it be permissible?
 Don't compromise my principle…Yeah Yeah.
 This kind of love is mythical;
 It's anything but typical.
 It's a craze you'd endorse; it's a powerful force.
 You're obliged to conform, 'cause there's no other choice.
 It use to look good to me but now I find it…
 Simply Irresistible…
 Simply Irresistible….She's all mine…
 There's no other way to go…
 Simply Irresistible.

906

Art Director: Rich Martel
Copywriter: Al Merrin
Producer: Tony Frere
Director: Leslie Dektor
Agency: BBD&O

GLASNOST

60 seconds
(Spoken in Russian)
SFX: Music
FATHER: Noise, noise, why all this noise?
KID: Hey Dude! Totally awesome day.
VO: (in English) Not very long ago, America introduced Pepsi to the Soviet Union…
OLD WOMAN: Look, look, what is this?
FATHER: Look at you! Why do you dress like that?
VO: (in English) …And while it may be quite a coincidence, a lot of refreshing changes have taken place ever since.
KID: Yo…Misha!
FATHER: Don't you have any normal friends? Kids!
VO: (in English) Pepsi…a generation ahead.
OLD WOMAN: Yuri…come on, lighten up.

907

Art Director: Donna Weinheim
Creative Director: Donna Weinheim
Copywriter: Jeff Alphin
　　　　　　Jane King
Producer: Ann Kurtzman
Director: Tony Kaye
Agency: Cliff Freeman & Partners
Client: Home Box Office/Comedy Channel

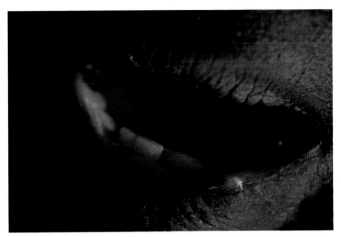

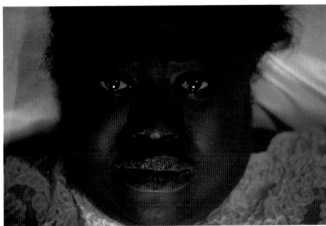

SNORING

60 seconds
SFX: Snoring; grunting
ANNCR: When life is rough, laugh it off with the new Comedy Channel. 24 hours a day. We're there when you need us.

908

Art Director: John Butler
　　　　　　Mike Shine
Creative Director: Bill Hamilton
Copywriter: Mike Shine
　　　　　　John Butler
Producer: Steve Amato
　　　　　　Trish Reeves
Agency: Chiat/Day/Mojo Advertising Inc.
Client: Soho Natural Sodas

NATURAL/ARTIFICIAL

45 seconds
SFX: Zydeco music

909

Art Director: Burint Ramany
Creative Director: Gerry Miller
Copywriter: Gerry Miller
Producer: Glant Cohen
Director: Leroy Koetz
Agency: Leo Burnett Co.
Client: Proctor & Gamble

910

Art Director: Susan Hoffman
Creative Director: Dan Wieden
David Kennedy
Copywriter: Geoff McGann
Agency: Wieden & Kennedy
Client: Nike

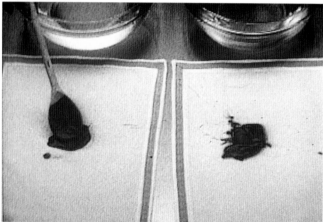

SPAGHETTI
45 seconds
SFX: Music
VO: Nobody's better in cold than All Temperature Cheer.

TENNIS LESSONS
60 seconds
INSTR: Today, we'll talk more about proper tennis procedure....Let's begin with the stroke. Always keeping your eye on the ball and maintaining a steady and bodied position. Keep...
SFX: Loud music
INSTR: ...Never, never try to hit too hard...
SFX: Loud music
INSTR: ...Avoid over-excitement.
SFX: Loud music
INSTR: In tennis, conservative attire is a must. Remember, tennis is a civilized sport, so always obey all court rules and regulations...
SFX: Loud music
INSTR: See...now you're on your way to really having fun.
SFX: Loud music
INSTR: Maybe we should go over this one more time...

911

Art Director: Tom Schwartz
          Rory Monaghan
Creative Director: Rory Monaghan
          Greg Taubenek
Copywriter: Jeff Sherman
Producer: Ron Nelken
Director: Leslie Dektor
Agency: Leo Burnett Co.
Client: United Airlines

SPEECH

60 seconds
BEN: I got a phone call this morning. From one of our oldest customers. He fired us. After 20 years. He fired us. Said he didn't know us anymore. I think I know why. We used to do business with a handshake—face to face. Now it's a phone call and a fax, and we'll get back to you later. With another fax, probably. Well, folks, something's gotta change. That's why we're going to set out for a little face to face chat with every customer we have.
SENIOR EXECUTIVE: But Ben, that's gotta be over 200 cities.
BEN: I don't care. Edwards…Ryan…(under) Nicholas…
ANNCR: If you're the kind of business that still believes personal service deserves a lot more than lip service…
BEN: (under) Give Joe my best.
ANNCR: …welcome to United. That's the way we've been doing business for over 60 years.
BEN: Willis.
GUY: Ben, where you going?
BEN: To visit that old friend who fired us this morning.
ANNCR: United. Come fly the friendly skies.

912

Art Director: Steve Stone
Creative Director: Jeffrey Goodby
          Rich Silverstein
Photographer: Don Peterman
Copywriter: David Fowler
Producer: Debbie King
Director: Jon Francis
Studio: Jon Francis Films

WHAT ELSE

60 seconds
WILL: What? What?
LADY: Dear Will, the Widow's Investment Club of Marin really appreciates those closing stocks in the afternoon paper.
WILL: It's not enough.
LADY: P.S. Will. July Pork Bellies…
OTHER LADY: Dump 'em.
SFX: Motorcycle engine
BIKER: Hey Will! Love that Friday Entertainment Section and its sensitive coverage of the local mime scene.
WILL: We've got to go further.
NUN: Dear William. I love the Neighborhood Section. Who was born, who got married, who got ripped off.
WILL: We've got to do more.
NUN: P.S. I can get you a police scanner. At cost.
BIKER: P.S. Thanks, Will. I'm sending you some steaks, man.
WILL: What? What more can we do to make this darn paper great?!

913

Art Director: John Butler
        Mike Shine
Creative Director: Bill Hamilton
Copywriter: Mike Shine
        John Butler
Producer: Steve Amato
        Trish Reeves
Agency: Chiat/Day/Mojo Advertising Inc.
Client: Soho Natural Sodas

NATURAL/ARTIFICIAL 1
30 seconds
SFX: Zydeco music

914

Art Director: Nick Scordato
        Ken Sausville
Copywriter: Jeanne Chinard
        Gordon Hasse
        Rich Wagman
        Walter Burek
Producer: Patti McGuire
Director: David Cornell
Agency: NW Ayer

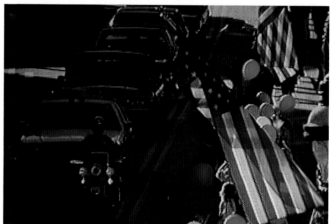

SMALL TOWN
2 minutes, 30 seconds
WOMAN VO: Oh, good morning congressman. No, that's all right.
We're all up. Here he comes.
MAN VO: When? Friday? You're kidding! Vicki do you speak Russian?
We've got company coming. We've got to get the word out.
LYRICS: How to get it done…
MAN VO: Order me some Russian flags. 1500. No, make it 2500.
LYRICS: How to get it done…
MAN VO: Patty's even quoted here. Says he's coming here to try her
apple pie.
WAITRESS VO: Yeah, they were here…
MAN VO: Oh, that kid wrote him…a letter, right? How's your story
coming? Are we gonna make the deadline?
LYRICS: We're there for you.
MAN VO: First Russian fax I've ever seen. Nice.
LYRICS: There for you. Yeah.
MAN VO: Big Bear's on his way.
WOMAN VO: Here comes the band!
LYRICS: How to get it done.

915

Art Director: Andy Dijak
Creative Director: Bob Kuperman
Copywriter: Dick Sittig
Producer: Vicki Blucher
              Karen Smith
Director: Brent Thomas
Agency: Chiat/Day/Mojo
Client: Eveready Battery Co.

916

Art Director: Michael Prieve
Creative Director: Dan Wieden
                    David Kennedy
Copywriter: Jim Riswold
Producer: Patti Greaney
            Bill Davenport
Director: Bob Giraldi
Agency: Wieden & Kennedy
Client: Nike

BUNNY/PLAYOFFS

20 seconds
1ST ANNCR: Don't be fooled by commercials where one battery company's toy outlasts the other's. The fact is, Energizer was never invited to their playoffs. Because nothing outlasts the Energizer. They keep going and going...
2ND ANNCR: Stop the bunny, please.
1ST ANNCR: ...and going, and going.

FORCE
30 seconds
SFX: Music

917

Art Director: Pam Cunningham
　　　　　　　Andy Dijak
Creative Director: Lee Clow
　　　　　　　Bob Kuperman
Copywriter: Steve Bassett
Producer: Richard O'Neill
Director: John St. Clair
　　　　　　Michael Werk
Agency: Chiat/Day/Mojo

Z CLEAN SHEET

30 seconds
SFX: Loud banging
ANNCR: This is where we started—a clean sheet of paper. No boundaries. No rules. No preconceived ideas. Just desire to build the best sports car in the world. A car for one driver in a thousand. The car destined to leave its mark.
SFX: Loud banging
ANNCR: The new Z. From Nissan.

918

Art Director: Peter Arnell
　　　　　　　Neal Slavin
Creative Director: Peter Arnell
Copywriter: Peter Arnell
Producer: Adrian Lichter
Director: Neal Slavin
Studio: Firebird Productions
Agency: Arnell/Bickford
Client: European American Bank

BLIND SOFTBALL

60 seconds
VO: I think that all of us are blind at one time or another, in the dark, or at night, or…mentally even sometimes, so this game makes the people come out of their shell.
SFX: Cheers; softball beeping
VO: People grow by playing this game.
SFX: Cheers; softball beeping
VO: It's like climbing the top of a mountain when you smack that thing, Bang-o.
SFX: Cheers
VO: One of the wonders of the game is to catch a fly ball. Anything you think is gonna happen will ultimately happen, right?
SFX: Cheers

919

Art Director: Andy Dijak
Mike Mazza
Creative Director: Bob Kuperman
Copywriter: Dick Sittig
Producer: Helen Erb
Ken Domanski
Director: Richard O'Neill
Agency: Chiat/Day/Mojo
Client: Nissan Motor Corp.

920

Art Director: Gary Yoshida
Copywriter: Bob Coburn
Producer: Gary Paticoff
Tena Montoya
Director: Henry Sandbank
Jeff Zwart
Klaus Lucka
Agency: Rubin Postaer & Associates
Client: American Honda Motor Corp.

IF I HAD A 240SX

30 seconds
240SX DREAMER: If I had a Nissan 240SX…I'd get a red coupe.—No!
A silver fastback. And I'd go for a spin up Route 7, the twisty part. Just
me and Elvis…maybe Mark. Heck, why not Ken Wahl! Yeah, me and
Ken…in my silver—no, red 240SX…driving into the sunset.

ON THE ROAD

30 seconds
SFX: Car engine; music
VO: If you think the new Honda Accord Coupe looks good on
television…you should see it on the road. You have to drive it to
believe it. The new Accord from Honda.

921

Art Director: Jeremy Postaer
Creative Director: Jeffrey Goodby
Photographer: Amir Hamed
Copywriter: Jeffrey Goodby
Ed Crayton
Producer: Debbie King
Director: Gary Johns
Studio: Johns & Gorman Films

922

Art Director: John Colquhoun
Steve Miller
Joe Sedelmaier
Creative Director: Cliff Freeman
Copywriter: Cliff Freeman
Rick LeMoine
Joe Sedelmaier
Agency: Cliff Freeman & Partners
Client: Little Caesars Enterprises

FOOTBALL

30 seconds
VO: It's been suggested that you might know more about us at U.C.
San Francisco if we had a sports program the way other schools do.
Take Dr. Nelson Artiga here....He oversees dental care and education
for thousands of underprivileged patients who might not have sought
treatment. Now if we had sports teams made up of remarkable
people like Dr. Artiga, you'd probably know all about us, right? Yeah,
probably not.

INSURANCE

30 seconds
ANNCR: Some pizza places have a lot of overhead. Trucks,
maintenance, drivers…insurance.
SFX: Clomp! Tire screeching
ANNCR: We don't have all that overhead at Little Caesars—that's
how we can afford to give you 2 great pan pizzas…
LITTLE CAESAR: Pan! Pan!
ANNCR: For one low price.

923

Art Director: Steve Stone
Creative Director: Jeffrey Goodby
Rich Silverstein
Photographer: Amir Hamed
Copywriter: Jeffrey Goodby
Producer: Cindy Fluitt
Director: Gary Johns
Studio: Johns & Gorman Films

924

Art Director: Keith Weinman
Creative Director: Larry Postaer
Copywriter: Karen Koritz
Producer: Joel Ziskin
Gary Paticoff
Director: Larry Bridges
Client: Bugle Boy Industries

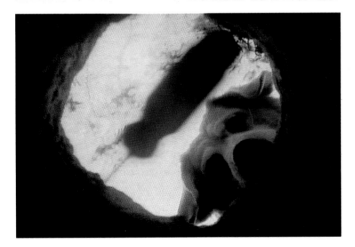

RUSTY'S GOT IT

30 seconds
SFX: Birds chirping; digging
DAD: Hey Honey, where's my red screwdriver?
MOM: Well, where did you leave it? Did you check your tool box?
DAD: No, it's not in my tool box. Hey kids, pardon me, have you seen my red screwdriver anywhere?
KID: Um…no.
DAD: Have you seen it? Have you?
OTHER KID: Uh-uh.
KID: Hey Dad, remember when you lost your glasses and they were just sitting there right on your face?
DAD: Very funny.
SFX: Digging

BEACH

30 seconds
SFX: Music; waves; seagulls
BUGLE BOY MAN: Hey, only a friend is gonna tell you but, you know, hanging out in that suit, well, you're attracting the wrong kind of attention….At a party, you got people offering you deals on kiwi farms instead of plates of hors d'oeuvres. I mean, loosen up. Like, like be yourself. Try changing your clothes for starters. Then, maybe, get a dog. A Bouvier…a Shar-Pei…something…

925

Art Director: Frank Costantini
Phillip Halyard
Creative Director: Hal Friedman
Michael Hart
Copywriter: Brian Sitts
Larry Volpi
Mimi Emilita
Agency: J. Walter Thompson
Client: Eastman Kodak

926

Art Director: Bob Barrie
Creative Director: Pat Burnham
Copywriter: Jarl Olsen
Producer: Char Loving
Director: Rick Dublin
Agency: Fallon McElligott
Client: Hush Puppies

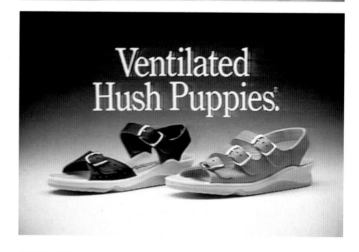

DADDY'S LITTLE GIRL

60 seconds
MAN SINGS: You're the end of the rainbow,
My pot of gold,
Daddy's little girl,
To have and to hold.
A precious gem, is what you are,
A ray of hope, a shining star.
You're as bright as the sunshine,
Morning's first light,
You warm my day and brighten my night.
You're sugar, you're spice, you're everything nice,
And you're Daddy's little girl.
VO: Don't the pictures of your lifetime deserve Kodak film?

VENTILATED HUSH PUPPIES

15 seconds
SFX: Urban street sounds; rumbling of train

927

Art Director: Jeff Hopfer
          Glenn Dady
Creative Director: Stan Richards
Copywriter: Mike Malone
Producer: Lisa Dee
Director: Leslie Dektor
Agency: Petermann-Dektor

928

Art Director: Leslie Caldwell
Creative Director: Mike Koelker
Copywriter: Mike Koelker
Producer: Steve Neely
Director: Leslie Dektor
Agency: Foote, Cone & Belding, San Francisco

ZION HARMONIZERS
30 seconds
MUSIC: The Zion Harmonizers singing

CHICAGO
60 seconds
SFX: Music
VO: The city.
JAZZ MAN: I don't know where it comes from ya know, jus' as long as it keeps coming, right?
YOUNG MUSICIAN: This is my bass note and this is my treble, what am I suppose to do?
JAZZ MAN: How old are you?
KID: 15.
JAZZ MAN: Wow?!

929

Art Director: Don Fibich
Copywriter: Chuck Withrow
Producer: Ann Russo
Roseanne Lowe
Celeste Sciortino
Director: Kenny Mirman
Agency: Wyse Advertising
Client: Cleveland Zoo

930

Art Director: Don Easdon
Dan Ahearn
Creative Director: Don Easdon
Bill Heater
Copywriter: Bill Heater
Craig Caldwell
Producer: Mary Ellen Argentieri
Director: Larry Robbins
Client: Nissan Infiniti

FACES

30 seconds
SFX: Music
VO: One of the most beautiful things about faces like these…is the look they'll bring to a face like this. The Cleveland Metroparks Zoo. It's wild.

LIGHT CHANGES IN FOREST

30 seconds
VO: We feel a customer should be able to enter an Infiniti showroom and feel, right away, a different kind of luxury experience. An experience perfectly unlike any showroom experience in the world. Shopping for a luxury car should be as luxurious as owning one. Infiniti.

931

Art Director: Sal DeVito
Creative Director: Lee Garfinkel
Copywriter: Lee Garfinkel
Producer: Rachel Novak
Director: Carlton Chase
Agency: Levine, Huntley, Schmidt & Beaver
Client: Beneficial

932

Art Director: Marv Lefkowitz
Creative Director: Agi Clark
Copywriter: Bob Elgort
Producer: Bob Smith
Director: Claude Mougin
Agency: LGFE
Client: Fasolino

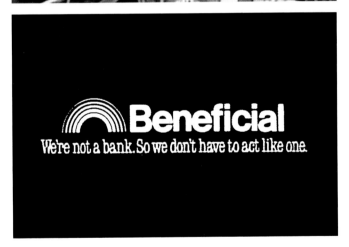

QADDAFI

30 seconds
ANNCR: Over the years, U.S. banks have loaned $20 million to people like this. $5.7 billion to people like this. $3 billion to people like this. But for 75 years, we've always believed it was more important to loan money to people like this.
Beneficial. We're not a bank. So we don't have to act like one.

ANGELINO

30 seconds
SPOKESMAN: Right now you wouldn't know a Fasolino from an Angelino…but Angelino is Italian for angel. And thank goodness they come in all sizes and shapes. And Fasolino is Italian for Pasta…which also comes in all sizes and shapes. Fasolino's. It's Italian for Pasta.

933

Art Director: Steve Montgomery
         Earl Cavanah
         Simon Bowden
Copywriter: Richard Kelley
         Mike Feinberg
         Larry Cadman
Agency: Scali, McCabe, Sloves
Client: Volvo

934

Art Director: Michael Prieve
Creative Director: Dan Wieden
         David Kennedy
Copywriter: Jim Riswold
Agency: Wieden & Kennedy
Client: Nike

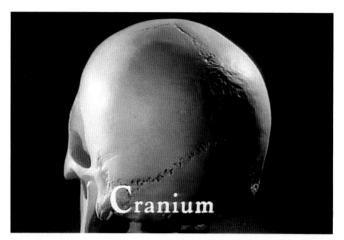

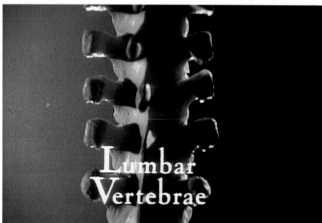

REPLACEMENT PARTS

30 seconds
VO: Drive a Volvo because replacement parts are hard to find.

CAN/CAN'T

30 seconds
SFX: Funk music
MARS: Yo! This is Mars Blackmon. And this is my main man Michael Jordan and this is a pair of hyped Air Jordans from Nike. This is something you can buy.
MARS (VO): And this is a patented vicious high-flying 360 slam dunk.
MARS: This is something you cannot do. Let me repeat myself. This you can buy.
MARS (VO): You cannot do this.
MARS: Can.

935

Art Director: Don Easdon
Creative Director: Don Easdon
⠀⠀⠀⠀⠀⠀⠀⠀⠀⠀Bill Heater
Copywriter: Bill Heater
Producer: Mary Ellen Argentieri
⠀⠀⠀⠀⠀⠀⠀Teri Hechter
Agency: Hill, Holliday
Client: Nissan Infiniti

936

Art Director: Sheri Olmon
Creative Director: Bill Hamilton
Copywriter: Marty Cooke
⠀⠀⠀⠀⠀⠀⠀Alan Platt
Producer: Andrew Chinich
⠀⠀⠀⠀⠀⠀Lee Weiss
Agency: Chiat/Day/Mojo Advertising Inc.
Client: New York Life

FLOCK OF GEESE

30 seconds

VO: An automotive designer looks at the shapes of nature, the soft lines. And because he sees things a certain way, those lines suggest an automobile design that is honest and natural. Where the driver is more important than the car itself. And what is discovered just watching nature, is an ancient Japanese notion of what is beautiful. It's called Infiniti.

SOCCER

30 seconds

TOM: I wanted to live in the Rocky Mountain region. I enjoy the great outdoors. I like to fish, play soccer.
MAN 1: What Tom does…he doesn't care if we make mistakes. He doesn't get down on anybody. He treats everybody fair.
MAN 2: It's all teamwork…no individual players.
ANNCR: A lot of these players depend on Tom Dater for their life insurance. He's been on their team for 10 years. And with New York Life for 18 years.
MAN 3: Why would I buy insurance from a stranger when I can buy it from the worst fullback in Boise?
ANNCR: New York Life. The company you keep.

937

Art Director: Pat Chiono
Bill Shea
Roger Rowe
Creative Director: Sean Fitzpatrick
Copywriter: Robert Woolcott
Rona Oberman
Paul Cappelli
Agency: McCann-Erickson
Client: Coca-Cola USA

CHRISTMAS TREE

60 seconds
KID (BRIAN BONSALL): Are you sure it's gonna work, Grandpa?
GRANDPA (ART CARNEY): Trust me, kid. I got a good feeling about this one.
KID: You mean like the time we took Grandma water skiing?
GRANDPA: (chuckle) Now, silver shovel, thank you, Grandma's fruitcake. And now, Grandpa's magic pine cone. In exactly two weeks, we should see something.
KID: Is it time, Grandpa?
GRANDPA: It's time. Let's go.

938

Art Director: Matt Smith
Creative Director: Ross Van Dusen
Copywriter: Jeff Billig
Producer: Harvey Greenberg
Director: Jeff Gorman
Agency: Chiat/Day/Mojo
Client: Worlds of Wonder

BASKETBALL

15 seconds
BOY #1: (laughs)
BOY #2 OC: C'mon man
BOY #1 OC: Sorry....Sorry....Sorry....Sorry....Nice shot.
BOY #2 OC: Oh oh!
SFX: Sports whistle
ANNCR: Substitution!!
SFX: Arena cheering
ANNCR: Kooky Katcher from Worlds of Wonder.

939

Art Director: Susan Hoffman
Creative Director: Dan Wieden
                David Kennedy
Copywriter: Geoff McGann
Agency: Wieden & Kennedy
Client: Nike

940

Art Director: Jerry Torchia
Creative Director: Mike Hughes
Copywriter: Andy Ellis
Producer: Morty Baran
Agency: The Martin Agency
Client: Signet Bank

MEET FELETIA

30 seconds
SFX: Organ music

CRONYN/TANDY

60 seconds
CRONYN: Apollinaire said, "Come to the edge." But they held back and they said, "It's dangerous." He said, "Come to the edge." And they said, "We may fall." And he said, "COME TO THE EDGE." So, they went to the edge and he pushed them...and they flew. Affirmation. And that's something I think we share, don't we?
TANDY: Who's doing the pushing?
CRONYN: Sometimes you push, sometimes I push. Isn't that right?
TANDY: Right!

941

Art Director: Dick Lemmon
　　　　　　　Mitch Gordon
Creative Director: Jan Zechman
Copywriter: Jan Zechman
Producer: Laurie Berger
Director: Ted Bokhoff
Studio: Cityworks
Client: State of Illinois

942

Art Director: Mike Martin
Creative Director: Jim Armstrong
Copywriter: Jim Armstrong
Producer: ProVideo
Agency: Armstrong Creative
Client: Madison Advertising Federation

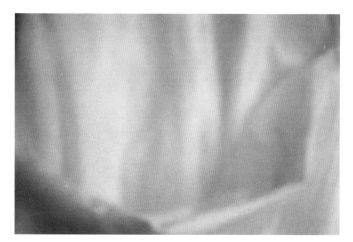

CRANE

30 seconds
SFX: Drum solo
VOICE OF CARL SANDBURG: This is one song of Chicago. Nothing like us ever was.

HE LOVES ME, HE LOVES ME NOT

15 seconds
VO: He loves me….He loves me not.
SFX: Tearing

943

Art Director: George Halvorson
Creative Director: George Halvorson
Copywriter: Tom Evans
Producer: Jim Geib
Director: Charlie Diercks
Agency: CME
Client: Boating Safety

944

Art Director: Brian Nadurak
Creative Director: Stan Richards
Copywriter: Marc Harty
Producer: Greg Lane
Director: Lol Creme
Agency: The Richards Group
Client: Texas Department of Health

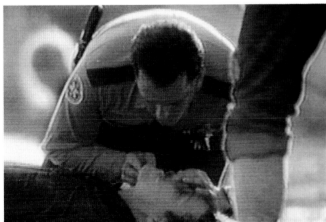

BREATH TEST

30 seconds
ANNCR: Last year, 473 drunk boaters failed to pass this breath test.

CHANGING FACES

30 seconds
WOMAN 1: You may have slept with me…
MAN 1: Or me, because if you've had two sex partners…
WOMAN 2: In the last year, and each of your partners…
MAN 2: Had two other partners the year before…
WOMAN 3: And so on for the last nine years…
MAN 3: It's as if you've slept with 512 people…
WOMAN 4: Any one of them could have given you the virus that causes AIDS…
MAN 4: Find out what to do now…
WOMAN 1: Call the toll-free Texas AIDSLINE. All calls are anonymous.

945

Art Director: John Lointi
Creative Director: Rick DeChant
Copywriter: Tom Woodward
Producer: Rick DeChant
Maura Mooney
Studio: Hi-Tech Productions
Agency: Liggett-Stashower
Client: United States Coast Guard

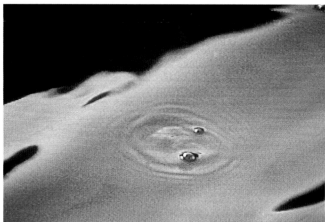

FLOATER

15 seconds
SFX: Steady, ominous tone
ANNCR: If you're wearing your life preserver in a boating accident, you'll be floating on top immediately.
If you're not wearing one, it might take a week or so.

946

Art Director: Charlotte Moore
Creative Director: Stephen Heller
Copywriter: Evelyn Monroe
Producer: Carol Hardin
Patti Greaney
Director: Bob Giraldi
Agency: Ogilvy & Mather
Client: Centers for Disease Control

REMOTE

60 seconds
MOM: When your father and I were married sex was a very different…
GIRL VO: I can tell by looking at her what she's going to say.
MOM: We dated for awhile before he had the nerve to kiss me…
GIRL VO: They went to a soda fountain and shared a straw…
MOM: …sex is a natural thing between two people…
MOM & GIRL VO: …who love each other.
SFX: Fast forward
GIRL VO: Fast forward through pregnancy and nice young men.
MOM: …young men who respect you.
SFX: Fast forward
GIRL VO: And now for the closing remarks.
MOM: …AIDS is one of them.
GIRL VO: Whoa!
SFX: Rewinding
MOM: There are risks in becoming sexually active. AIDS is one of them. Theresa, let's start at the beginning. HIV is the name of the virus that causes AIDS…
ANNCR: We can help you talk about AIDS. Call for a guide.

947
Art Director: Mike Martin
Creative Director: Jim Armstrong
Copywriter: Jim Armstrong
Producer: ProVideo
Agency: Armstrong Creative
Client: Madison Advertising Federation

948
Art Director: Tim Musta
Copywriter: Jan Pettit
Producer: LuAnn Truso
Studio: Northwest Teleproductions
Agency: Miller Meester Advertising
Client: Tom Thumb

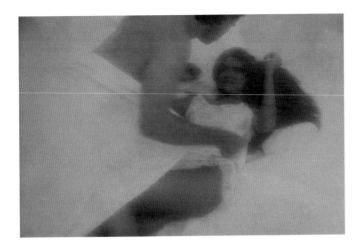

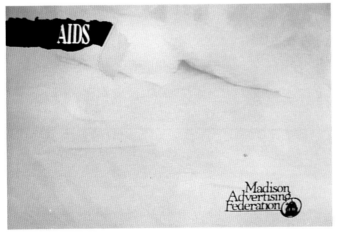

GARY'S ON HIS DEATHBED

15 seconds
VO: Gary is on his deathbed.
SFX: Tearing

NIGHT CALLER

30 seconds
SFX: Phone ringing throughout
VO: As the parent of a teenager, who would you rather hear from in the middle of the night? The police department? The emergency room? The coroner? Or...
SFX: Ringing stops, phone is picked up
TEENAGER VO: Mom? I'm at a party. Could you, uh, come and get me?
VO: When your kids aren't OK to drive, make it OK to call. This message brought to you by Tom Thumb.

949

Art Director: Richard Ostroff
Creative Director: Allan Beaver
                                Lee Garfinkel
Copywriter: Amy Borkowsky
Producer: Rachel Novak
Director: Mark Story
Agency: Levine, Huntley, Schmidt & Beaver
Client: Ad Council

FRYING PAN

30 seconds
VO: Last year, 400,000 women killed their husbands with a frying pan.
Reduce your intake of high-fat fried foods and reduce your risk of
cancer and heart disease.
For a free booklet on low-fat eating, call 1-800-EAT-LEAN.

950

Art Director: Doug Johnson
Creative Director: Gary Dixon
Photographer: Brian Capener
Copywriter: Stan Ferguson
Producer: Jim Rutherford
Director: Stan Ferguson
Agency: Bonneville Media Communications
Client: LDS Church

HARD LESSON

60 seconds
NEW FATHER VO: Dear Mom, thanks for helping Janet and me with
the new baby the past two weeks. You were there, as always....But,
there was a time when I wasn't sure I wanted your help. Remember
when we walked all the way to town and back? And then you
discovered the new toy I had.
WOMAN: Um...where did you get that?
NEW FATHER (AS A CHILD): From the store...
WOMAN: I didn't know you had any money...
NEW FATHER VO: I didn't have any money....Taking that toy back was
one of the hardest things I ever had to do.
NEW FATHER (AS A CHILD): I took this, and I'm sorry.
OWNER: It takes a big man to face up to a mistake, son. But, bringing it
back was the right thing to do.
NEW FATHER VO: Thanks, Mom, for teaching me the hard lessons.
ANNCR: Family values...pass them on. Your children need them now
more than ever. From The Church of Jesus Christ of Latter-day Saints.

951
Art Director: Richard Ostroff
Creative Director: Allan Beaver
Lee Garfinkel
Copywriter: Amy Borkowsky
Producer: Rachel Novak
Director: Phil Marco
Agency: Levine, Huntley, Schmidt & Beaver
Client: Ad Council

952
Art Director: Gary Johnston
Mark Sitley
Creative Director: Robin Raj
Copywriter: Robin Raj
Producer: Mark Sitley
Julie Hampel
Director: Bob Giraldi
Agency: Chiat/Day/Mojo Advertising Inc.
Client: National Coalition for the Homeless

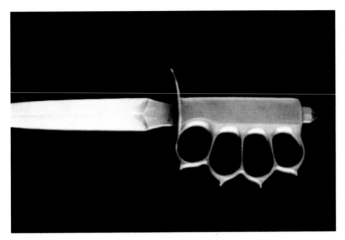

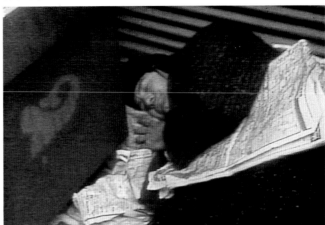

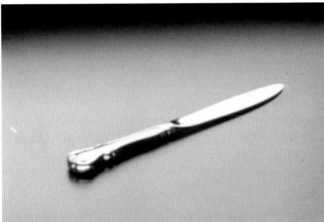

KNIVES

30 seconds
VO: The stiletto. Outlawed in most major cities. The trench knife. It boasts a seven-inch, solid steel blade. The survival knife. Designed to cut through virtually anything. Yet, the most dangerous knife of all may be this one.
For a free booklet on how to reduce your risk of cancer and heart disease through low-fat eating, call 1-800-EAT-LEAN.

LIFESTYLES OF THE HOMELESS

60 seconds
ROBIN LEACH VO: Say, what's it like to live a life of complete independence? George Rutallo knows. Yes. Every morning he wakes up to a commanding view of Third Avenue. A panoramic vantage he must pay dearly for. It's here he rubs shoulders with the power elite. A perfect location, close to restaurants and shopping. George's digs are nothing if not spacious, and he shares them freely with family, friends, even total strangers. His bedroom sleeps hundreds, and a spectacular dining room caters to literally thousands. Yes, Mr. Rutallo is living like there's no tomorrow. It's a world of scenic make-believe. But for George this is no fairy tale. It's just a little place he calls home. What can you do about the 3 million Americans living in our streets? You can pick up the phone and call Washington.
ANNCR: What can you do about the 3 million men, women and children living in our streets? You can write the National Coalition for the Homeless.

953

Art Director: David Page
Creative Director: Jeffrey Goodby
Photographer: Barney Colangelo
Copywriter: David O'Hare
Producer: Cindy Fluitt
Director: Jeffrey Goodby
Studio: Fleet Street Pictures

954

Art Director: Mary Mentzer
Tim Musta
Copywriter: Jan Pettit
Producer: LuAnn Truso
Studio: Northwest Teleproductions
Agency: Miller Meester Advertising
Client: Tom Thumb

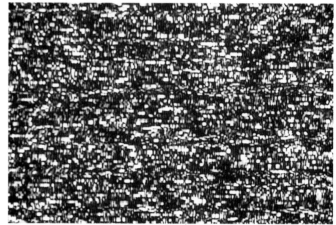

TOBY

30 seconds
MAN: What's wrong?
WOMAN: That was the Fowlers. Gretchen's pregnant; they think Toby's the father.
MAN: How do they know?
WOMAN: He's over there every night. And when he's not, he's out running around.
MAN: He's young.
WOMAN: He's out of control.
MAN: What do you want me to do, chain him up in the backyard?
WOMAN: If that's what it takes to stop this selfishness…wait, it's him.
VO: Will you please get your dog fixed. It's painless, it's cheap, and, well, he's just not going to do it himself.

REASONS FOR PEACE

30 seconds
ANNCR: Between the U.S. and the Soviet Union, we have a combined total of 24,562 nuclear warheads. And, while that's a very powerful reason for disarmament, there's one even more powerful. We also have a combined total of 133 million children.
This message brought to you by Tom Thumb.

955

Art Director: Wendy Hansen
Creative Director: Lyle Wedemeyer
Copywriter: Lyle Wedemeyer
Director: Rick Dublin
        Eric Young
        Kevin Smith
Agency: Martin/Williams
Client: Minnesota Department of Health

956

Art Director: Allen Kay
Creative Director: Lois Korey
Copywriter: Neil Leinwohl
Producer: Milda Misevicius
Director: Henry Sandbank
Studio: Sandbank & Partners
Client: Members Only

ANIMALS

30 seconds
ANNCR: If you think this looks ridiculous, remember…smoking is just as unnatural for you as it is for them.

BADGE

30 seconds
SFX: Police radio transmissions and echoed gunfire
VO: This message has been brought to you by Members Only.

957
Art Director: Ron Fisher
            April Norman
Creative Director: Ron Fisher
Photographer: Glenn Bewley
Copywriter: Virgil Shutze
Producer: Dottie Martin
Director: Jimmy Collins
Agency: HutchesonShutze
Client: Atlanta's Table

958
Art Director: Robert Valentine
Designer: Robert Valentine
Illustrator: Chesley McLaren
Producer: Kelly Mosley
            Nancy Lawrence

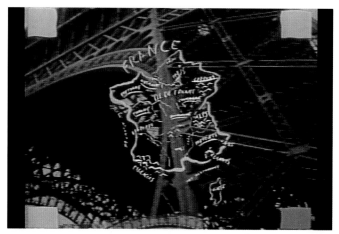

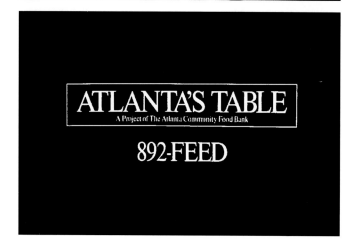

WORK FOR FOOD

30 seconds
NARRATOR: He carried a sign that said, ''I'll work for food.'' Hard times had cinched his belt halfway around again. Pants hung low on his hips. I tried to look away, but couldn't. He didn't seem to mind. He just looked at me for a long minute, then the light changed.
ANNCR: Help drive hunger from the face of Atlanta. Give to Atlanta's Table.

VIVE LA FRANCE

1 minute, 19 seconds
MUSIC: ″La Vie En Rose″

959

Art Director: Ron Arnold
Creative Director: Ron Arnold
Copywriter: Patti Goldberg
Producer: Kathryn Speiss
Director: Eli Noyes

960

Art Director: Tony Smith
Creative Director: Tony Smith
Copywriter: Jonathan Young
Producer: Ed Galvez
　　　　　 Kathy Wheelock
Director: Drew Takahashi
Agency: McCann-Erickson
Studio: Colossal Pictures
Client: National Dairy Board

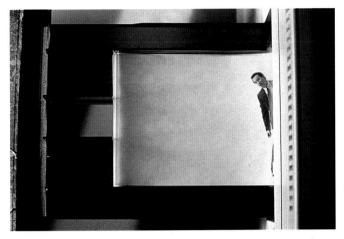

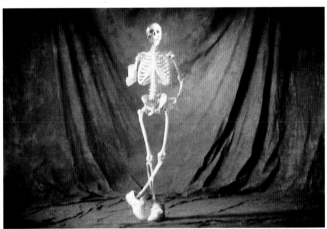

FLIP CARD MAN

30 seconds

MAN: All Mita makes are great copiers. Which may be why nearly 9 out of 10 people who own them, love them. I know I do. I don't worry about coming out too dark, too light, crumpled, or not coming out at all. In fact, I always look 100%. Sometimes even 151%. At Mita, all we make are great copiers.

PRESTON CHANGO

30 seconds

PRESTON CHANGO: I know I should drink milk 'cause it will help me grow up big and strong. Milk's got stuff that's good for my bones and stuff that's good for my muscles. And I guess that's okay, but I'm more interested in having fun! That's what makes milk so neat; you can drink a lot of it and it tastes cool. Milk can be a real pick-me up! Milk, it does a body good.

961

Art Director: Jeffrey Bacon
　　　　　　　John O'Brien
Photographer: Bob Graham
Director: Jim Edwards
Agency: Cimarron/Bacon/O'Brien
Client: Bacon/O'Brien Design

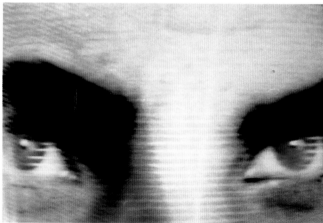

BITS AND PIECES

5 minutes
JOHN: Bits and pieces.
JEFF: Yes, bits and pieces....I think the company was founded on the orange. I lost my roommate, Pete, an ordinary naval orange took Pete's head off. I needed a new roommate, from then on we just hung out.
JOHN: Pete's never been the same.
JEFF: I would wake up at three in the morning and just have to do a painting. It used to drive my parents nuts.
JOHN: I would wake up in the morning and just have to draw underneath the table with crayons.
JEFF: ...The thing that we're good at is making things.
JOHN: It's all about quality. How you see things....The final concept.
JEFF: I don't want to do it if we're not going to do it better than anyone else would do it.
JOHN: It's finished when we feel it.
JEFF: John beaned Pete in the head with an orange and that's what we want to do.
JOHN: Bits and pieces of bits and pieces.
JEFF: We just want to hit the top, that's exactly where we want to be.

962

Art Director: Marty Weiss
Creative Director: Marty Weiss
　　　　　　　　　Nat Whitten
Copywriter: Nat Whitten
Producer: Marty Weiss
　　　　　　Nat Whitten
Director: Andy Parke
　　　　　　Laura Belsey
Agency: Weiss, Whitten Inc.

WEISS, WHITTEN PROMOTIONAL REEL

5 minutes, 35 seconds
MRS. WEISS: I am Helen Weiss.
MR. WEISS: And I am Bernie Weiss. We are the parents of Martin Weiss.
MR. WHITTEN: I'm Benjamin Whitten.
MRS. WHITTEN: And I'm Jane Whitten.
MRS. WEISS: Whitney is a writer and my son is an art director.
INTERVIEWER: Could you tell us what business your son is starting?
MR. WEISS: No, I'm not sure what kind of business he's getting into.
MRS. WEISS: That was Marty Weiss' first print ad. But then I thought to myself, what's he mean, artist? He's gonna grow up a bum...
MR. WEISS: We do have some items he doesn't let us throw out...
INTERVIEWER: What is it?
MR. WEISS: I don't know what it is.
MRS. WHITTEN: Call Weiss, Whitten, they're tops.
MR. WHITTEN: That could be better. More enthusiasm.
MRS. WHITTEN: Call Weiss, Whitten, they're tops.
MR. WHITTEN: No, don't stop on "toopps"...call Weiss, Whitten, they're tops...tops...tops...
MRS. WHITTEN: Stacato...call Weiss, Whitten, they're tops.

963

Art Director: David Hukari
Photographer: Fred Vanderpoel
Copywriter: Frank Priscaro
Producer: Fred Vanderpoel
Director: Fred Vanderpoel
Agency: Priscaro & Hukari
Client: Infoworld

964

Art Director: Robert Barthelmes
Producer: Suzanne Bauman
Director: Suzanne Bauman
Studio: Soulstar Films
Client: *Vogue* Magazine

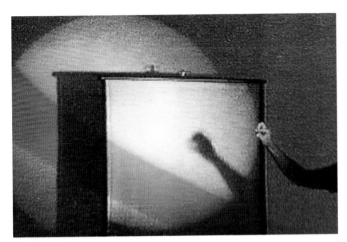

TEST CENTER SPIES

11 minutes, 4 seconds
1ST VO: Swanky-Flueger Investigations presents Case B-701, the InfoWorld Test Center.
2ND VO: We sent our crack crew in disguised as the Industrial Light Pollution Council…
ERNIE: You have a test center downstairs….Why?
SACKS: Well, computer products have become pretty complicated, so we needed a way to test them accurately…
2ND VO: Now, who's…this?
1ST VO: Must be Lauren Black, Director of the Test Center.
ERNIE: How many products do you test…?
BLACK: We test between 700 and 800 a year…
2ND VO: Oh, this is Michael Miller, he's the—
MILLER: I'm Michael Miller, Executive Editor…
2ND VO: Told you.
MILLER: …in charge of all the reviews here.
1ST VO: In summation…shut that thing off!
2ND VO: Well, I…ah…would…if I…
1ST VO: There! You did it!

IN VOGUE

11 minutes, 34 seconds
ANDRE LEON TALLEY: It's a more relaxed *Vogue,* more relaxed about make-up, hair. Things are not as preconceived. Accidents happen, and most often, accidents are big successes.
ANNA WINTOUR: I don't want that kind of plastic image of the perfect woman anymore. I think that we're all smarter than that…
ALEXANDER LIBERMAN: I think fashion now comes from the youth. It's the youth that dares.
TALLEY: In the '60s when Diana Vreeland was here, fashion only came from one place: her mind, her fantasy, and Paris….Now fashion comes from Paris, Milan, Tokyo…down the street…MTV…Madonna.
WINTOUR: If you look back at *Vogue*'s history, the features have always been very important. And I feel that it's the substance and the tone of the features that has set *Vogue* apart from other magazines.
LIBERMAN: …As they take 20 shots, photographers don't really see what they take. They hope they're getting something. I think that's how we capture the spirit of the time: by these fleeting instants where a model becomes herself, or it's catching a woman in life as if unobserved. This, for me, is the concept of modern creativity.

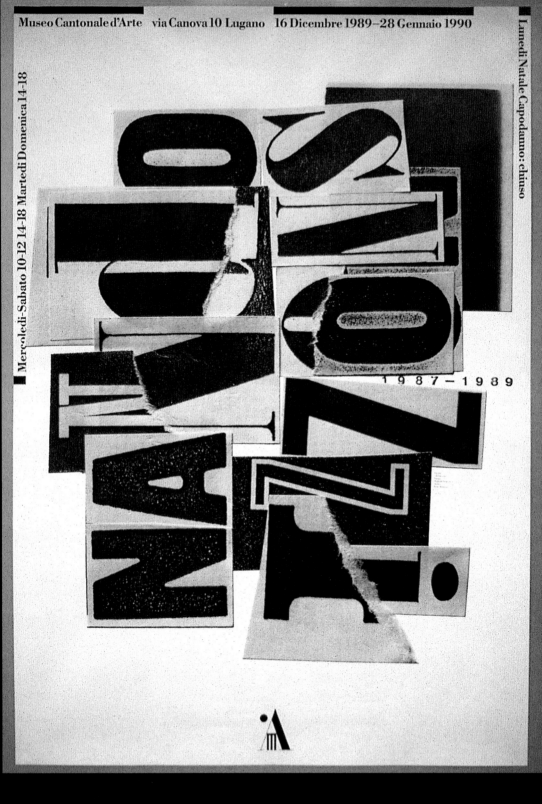

Museo Cantonale d'Arte   via Canova 10 Lugano   16 Dicembre 1989–28 Gennaio 1990

Lunedi Natale Capodanno: chiuso

Mercoledi-Sabato 10-12 14-18 Martedi Domenica 14-18

1987 – 1989

965 Gold
Art Director: Bruno Monguzzi
Designer: Bruno Monguzzi
Studio: Bruno Monguzzi
Client: Museo D'Arte

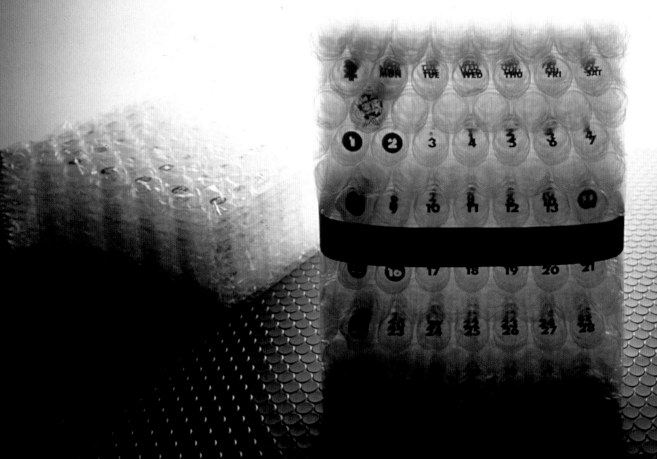

Sveriges största morgontidning.

T-CENTRALEN

Sveriges största morgontidning.

Sveriges största morgontidning.

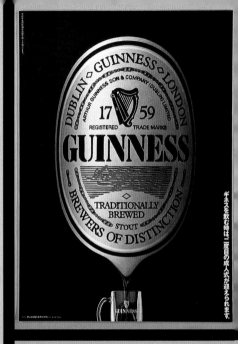

ギネスを飲む時は、女の人

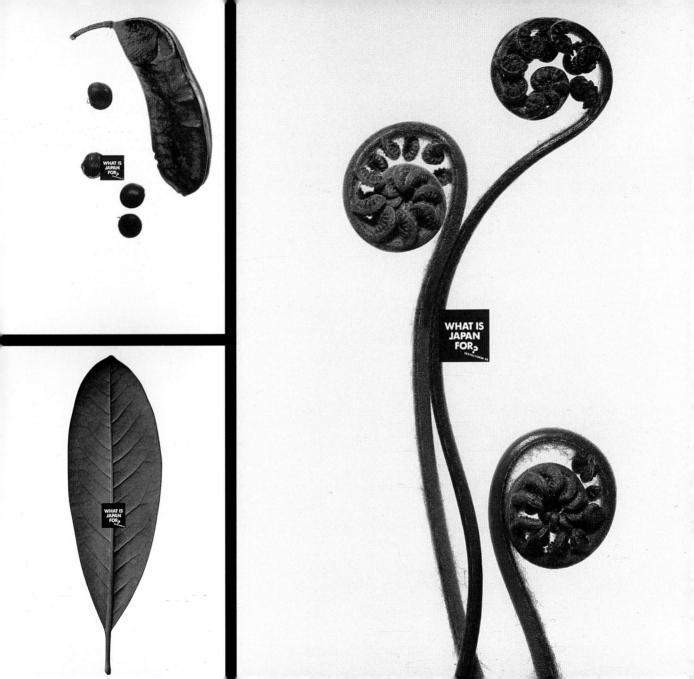

WHAT IS
JAPAN
FOR?

WHAT IS
JAPAN
FOR?

WHAT IS
JAPAN
FOR?
DENTSU FORUM '95

972 Distinctive Merit
Art Director: Gavino Sanna
Creative Director: Gavino Sanna
Copywriter: Franco Bellino
Producer: Franco Bellino
Agency: Young & Rubicam Italia SpA
Client: EDIT Editoriale Italiana

973 Distinctive Merit
Art Director: Neil French
Creative Director: Robert J. Speechley
Copywriter: Neil French
Producer: Sarah Uduwella
Cohorts Melbourne
Agency: The Ball WCRS Partnership
Client: Parker Pen

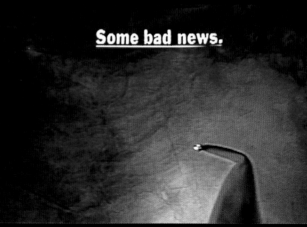

974
Art Director: Börje Stille
Copywriter: Ingemar Johannesson
Agency: Johannesson & Stille AB
Client: Folksam

975
Art Director: Toshio Iwata
Designer: Yoshihiro Ohkubo
Illustrator: Bungo Saito
Copywriter: Hiromi Tanaka

		Tid Time	Destination	Linje Flight	Pir/ Gate
●	⌒	8:00	STÖLD	B313	A6
●	⌒	8:25	SJUKDOM	F791	B1
	⌒	9:05	RÅN	U481	A7
		9:40	RESEAVBROTT	A415	B3
	⌒	10:10	STÖLD	S101	A8
	⌒	10:30	SJUKDOM	U413	C1
	⌒	10:50	RÅN	G891	A3
	⌒	11:05	RESEAVBROTT	H585	B2
	⌒	11:35	STÖLD	C432	A1
	⌒	12:00	SJUKDOM	E932	A5
	⌒	12:20	RÅN	B493	C3
	⌒	12:50	RESEAVBROTT	A491	B7
	⌒	13:10	STÖLD	F381	B5
	⌒	13:40	SJUKDOM	K418	A2
	⌒	14:10	RÅN	L301	C4
	⌒	14:25	RESEAVBROTT	S413	A9
	⌒	14:50	STÖLD	U793	B4

Åk inte dit.

FOLKSAM

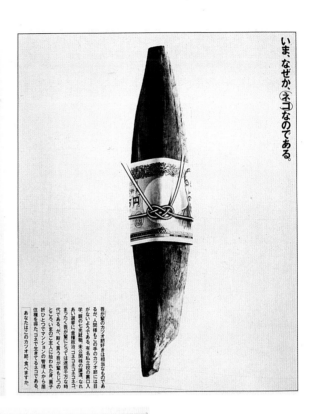

976
Art Director: André Plaisier
Creative Director: G. Van Der Stighelen
Illustrator: Edmond Tang
Copywriter: Eric Debaene

977
Art Director: Martin Spillmann
Creative Director: Hansjörg Zürcher
Copywriter: Gaby Girsberger
Agency: Advico Young & Rubicam
Client: Ringier AG

978
Art Director: John Finn
Illustrator: Jeremy Fisher
Agency: Batey Ads
Client: Singapore Airlines

979
Art Director: Clas Engwall
Creative Director: Lasse Collin
Photographer: Bengt Eriksson
Copywriter: Lasse Collin
Agency: Collin Annonsbyrå
Client: Ecco, Sverige

980
Art Director: Doug Bramah
Creative Director: Gary Prouk
Photographer: Vincent Noguchi
Copywriter: Bill Keenan
Agency: Scali, McCabe, Sloves (Canada) Ltd.
Client: Harvey's of Bristol (Export) Ltd.

981
Art Director: Arturo Massari
Creative Director: Andrea Concato
Photographer: Chris Broadbent
Copywriter: Gianluca Nappi
Agency: TBWA Italia SpA
Clieni: Carpene' Malvolti

982
Art Director: Fernando Lion
Creative Director: José Zaragoza
Helga Miethke
Photographer: Moacyr Lugato
Copywriter: Antonio Paes
Luciana Sales
Agency: DPZ-Propaganda
Client: Deca

983
Art Director: Masamichi Yoshino
Creative Director: Masamichi Yoshino
Designer: Masamichi Yoshino
Photographer: Takayuki Watanabe
Copywriter: Ryoichi Akiba
Agency: Dentsu Inc.
Client: Mitsubishi Pencil Co., Ltd.

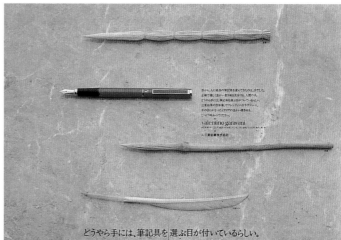

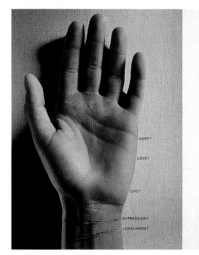

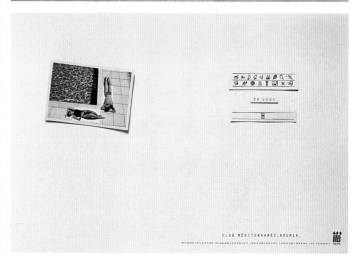

984
Art Director: Paul Shearer
Photographer: Paul Bevitt
Copywriter: Rob Jack
Agency: Butterfield, Day, DeVito, Hockney

985
Art Director: Andrew Lees
Creative Director: Andrew Lees
Copywriter: Chris Cudlipp
Agency: Chiat/Day/Mojo
Client: Club Mediterranee

986
Art Director: Nigel Rose
Creative Director: John O'Donnell
Photographer: Nadav Kander
Agency: Collett Dickenson & Pearce
Client: Benson & Hedges

987
Art Director: Andrew Lees
Creative Director: Andrew Lees
Designer: Andrew Lees
Copywriter: Andrew Lees
Agency: Chiat/Day/Mojo
Client: Club Mediterranee

988
Art Director: Dave Baldwin
Creative Director: Chris Whittaker
John O'Sullivan
Photographer: Duncan Sim
Copywriter: Pete Cass
Agency: KHBB
Client: Gallo Wines

989
Art Director: Stephan Auer
Creative Director: Carlos Obers
Designer: Stephan Auer
Photographer: Dieter Eickelpoth
Copywriter: Rita Obers
Agency: RG Wiesmeier
Client: Elbeo Werke

990
Art Director: Koji Mizutani
Designer: Osamu Kitajima
Ichiro Mitani
Photographer: Sachiko Kuru
Agency: Blue International Co. Ltd.

991
Art Director: Haruyuki Aoki
Creative Director: Haruyuki Aoki
Designer: Keiko Nagano
Photographer: Keisuke Minoda
Copywriter: Shinichi Enami
Agency: Dentsu Inc.
Client: Wako

992
Art Director: Peter Heßler
Creative Director: Peter Heßler
　　　　　　　　Jochen Beithan
Photographer: Mane Weigand
Copywriter: Cornelia Arnold
　　　　　　　Jochen Beithan

993
Art Director: Peter Heßler
Creative Director: Peter Heßler
                  Jochen Beithan
Photographer: Günter Pfannmüller
Copywriter: Jochen Beithan

994
Art Director: Gavino Sanna
Creative Director: Gavino Sanna
Photographer: Leo Torri
Copywriter: Gaspare Giua
Agency: Young & Rubicam Italia SpA
Client: Castelli SpA

995
Art Director: Helga Miethke
Creative Director: José Zaragoza
Helga Miethke
Photographer: Manolo Moran
Copywriter: Paulo Leite
Agency: DPZ-Propaganda
Client: Hering

A menina dos olhos nunca esteve tão bonita atrás de um óculos.

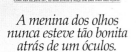

Espelho, espelho meu, existe astigmatismo mais charmoso do que o meu?

Sua miopia nunca recebeu um assobio na rua?

996
Art Director: Roberto Cipolla
Creative Director: Francesc Petit
Paulo Ghirotti
Photographer: Luiz Crispino
Copywriter: Ruy Lindenberg
Agency: DPZ-Propaganda
Client: Colorcenter

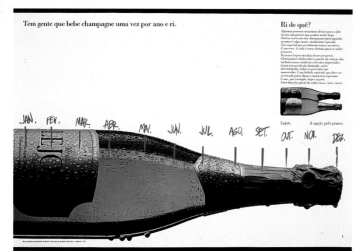

Tem gente que bebe champagne uma vez por ano e ri.

Ri de quê?

JAN. FEV. MAR. ABR. MAI. JUN. JUL. AGO. SET. OUT. NOV. DEZ.

Lejon.   A opção pelo prazer.

997
Art Director: Marcello Serpa
Creative Director: Francesc Petit
                    Paulo Ghirotti
Photographer: Andreas Heiniger
Copywriter: Paulo Ghirotti
              Luiz Toledo
Agency: DPZ-Propaganda
Client: Heublein

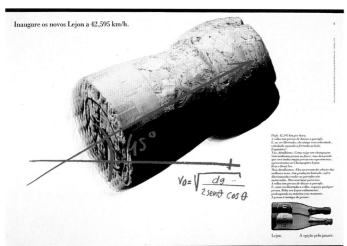

Inaugure os novos Lejon a 42.595 km/h.

$$V_0 = \sqrt{\frac{dg}{2\,sen\theta\,cos\theta}}$$

Lejon.   A opção pelo prazer.

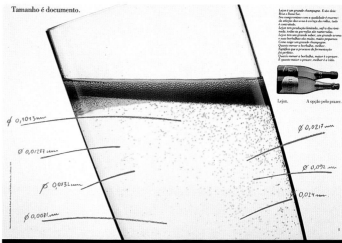

Tamanho é documento.

ϕ 0,1013 mm
ϕ 0,01289 mm
ϕ 0,00132 mm
ϕ 0,0081 mm
ϕ 0,0217 mm
ϕ 0,092 mm
0,024 mm

Lejon.   A opção pelo prazer.

VOCÊ SÓ TEM UMA VIDA.

CUIDE BEM DELA.

USE CINTO DE SEGURANÇA.

VOCÊ SÓ TEM UMA VIDA.

CUIDE BEM DELA.

CRIANÇAS SÓ NO BANCO DE TRÁS.

VOCÊ SÓ TEM UMA VIDA.

CUIDE BEM DELA.

NÃO BEBA ANTES DE DIRIGIR.

998
Art Director: Roberto Cipolla
Creative Director: Francesc Petit
                    Paulo Ghirotti
Photographer: Andreas Heiniger
Copywriter: Ruy Lindenberg
Agency: DPZ-Propaganda
Client: General Motors

999

Art Director: José Zaragoza
Creative Director: José Zaragoza
             Helga Miethke
Photographer: Moacyr Lugato
Copywriter: Antonio Paes
Agency: DPZ-Propaganda
Client: Artex

A COBERTURA DOS SEUS SONHOS.   LENÇÓIS ARTEX.

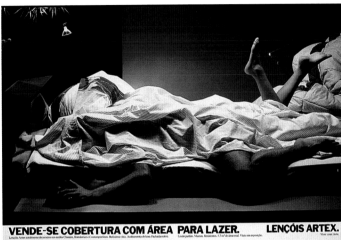

VENDE-SE COBERTURA COM ÁREA PARA LAZER.   LENÇÓIS ARTEX.

Extintor de incêndio.

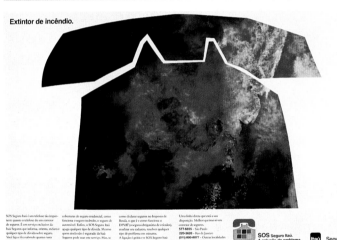

SOS Seguro Itaú.
A solução do problema.   Itaú Seguros

Saída de emergência.

SOS Seguro Itaú.
A solução do problema.   Itaú Seguros

Pára-choque.

SOS Seguro Itaú.
A solução do problema.   Itaú Seguros

1000

Art Director: Marcello Serpa
Creative Director: Francesc Petit
             Paulo Ghirotti
Copywriter: Luiz Toledo
Agency: DPZ-Propaganda
Client: Itaú seguros

1001
Art Director: Helga Miethke
Creative Director: José Zaragoza
           Helga Miethke
Photographer: Manolo Moran
Copywriter: Paulo Leite
Agency: DPZ-Propaganda
Client: Hering

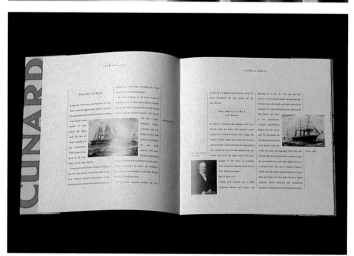

1002
Art Director: David Pocknell
Designer: Mark Welby
           Jonathan Russell

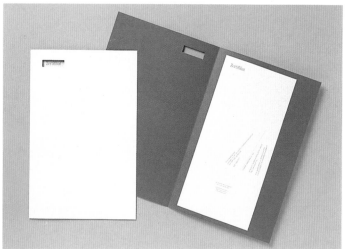

1003
Art Director: Klaus Winterhager
Client: Zanders Feinpapiere AG

1004
Art Director: Planungsteam K. Nengelken
Agency: Planungsteam K. Nengelken
Client: Zanders Feinpapiere AG

1005
Art Director: György Kara
Designer: György Kara
Photographer: Géza Molnár
Client: Artex

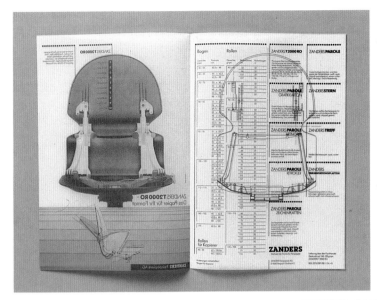

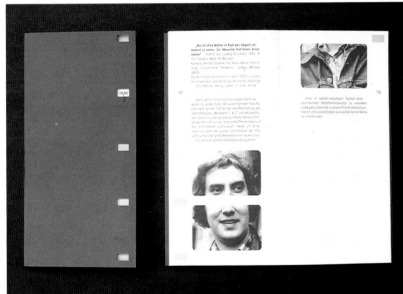

1006
Art Director: Holger Giffhorn
　　　　　　V. Thomas Serres
Creative Director: Holger Giffhorn
　　　　　　V. Thomas Serres
Designer: Holger Giffhorn
　　　　　　V. Thomas Serres
Agency: Giffhorn V. Serres
Client: Kultusministerium des Laudes Nordrheim

1007
Art Director: Peter Horlacher
Creative Director: Peter Horlacher
Designer: Peter Horlacher
Copywriter: H. J. Nieber
　　　　　　P. Wiechmann
　　　　　　R. W. Trowitzsch
Client: Bit-Verlag

1008

Art Director: Richard Henderson
Creative Director: Flett Henderson & Arnold
Designer: Flett Henderson & Arnold
Photographer: Ray Kinnane
Copywriter: Michael Heffernan
            Pat Gringer
Agency: Flett Henderson & Arnold
Client: Flett Henderson & Arnold

1009

Art Director: Michael Johnson
Creative Director: Kit Cooper
Designer: Michael Johnson
Photographer: Derek Seawood
Copywriter: Len Weinreich
Studio: Sedley Place
Client: BWBC & Co.

1010

Art Director: Katsu Asano
Creative Director: Katsu Asano
Designer: Kinue Yonezawa
Photographer: Bungo Saito
Copywriter: Katsu Asano
Agency: ASA 100 Co.
Client: Lunetta BADA

1011

Art Director: Lynn Trickett
            Brian Webb
Designer: Colin Sands
Photographer: Glynn Williams
Agency: Trickett & Webb
Client: Computer Cab

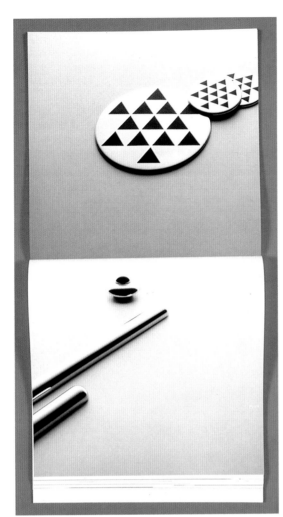

1012

Art Director: Shin Matsunaga
Designer: Shin Matsunaga
Photographer: Noritoyo Nakamoto
Client: Daichi Co., Ltd.

1013

Art Director: Hiroaki Nagai
Creative Director: Taosa Tohgura
　　　　　　　　　Satoru Miyata
Photographer: Tsutomu Wakatsuki
Copywriter: Hiroshi Mitsui
Agency: Commons Co. Ltd.
Client: Yokohama Rubber Co., Ltd.

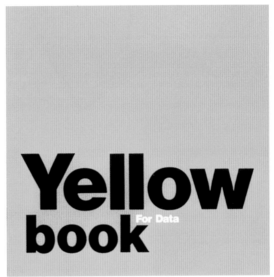

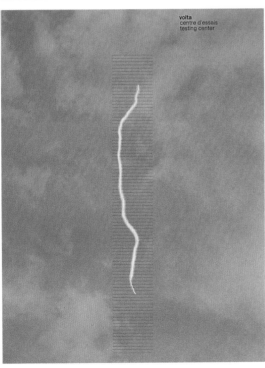

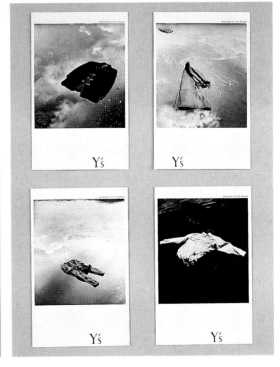

1014

Art Director: Jean-Marc Barrier
Creative Director: Jean-Marc Barrier
Designer: Jean-Marc Barrier
Photographer: Jean-Marc Barrier
Client: Merlin Gerin SA

1015

Art Director: Hisao Sugiura
Creative Director: Yohji Yamamoto
Designer: Hisao Sugiura
　　　　　　Studio Super Compass Ltd.
Photographer: Loren Hammer
Studio: Studio Super Compass Ltd.
Client: Y's

1016
Art Director: Koji Mizutani
Designer: Hirokazu Kuvelodyashi
Photographer: Yoshihiko Ueda
Copywriter: Kdoru Izima
Client: Melrose Co. Ltd.

1017
Art Director: Gavino Sanna
Creative Director: Gavino Sanna
Photographer: Mario Zappalà
Agency: Young & Rubicam Italia SpA
Client: Castelli SpA

1018
Art Director: Hiromi Inayoshi
Creative Director: Toru Ando
                    Yukuo Sato
Designer: Hiromi Inayoshi
Illustrator: Jean-Michel Folon
Agency: Dentsu Inc.
Client: Mitsukoshi Ltd.

1019
Art Director: Yoshiaki Bando
Designer: Yoshiaki Bando

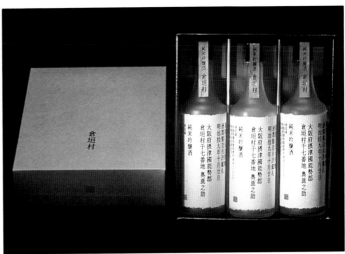

1020
Art Director: Belinda Duggan
Designer: Belinda Duggan
Client: John Harvey & Sons

1021
Art Director: Yoshitomo Ohama
Designer: Kazunori Umezawa

1022
Art Director: Frances Lovell
Creative Director: Duncan D. Bruce
Designer: Frances Lovell
Client: Black's Photo Corp.

1023
Art Director: James Gardiner
Creative Director: Ian Woodyer
Designer: James Gardiner
Ian Woodyer
Client: Caledonian Brewery

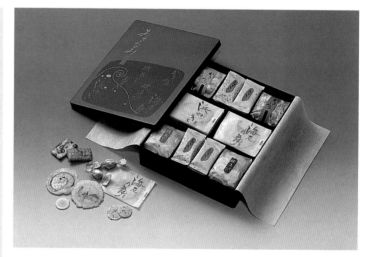

1024
Art Director: John Blackburn
Designer: John Blackburn
Client: Taylor Fladgate

1025
Art Director: Koko Nabatame
Creative Director: Koko Nabatame
Designer: Nabatame Design Office
Client: Nakamuraya Co., Ltd.

1026
Art Director: Akio Okumura
Designer: Akio Okumura
Client: Kazu Jewelry Design Studio

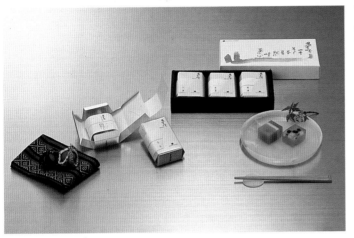

1027
Art Director: Kazuki Maeda
Designer: Seiichi Maeda
　　　　　Kenichi Tawaratsumiia

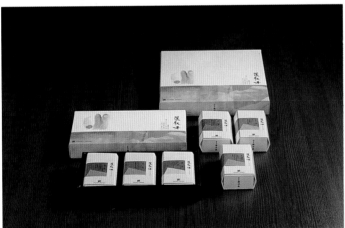

1028
Art Director: Ken Miki
Creative Director: Takuya Kihara
Designer: Ken Miki
　　　　　Junji Osaki
Client: Be-In International Inc.

1029

Art Director: John Blackburn
Designer: Belinda Duggan
　　　　　Tom Sutherland
Illustrator: Colin Elgie
　　　　　Jean-Paul Tibbles
　　　　　Jane Thompson
Agency: Blackburn's Ltd.
Client: Berry Bros. & Rudd

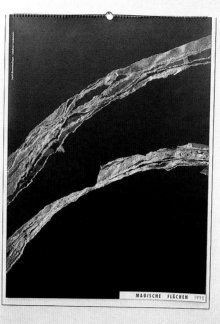

1030

Art Director: Michael Domberger
Designer: Michael Domberger
Illustrator: Peter Anderson
Client: Offizin Scheufele

1031

Art Director: Don Friedrich
Designer: Don Friedrich
Photographer: Franz Wagner
Client: Wagner Siebdruck

1032

Art Director: Manfred Grupp
Creative Director: Manfred Grupp
Designer: Gret Lengerer
Photographer: Claude Bornand
Copywriter: Michael Thevoz
Studio: Papierfabrik Scheufelen GmbH & Co.

1033

Art Director: Holger Nicolai
        Wolfgang Heuwinkel
Designer: Holger Nicolai
        Wolfgang Heuwinkel
Photographer: Hans Hansen
Copywriter: F. Mellinghoff
Agency: Nicolai Werbeugentur, Hamburg
Client: Zanders Feinpapiere AG

1034

Art Director: Thomas Bartsch
Creative Director: Thomas Bartsch
Designer: Thomas Bartsch
Agency: Illuverlag
Client: Illuverlag

1035

Art Director: Gary Martin
Creative Director: Andrew Niccol
Photographer: Andreas Heumann
Copywriter: Mark Goodwin
        Andrew Niccol
Agency: BBDO London
Client: Dormeuil

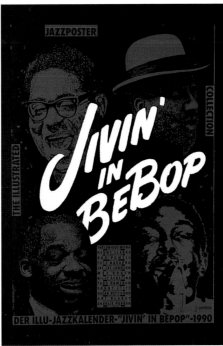

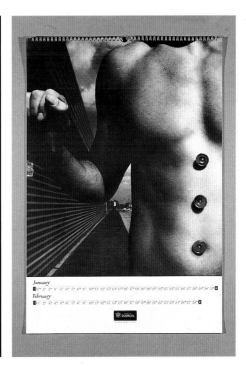

1036

Art Director: Toshihiko Maejima
Designer: Toshihiko Maejima
Photographer: Dominique Issermann
Agency: Dentsu Inc.
Client: Tasaki Shinju

1037

Art Director: Shin Matsunaga
Designer: Shin Matsunaga
Client: Nippon Telephone & Telegram Corp.

1038
Art Director: Shin Matsunaga
Designer: Shin Matsunaga
Client: Nippon Telephone & Telegram Corp.

1039
Art Director: Alan Fletcher
Creative Director: Alan Fletcher
Designer: Alan Fletcher
Illustrator: Alan Fletcher
Client: Pentagram
G & B Arts

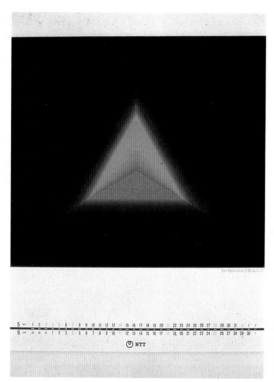

1040
Art Director: Martyn Hey
Photographer: Stuart Redler
Studio: Giant
Client: Kuwait Petroleum

1041
Art Director: Margaret Calvert
Designer: Peter Willberg
Jason Godfrey
Illustrator: Various
Studio: Royal College of Art
Client: IBM Germany

1042
Art Director: Sakutaro Nakagawa
Creative Director: Naotake Bando
Designer: Yutaka Oshiro
　　　　　　Hitoshi Hirano
Copywriter: Sakutaro Nakagawa
Studio: Word Shop Inc.
Client: Misawa Homes Co., Ltd.

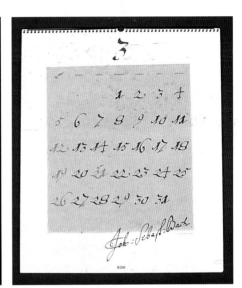

1043
Art Director: Norico Hirai
Designer: Tsutomu Nakazato
Illustrator: Fumihiko Enokido
Studio: Core Produce Ltd.
Client: Bell & Howell Japan

1044
Art Director: Ian Jensen
Creative Director: Noel Harris
Designer: Ian Jensen
Copywriter: Don Blackley
Agency: Chiat/Day/Mojo
Client: Chiat/Day/Mojo

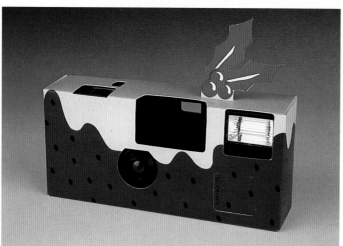

1045
Art Director: Klaus Wuttke
Designer: Eileen Robertson
        Christiane Ella
Illustrator: Eileen Robertson
Agency: Klaus Wuttke & Partners Ltd.
Client: Klaus Wuttke & Partners Ltd.

1046
Art Director: Tom Meenaghan
Creative Director: Tom Meenaghan
Designer: Tom Meenaghan
Illustrator: Mary Murphy
Studio: Designworks
Client: Guinness Corp. Affairs

1047
Art Director: Glenn Tutssel
Creative Director: Glenn Tutssel
Designer: Glenn Tutssel
Illustrator: Harry Willock
Agency: Michael Peters & Partners
Client: Tutssel/Warne

1048
Art Director: Richard Clewes
Designer: Richard Clewes
Agency: 360 Degrees
Client: Peter Hutchings Photography

1049
Art Director: Tom Meenaghan
Creative Director: Joanne Hugo
Designer: Joanne Hugo
Illustrator: Mary Murphy
Copywriter: Mary Murphy
Studio: Designworks
Client: Wiggins Teape

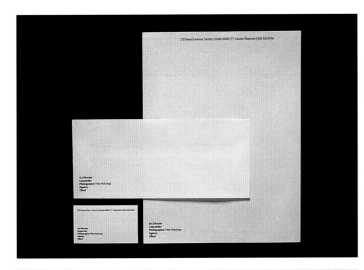

1050
Art Director: Béatrice Mariotti
Creative Director: Béatrice Mariotti
Designer: Béatrice Mariotti
Agency: Carre Noir
Client: Le Bon Marché

1051
Art Director: Catherine Pike
Illustrator: Raffi Anderian
Brett Lodge
Publication: The *Toronto Star*

1052
Art Director: Hans-Georg Pospischil
Designer: Peter Breul
Bernadette Gotthardt
Illustrator: Fernando Botero
Photographer: Abe Frajndlich

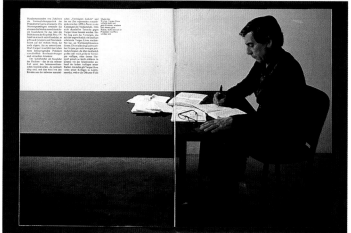

1053
Art Director: Hans-Georg Pospischil
Designer: Peter Breul
        Bernadette Gotthardt
Illustrator: Heinz Edelmann

1054
Art Director: Hans-Georg Pospischil
Creative Director: Seymour Chwast
Designer: Seymour Chwast
Illustrator: Seymour Chwast
Studio: The Pushpin Group
Client: Frankfurter Allgemeine Magazin

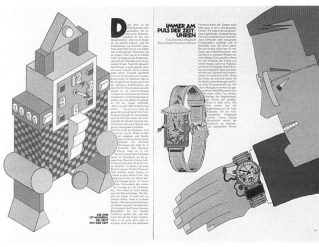

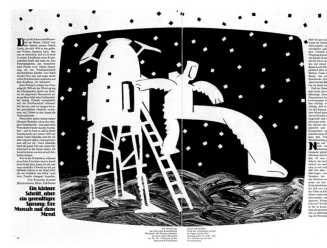

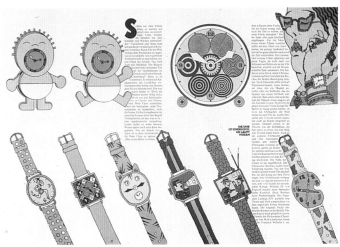

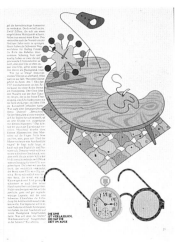

1055

Art Director: Hans-Georg Pospischil
Designer: Peter Breul
        Bernadette Gotthardt
Illustrator: The Pushpin Group

1056

Art Director: Hans-Georg Pospischil
Designer: Peter Breul
        Bernadette Gotthardt
Photographer: Jürgen Röhrscheid

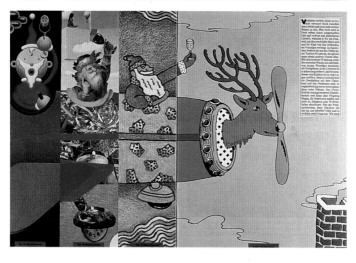

1057
Art Director: Hans-Georg Pospischil
Designer: Peter Breul
　　　　Bernadette Gotthardt
Illustrator: Brad Holland

1058
Art Director: Hans-Georg Pospischil
Creative Director: Seymour Chwast
Designer: Seymour Chwast
Illustrator: Seymour Chwast
Studio: The Pushpin Group
Client: Frankfurter Allgemeine Magazin

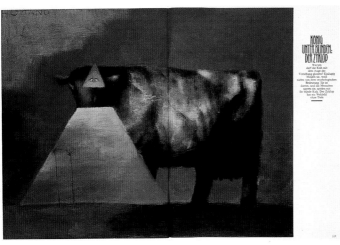

1059
Art Director: Hans-Georg Pospischil
Designer: Peter Breul
Bernadette Gotthardt
Illustrator: Hans Hillmann

1060
Art Director: Hans-Georg Pospischil
Creative Director: Seymour Chwast
Designer: Seymour Chwast
Illustrator: Seymour Chwast
Agency: The Pushpin Group
Client: Frankfurter Allgemeine Magazin

1061
Art Director: Hans-Georg Pospischil
Designer: Peter Breul
       Bernadette Gotthardt
Illustrator: Heinz Edelmann

1062
Art Director: David Hillman
Creative Director: David Hillman
Designer: David Hillman
       Amanda Bennett
Client: Barrie & Jenkins

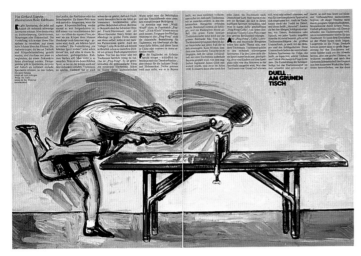

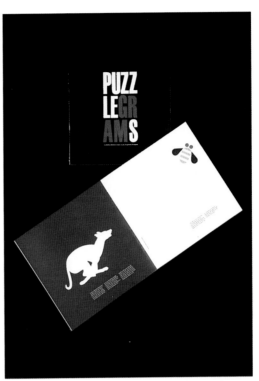

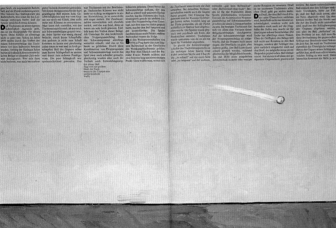

1063
Art Director: François Fabrizi
Studio: Studio Fabrizi

1064

Art Director: Shin Matsunaga
Designer: Shin Matsunaga
Publication: The Works of Shin Matsunaga
New York 1989

1065

Art Director: Brigette Sidjanski
Illustrator: Stasys Eidrigevicius
Client: Nord-Sud Verlag

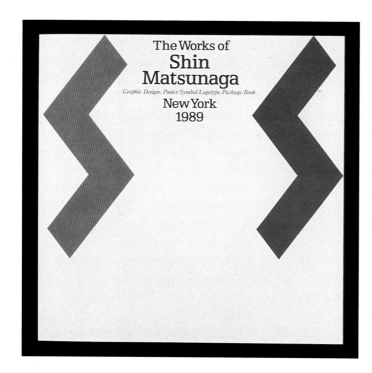

1066

Art Director: Ikko Tanaka
Designer: Ikko Tanaka
Photographer: Irving Penn
Client: Issey Miyake International Inc.

1067

Art Director: Pieter Brattinga
Designer: Pieter Brattinga
Producer: J. Vender Wolk C.S.
Publication: Joh. Enschedé

1068
Art Director: Joseph Pölzelbauer
Designer: Joseph Pölzelbauer
Copywriter: Rolf Müller
　　　　　 Martin Pflaum
　　　　　 Otl Aicher
Client: Karl Schillinger

1069
Art Director: Philip Hartley
　　　　　 Peter Stimpson
Creative Director: Philip Hartley
　　　　　　　　 Peter Stimpson
Designer: Philip Hartley
　　　　　 Peter Stimpson
Photographer: Various
Client: Elf Petrole

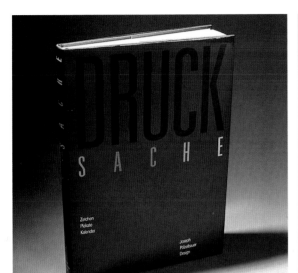

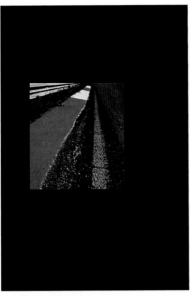

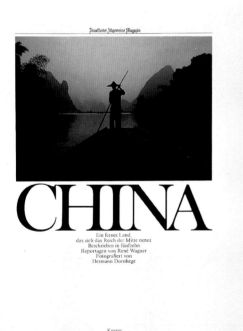

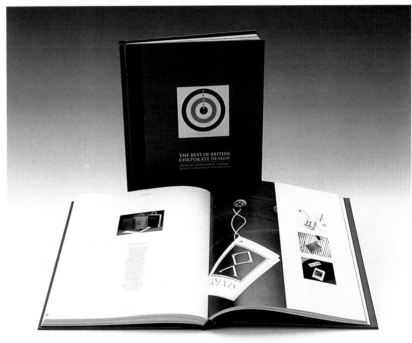

1070
Art Director: Hans-Georg Pospischil
Designer: Bernadette Gotthardt
Photographer: Hermann Dornhege

1071
Art Director: Marcello Minale
Designer: Ian Glazer

1072
Art Director: Katsuhiro Kinoshita
Designer: Katsuhiro Kinoshita
Photographer: Hashi
Publication: Fukutake Publishing Co., Ltd.

1073
Art Director: Kijuro Yahagi
Designer: Kijuro Yahagi
Client: Shigeru Ban Architect

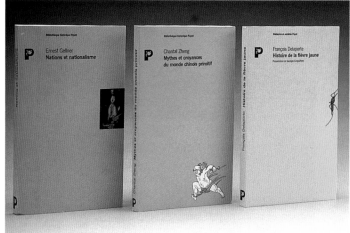

1074
Art Director: John McConnell
Creative Director: John McConnell
Designer: John McConnell
        Justus Oehler
Client: Editions Payot

1075
Art Director: John McConnell
Creative Director: John McConnell
Designer: John McConnell
        Justus Oehler
Client: Editions Payot

1077
Art Director: Dianne Eastman
Creative Director: Brian Harrod
          Ian Mirlin
Photographer: Bert Bell
Copywriter: Bill Daniel
Agency: Harrod & Mirlin
Client: Levi Strauss

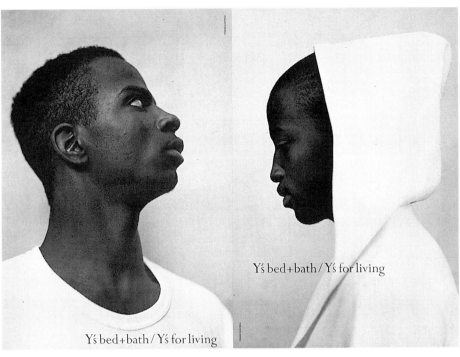

1078
Art Director: Hisao Sugiura
Creative Director: Goichi Hayashi
Designer: Hisao Sugiura
          Studio Super Compass Ltd.
Photographer: Kurt Markus
Studio: Studio Super Compass Ltd.
Client: Y's for Living

1079
Art Director: Dianne Eastman
Creative Director: Brian Harrod
          Ian Mirlin
Photographer: Bert Bell
Copywriter: Bill Daniel
Agency: Harrod & Mirlin
Client: Levi Strauss

1080
Art Director: Michio Miyabayashi
Creative Director: Michio Miyabayashi
Designer: Michio Miyabayashi

1081
Art Director: Rob Sluijs
Copywriter: Ton Druppers
Agency: KKBA
Client: Minolta

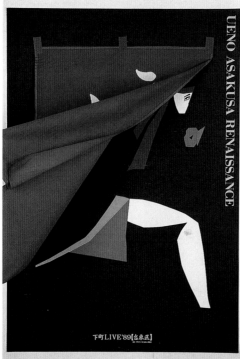

1082
Art Director: Yutaka Oshiro
Creative Director: Michimasa Kamimura
Designer: Yutaka Oshiro
Illustrator: Yutaka Oshiro
Copywriter: Michimasa Kamimura
Agency: Dentsu Inc.
Client: Taito-ku Municipal Office

1083
Art Director: Mitsuo Katsui
Illustrator: Masahiko Fujii
Photographer: Mamoru Horiguchi
Copywriter: Robert A. Mintzer

1084
Art Director: Peter Pócs
Designer: Peter Pócs
Photographer: László Haris
Copywriter: Peter Pócs
Client: SZDSZ

1085
Art Director: Kyösti Varis
Creative Director: Kyösti Varis
Designer: Kyösti Varis
Illustrator: Kyösti Varis
Agency: Varis & Ojala Oy
Client: Lahti Organ Festival

1086
Art Director: Bruno Monguzzi
Designer: Bruno Monguzzi
Studio: Bruno Monguzzi
Client: Kunsthaus Zurich

1087
Art Director: Takuya Ohnuki
Creative Director: Susumu Miyazaki
Shinsuke Kasahara
Designer: Soichi Akiyama
Yuji Masuda
Photographer: Herb Ritts
Copywriter: Masakazu Taniyama
Agency: Hakuhodo Inc.
Client: Sanraku Co., Ltd.

1088
Art Director: Noriko Amagai
Creative Director: Kōzō Koshimizu
Designer: Shigeharu Yamauchi
Photographer: Tamotsu Fujii
Copywriter: Kōzō Koshimizu

1089
Art Director: Niklaus Troxler
Creative Director: Niklaus Troxler
Designer: Niklaus Troxler
Illustrator: Niklaus Troxler
Copywriter: Niklaus Troxler
Studio: Grafik-Studio Niklaus Troxler
Client: Jazz in Willisau

Willisau, Sonntag 5. März 89, 17.00 Uhr, im Hotel Mohren

Anthony Braxton Trio feat. Adelhard Roidinger, Tony Oxley

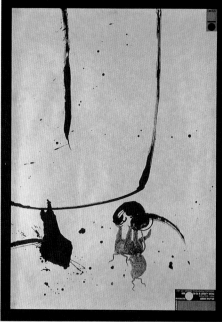

1090
Art Director: Takaharu Matsumoto
Creative Director: Takaharu Matsumoto
Designer: Takaharu Matsumoto

1091
Art Director: Fumihiko Enokido
Designer: Fumihiko Enokido
Illustrator: Fumihiko Enokido

1092
Art Director: Sandy Choi
Designer: Sandy Choi
Copywriter: Shona Brian-Boys

1093
Art Director: David Hillman
Creative Director: David Hillman
Designer: David Hillman
    Karin Beck
Copywriter: David Gibbs
Client: Design Council

1094
Art Director: Seymour Chwast
Designer: Seymour Chwast
Agency: The Pushpin Group
Client: Zanders Feinpapiere AG

1095
Art Director: Noriyuki Tanaka
    Yasuhiro Sawada
Creative Director: Noriyuki Tanaka
Designer: Noriyuki Tanaka
    Yasuhiro Sawada
Illustrator: Noriyuki Tanaka
Photographer: Senji Urushibata
Client: Noriyuki Tanaka

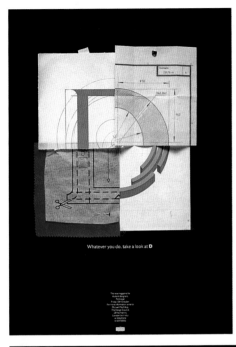

1096
Art Director: Makoto Saito
Designer: Makoto Saito
Photographer: Kazumi Kurigami
Agency: Cohwa International Co., Ltd.
Client: Shochiku Co., Ltd.

1097
Art Director: Daisuke Nakatsuka
Creative Director: Daisuke Nakatsuka
Designer: Wataru Hayakawa
Photographer: Eiichiro Sakata
Copywriter: Daisuke Nakatsuka
Client: Dai-ichi Mutual Life Insurance Co.

1098
Art Director: Ducki Krzysztof

1099
Art Director: Ikko Tanaka
Designer: Ikko Tanaka
Client: Takenaka Corp.

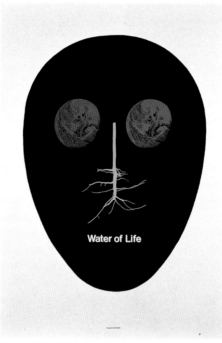

1100
Art Director: Kijuro Yahagi
Designer: Kijuro Yahagi
Client: Tokyo Kaisen Market

1101
Art Director: Ken Miki
Designer: Ken Miki

1102
Art Director: Masakazu Tanabe
Designer: Masakazu Tanabe
Illustrator: Masakazu Tanabe
Client: The Poster Execution Committee

1103
Art Director: Kenichi Samura
Creative Director: Kenichi Samura
Designer: Kenichi Samura
Client: Issey Miyake International Inc.

1104
Art Director: Niklaus Troxler
Creative Director: Niklaus Troxler
Designer: Niklaus Troxler
Illustrator: Niklaus Troxler
Copywriter: Niklaus Troxler
Agency: Grafik-Studio Niklaus Troxler
Client: Jazz in Willisau

1105
Art Director: K. Domenic Geissbuhler
Creative Director: K. Domenic Geissbuhler
Designer: K. Domenic Geissbuhler
Illustrator: K. Domenic Geissbuhler
Studio: K. Domenic Geissbuhler
Client: Zurich Opera House

1106
Art Director: Ducki Krzysztof

1107
Art Director: Kenichi Samura
Creative Director: Kenichi Samura
Designer: Kenichi Samura
Photographer: Chikao Todoroki
Publication: Bijutsu Shuppan-Sha Co., Ltd.

1108
Art Director: Shin Matsunaga
Designer: Shin Matsunaga
Client: JAGDA

1109
Art Director: Niklaus Troxler
Creative Director: Niklaus Troxler
Designer: Niklaus Troxler
Illustrator: Niklaus Troxler
Copywriter: Niklaus Troxler
Agency: Grafik-Studio Niklaus Troxler
Client: Jazz in Willisau

1110
Art Director: Tadanori Itakura
Designer: Tadanori Itakura
Photographer: Yasunori Saito
Client: Lexis Editorial Office

1111
Art Director: Holger Matthies
Creative Director: Holger Matthies
Designer: Holger Matthies
Illustrator: Holger Matthies
Client: Theater Oberhausen

1112
Art Director: Osamu Furumura
Designer: Kenichi Yoshida
Illustrator: Osamu Furumura
Copywriter: Osamu Furumura
Client: Imayo Co. Ltd.

1113
Art Director: Takaharu Matsumoto
Creative Director: Takaharu Matsumoto
Designer: Takaharu Matsumoto

1114
Art Director: Cecile Rusterholtz
　　　　　 Laure Predine
Photographer: Claude Sauvagot
Studio: Tatoo
Client: Enfants du Monde

1115
Art Director: Atsushi Ebina
Creative Director: Atsushi Ebina
　　　　　 Mitsugu Hiroki
Designer: Atsushi Ebina
Illustrator: Atsushi Ebina
Copywriter: Hitoshi Yasui
Studio: Verve Inc.
Client: Herald Ace

1116
Art Director: K. Domenic Geissbuhler
Creative Director: K. Domenic Geissbuhler
Designer: K. Domenic Geissbuhler
Illustrator: K. Domenic Geissbuhler
Studio: K. Domenic Geissbuhler
Client: Zurich Opera House

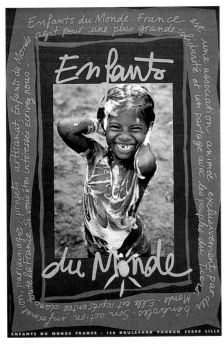  

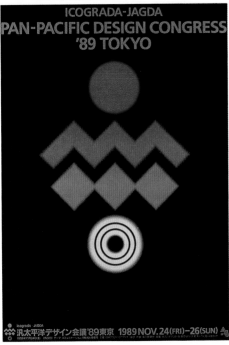 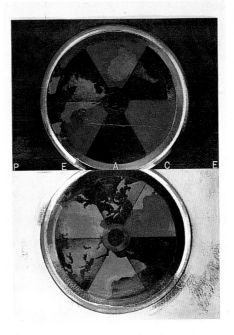 

1117
Art Director: Shin Matsunaga
Designer: Shin Matsunaga
Client: JAGDA
　　　　 ICOGRADA

1118
Art Director: Noriyuki Tanaka
　　　　　 Kentara Honzawa
Creative Director: Noriyuki Tanaka
Designer: Noriyuki Tanaka
　　　　　 Kentara Honzawa
Illustrator: Noriyuki Tanaka

1119
Art Director: Masaaki Izumiya
Creative Director: Masaaki Izumiya
Designer: Hiroshi Yonemura
Photographer: Yoshihiko Ueda
Copywriter: Mitsuhiro Koike
Agency: Hakuhodo Inc.
Client: Dai-ichi Mutual Life Insurance Co.

1120
Art Director: Toshiyasu Nanbu
Designer: Toshiyasu Nanbu
Client: Taste

1121
Art Director: Shin Matsunaga
Designer: Shin Matsunaga
Photographer: Noritoyo Nakamoto
Client: Takenaka Works Co., Ltd.

1122
Art Director: Kijuro Yahagi
Designer: Kijuro Yahagi
Client: Takeo Co., Ltd.

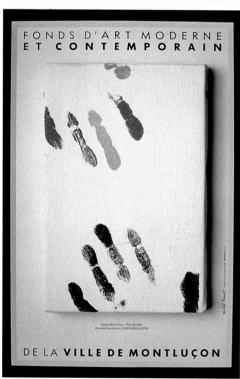

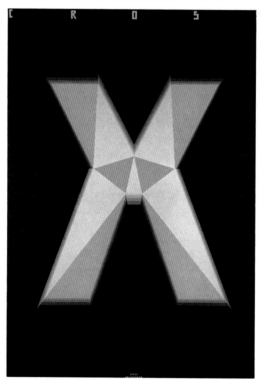

1123
Art Director: Michel Bouvet
Creative Director: Michel Bouvet
Designer: Michel Bouvet
Photographer: Françis Laharrague
Client: Ville de Montluçon

1124
Art Director: Shin Matsunaga
Designer: Shin Matsunaga
Client: Daiichishiko Co., Ltd.

1125
Art Director: Alan Fletcher
Creative Director: Alan Fletcher
Designer: Alan Fletcher
          Debbie Martindale
Illustrator: Alan Fletcher
Client: Geers Gross

1126
Art Director: Henry Steiner
Creative Director: Michael McLaughlin
Designer: Henry Steiner
Photographer: John Thomson
Client: Artspec Imaging Ltd., New Zealand

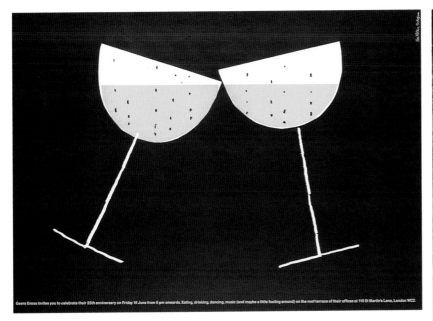

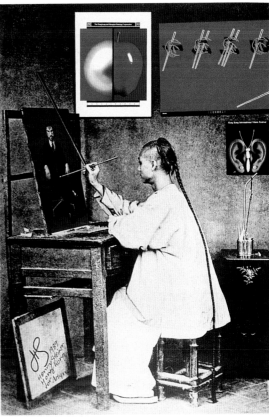

1127
Art Director: Andrew Lees
          Jackie Coates
Creative Director: Andrew Lees
Designer: Andrew Lees
Copywriter: Andrew Lees
          Chris Cudlipp
Agency: Chiat/Day/Mojo
Client: Club Mediterranee

1128
Art Director: Alain Le Quernec
Designer: Alain Le Quernec
Client: Artis

1129

Art Director: Andrew Lees
         Jackie Coates
Creative Director: Andrew Lees
Copywriter: Chris Cudlipp
         Andrew Lees
Agency: Chiat/Day/Mojo
Client: Club Mediterranee

1130

Art Director: Mervyn Kurlansky
Creative Director: Mervyn Kurlansky
Designer: Mervyn Kurlansky
Client: Polish Government

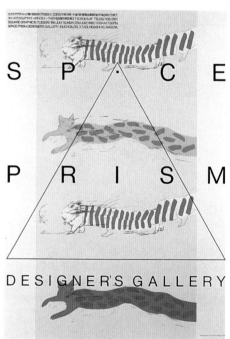

1131

Art Director: Heinz Handschick

1132

Art Director: Börje Stille
Copywriter: Ingemar Johannesson
Agency: Johannesson & Stille AB
Client: Folksam

1133

Art Director: Masakazu Tanabe
Designer: Masakazu Tanabe
Illustrator: Masakazu Tanabe
Client: Designer's Gallery Space Prism

1134
Art Director: Börje Stille
Copywriter: Ingemar Johannesson
Agency: Johannesson & Stille AB
Client: SIS

1135
Art Director: José Bulnes
　　　　　　Antoine Robaglia
Studio: Information et Enterprise
Client: Matra

1136
Art Director: Minoru Niijima
Designer: Minoru Niijima
Client: Kanazawa Sculpture Exhibition Committee

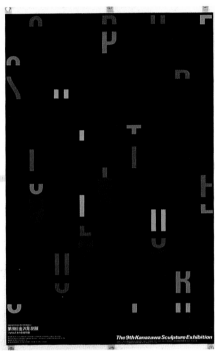

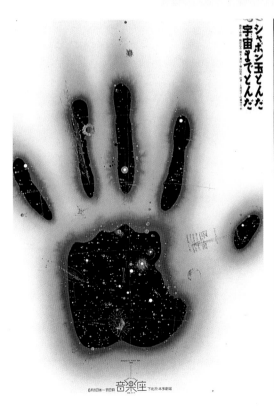

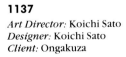

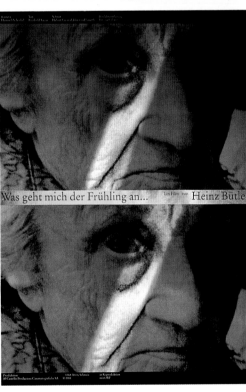

1137
Art Director: Koichi Sato
Designer: Koichi Sato
Client: Ongakuza

1138
Art Director: Bruno Monguzzi
Designer: Bruno Monguzzi
Photographer: Bruno Monguzzi
Client: Al Castello

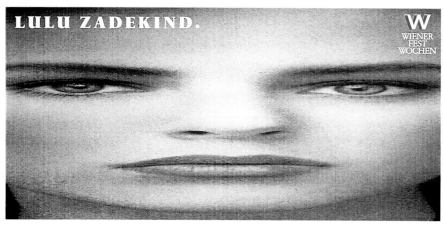

1139
Art Director: Klaus Erwarth
Creative Director: Mariusz Jan Demner
Designer: Andreas Miedaner
Photographer: Stockfoto
Copywriter: Mariusz Jan Demner
Agency: Demner & Merlicek
Client: Wiener Festwochen

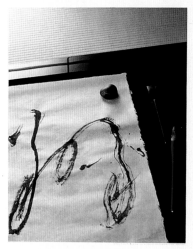

1140
Art Director: Bret Granato
Creative Director: Greg Starr
Designer: Eiki Hidaka
Photographer: Yukio Shimizu
Studio: Emphasis, Inc.
Client: Japan Airlines

1141
Art Director: Daisuke Nakatsuka
Creative Director: Daisuke Nakatsuka
Designer: Wataru Hayakawa
Photographer: Bishin Jumonji
Copywriter: Nobuko Tsunematsu
　　　　　　　Hideo Okano
Agency: Nakatsuka Daisuke Inc. Advertising
Client: Rengo Co., Ltd.

1142
Art Director: Toshihiko Maejima
Creative Director: Toshihiko Maejima
Designer: Toshihiko Maejima
Photographer: Toshihiko Maejima
Copywriter: Toshihiko Maejima
Agency: Dentsu Inc.
Client: Japan Design Committee

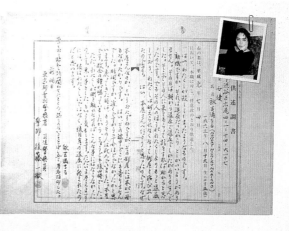

1143
Art Director: Tetsu Goto
Creative Director: Masaaki Tsuruho
Designer: Hisashi Katsumura
Photographer: Seo Takashi
Copywriter: Masaaki Tsuruho
Agency: Dentsu Inc.
Client: Kodansha

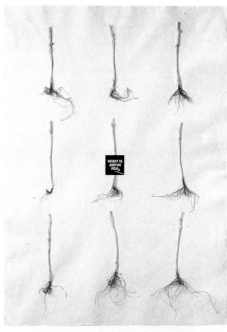

1144
Art Director: Shotaro Sakaguchi
                Katsumi Yutani
Creative Director: Katsumi Yutani
Designer: Keizo Tada
            Shotaro Sakaguchi
Photographer: Hatsuhiko Okada
Copywriter: Taketo Suzuki
Agency: Dentsu Inc.
Client: Dentsu Inc.

1145
Art Director: Shotaro Sakaguchi
          Katsumi Yutani
Creative Director: Katsumi Yutani
Designer: Keizo Tada
          Shotaro Sakaguchi
Photographer: Hatsuhiko Okada
Copywriter: Taketo Suzuki
Agency: Dentsu Inc.
Client: Dentsu Inc.

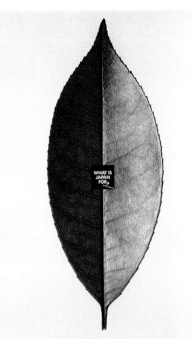

1146
Art Director: Kiyoshi Ohmori
Creative Director: Takeshi Yoneshima
Designer: Kiyoshi Ohmori
Photographer: Naohiko Hoshino
Copywriter: Takeshi Yoneshima

1147
Art Director: Koji Mizutani
Creative Director: Masatoshi Ikeda
Designer: Osamu Kitajima
Photographer: Yoshihiko Ueda
Agency: Dentsu Inc.
Client: Ana's

1148
Art Director: Yoshihiro Kobayashi
Creative Director: Noboru Kimura
Designer: Yoshihiro Kobayashi
Photographer: Tsutomu Wakatsuki
Copywriter: Miyuki Otomo
Client: Suntory Ltd.

1149
Art Director: Katsu Asano
Creative Director: Katsu Asano
Designer: Kinue Yonezawa
Photographer: Bungo Saito
Copywriter: Katsu Asano
Agency: ASA 100 Co.
Client: Japan Graphic Designers Association Inc.

1150
Art Director: Manfred Grupp
Creative Director: Erwin Fieger
Designer: Erwin Fieger
Photographer: Erwin Fieger
Copywriter: Erwin Fieger
Producer: AWS Ditzingen-Heimerd

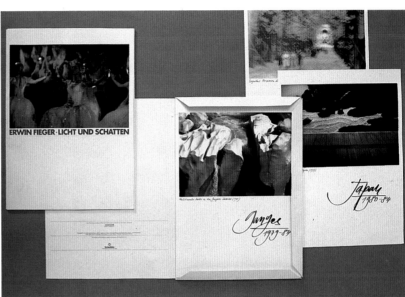

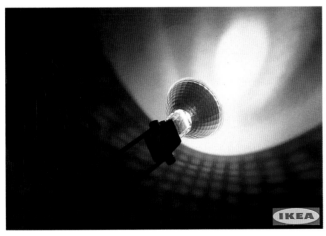

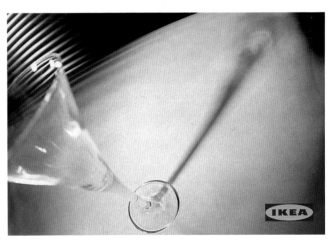

1151
Art Director: Helmut Klein
Creative Director: Edmund Petri
Designer: Gabi Wagner
Photographer: Helmut Klein
Agency: Young & Rubicam
Client: IKEA

1152
Art Director: Norbert Herold
Creative Director: Norbert Herold
Photographer: Monika Robl
Agency: Heye & Partner
Client: Optyl GmbH

1153
Art Director: Sigi Mayer
Creative Director: Sigi Mayer
Designer: Sigi Mayer
Photographer: Horst M. Stasny
Copywriter: Horst M. Stasny
Agency: Sigi Mayer
Publication: Modern Times Magazine

1154

Art Director: Darrel Shee
           Bill Martin
Creative Director: Gary Prouk
Copywriter: Bill Martin
Producer: Anne Phillips
Director: Richard Unruh
Studio: Partners Film Co. Ltd.
Agency: Scali, McCabe, Sloves (Canada) Ltd.
Client: Labatt Brewing Co. Ltd.

1155

Art Director: Noel Harris
Creative Director: Noel Harris
Copywriter: Harry Scott
Producer: Harry Scott
Director: Michael Ellis
Agency: Chiat/Day/Mojo
Client: Toyoto Motor Corp.

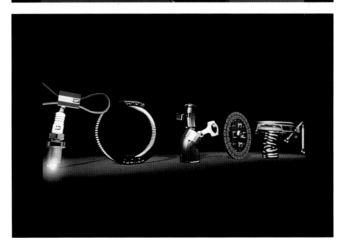

APE

30 seconds
LYRICS: Once I had a secret love,
    That lived within the heart of me.
    All too soon my secret love,
    Became impatient to be free.
VO: Carlsberg. Unbelievably good beer.

TOYOTA PARTS

30 Seconds
SFX: Latin American Music
VO: Toyota genuine parts and quality service…the only way to keep the feeling.

1156

Art Director: Randy Diplock
Creative Director: Gary Prouk
Photographer: Stanley Mestel
Copywriter: Randy Diplock
Producer: Sylvia Maguire
Director: Greg Sheppard
Agency: Scali, McCabe, Sloves (Canada) Ltd.
Client: Canadian Childrens Foundation

1157

Art Director: Neil French
Creative Director: Neil French
Copywriter: Neil French
Producer: Han Chew
Director: Neil French
Agency: The Ball WCRS Partnership
Client: Singapore Tourism Promotion Board

NOT IN SERVICE

30 seconds
SFX: Rain
VO: In Canada, like other countries, child abuse exists. The abuse can range from verbal to sexual. In fact, 1 in 8 Canadian kids are victims. And like other countries, we have a child helpline. But there is a difference.
BELL RECORDING: I'm sorry, the number you have dialed is not in service….I'm sorry, the number you have dialed is not in service.

SMILE

30 seconds
VO: Every year, tourism brings in 4 billion dollars to Singapore. And, it's up to everyone of us to keep it coming. But, of course, it isn't just a smile that matters, it's an attitude. And that's why we have The Singapore Tourism Awards. So, next time you meet a visitor, give him your billion dollar smile.

1158
Art Director: Kayleen Flanigan
Creative Director: Rob Freebody
            Mark Busse
Photographer: Annie Westbrook
Copywriter: Melinda Kerr
Producer: Anne Hughes
            Catherine Hancock
Director: John Ware
Agency: Foote, Cone & Belding

1159
Art Director: Richard Dearing
Creative Director: Ray Ross
Designer: Richard Dearing
Illustrator: Justin Robson
Copywriter: Don Blackley
Producer: Di Kelly
Director: Peter Macintosh
Agency: Clemenger Sydney
Client: Ricegrowers Association

POWER

30 seconds
VO: The new Mazda T-Series not only…
SFX: Loud rumble of traffic; horns tooting
VO: …has a powerful four liter…
SFX: Gear change
VO: …direct injection engine and a split shift subtransmission…
SFX: Clunk
VO: …that gives you the control of ten gear ratios.
SFX: Gear change
VO: It also carries an unbeatable 12 month unlimited kilometer warranty. Making it a very powerful proposition indeed.
SFX: Traffic
VO: The new Mazda T-Series. You get more from Mazda.

HEALTH

30 seconds
VO: There is one food that's as natural as corn on the cob…with far less sugar. It's as cheap as chips…with a lot less fat. It's as convenient as a can of beans…with a lot less salt. And, it's as easy to cook as a boiled egg…with no cholesterol at all. It's rice. Yes, rice. Grown in Australia by Sunrice.

1160
Art Director: Darren Warner
Creative Director: Gary Prouk
Copywriter: David Martin
Producer: Leslie Collie
Director: Steve Chase
Studio: Champagne Pictures
Agency: Scali, McCabe, Sloves (Canada) Ltd.
Client: William Neilson Ltd.

1161
Art Director: Yuzuru Mizuhara
Creative Director: Wataru Tsuchiya
Copywriter: Atsushi Sugimoto
Producer: Tsuneo Usui
Director: Yuzuru Mizuhara
Agency: Hakuhodo Inc.
Client: Canon

TWO SPEEDS

30 seconds
SINGER: Live my life
  The two speed way.
  It may come easy.
  It may go the long way.
  Just don't tell me the way to go.
  I could take it fast or I could take it slow.
  I could take it fast.
  I could take it slow.
  I could make it last.
  I could make it go.
  Just do what you do.
  The two speed way.

STRAWBERRY

30 seconds
VO: You may find it hard to believe, but everything around me is a copy. This high resolution is networked with a computer. It's here—the Canon Pixel Duo.

1162

Art Director: Mick DeVito
Copywriter: Derek Day
Producer: Sarah Shaw
Agency: Butterfield, Day, DeVito, Hockney

1163

Art Director: Anne Baxendale
Creative Director: Chris Whittaker
John O'Sullivan
Copywriter: Paul Wadey
Producer: Clare Hunter
Director: Ian McKenzie
Agency: KHBB
Client: Uniroyal Tires

LOOK AFTER YOUR HEART

50 seconds
SONG: ''Stop in the Name of Love''
VO: Eat too much, smoke, do too little, and it may not just be *your* heart you hurt.
So make a new start. And look after your heart.

BRIBERY

30 seconds
SFX: Rain pounding; then the sound of a heavy crane
VO: In the wet, you can't choose a better tire than a Uniroyal.

1164

Art Director: Dave Baldwin
Creative Director: Chris Whittaker
John O'Sullivan
Copywriter: Pete Cass
Producer: Clare Hunter
Director: Ian Giles
Agency: KHBB
Client: Nouvelee

1165

Art Director: Rohan Caesar
Creative Director: Robin Archer
Designer: Sue Hitchcock
Copywriter: Joe Di Stefano
Producer: Film Graphics
Director: Phil Meatchem
Agency: SSB Advertising
Client: Colonial Mutual

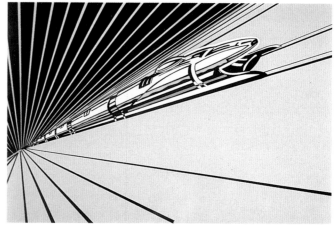

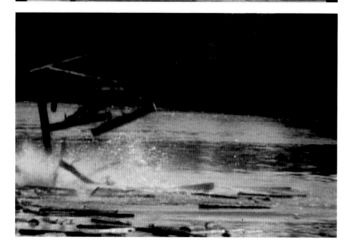

REVERSING LOGS

30 seconds
VO: Nouvelle announces a new kind of toilet tissue. It's very soft. It's very strong. It's even a little longer. The big difference is our toilet tissue is made from 100% recycled paper. So to make Nouvelle we don't have to cut down any more trees. Nouvelle Toilet Tissue. Soft on humans, not so hard on Mother Nature.

TRAIN

60 seconds
SFX: Station noises, crowds, whistles; then dramatic music
VO: In 1873, an Australian company started out with a vision. To forge a large insurance and financial services group built on security and strength.
SFX: Musical crescendo
VO: Today, it has evolved into a diverse financial force with $7.3 billion worth of assets worldwide. That company is the Colonial Mutual Group. A powerful, modern company that can look forward, because like few others it comes from a position of strength. The Colonial Mutual Group. Building on strength.

1166
Art Director: Richard Clewes
Creative Director: Richard Clewes
Copywriter: Richard Clewes
Producer: Charlene Kidder
Director: Greg Sheppard
Agency: 360 Degrees
Client: Credit Valley Hospital

1167
Art Director: Veronika Classen
Creative Director: Klaus Erich Küster
Copywriter: Veronika Classen
Producer: Käthe Pietz
Director: Lester Bookbinder
Agency: Michael Conrad & Leo Burnett
Client: Braun AG

HEALTHY CONTRIBUTION

30 seconds
SFX: Operating Room sounds
VO: Recently, in Mississauga, The Credit Valley Hospital broke new ground in medicine. Of course, we can't finish Phase Two Expansion without your assistance. Please, make a healthy contribution to The Credit Valley Hospital.

BEO

30 seconds
SFX: Alarm clock beeping
BEO: Shut up!!!
VO: Braun voice control stops at a word.

1168

Art Director: Shigenori Arakawa
Creative Director: Wataru Tsuchiya
Designer: Toshikazu Ieda
Photographer: Satoshi Seno
Copywriter: Natsuko Kazami
Producer: Shinji Mita
Director: Jun Asakawa
Agency: Hakuhodo Inc.
Client: Meiji Mutual Life Insurance Co. Ltd.

1169

Art Director: Ryo Honda
Creative Director: Yasuhiro Ohnishi
Designer: Yasuhiko Yamamoto
Photographer: Toshio Yamaguchi
Copywriter: Ryo Honda
Producer: Ryoichi Manmi
Director: Yasuhiko Yamamoto
Agency: Dentsu Inc.
Client: Fuji Xerox Co., Ltd.

DENTAL INSURANCE

30 seconds
CHILDREN: Teeth!
VO: They are fine when they are healthy.
CHILDREN: Cavities! Teeth fell out! A denture!
VO: Dependable!
CHILDREN: Teeth!
VO: Dental Insurance by the Meiji Mutual Life.

CARP SWIMMING ON PAPER

30 seconds
VO: Apply colors with an electronic palette. Increase the number.
Change the size. Documents can have new colors. Just a little fantastic.
XEROX's color copier Palette. Now on sale.

1170

Art Director: Richard Dearing
Creative Director: Ray Ross
Designer: Richard Dearing
Illustrator: Justin Robson
Copywriter: Gary Graf
Producer: Ron Spencer
Director: Peter Macintosh
Agency: Clemenger Sydney
Client: Ricegrowers Association

1171

Art Director: Jacob Cajaiba
Photographer: Klaus Meewes
Copywriter: Jacob Cajaiba
Producer: Ines Angiolillo
Director: Ernani Bessa
Agency: Salles/Inter-Americana
Client: ADVB

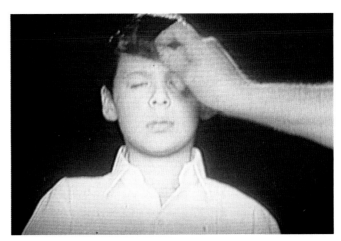

MADE IN AUSTRALIA

30 seconds
VO: There is something we export to the Orient that they really love…
and it's not a cuddly toy. Something they pay top dollar for…and it's
not liquid gold. Something they keep coming back for, again and again
…and it's not a boomerang. It's rice. Sunlong Rice…the only rice
Australia exports to the experts.

CHAPLIN

30 seconds
SFX: Drumroll
ANNCR: A child's future depends on you. Without affection…without
love…the only thing he is going to give back to the world…is hate and
violence.
SFX: Music reminiscent of Charlie Chaplin films
ANNCR: But if you give him love and affection…one day, he is going to
give it all back to you and the world in which you live.

1172

Art Director: Richard Dearing
Creative Director: Ray Ross
Designer: Richard Dearing
Illustrator: Justin Robson
Copywriter: Don Blackley
Producer: Di Kelly
Director: Peter Macintosh
Agency: Clemenger Sydney
Client: Ricegrowers Association

1173

Art Director: Jeff Layton
Creative Director: Boris Damast
Designer: Jeff Layton
Copywriter: Boris Damast
Producer: Gordon Stanway
Director: John Mastromonaco
Agency: Baker Lovick Advertising
Client: The Act Foundation

NUTRITION

30 seconds
VO: There's one food that provides protein to more people in the world than any other…and it's not fish. Fiber to more people in the world…and it's not bread. Energy to more people…and it's not red meat. And vitamins and minerals to more people in the world than any other…and it's not fresh fruit. It's rice. Yes rice. Grown in Australia by Sunrice.

JULIE

30 seconds
ANNCR: This is Julie. She's 12. Recently she saved a heart attack victim. Because she knew the simple skill of CPR. Learning CPR only took 4 hours out of Julie's life. In return she saved someone else's. Her father's. CPR. The reward of a lifetime. Anyone can learn it. Phone and find out how.

1174

Art Director: Peter van den Engel
Copywriter: Martijn Horvath
Producer: Frits Harkema
Director: Flip van Vliet
Agency: DMB&B Amsterdam
Client: Bavaria B.V.

1175

Art Director: Ikuo Amano
Creative Director: Serge Lutens
Designer: Yoshikatsu Okamoto
       Yutaka Kobayashi
Photographer: Serge Lutens
Copywriter: Koichi Tsuchiya
Producer: Masaaki Sato
       Tadashi Ichihashi
       Takanobu Shiraishi

CONFERENCE

30 seconds
SFX: Various gurgling noises; the sounds of a bottle being opened and a glass being filled

PERSPECTIVE

60 seconds
VO: Brown, which has been stolen from the museum… Inoui

1176

Art Director: Terry Cheverton
Creative Director: Stuart Byfield
Copywriter: Paul Hand
Producer: Maureen Gibby
Director: Salik Silverston
Agency: Grey Advertising
Client: Salvation Army

1177

Art Director: Masatake Satomi
Creative Director: Toshiaki Nozue
Designer: Junichiro Akiyoshi
Photographer: Toshio Tateishi
Copywriter: Mamoru Kusakawa
         Izuru Toi
Producer: Hiroshi Yoshida
Agency: Dentsu Inc.
Client: Matsushita Electric Industrial Co., Ltd.

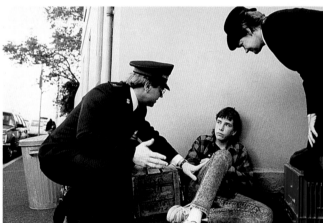

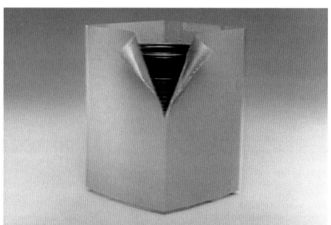

BREAK THE SPELL

90 seconds

VO: He was 14, he was 16, he was somebody's son.
    For a dollar he'd do anything for anyone.
    He asked is this living or am I in hell,
    God help me, God listen, please break the spell.
    He didn't care about Gucci or a Merc in the drive,
    His main interest was staying alive.
    Come night he'd sleep wherever he fell.
    God help me, God listen, please break the spell.
    The pills looked inviting, they whispered their charms,
    If only he could be held gently in somebody's arms.
Thank God for the Salvos.

TAP DANCE

60 seconds

SFX: Tapping

VO: This floor is made of a newly developed, vibration-reducing steel plate that absorbs sound. No matter how hard he dances, he can hardly make himself heard. Using this material we've created a quieter washing machine with less vibration. The debut of the quiet, quiet National Washing Machine Day. Nowadays, you should choose washing machines by their sound.

1178

Art Director: Stuart Byfield
Creative Director: Stuart Byfield
Greg Harper
Copywriter: Greg Harper
Producer: Helene Nicol
Director: John Lyons
Agency: Grey Advertising
Client: Transport Accident Commission

1179

Art Director: Katsumi Shibata
Creative Director: Koichiro Hara
Designer: Mamoru Kusakawa
Photographer: Toshio Tateishi
Copywriter: Hiroki Fukue
Producer: Hideo Kaneko
Director: Katsumi Shibata
Agency: Dentsu Inc.
Client: Gekkeikan Sake Co., Ltd.

THE GIRLFRIEND

60 seconds
SFX: Hospital noises
KAREN: They drink too much, they drive, they smash up their cars, people they care about…and if they survive…they have to live with it…that's the real tragedy…
VO: If you drink then drive, you're a bloody idiot.

FLOWERS, BIRDS, WIND, MOON

60 seconds
VO: Flower, bird, wind, moon.
Feelings blossom as a flower, before one knows,
Wishes take flight like a bird, even farther it goes.
A dream carried on a breeze relentlessly free,
Our fancy attracted by the moon, a tempting mystery.
Japan overflows with things to charm the senses. The Japanese sake Gekkeikan satisfies the sensitive mind of the Japanese.

1180

Art Director: Junichiro Akiyoshi
Creative Director: Satoshi Tarumi
Photographer: Toshio Tateishi
Copywriter: Satoshi Tarumi
　　　　　　　Ryoji Hagiwara
Producer: Hiroshi Yoshida
Director: Tsutomu Iwamoto
Agency: Hakuhodo Inc.
Client: Matsushita Electric Industrial Co., Ltd.

1181

Art Director: Junichiro Akiyoshi
Creative Director: Tetsuo Hashimoto
Photographer: Toshio Tateishi
Copywriter: Shigeru Koyama
　　　　　　　Masaki Inoue
Producer: Hiroshi Yoshida
Director: Masatake Satomi
Agency: Hakuhodo Inc.
Client: Matsushita Electric Industrial Co., Ltd.

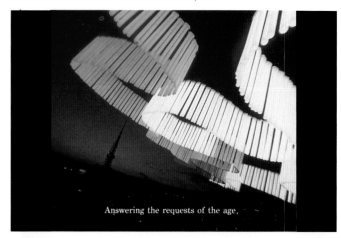

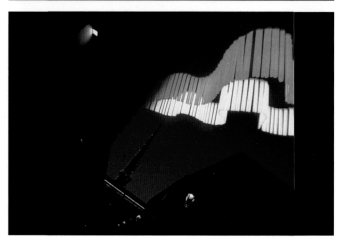

A FEAST OF LIGHT

60 seconds
VO: Meals can be a visual feast when their vivid colors are highlighted by the National Gourmet Lamp. National has created a lamp that makes food look delicious. Eat up!

AN AURORA OF LIGHT

60 seconds
VO: Have you heard? National's high precision bridge technology has created the Twin Fluorescent Lights series. An aurora of lights has begun to dance. New undulations of light will change the Japanese night. Total manufactured: 5,700,000. Answering the requests of the age, the light leader. The National Twin Fluorescent Light.

1182

Art Director: Roberto Fiamenghi
Creative Director: Gavino Sanna
Copywriter: Andrea Ruggeri
　　　　　　　Piera Teatini
Producer: Roberta Caimi
Director: Cesare Monti
Agency: Young & Rubicam Italia
Client: EDIT Editoriale Italiana

1183

Art Director: Sabine Kalchmair
Photographer: Thomas Albrecht
Copywriter: Johannes Kastner
Producer: Wirz & Fraefel Prod. AG
Director: Ernst Wirz
Agency: Kastner & Partner
Client: Wella AG

WON'T LET YOU REST IN PEACE
15 seconds
SFX: Ominous music

VERANDA
45 seconds
SFX: Music
WOMAN: Incidentally, the only important thing in this film is my hair,
VO: For clever heads, it's just got to be Design. Hairstyling from Wella.
Either you have Design or you don't.

1184

Art Director: Richard Dearing
Creative Director: Ray Ross
Illustrator: Justin Robson
Copywriter: Don Blackley
            Gary Graf
Producer: Di Kelly
Director: Peter Macintosh
Agency: Clemenger Sydney
Client: Ricegrowers Association

1185

Art Director: Rohan Caesar
Creative Director: Robin Archer
Designer: Sue Hitchcock
Copywriter: Joe Di Stefano
Producer: Film Graphics
Director: Phil Meatchem
Agency: SSB Advertising
Client: Colonial Mutual

HEALTH

30 seconds
VO: There is one food that's as natural as corn on the cob…with far
less sugar. It's as cheap as chips…with a lot less fat. It's as convenient as
a can of beans…with a lot less salt. And, it's as easy to cook as a boiled
egg…with no cholesterol at all. It's rice. Yes, rice. Grown in Australia
by Sunrice.

TRAIN

45 seconds
SFX: Station noises, crowds, whistles; then dramatic music
VO: In 1873, an Australian company started out with a vision. To forge
a large insurance and financial services group built on security and
strength.
SFX: Musical crescendo
VO: Today, it has evolved into a diverse financial force with $7.3 billion
worth of assets worldwide. That company is the Colonial Mutual
Group. A powerful, modern company that can look forward, because
like few others it comes from a position of strength. The Colonial
Mutual Group. Building on strength.

1186

Art Director: Fumichika Kato
Creative Director: Tokihiko Okamoto
Designer: Tsuguya Inoue
Photographer: Minsei Tominaga
Copywriter: Hiroyuki Yoshimura
Producer: Yoji Watanabe
Director: You Sato
Agency: Dentsu Inc.
Client: Cosmo Securities Co., Ltd.

1187

Art Director: Masahiko Satoh
Miyako Maekita
Creative Director: Ryoji Nakagawa
Photographer: Hiroshi Machida
Copywriter: Masahiko Satoh
Miyako Maekita
Producer: Yoshitada Kohchi
Director: Shinya Nakajima
Agency: Dentsu Inc.

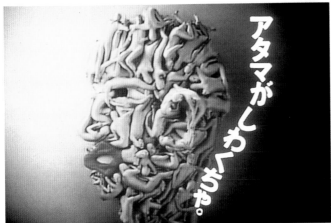

THE ANTENNA MAN

15 seconds
VO: Our antennae to the future react so sensitively that our brains tingle. Our heads are full of crinkles. Cosmos Securities.

MUSIC BOX

60 seconds
VO: If any one of these tines were missing, this music box would not play. With Toray, the strength of the 17 fields of enterprise represented by these tines are brought together to play one beautiful melody. Each one is crystal harmony, that's Toray.

1188
Art Director: Tony Beckly
Creative Director: Allan Crew
Copywriter: Julian Lloyd
Producer: Susie Cole
Director: Video Paint Brush
Agency: Lintas, Melbourne
Client: Schizophrenia Foundation

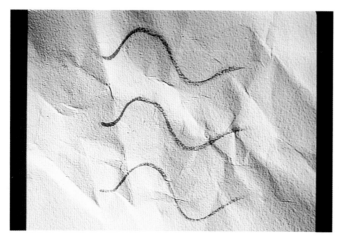

KIM

30 seconds

VO: For most of us the thought that our brains might malfunction is so
frightening we don't like to think about it. But many thousand
Australians will develop a disease which will make them think
differently about the world. And the world think differently about
them. Yet Schizophrenia is a disease like any other, except it affects
your brain, not your body. There's much we can do. For a start, we can
think differently about it.

PRESIDENT'S MESSAGE

It's hard to believe, but the Art Directors Club has been around for almost seventy years. I am fortunate to have a copy of an *Annual* from the early 20s. When you go through its pages, you get much the same feeling as when you leaf through this volume. They both have an air of authority, of final say about our profession. I think this special quality has never changed and is very much alive today. Sure, we have had competition from other organizations, but to me, at least, none have gained and maintained the importance of The Club.

To go back half way through our history, I remember the festive awards lunches held at the Waldorf-Astoria Ballroom over thirty years ago. There was an air of excitement around that room as the winners were called up that may not be duplicated in these more sober times, but it is still a landmark in an art director's career to be included in the yearly exhibition and in the *Annual,* which has remained the definitive chronicle of this profession.

All this tradition notwithstanding, we have gradually added many activities to make the club part of today's environment. The increasingly global aspects of advertising and design created the need for an international show judged by a jury from around the world. Their choices are also included in this book.

Activities to promote the participation of students and younger members are a priority on my list. We must provide for an enthusiastic and orderly succession. A new journal is being published and there are plans for a national conference.

The Board of Directors, the judges, the committee members, and especially the staff have given a lot of their time and knowledge to our club. If only for very selfish reasons, everyone in our profession must stay involved and keep the club a focus and a mainstay of our activity.

Henry Wolf

ART DIRECTORS CLUB

Staff

Executive Director
Diane Moore

Associate Director
Verice Weatherspoon

House and Project Manager
Leslie Buchan

Public Relations and Media Manager
Daniel M. Forté

Exhibition Manager
Jeri Zulli

Associate Exhibition Manager
Jonathan Gregory

House Assistant
Glenn Kubota

Exhibition Assistant
Denise Burns

Bookkeeper
Benny Carrasquillo

Administrative Assistant
Tracey Thomas

Chef
Chuck Lobl

Waitress
Margaret Busweiler

Advisory Board

Robert H. Blattner
William P. Brockmeier
Ed Brodsky
William H. Buckley
David Davidian
Lou Dorfsman
Walter Grotz
Jack Jamison
Walter Kaprielian
Andrew Kner
George Lois
John Peter
Eileen Hedy Schultz
Robert Smith
William Taubin

Executive Board 1989-90 Officers

President
Henry Wolf

First Vice President
Kurt Haiman

Second Vice President
Richard Wilde

Secretary
Ruth Lubell

Treasurer
Martin Solomon

Assistant Secretary/Treasurer
Peter Hirsch

Executive Committee

Robert Best
Seymour Chwast
Lee Epstein
Blanche Fiorenza
Sara Giovanitti

Committees and Chairpeople

69th Annual Judging
Lyle Metzdorf

Agency Relations
Kurt Haiman
Lee Epstein

Constitution
Jack Jamison

Call for Entries
McRay Magleby

Gallery
Richard Wilde

Hall of Fame Management
William Buckley

Hall of Fame Selection
Milton Glaser

Hall of Fame Patrons
Walter Kaprielian

4th International Judging
Karl Steinbrenner

Membership
Sal Lazzarotti
Carol Ceramicoli

Portfolio Review
Lee Epstein

Japanese Traveling Show
Shin Tora

Speaker Luncheons
Dorothy Wachtenheim

Newsletter
Sara Giovanitti
Seymour Chwast

ADC PUBLICATIONS PRESIDENT'S MESSAGE

The Art Directors Club's 69th *Annual,* which also includes the 4th Annual International Exhibition, marks the second year in our very successful relationship with Rotovision, who through their extensive international distribution network sold out every copy of last year's edition! I'm certain the book you now hold in your hands will be no exception.

McRay Magleby, the talented, award winning graphic designer from Brigham Young University Graphics did the striking cover and section dividers. Our panels of national and international judges were very selective this year, making for an even better publication.

My thanks go out to the ADC Publications Board, Pearl Lau, James Craig, Hugh O'Neill and Phil Thurman, and Executive Board liaison, Richard Wilde. A book of this magnitude could never have been published were it not for the invaluable assistance from the club's Diane Moore, Jeri Zulli and Dan Forté. We sincerely hope you enjoy this year's edition of the "Bible" of visual communication.

Dorothy Wachtenheim,
President, ADC Publications

JUDGES OF THE 69TH ANNUAL EXHIBITION

ADVERTISING
Carl Ally
Laurie Bleier
Dick Calderhead
David Davis
Lee Epstein
Elissa Querze
Michael Scheiner
Martin Solomon
John Steffy

EDITORIAL
Robert Barthelmes
Walter Bernard
Michael Brock
Bob Ciano
Carl Fischer
Claudia Lebanthal
D. J. Stout
David Walters
Fred Woodward

GRAPHICS
Charles Anderson
Peter Bradford
Lou Dorfsman
David Enock
Vance Jonson
Tana Kamine
Kiyoshi Kanai
Marie Christine Lawrence
Richard Moore
Minoru Morita
David November
Shin Tora

PROMOTION
Laura Bell
Carolyn Crimmins
Lynda Decker
Holly Jaffee
Andy Kner
Emil Micha
Jim Shefick

TELEVISION
Jerry Cotts
Ken Ferris
Harvey Gabor
Frank Ginsberg
Gary Goldsmith
David Jenkins
Jan Koblitz
Walter LeCat
Tom Monahan
Charlie Piccirillo
Robin Raj
Tina Raver
Phyllis Robinson
Nat Russo
Mort Sharfman
Michael Smith
Bob Smith
Karl Steinbrenner
Jerry Whitley

69th Annual Exhibition Chairpersons. Standing (left to right): Lou Dorfsman, Design; Carl Ally, Advertising; Andrew Kner, Promotion; Carl Fischer, Editorial. Seated (left to right): Lyle Metzdorf, Chairman; Phyllis Robinson, Television.

ART DIRECTORS CLUB 69TH NATIONAL JUDGING

In 1960, I saw my first *Art Directors Annual* and thought it was wonderful. Through the years, the ADC's *Annuals* have inspired me to do better creative work. So it is truly an honor and a privilege to have been this year's show chairman.

Hopefully, the work in this *Annual* will prove to be an inspiration to many future art directors. The *Art Directors Annuals* are also historically important because they are the only books that record the best in advertising, design, editorial, promotion and television in one volume.

This year's show, the 69th Annual Exhibition, received 14,075 entries including 24 hours of television from all over America. About 68% of the entries came from outside New York. It took 55 judges two weekends of soul-searching to select the 962 pieces that are in this *Annual.* They awarded 17 Gold, 45 Silver and 79 Distinctive Merit.

Not all categories received top awards. In fact, the club had no restrictions on how many pieces to select. This allowed the judges to pick only the best work. And picky they were! As a result, we ended up with a very good, quality show.

In order to select outstanding work, the judges used excellence in the following areas as a guide:

1. Concept
2. Art Direction
3. Design
4. Execution

I feel confident that few award shows have ever had better qualified section chairpersons for the judging than this year's exhibition. Thanks to Carl Ally, Advertising, Lou Dorfsman, Design, Carl Fischer, Editorial, Andrew Kner, Promotion and Phyllis Robinson, Television. Their leadership and expertise were invaluable. Thanks also to our judges. They were chosen by selecting top people with track records for producing award winning work. They came from within the club, outside the club and across the country.

And last, but not least, a special thanks to Ms. Diane Moore, the ADC's executive director, Ms. Jeri Zulli, exhibition manager, her staff and to Dan Forté for his help with the television judging. Through the combined efforts and talents of the ADC, you hold in your hands the best advertising, design, editorial, promotion and television done in 1989.

Lyle Metzdorf,
Chairman, 69th Annual Exhibition

JUDGES OF THE 4TH ANNUAL INTERNATIONAL EXHIBITION

Per Arnoldi
Ken Cato
Barry Day
Benoit Devarrieux
Gene Federico*
Kasumasa Nagai
Istvan Orosz
Francesc Petit
Gavino Sanna
Henry Steiner
Yarom Vardimon
Henry Wolf*
Maxim Zhukov

*Member of ADC Hall of Fame

ART DIRECTORS CLUB 4TH ANNUAL INTERNATIONAL EXHIBITION

This year marks the fourth exciting time the Art Directors Club of New York has been accepting, judging and exhibiting advertising, promotion, editorial and television communications from all over the world.

In 1984, when I was first given the go ahead from the Board of Directors to establish a long overdue international exhibition, it was the realization of a dream I'd had for several years. The idea came about while working overseas in Latin America, Japan and Southeast Asia with some temporary assignments in Europe. So much great work was being done in those areas that I felt it was imperative for the New York Art Directors Club to recognize that fact and honor the best.

What is particularly thrilling is to see the expertise and sophistication with which these communications are being accomplished. The recent geopolitical upheavals and dramatic changes we've witnessed in Europe, Asia, Latin America and Africa have such wide ranging effects that the next few years will be even more exciting. And it's more and more commonplace to see commercials and advertising production film crews popping up in once forbidden places.

We are seeing enormous changes in how the world perceives itself. And we—you and I, comrades—will aid and abet those changes for good or not so good.

The process will be fascinating, enlightening, informative and instructive. We'll continue to learn about each other and learn, underneath it all, that people the world over want to live better. Each year that we receive your entries from overseas, and a new international panel of judges makes its selections, we are seeing better and better work being done in more and more countries.

We'd like to see more representation from more countries. We'd like to see more of the best. We'd like you to enter your own work and we'd like to see you accept your Gold or Silver award at the next gala presentation here in New York.

We'd also like you to help us spread the word that every year during the month of December, we accept entries to the ADC International Exhibition of Advertising, Editorial, Graphic Design and Television.

Thank you for your enthusiastic response to our International Exhibition. And thank you for having helped make a dream come true.

Karl H. Steinbrenner,
Chairman,
4th Annual International Exhibition

A distinguished panel of experts review the submissions to the 4th Annual International Exhibition.

The ADC Traveling Show kicked-off its 1989 season at St. Louis's Loretto Hilton on the campus of Webster University. Over 500 people attended the opening night reception.

Photo: Bill Stover

TRAVELING SHOW

Last year's 68th Traveling Exhibition made successful stops in various cities in the United States and Japan. Among the places that played host to large opening night crowds in our country were:

The American Advertising Museum,
Portland, Oregon
Art Institute of Fort Lauderdale,
Fort Lauderdale, Florida
Art Institute of Houston, Houston, Texas
Art Institute of Pittsburgh,
Pittsburgh, Pennsylvania
San Antonio Advertising Federation,
San Antonio, Texas
Not Just an Art Directors Club,
St. Louis, Missouri

The club's 68th Annual Exhibition combined with the 3rd International Annual Exhibition toured extensively throughout Japan with the help of ADC members and goodwill ambassadors Minoru Morita and Shin Tora. Throngs of Japanese graphic designers and advertisers enjoyed shows in Nagoya's International Design Expo, Osaka's Design Center and at Tokyo's Gallery 7.

Anyone interested in sponsoring the club's national show may contact the exhibition department for further information.

GALLERY COMMITTEE

The Art Directors Club Gallery has emerged as one of the most important galleries exhibiting work from the visual communications industry. The exhibitions are varied, covering a wide range of shows from student work to international exhibits. The gallery openings have served as the meeting place for club members as well as enriched the advertising and graphic design community at large.

ADC Hall of Fame Show

ADC National & International Exhibitions

ADC/VCEF Benefit Art Exhibition & Auction

Association of Graphic Arts Show

Club of American Collectors Antique French Poster Exhibition & Sale

DESI Awards

Dimensional Illustrators Exhibition

Japanese Poster Show from Kyushu Graphic Design Association

Kazumasa Nagai & Nippon Design Center "Exhibition 90"

Package Design Council Exhibition

Society of Publication Designers Illustration & Photography Show

SVA Illustration & Photography Exhibition

SVA Photography Show

SVA Student Portfolio Exhibition

Richard Wilde,
Gallery Chairman

Club of American Collectors gallery exhibit and sale, "One Century of Advertising Art," showcasing rare French posters.

Luncheon speaker Sam Antupit of Harry Abrams with Luncheon Committee member Pearl Lau.

Luncheon speaker Louise Fili   *Photo: Dan Forté*

LUNCHEON COMMITTEE

The creative industry is growing and expanding. New markets, new mediums, new people. I'm happy to report that the Art Directors Club is in step. During the year, we have introduced some new faces to show how computer animation is working for entertainment and research purposes (R. Greenberg and Associates). We've demonstrated how graphic designers can become experts in all levels of communication, as with the Access Guides (Richard Saul Wurman).

Lunchtime at the club has gone from the sublime (Peter Vitale, photographer for *Architectural Digest*) to the ridiculous (Michael Frith and the Muppets). There are two sides to every story, especially in design. The classic magazine designer represented by Walter Bernard and the off-beat represented by Fred Woodward of *Rolling Stone* are lunch speakers in point.

With presentation always being the key and the first thing taught in art school, it's a special pleasure to have people such as Nigel Holmes, who turned around the look of charts and graphs. Statistical information has never been the same! In opposition, we have the design of big, beautiful coffee table books by Sam Antupit of Harry Abrams. Of course, once you learn something, turn it upside down and throw it out the window with the Ad Brats, Richard Kirshenbaum and Julian Bond. Two prominent members of our club, Hall of Famer Lou Dorfsman and past president and BSB's senior promotion art director Andrew Kner, also took the time to enlighten our large luncheon gatherings.

Our lunchtime lectures at the club are by far the best on-going and consistent forum for learning, growing and meeting new people. It's the best deal in town for getting that blend of fun, education and delicious lunches! Thanks to our fellow committee members: Scott Menchin, Dale Moyer, Susan Newman, Robin Sweet, our chairperson Dorothy Wachtenheim and the club's staff for making our speaker lunches so special.

Pearl Lau,
Committee Member

Dorothy Wachtenheim,
Chairperson

PORTFOLIO REVIEW

Springtime is always a tough time for graduating seniors. A scary time when the womb of the school is displaced by the nakedness of job hunting. A disillusioning time when averages and grades don't matter--when all that really counts is the portfolio.

That's why the Art Directors Club sets aside a series of Mondays and Fridays in mid-spring to give seniors a chance to go one-on-one with professional art directors and designers. They hear critiques, argue back, get a feel for the real and then, hopefully, improve their portfolios based on what they've experienced.

Everybody involved gains. The participating schools, FIT, Kean College, Kutztown University, Moore College of Art & Design, New York City Technical College, CW Post College, Pratt Manhattan, University of Delaware, University of Massachusetts and Youngstown State University all get to see how well they're preparing their students and to detect possible lapses in their curriculum.

The volunteer professionals have a chance to gauge and screen the upcoming talent and to see how far the new generation of creatives will push the status quo. And, of course, the graduates will learn that the industry is a spectrum of creative tastes, temperaments and personalities. The sooner they learn to perfect and trust their own talents and instincts, the better.

Lee Epstein,
Chairman, Portfolio Review

Alan Zwiebel reviews a student's portfolio.   *Photo: Dan Forté*

1990 VCEF SCHOLARSHIP RECIPIENTS

THE COOPER UNION
Paul Carlos
Thomas Ferraro
Agnieszka Jane
Charles Robertson
Reva Weiss

FASHION INSTITUTE OF TECHNOLOGY
Sonia Biancalani
Shardona Hebblethwaite
Raffaella Isidori
Doreen Serpico

NEW YORK CITY TECHNICAL COLLEGE
Allene Edwards
(Roz Goldfarb Award)
Camilo Fajardo
Alicia Fernandez
Agnes Laygo
Xing Hong Lin
(Ruth Lubell Award)
Anamika Sharma
Paul Viola

PARSONS SCHOOL OF DESIGN
Glennys Anglada
Ron De La Pena
(Book of the Month Club Award)
Pauline Demanche
Christopher Follett
(Book of the Month Club Award)
Claudine Guerguerian
Bonnie Lau
(Richard Taubin Award)
Toshiya Masuda
(Book of the Month Club Award)
Ezra Petronio
(Richard Taubin Award)
Nobuyuki Suzuki
Cheung Tai
(Richard Taubin Award)
Siung Fat Tjia

PRATT INSTITUTE
Christopher Bean
Mateo Mulcare
Susie Shon

PRATT MANHATTAN
Mary Margaret Fraser
Anna M. Mondragon
Ann Y. Song
Esther D. Weitzman

SCHOOL OF VISUAL ARTS
Abigail Aron
Robert Carducci
Thomas Gianfagna
Robert Hawse
Mikko Meronen

VISUAL COMMUNICATORS EDUCATION FUND

Since its very inception 69 years ago, the Art Directors Club has worked towards the creation and execution of scholarships for promising art students in the various schools in the New York area.

The funding for these scholarships has never been an easy job, but one that has always succeeded in one way or another. The scholarships have provided great satisfaction to the members of our VCEF committees and given great help to those worthy students who have received them.

In recent years, while donations from corporations have become more difficult to attain, the committee has instituted several innovative ways of allowing us to continue this most important aspect of our club's being.

One dollar from every entry into the Art Directors Club Annual Exhibition goes directly to the VCEF for scholarships. An annual art auction to which members and friends contribute a piece of their talents in the form of a drawing, painting or photograph for auction has become another source of income.

The VCEF committee encourages the Art Directors Club membership, the corporations who so badly need good art directors for their own success and futures, and the related suppliers, friends and beneficiaries of good art direction to consider an annual donation to this worthy cause.

This year, upwards of $15,000 will have been given to deserving art students. These dollars are not easily gotten. The fund needs your help so it can help support and inspire the talents of tomorrow.

It is our goal to collect enough funding in the next five years to institute an endowment that will be self-perpetuating. One that will insure scholarships for years to come, no matter what economic factors come into play.

The VCEF wishes to extend its sincere gratitude to those who have helped us achieve the measure of success we already have and ask everyone who hasn't, to consider helping us obtain our goal of a permanent endowment.

The students listed here are the recipients of this year's scholarships. They are the latest of a long list that this VCEF Committee has full intentions of making longer and longer in the years to come.

Walter Kaprielian,
President,
Visual Communicators Education Fund

Photo: Dan Forté

VCEF President Walter Kaprielian with 1990 VCEF Scholarship winners.

Photo: Dan Forté

VCEF Scholarship recipient receives her certificate and Art Directors Annual *as Diane Moore, Walter Kaprielian and Martin Solomon look on.*

ADC NATIONAL MEMBERS

A

Rea Ackerman
Kazuhiko Adachi
Donald Adamec
Tina Adamek
Gaylord Adams
Steven Adams
Patricia Addiss
Peter Adler
Charles Adorney
Betty Alfenito
Leslie Alfin-Klein
Lorraine Allen
Carlo Ammirati
Joseph Anderson
Gennaro Andreozzi
Al Anthony
Robert Anthony
Frank S. Arcuri
Arnold Arlow
Dennis M. Arnold
Herman Aronson
Rochelle L. Arthur
Tadashi Asano
Marvin Asch
Seymour Augenbraun
Joel Azerrad

B

Jeff Babitz
Alberto Baccari
Robert O. Bach
Ronald Bacsa
Priscilla Baer
Frank Baker
Ronald Ballister
Don Barron
Robert Barthelmes
Gladys Barton
Matthew Baslie
Wendy Bass
Mary K. Baumann
Allan Beaver
Dolores Bego Kluga
Ephram E. Benguiat
Edward J. Bennett
Laurence Key Benson
Bill Berenter
John Berg
Sy Berkley
Pamme J. Berman
Walter L. Bernard
Barbara Bert
Peter J. Bertolami
Frank Bertulis
Robert Best
Roger Black
Janet Blank
Peter J. Blank
Robert H. Blattner
Robert H. Blend
Anthony Bloch
Bruce Bloch
David S. Block
Arnold Blumberg
Robert Bode
Ronne Bonder
George Warren Booth
Jeroen Bours
Harold A. Bowman
Carolyn Bowyer
Doug Boyd
Douglas C. Boyd

Jean L. Brady
Simeon Braguin
Fred J. Brauer
Al Braverman
Barry Braverman
Angela Reed Breese
Lynn Dreese Breslin
William P. Brockmeier
Ed Brodsky
Ruth Brody
Adrienne G. Brooks
Joe Brooks
Annette S. Browdy
T. Courtney Brown
Robert Bruce
Bruno E. Brugnatelli
Lee Buchar
William Buckley
Aaron Burns
Herman F. Burns
Laurie Burns
Cipe P. Burtin

C

Bill Cadge
Albert J. Calzetta
Arline Campbell
Bryan Canniff
Andrew Cantor
Michael R.
    Capobianco
Tony Cappiello
Thomas Carnase
William F. Carrig
David E. Carter
Ralph Casado
Angelo Castelli
John R. Centanni
Carol F. Ceramicoli
Edward Cerullo
Anthony
    Chaplinsky Jr.
Ilene Brown Charella
Vivian Chen
Richard S. Chesler
Roberta Chiarella
Younghee Choi
Shui-Fong Chong
Alan Christie
Hoi Ling Chu
Stanley Church
Seymour Chwast
Bob Ciano
Jon Cisler
Herbert H. Clark
Thomas F. Clemente
Mahlon Cline
Victor Closi
Joel Cohen
Joseph R. Coleman
Michael Coll
Eleanor Colston
Catherine Connors
Daniel Cooperbey
Dinah Coops
Lee Corey
Eva Costabel
Sheldon Cotler
Ron Couture
Phyllis Richmond Cox
Robert Cox
Thomas J. Craddock
James Craig

Meg Crane
Brian A. Cranner
Constance Craven
Bob Crozier
Louis F. Cruz
Jerry Cummins
Ethel R. Cutler
Gregory F. Cutshaw

D

Russell J. D'Anna
Royal Dadum
Deborah Dalton
Derek Dalton
Wendy Damico
David Davidian
Kathryn Davidian
David Davis
Herman Davis
Joseph Davis
Paul Davis
Philip Davis
Jan DeChabert
Perri L. DeFino
Erik DeMartino
Faye M. DeSanto
Lynda Decker
Robert Defrin
Joseph Del Sorbo
Jerry Demoney
Michael Denapoli
Diane Depasque
David Deutsch
Frank M. Devino
Francis J. Devito
Peter J. Deweerdt
Dennis DiVincenzo
Charles Dickenson
Carolyn Diehl
Edward P. Diehl
John F. Dignam
Lou Donato
Chel Dong
Louis Dorfsman
Marc Dorian
Kay Elizabeth Douglas
Andra Douglas
Nick Driver
Rina Drucker
Fae Ellen Druiz
Ann Dubiel
Donald H. Duffy
William R. Duffy
Laura K. Duggan
Rosalyn C. Dunham
Patrice Dunn
Rudolf Dusek
Michael Dweck

E

Stephen T. Eames
Heidi Eckman
Bernard Eckstein
Peter Edgar
Don Egensteiner
Jack Ehn
Antonie Eichenberg
Zeneth Eidel
Stanley Eisenman
Robert Eisner
Jane Eldershaw
Judith Ellis
Wallace W. Elton
Jack Endewelt
David Epstein
Lee Epstein

Shirley Ericson
Lois A. Erlacher
Suren Ermoyan
Robert H. Essel
June Evers

F

Kathleen Quinn Fable
Joseph Fama
Rose Farber
Judy Fendelman
Michael Fenga
Roger Ferritter
Michael Fidanzato
William F. Finn
Blanche Fiorenza
Gon Firpo
Carl Fischer
Wayne Fitzpatrick
John Flanagan
Morton Fleischer
Gilbert D. Fletcher
Donald P. Flock
John Fraioli
Stephen O. Frankfurt
Richard G. Franklin
Frederic B. Freyer
Ruby Miye Friedland
Beverly Friedman
Michael K. Frith
Oren Frost
Paul Fuentes
Neil Fujita
Leonard W. Fury

G

Harvey Gabor
Raymond M. Gaeta
Robert Gage
Rosemarie Galioto
Danielle Gallo
Gene Garlanda
David Gatti
Joseph T. Gauss
Alberto P. Gavasci
Howard Geissler
Charles Gennarelli
Robert J. George
Joseph Gering
Michael Germarkian
Linda Gersch
John Geryak
Victor Gialleonardo
Edward Gibbs
Carol Bonnie Gildar
Donald Gill
Peter C. Gilleran
Frank C. Ginsberg
Sara Giovanitti
George Giusti
Milton Glaser
Eric Gluckman
Marc Gobe
Bill Gold
Irwin Goldberg
Les Goldberg
Roz Goldfarb
Eli W. Goldowsky
Jo Ann Goldsmith
Joanne Goodfellow
Laura J. Goodman
Cyd Gorman
Rhonda Gotthainer
Diana Graham
Richard Grider
Jack Griffin

Glenn P. Groglio
Walter Grotz
Susan Grube
Nelson Gruppo
Rollins S. Guild
Jean - Manuel Guyager

H

Steven Haas
Jane Haber
Hank Hachmann
Robert Hack
Kurt Haiman
Graham Halky
Bruce W. Hall
Evertt Halvorsen
Shoichiro Hama
Edward Hamilton
Frances M. Hamilton
Paul Hartelius Jr.
George Hartman
Alan Hartwell
Barry Hassell
Dorothy Hayes
Saul Heff
William G. Heinrich
Amy Heit
Shelley L. Heller
Steven Heller
William J. Hendricks
Randall Hensley
Robert S. Herald
Louis F. Hernandez
Susan Herr
James J. Herrmann
Chris Hill
Peter M. Hirsch
Jitsuo Hoashi
Roland Hodes
Marilyn Hoffner
Leslie Hopkins
Steve Horn
William David Houser
Paul Howard
Julie Hubner
Thomas M. Hughes
Wayne Hulse
Jud Hurd
Gary Husk
Melanie
    Jennings Husk
Steff Hynek

I

Tom J. Ide
Ana J. Inoa
Henry Isdith
Edward Israel

J

Harry Jacobs
Melissa Jacoby
Holly Jaffe
Lee Ann Jaffee
Jack Jamison
John C. Jay
Bill Jensen
Patricia Jerina
Barbara John
Shaun Johnston
Anne M. Jones
Bob Jones
Roger Joslyn
Len Jossel
Barbara L. Junker

K

Nita J. Kalish
Kiyoshi Kanai
Walter Kaprielian
Judy Katz
Ward Kelvin
Alice Kenny
Nancy Kent
Myron W. Kenzer
Ellen Sue Kier
Bok-Young Kim
Soon Kim
Judith Klein
Mark Kleinfeld
Hilda Stranger Klyde
Andrew Kner
Henry Knoepfler
Ray Komai
Robert F. Kopelman
Kati Korpijaako
Oscar Krauss
Helmut Krone
Thaddeus B. Kubis
Bill Kuchler
Anna Kurz

L

Howard La Marca
Lisa LaRochelle
James E. Laird
Abril Lamarque
David R. Lance
Joseph O. Landi
David Langston
Michael Lanotte
John Larkin
Pearl Lau
Kenneth H. Lavey
Marie Christine
    Lawrence
Sal Lazzarotti
Daniel Lee
Ed Lee
Diane Elizabeth
    Lemonides
John Lenaas
Robert C. Leung
Richard Levenson
Joanne Levey
Alexander Liberman
Susan Llewellyn
George Lois
Henry R. Loomis
Dennis Lopez Luna
George Gilbert Lott
Robert Louey
Jackson Lowell
Alfred Lowry
Ruth Lubell
John Lucci
Richard Luden
John H. Luke
Thomas R. Lunde
Larry Lurin
Robert W. Lyon Jr.
Michael J. Lyons

M

Charles MacDonald
Richard MacFarlane
David H. MacInnes
Frank Macri
Sam Magdoff
Louis Magnani
Carol A. Maisto
Anthony Mancino
Jean Marcellino
John Margeotes
David R. Margolis
Jack Mariucci
John S. Marmaras
Andrea Marquez
Hector Marrero
Daniel Marshall
William R. Martin
Michael Mastros
Theodore Matyas
Andrea Freund Mauro
Marce Mayhew
Victor J.
    Mazurkiewicz
William McCaffery
Sheila McCaffery
Constance McCaffrey
Eileen McClash
Brian P. McDermott
Mark S. McDowell
Philip P. McKenna
Scott A. Mednick
William Meehan
Nancy A. Meher
Scott Menchin
Mario G. Messina
Alice Messinger
Lyle Metzdorf
Jackie Merri Meyer
Emil T. Micha
Eugene Milbauer
Anistatia R. Miller
Lawrence Miller
John Milligan
Isaac Millman
Wendell Minor
Michael Miranda
Pamela E. Mitchell
Leonard J. Mizerek
Allan Mogel
Joseph Montebello
Richard Moore
Paul D. Moran
Viorel Moraru
Jeffrey Moriber
Minoru Morita
Mami Morooka
Leonard Morris
William R. Morrison
Thomas Morton
Roger Paul Mosconi
Louie Moses
Roselee Moskowitz
Chet Moss
Geoffrey Moss
Tobias Moss
Dale Moyer
Robbi G. Muir
Virginia
    Murphy-Hammill
Ralph J. Mutter

N

William Naegels
Daniel Nelson
John Newcomb
Andrew M. Newman
Susan E. Newman
Stuart Nezin
Mary Ann Nichols
Raymond Nichols
Joseph Nissen
Evelyn C. Noether
David November

O

Frank O'Blak
John O'Neil
Hugh O'Neill
Kevin James O'Neill
Jack W. Odette
Noriyuki Okazaki
John Okladek
Susan Alexis Orlie
Luis Ortiz
Nina Ovryn
Bernard S. Owett

P

Onofrio Paccione
Zlata W. Paces
Sharon Padua
Robert Paganucci
Robert A. Paige
Brad Pallas
Roxanne Panero
Jacques Parker
Paul E. Parker Jr.
Grant Parrish
Kathleen Pascoe
Charles W. Pates
Arthur Paul
Leonard Pearl
Alan Peckolick
B. Martin Pedersen
Carol Peligian
Meryl Penner
Vincent Pepi
Pierre Pepin
Paul Perlow
Bea Perron
Harold A. Perry
Roberta Perry
David S. Perry
Victoria I. Peslak
John Peter
Christos Peterson
Robert Petrocelli
Theodore D. Pettus
Stephanie Phelan
Allan Philiba
Alma M. Phipps
George Pierson
Michael Pilla
Ernest Pioppo
Peter Pioppo
Robert Pliskin
Raymond Podeszwa
George Polk
Richard Portner
Louis Portuesi
Fran Posen
Anthony Pozsonyi
Benjamin Pride
Bob Procida
Rory James Pszenitzki

Q

Charles W. Queener
Elissa Querze
Anny Queyroy
Mike Quon

R

Judith G. Radice
Paul Rand
Elaine Raphael
Robert C. Reed
Samuel Reed
Sheldon Reed
Patrick Reeves
Herbert O. Reinke
Ann Marie Renzi
David Rhodes
Edward E. Ricotta
Arthur Ritter
Valerie Ritter
Kenneth Roberts
Judy Roberts
Ray Robertson
Bennett Robinson
Lennox I. Robinson
Harry Rocker
Harlow Rockwell
Randy Rodriguez
Andy Romano
Cory L. Rosenberg
Lee Rosenberg
Barbara Rosenthal
Herbert M. Rosenthal
Charles Rosner
Andrew Ross
Richard J. Ross
Richard Ross
Arnold Roston
Cynthia Rothbard
Iska Rothovius
Mort Rubenstein
Randee Rubin
Thomas P. Ruis
Robert Miles Runyan
Henry N. Russell
Albert Russo
Don Ruther
Thomas Ruzicka

S

Stewart Sacklow
Moriyoshi Saito
Robert Saks
Tracey Salaway
Richard M. Salcer
Ludvic Saleh
Robert Salpeter
Karen Salsgiver
Ina Saltz
George Samerjan
Carmine Santandrea
Jim Santandrea
Audrey Satterwhite
Xavier Saucedo
Hans Sauer
Mike Saz
Sam Scali
Peter Scannell
Ernie Scarfone
Paula Scher
Glen Scheuer
Mark Schimmel
Klaus F. Schmidt
Joyce Schnaufer
Beverly Faye Schrager
Sharon Schuermann
Carol Schulter
Eileen Hedy Schultz
Nancy K. Schulz
Victor Scocozza
Ruth Scott
William C.
    Seabrook III
David M. Seager
Ann Secor
J. J. Sedelmaier
Leslie Segal
Sheldon Seidler
Amy Seissler
John L. Sellers
Kaede Seville
Kevin M. Shea
Alexander Shear
Minoru Shiokawa
Jerry Siano
Louis Silverstein
Milt Simpson
Meera Singh
Len Sirowitz
Jack Skolnik
Elizabeth F. Slott
Paul Slutsky
Carol Lynn Smith
Robert S. Smith
Edward Sobel
Andrew Sokol
Martin Solomon
Harold Sosnow
Carmen Soubriet
Michelle R. Spellman
Lisa A. Speroni
Victor E. Spindler
Martin St. Martin
David Stahlberg
Shelley LaRoche
    Stansfield
Mindy Phelps Stanton
Karsten Stapelfeldt
Alexander Stauf
Lynn Steck
Irena S. Steckiv
Emily Stedman
Douglas Steinbauer
Karl H. Steinbrenner
Karl Eric
    Steinbrenner Jr.
Vera Steiner
Barrie Stern
Charles M. Stern
Henrietta Stern
Gerald Stewart
Linda Stillman
Bernard Stone
Otto Storch
William Strosahl
Brenda Suler
Ken Sweeny
Robin Sweet
Janice Sztabnik

T

Barbara Taff
Daniel L. Tagbo
Robert Talarczyk
Wendy Talve Reingold
Norman Tanen
Jo Ann Tansman
Melissa K. Tardiff
Melcon Tashian
Bill Taubin
Jack George Tauss
Mark Tekushan
Ciro Tesoro
Neli Thalasinos
Richard Thomas
Bradbury Thompson
Paula Thomson
Geraldine Thordsen
John Philip Thurman
Harold Toledo
Shinichiro Tora
Victor Trasoff
Joanne Trovato
Susan B. Trowbridge
Joseph P. Tully
Anne Twomey

U

Catherine Ullmann
Claire Ultimo
Frank Urrutia

V

Michael Valli
A. Barbara
Vaughn-Davis
Haydee N. Verdia
Massimo Vignelli
Frank A. Vitale
David Vogler
Constance
Von Collande
Barbara Von Schreiber
Thuy Vuong

W

Dorothy
Wachtenheim
Allan R. Wahler
Ernest Waivada
Jurek Wajdowicz
Joseph O. Wallace
Paul Waner
Kenneth Wasserman
Laurence S. Waxberg
Jessica Weber
Tricia Weber
Art Weithas
Theo Welti
Karl M. Wessel
Stephen Wierzbicki
Gail Wiggin
Richard Wilde
Rodney C. Williams
Jack Williamson
Anna Willis
Lauren Winarsky
David Wiseltier
Rupert Witalis
Henry Wolf
Laura Woods
Elizabeth Woodson
Orest Woronewych
Michael K. Wright

Y

Ronny Yakov
Ira Yoffe
Zen Yonkovig

Z

Bruce Zahor
Carmile S. Zaino
Gary Zamchick
Paul Zasada
Elaine Zeitsoff
Maxim Zhukov
Mikael T. Zielinski
Cynthia Zimpfer
Bernie Zlotnick
Richard Zoehrer
Alan Zwiebel

ADC AFFILIATE MEMBERS

Avon Products Inc.
Perry C. Zompa
Timothy J. Musios

NYC Technical College
Robert Holden

Omnicom Group Inc.
Pamela Manser

Parsons School of Design
Albert Greenberg
David Levy

Peter Rogers Associates
Dee Paul
Lisa Zaslow
Peter Rogers

School of Visual Arts
Leslie Brooks

Toppan Printing Co., Ltd.
Ryuichi Minakawa
Takeo Hayano
Teruo Tanabe

Union Camp Corporation
Robert Todd

ADC INTERNATIONAL MEMBERS

Argentina
Daniel Verdino

Australia
Leighton D. Gage
Ron Kambourian

Austria
Franz Merlicek
Helmut Klein
Mariusz Jan Demner

Bermuda
Paul R. Smith

Brazil
Adeir Rampazzo
Oswaldo Miranda

Canada
I. L. Fraiman
John D. Brooke
Ran Hee Kim

Denmark
Peter Von Schilling

England
Celia Frances Stothard
Jean Govoni
Keith Murgatroyd
Len Sugarman
Roland Schenk

France
Jean Chambers

Germany
Olaf Leu

Holland
Pieter Branttiga

India
Brendan Pereira
Kosala Rohana
Wickramanayake

Israel
Asher Kalderon
Dan Reisinger

Italy
Titti Fabiani

Japan
Akihiro H. Yamamato
Akio Hirai
Akio Okumura
Elman Chan
Hideo Mukai
Hideyuki Kaneko
Ikko Tanaka
Joji Yamamoto
Katsumi Asaba
Kazuki Maeda

Keisuke Nagatomo
Keizo Matsui
Makoto Nakamura
Masakazu Tanabe
Masato Watanabe
Masuteru Aoba
Michio Iwaki
Michio Nakahara
Mitsuhiko Kotani
Mitsutoshi Hosaka
Motoaki Okuizumi
Norio Uejo
Pete Kobayashi
Ryohei Kojima
Satoru Fujii
Seiji Sugii
Shigeo Okamoto
Shigeshi Omori
Shin Matsunaga
Soji George Tanaka
Susumu Sakane
Takaharu Matsumoto
Takahisa Kamijyo
Takao Matsumoto
Takeo Yao
Takkeshi Ohtaka
Teruaki Takao
Terunobu Fukushima
Tetsuro Itoh
Toshio Iwata
Toshiyuki Ohashi
Yasuharu Nakahara
Yasuo Suzuki
Yasuyuki Ito
Yoshikatsu Kosakai
Yuji Baba
Yusaku Tomoeda

Mexico
Diane Garcia De Tolone
Felix Beltran
Luis Efren
Ramirez-Flores

Philippines
Emily A. Abrera

Republic of Singapore
Chiet-Hsuen Eng

Switzerland
Bilal Dallenbach
Fernand Hofer
Moritz Jaggi

West Germany
Hans-Georg
Pospischil

West Malaysia
Peter Wong

INDEX